Penguin Books

The Ackerman Guide

Roy Ackerman has been involved in different aspects of the catering industry over many years. He started in the trade as a commis chef, trained in all departments of the kitchen as an apprentice and worked in England, France and other parts of Europe. In 1976 he opened his first restaurant in Oxford and within three years he opened three more, all the time working on a variety of other projects.

In 1980 he joined Kennedy Brookes plc and became Deputy Chairman responsible for development and new projects, amongst other things. The Company has a very successful record in various types of catering including restaurants, brasseries and hotels.

Recently, Roy Ackerman has originated and presented a 6-part television documentary, *The Chef's Apprentice*, a history of food which is being networked on Independent Television in 1987.

Roy Ackerman is a well-known figure within the catering trade and in 1985 he was awarded the Special Prize at the Hotel and Catering Awards, and was elected Fellow of the Hotel and Catering Institute. In November 1986 he was elected Chairman of the Restaurateurs Association of Great Britain, and is a frequent campaigner for change in the licensing laws. He is also co-Chairman of the Henley Festival of Music and the Arts.

Roy Ackerman

The Ackerman Guide

to the Best Restaurants and Hotels in the British Isles

Penguin Books

Penguin Books Ltd, Harmondsworth, Middlesex, England
Viking Penguin Inc., 40 West 23rd Street, New York, New York 10010, U.S.A.
Penguin Books Australia Ltd, Ringwood, Victoria, Australia
Penguin Books Canada Limited, 2801 John Street, Markham, Ontario, Canada L3R 1B4
Penguin Books (N.Z.) Ltd, 182-190 Wairau Road, Auckland 10, New Zealand

First published 1987
Copyright © Alfresco Leisure Publications plc, 1987
All rights reserved

Designed, edited and produced by Pilot Productions Ltd, London W1
Illustrated by Chris Ackerman-Eveleigh

Made and printed in Hong Kong by Mandarin Offset Marketing Ltd.
Typeset in Century by Saxon Printing Ltd, Derby DE1 1DD

Contents

St George's House,
Croydon, Surrey.

Nestlé are delighted
to be associated with
Roy Ackerman's new Guide.
Through its novel and
informal approach, the
Guide enhances your pleasure
in finding new venues and
discovering the wealth of
gastronomic opportunities
available throughout the
British Isles.
'Bon Appetit.'

Using our world-wide
resources in the
pursuit of excellence.

Nestlé

THE NESTLÉ COMPANY LTD. St. George's House, Croydon, Surrey CR9 1NR. 01-686 3333.

Introduction

A number of factors contributed to my decision to put this book together. Having been involved in the restaurant and catering trade for most of my life, I have sometimes been astonished at the inaccuracies and injustices done to many chefs and restaurateurs in various food guides and articles.

I'm amazed when I hear that some inspectors on other food guides boast they've eaten perhaps 6 meals in a day, in an effort to get to all the places they have to visit. Frankly, I do not think it possible to enjoy the experience or the style of an establishment if moving at this pace. It is necessary to sample the *whole* experience rather than just the first course in one, the main course in another, perhaps a pudding in a third. How can you possibly experience what the normal customer will feel if you are under this strain and restriction? I fail to see how anyone, however able they might be, can sum up the ambient qualities of a restaurant in half an hour. Food, wine, company and the ambience of a restaurant are things to be savoured and enjoyed over a period of time.

I am also astonished by reports of certain organisations using students fresh from catering college. In some cases, people with a minimum grounding in the catering trade have taken vacation jobs to 'inspect' establishments whose chefs, sometimes several years their senior and who have been trained over many years in the science and art of cooking, are subjected to a cursory and uninformed judgement. I also know of one magazine that has published a restaurant column under one named food writer when, in fact, three young ladies, all under the age of 21, were employed to review the selected restaurants. Given the limitations of their experience, I cannot believe that, however intelligent they might have been, they could possibly have judged the calibre and standard of cuisine in a restaurant fairly and professionally.

Moreover, journalists who flay restaurateurs with harsh words in print, never consider the fact that the printed word stays around for a long time. A negative judgement formed on a one-off visit to a restaurant can mean that the restaurant suffers for many months or even years in the future for a temporary shortcoming.

For this reason I have only included places that I feel I can talk positively about, and hopefully year by year this can be expanded to a much larger group.

So, in writing this guide, I was motivated by a wish to give an accurate and balanced appraisal of the opportunities for eating out and enjoying yourself in a variety of places throughout Great Britain. In doing this, I have used a small team of reviewers who have worked with me over a number of years and whose judgement I trust and who understand what I am seeking in standards of cuisine, atmosphere and service. I have visited the majority of places myself, particularly those in the 'Best' sections and the ones which have special mentions in the book.

The selection process

In the course of our travels, we have obviously visited many places in the UK that we have not included in this book. We have tried to assess each establishment on its own merit, not just for its food but for its ambience, architectural style, attitude of staff, state of décor and general air of welcome and positiveness. This means we have been able to include establishments for different reasons. However, if we were unable to find any of the above criteria in an establishment, rather than write something negative we have left the review out altogether.

You will find a 'General Listing' section at the back of the book which lists other establishments in the area that have not been reviewed in the book, or visited only once, and includes hotels, restaurants and historic inns.

Layout of the book

The main review section of the book is split into 2 sections: 'Establishments in London'; and 'Establishments in the British Isles outside London'.

'Establishments in London' includes a section called 'The Best of London'. 'The Best of London' is a round-up of my personal favourites, and includes restaurants, grand hotels and their restaurants, and modern style hotels with particularly good restaurants.

'Establishments in the British Isles' includes a selection of 'The Best of the British Isles' and again it is a section devoted to my favourite places.   The full British Isles section includes not only restaurants, but country house hotels, hotels, restaurants with rooms and historic inns, listed alphabetically by county and town.

This leads on to 'The Best Country House Hotels' section where I have again put together my favourites, both for the food and for the ambience and architecture. All the establishments in this section I would willingly revisit, some for the food and service, some mainly for the ambience, but all are distinctive in at least 2 of these respects.

The establishments listed in the 'Best' sections are not necessarily in alphabetical or preferential order.

LIST OF THE BEST
London Restaurants
L'Arlequin
Chez Nico
Le Gavroche
Hilaire
Inigo Jones
Kalamaras
Langan's Brasserie
La Poule au Pot
Rue St Jacques
Le Suquet
La Tante Claire
La Croisette

9

London's Grand Hotels and their Restaurants
Claridge's
The Connaught
The Dorchester
The Hyde Park
The Ritz
The Savoy

Other London Hotels with Recommended Restaurants
The Capital, Capital Hotel
The Chelsea Room, Hyatt Carlton Tower
90 Park Lane, Grosvenor House Hotel
Le Soufflé, Hotel Inter-Continental

Best Restaurants in the British Isles Outside London
The Altnaharrie Inn
The Carved Angel
Hintlesham Hall
Le Manoir aux Quat'Saisons
Michael's Nook
Peacock Vane
The Seafood Restaurant
Shipdham Place
The Walnut Tree Inn
The Waterside Inn
The Old Woolhouse

Best Country House Hotels
Ballymaloe
Bodysgallen
Chewton Glen
Cromlix House
Gidleigh Park
Hambleton Hall
Homewood Park
Hunstrete House
Inverlochy Castle
Middlethorpe Hall
Sharrow Bay

Regional introductions
We have split up the British Isles into 8 different sections and have tried to illustrate the types of food that historically have been associated with the areas and indicated where the food is available now. If you're prepared to look, you can sometimes find regional foods in restaurants, sometimes in local shops or alternatively in the homes of people who live in these areas. I hope these sections will prove beneficial in seeking out the natural and local flavour of the area. Bon appétit!

Assessment

It is not for me to set myself in judgement on the likes of Roux, Mosimann, Koffman or Blanc, but to try and include for the reader what I consider the best restaurants of their kind in their various areas. Therefore I have not used a star rating system but awarded instead a 4-leaf clover to each of the restaurants I regard as being the best in their category, some for the finest food and others for the food and ambience combined.

The 4-leaf clover symbol

The 4-leaf clover has been chosen because it is a symbol of luck and is a rare find. There is always a degree of luck involved when the total combination of good ambience, excellent food, wine and service, and the humour and mood of the customer makes the perfect lunch or dinner; in other words, when everything comes together to create the perfect meal and occasion.

Pricing system

The little symbol at the top right of every review is a close approximation of the cost of a 3-course dinner for 2, without wine. Where possible we have quoted the set menu price.

Architecture and food

I am sure that I am not alone in thinking that the architecture of the building where I am eating plays a tremendous part in the overall effect of the experience. Whilst in cities we are quite used to finding places which are tucked away around the corner or perhaps even in a parade of shops, when you get out into the country restaurant and hotel architecture comes into its own. My own choices - where I feel most at home with the style of the house - are Hintlesham Hall and Hunstrete House, both of which have the most elegant of exteriors. Thornbury Castle, along with Inverlochy Castle, are probably the most impressive in their style, and perhaps Cliveden and Ston Easton Park the grandest.

Of smaller places which have an unassuming exterior and absolute magic in the kitchen, The Old Woolhouse, Northleach, has to be one of my favourites, and for good country flavours, The Walnut Tree Inn at Llandewi Skirrid. The illustrations in the book will hopefully convey some of the feeling of the architecture to help you choose your own potential favourites.

Eating out is as much to do with you as with the restaurant
Driving like a maniac to get to the restaurant on time, or preceding a special dinner surprise with an over-extended business lunch; someone blocking your car while you're trying to get out of the garage, or an argument exploding on the way to the restaurant - these and situations like these unerringly make an evening unsuccessful, and can quite easily overspill into the atmosphere of the dining room. So mixing all the ingredients together for a successful meal can require a degree of luck as well as the skill of the restaurant staff.

There are many factors that contribute to an enjoyable eating experience besides good food, wine, ambience, pleasant staff and luck, one such factor is you - the customer.

Dress code is important to the atmosphere and overall effect of a restaurant and it is worth making an effort to dress correctly for the occasion whether it is casual or formal. Some extreme comments have been made for and against smoking in restaurants. As a non-smoker, but with friends that do smoke, there is a middle line where consideration for other people comes into account. It must be obvious to the most thick-skinned pipe or cigar smoker that if they have eaten early and other people in the restaurant have just arrived and started their meal, blowing smoke over their table is bound to detract from the pleasure of eating. The ridiculous suggestion by one journalist that all restaurants should, by law, have air conditioning installed takes no account of the variety in size of restaurants or the architectural problems of some of our older buildings, or indeed the cost, which may be prohibitive for some owners.

The trade historically
The culinary world of today owes much to the famous French chefs who, through the ages, have travelled from their own shores to teach some of the less culinarily inspired nations about food. There is no doubt that the culinary influences of such French geniuses as Carême, Escoffier, Soyer and others, have helped form the basis of international cuisine. If one is tracing recent culinary history it's very interesting to see how the British influence has developed over the years and has brought forward some exciting talent in the form of a new wave of young British chefs who have been trained by the likes of Michel and Albert Roux, Anton Mosimann, Michel Bourdin, Richard Shepherd, George Perry-Smith and Kenneth Bell, amongst others. These are not carbon copies, but individuals who have learnt the basics and the artistry of such masters and then developed their own particular taste and style. Among British chefs to have achieved recognition are Stephen Ross of Homewood Park, perhaps one of the best exponents of the new British cuisine, Ian McAndrew, Paul Gayler, Philip Britten, John Webber, David Cavalier from Pebbles, Aylesbury and Peter Chandler from Paris House, Woburn.

For even younger chefs!
Every year the Restaurateurs Association of Great Britain holds a competition to find the Young Waiter and Young Chef of the Year to encourage youngsters in the trade to further their careers. This competition gives them the opportunity to enter and compete with people of their own age group, at both local and national level. Winners receive study trips in Great Britain and Europe as well as cash prizes.

A personal view on restaurants and eating out

I've used, by way of comparison, some references from a guide book to london hotels and restaurants – *The Restaurants of London* by Eileen Hooton-Smith – published in 1928, and the extracts I have included seem to be as relevant now as when they were written. An interesting fact that arose when reading the book is that the majority of places operating in 1928 have long since disappeared. Establishments have either been pulled down to make way for major new developments, or perhaps owners have simply retired and shut up shop. The catering trade, whilst in many ways a rewarding one, takes its physical and mental toll on the restaurateur and chef. Sometimes they simply have to stop and go away to regain their composure or joie de vivre; it's a trade where you see people both at their very best and often their very worst.

The nature of the catering trade is cyclical, like many other businesses there are good times and bad, but hopefully there will always be a market for dining out and as we move towards a way of life that includes far more leisure time than hitherto, probably a larger amount of disposable income will be spent on eating and drinking. There is no doubt that in this country in recent years, knowledge of gastronomy and the practice of eating out has increased enormously. There are many reasons for this. The last decade has seen a tremendous increase of interest in the world of food, cooking and wine, caused not only by the fact that food journalism and photography has leapt forward dramatically, but also that the catering industry has been one of the fastest growing industries in this country. As well as the increasing influence of overseas travel on the average person's expectations, one of the other contributing factors has been the advent of ethnic cuisine and the steak bars of the early 1950s and '60s. This helped to dissolve the world of mystery that surrounded the largely foreign habit of eating out. A whole generation who had not been trained or taught or encouraged to eat out, for once could go into a restaurant and not be embarrassed about how to pronounce the name of a certain dish or not worry about the overall price of the meal - it was clearly marked to include a starter and a pudding. This was a beginning that taught people that eating out could be fun and from there they perhaps graduated to other styles of eating to benefit everyone from consumer to supplier.

The number of restaurants now available has increased dramatically especially with the late entry on the scene of the brewers - those monoliths of business - who have recently begun

to realise that reasonably priced food attractively served, increases the sale of drink by encouraging a greater number of people to enjoy the *total* experience of an evening. Let's hope they don't get involved with too many extreme schemes and waste too much of their money on ideas which have already been tried by some restaurateurs, thereby discouraging them from investing in what should be a growing part of their trade. The return to the old-fashioned brewing values of pride in their product could be reflected so easily in an honest approach to the types of food they offer.

On the human resources side, technical colleges are working much more closely with the industry than before, and turning out craft students who are badly needed. We seemed to go through a time when everyone wanted to be a manager with graduate status and no-one wanted to learn the craft of the kitchen. This, hopefully, is on the turn, helped by some of the nationally and internationally known chefs who spend time not only training teams of youngsters in their own kitchens but also in encouraging young students, judging competitions and generally endorsing the fact that catering is a healthy, respectable and worthwhile trade to be in.

There is a greater awareness in this country the need to use good, fresh raw product as the basis of sound cooking. Producers and suppliers are now realising that if they cannot produce locally and are not prepared to meet the standards demanded, then today's chef is prepared to go further afield to find ingredients.

Restaurant changes

We have done our best, by much correspondence and telephone communication with the various establishments, to check that the information in this book is accurate. At the time of going to press, we are confident that it is. Alfresco Leisure Publications plc takes full responsibility for the contents of *The Ackerman Guide*.

When we have reproduced part of a menu or mentioned certain dishes in the review, we cannot guarantee that they will necessarily be available on your visit, and in the majority of cases the menus will be far more comprehensive than the extracts we have chosen.

It is possible that the owner, the chef or the restaurant manager will have changed by the time you visit the establishment. Also, styles of food may gradually alter over a period of time, especially if a chef with a different style of cooking or presentation has taken over the kitchen.

We assume that in most cases you will book before arriving at the establishment and therefore it is advisable, when telephoning to make your booking, to check on any points you feel are important to the enjoyment of your visit.

London

The nation's capital is the central meeting point of ideas and cultures, a melting pot for all these things and more. And, culinarily speaking, it has a certain character and purpose of its own, namely the distribution of the exotica coming into its ports. The great markets of Smithfield, Leadenhall, Covent Garden, and Billingsgate are serviced by public houses which even now are able to observe a separate version of licensing laws so that it is possible to get a substantial fry-up of eggs, bacon, sausages, potatoes, mushrooms, tomatoes, and fried bread, washed down by copious amounts of ale, at an ungodly hour of the day - ungodly, that is, unless you've been up half the night, in which case it is a perfectly normal lunch.

Such fare as jellied eels, pie and mash with vinegar liquor, is more traditional porters' fare, and there are still shops serving this menu, notably in the East End, the City, Wandsworth and Greenwich. And also still to be seen on London's streets, especially wherever crowds gather, are stalls of cockles, mussels, whelks, whitebait, and jellied eels, or in winter hot chestnuts from a brazier. All these traditions go way back to the days of the itinerant pie man.

Much eating was done in London's clubs, exclusive to the capital, and certain dishes now absorbed into the lore of London derive their names from them, giving us Reform Sauce and Reform Cutlets, and Boodles Orange Fool. Even if they don't bear that name, other fare is redolent of the club or chop house atmosphere: boiled beef and carrots, steak and kidney pudding, or mixed grill, Greenwich whitebait, toad in the hole (though made with chops or kidneys rather than sausages), even London Particular, a thick pea soup reminiscent of the consistency of London's fog before the clean air legislation. Even if the meals began as the cockney working man's food, the better off took them to their stomachs.

Business was done in clubs, and much business stemmed from the tea and coffee trades. Indeed, coffee houses were originally merely places of barter, with the refreshment aspect coming later. The former Lloyds of London building was on the site of one of the earliest coffee houses.

The capital seems to have contributed less towards tea-time than other areas - perhaps because of a less harsh climate and more plentiful food in general - but those items that have survived are certainly distinctive, stemming from days when, apart from the City itself, the area was more a collection of villages. From Chelsea came the bun, a yeasted curranty dough, rolled up, cut into slices, the slices then baked in batches alongside each other. It's enormously popular nationwide, mass-produced by most bakeries, but few people when they eat one now think of it as coming from a part of London.

On the other hand, Maids of Honour have a totally different tradition. They are not so commonly found, and have such a history attached to them that you hardly get the chance to eat one without being aware of the fact! The best place to get them is undoubtedly where they were first made, at Newens Tea Shop (sometimes also called The Original Maids of Honour Shop),

Kew Road, Richmond. They were devised for Henry VIII, whose figure bears out his love of good food, and for whom the parkland around was stocked with deer, and the end product is a warm flaky pastry case with a sweet cheese filling.

Nowadays, however, 'quality' and 'variety' must be the by-words for London, with markets and small traders making every conceivable foodstuff available to the capital, provided you know where to look. Obvious ones are Soho for Chinese, Kilburn for West Indian, Southall for Indian spices; and dotted around are individual shops selling for instance Middle Eastern pastries, Polish delicatessen, Portuguese products, Provençal herbs. It is now often easier to get such local produce in London than in its place of origin.

Street markets are places where it is usually worth spending some time, and you might visit any of these:

Albert Wharf, SW11 (Mon - Sat)
Berwick Street, W1 (Mon - Sat)
Camden Lock, NW1 (Sat + Sun)
Camden Passage N1 (Wed + Sun)
The Cut, SE1 (Mon - Sat)
Lambeth Walk, SE11 (Fri + Sat)
Leadenhall Market, EC3 (Mon - Fri)
North End Road, SW6 (Mon - Sat)
Petticoat Lane, E1 (Sun)
Portobello Road, W11 (Mon - Sat)
Tachbrook Street, SW1 (Mon - Sat)
Wentworth Street, E1 (Mon - Sat)

The wholesale markets are not generally open to the public for purchasing, but nevertheless the atmosphere in the area is certainly exciting:

Billingsgate (fish), E14
New Covent Garden (fruit & vegetables), SW8
Smithfield (meat), EC1
Spitalfields (fruit, vegetables & flowers), E1

Stores like Harrods, and Fortnum & Mason, are places to go for virtually anything you care to name, but they are now finding suburban rivals. For cheese, your first port of call might be Paxton & Whitfields of St James's; and there's now also a Real Cheese Shop in Barnes, handy for South-West Londoners, and it's not far from a coffee roasters, if you cannot get up to Carwardine's, or Higgins in South Molton Street. Certain areas have whole pockets of good stores, thus St James', Belgravia, parts of Fulham and King's Road, Covent Garden and Neal's Yard are real havens for food lovers. The list is endless, and it shows a heartening revival of interest in good eating and good food.

HISTORIC HOUSES OPEN TO THE PUBLIC

Apsley House, Piccadilly
Chiswick House, Chiswick
Fenton House, Hampstead
Ham House, Ham
Hampton Court Palace, Hampton
Kenwood, Hampstead
Marble Hill House, Twickenham
Osterley Park House, Osterley
Syon House, Brentford

Best Restaurants in London

There are as many restaurants of infinite variety in London as in any other capital city, ranging from the very best classic French cuisine through to most varieties of ethnic cuisine. To include a selection of the large variety of ethnic restaurants available would require a far larger volume than this, so we have restricted our choice to the best European cuisines, and have left it to our guest chefs to pick their favourite ethnic restaurants.

London hotels can be split into several categories, grand hotels of character and tradition, small distinctive hotels with style and their own ambience, and luxury international hotels of mainly modern construction and design.

The grand hotel range includes hotels of which the capital is, and should be, justly proud, as in most respects they equal the best in the world, and act as a showcase for the best of British hospitality. In the past decade, the improvements and refurbishments of décor, standard of food and general competence and service have improved beyond recognition. There are, of course, legendary names amongst them and I rarely fail to get excited when I step through the portals of The Savoy, The Ritz or The Connaught.

The smaller distinctive hotels are very special for visitors from abroad or the UK and carry on a tradition that is unique. They range from Duke's Hotel tucked away in St James's, to Brown's Hotel in Mayfair, originally a terrace of Victorian houses, to the relative newcomers who have created their own individual and distinctive style. One such is The Capital, which has operated in Knightsbridge for 15 years, and Blakes in Kensington.

The international-style hotels have their own following and offer the very best in the latest modern designs and facilities, and in some cases their food is superior to that of their world-wide counterparts. The Inter-Continental and The Hyatt Carlton Tower are prime examples of well-managed, large modern hotels with food of a high standard.

La Tante Claire   SW3

68 Royal Hospital Road SW3 4LP
01-352 6045/351 0227

Closed: Sat + Sun; Bank Holidays; 10 days Easter; 3 weeks Aug; 10 days
          Christmas/New Year
Last
Orders: lunch (2.00pm); dinner (10.00pm)

one of my favourite restaurants

Much has been written of Pierre Koffman, but despite specula-
tion to the contrary, when the enlarged Tante Claire opened
there was no doubt that he remained supreme in the kitchen.
With a larger number of covers to cater for, the food is always
exciting and often in unique combination, honest in quantity and
quality. Pierre is a man dedicated to his kitchen which leaves the
front of house to Jean-Pierre Dorantet, whose knowledgeable
explanation of some of the more unusual dishes enhances the
pleasure of eating here. The décor is very different from the old
Tante Claire and different from most restaurants of this calibre,
but it works surprisingly well and provides a restful backdrop
for one of my favourite London restaurants. It has a cool and
refreshing feel to it which does not detract from its intimacy.
    Underlying Pierre's cooking is a basic French belief in the true
value of good ingredients, as seen in his pied de cochon farci aux
morilles, mousseline de brocoli. And the presentation on the
plate is lovingly achieved. A credit to his capabilities is his
delicate treatment of marbré de foie gras et langue de veau,

L^A TANTE CLAIRE

VOL-AU-VENT DE FOIE GRAS, BETTERAVES ROUGES
ET POINTES D'ASPERGES AU VINAIGRE DOUX 14.50

GRILLADE DE COQUILLES ST JACQUES
A L'EMULSION DE POIVRES 11.50

MARBRE DE FOIE GRAS ET LANGUE DE VEAU,
PETITS OIGNONS ET RAISINS 14.00

PETIT PANIER DU JARDINIER
AU PARFUM DE CORIANDRE 8.50

SALADE DE LANGOUSTINES, HARICOTS
MAGRET ET TRUFFE 12.50

TRANCHES DE SAUMON CRU
A LA CRÈME DE CIBOULETTES ET CAVIAR 12.50

FRIVOLITÉS DE LA MER 10.50

CHINOISERIE DE BAR AUX PETITS LÉGUMES 15.30

MINUTE DE ROUGET AUX GRAINES DE CUMIN
ET CELERI FRIT 14.50

MIGNONS DE LOTTE AUX CÂPRES,
TOMATES ET SAFRAN 13.80

PAVE DE SAUMON SAUVAGE RÔTI AVEC
SON JUS DE CRESSON 14.50

CIVET DE HOMARD
AU VIN DE MADIRAN ET JEUNES POIREAUX

AIGUILLETTE DE TURBOT
CLOUTÉ À LA FAÇON BOUCANNIÈRE 15.10

PIGEONNEAU RÔTI ROYALE
AVEC SES LÉGUMES CONFITS 15.80

PIED DE COCHON FARCI AUX MORILLES
MOUSSELINE DE BROCOLI 13.90

AIGUILLETTES DE CANARD
POÊLÉES AUX ENDIVES 15.30

CASSOLADE DE LAPEREAU AUX LANGOUSTINES
ET POIS GOURMANDS 13.80

PIÈCE DE BOEUF À LA FONDUE D'ÉCHALOTES,
GRATIN D'ÉPINARDS ET ARTICHAUT 15.10

SELLE DE CHEVREUIL AU CHOCOLAT NOIR
ET VINAIGRE DE FRAMBOISES 15.90

CARRÉ D'AGNEAU AUX ÉPICES
ET TIAN DE LÉGUMES 14.50

CROUSTIS DE RIS DE VEAU
BRUNOISE TRUFFÉE ET ÉPINARDS 14.40

MINIMUM CHARGE £25.00 PER PERSON
VAT AND SERVICE INCLUDED

NO PIPE SMOKING
IF YOU SMOKE
DO SO WITH CONSIDERATION FOR OTHER GUESTS

petits oignons et raisins - certainly not an everyday dish to the average English person! There is a choice of 7 starters, 6 fish dishes and 8 meat dishes, all with their own individual style and flavour. The wide range of fish dishes offered again gives Pierre an excellent platform from which to show his skills.

There is an excellent wine list with some unusual and bargain priced wines from Savoie, Camargue, Bandol, Cahors and Jurançon.

I suspect that Koffman has spent as much on his kitchen as on the front of house and with this standard of quality, who would blame him! Minimum charge is £25.00 per head which you will really look forward to spending. You need to book substantially ahead unless you are lucky enough to live locally and pick up a rare cancellation the same evening - I'm going to regret giving you this tip!

Le Gavroche W1

43 Upper Brook Street, W1Y 1PF
01-408 0881/499 1826 ♣ £90

— style & panache

Closed: Sat + Sun; Bank Holidays; Christmas/New Year
Last
Orders: lunch (2.00pm); dinner (11.00pm) *in elegant surroundings*

It seems strange to talk about Albert Roux and then about Michel Roux as opposed to 'the Roux brothers', but they are indeed separate both in personality and in life styles. However they are inextricably linked by their regard and admiration for each other. If you are talking with either of them about food or restaurants, it's very rare that the other brother is not mentioned. They have been working as a team for over 20 years, but success did not come immediately, as London was not quite used to the classic and well-presented cuisine of the Rouxs. Initially Le Gavroche established itself over a period of time in Sloane Street before moving to its more prestigious location in Mayfair, leaving the set menu of Gavvers in its place.

after Bewick

Gavroche

Albert Roux, a quiet modest man, is a brilliant cook, no mean businessman and still very much the driving force behind Le Gavroche. He inspires from behind the scenes, and it is to his great credit that his was the first 3-star Michelin restaurant in Great Britain. I would like to think that this is not only because of the standard of cuisine, service and décor at Le Gavroche, but also because of all the years of hard work and effort, plus the creative talent of this man, and the inspiration that has been passed on to the whole school of chefs who have started on their own having served apprenticeships with the Rouxs.

However, on to the restaurant itself, which is in the capable hands of Silvano Giraldin at the front of house with his well-trained professional staff who really understand what service is about. Perhaps have a drink in the upstairs bar whilst waiting to order or instead in the more loungey atmosphere of the reception area downstairs. There are comfortable armchairs and sofas, warm soft lighting, and an air of being with people who have come to experience this exceptional food as well as to enjoy themselves; for it is possible to enjoy yourself at Le Gavroche. Although I accept that some of the other tables might be adorned by the international expense account brigade, who are trooping around the best 3-stars in the world, this one happens to be in London, so it belongs more to us than to them. It is an example of an establishment that having reached the pinnacle now has the even harder task of remaining there, and improving on the incredibly high standards of cuisine and service it has already achieved.

The lesson I would like to teach to quite a lot of the younger chefs who are making a living for themselves outside London is that whatever your style of décor, and however luxurious your restaurant might be, it all comes down to the quality of raw product, the flavours that are extracted from it, as well as the presentation on the plate. Albert Roux, Steven Doherty and their team in the kitchen manage all of this, and they're busy with lunch and dinner 5 days a week.

Merely describing the food does not really do it justice, but if one has to pick some favourites from the menu, the ragoût de langoustines aux vermicelli is quite sensational, the gâteau de deux mousses de légumes is as good as you'll find anywhere in the world, and if you want to try a true symphony of fish, try the symphonie de la mer à la crème de fenouil. Simpler dishes aren't forgotten, with the poulet fermier sauté en cocotte aux lentilles et au thym amongst the dozen or so entrées. The special dishes of the day can also be quite sensational, for example the cotelette de pigeonneau au foie gras avec sa salade de légumes au vinaigre de vin rouge, and the canard de Challans rôti avec sa sauce à la moutarde aux herbes de potager. There is a set price lunch for around £20.00, and the incredible Menu Exceptionnel for 2 people will give you a good insight into the mysteries and talent of this kitchen.

The wine list is extensive and what one would expect from a restaurant of this reputation, and there are a number of half bottles in most varieties. A knowledgeable sommelier or Monsieur Giraldin himself will be only too pleased to help you with your selection.

If you're from out of town and really feel like making a stay of it, the Roux brothers run on a management basis an enterprise called 47 Park Street, which is above Le Gavroche. Behind this Edwardian façade there are some exceptionally good rooms, in total 54 first-class suites or apartments comprising 1 or 2 bedrooms, their own kitchen and bathroom, and most also having a good-sized living room. They are beautifully designed and decorated, and if you wish you can arrange for your own dinner party to be served in the apartment or even in the private reception room, which is again elegantly furnished. The food, of course, comes from Le Gavroche.

Chez Nico   SW8

129 Queenstown Road SW8
01-720 6960

one of the best young British chefs ♣ £70

Closed: lunch (Sat, Sun + Mon); dinner (Sun);
Bank Holidays; Easter; Christmas; 3 weeks during
Summer
Last
Orders: dinner (10.45pm)

It's so nice to be writing again about a young English chef, and Philip Britten is a young man with great ability who should go right to the top. A quiet man who supervises an equally young team, he keeps himself to himself and stays largely in the kitchen which is, he believes, his rightful place. He admires Nico Ladenis' style, and after 4 years of working with him has obviously got to know it well. But that, plus his time with Anton Mosimann at The Dorchester, has not stopped him developing his own individual dishes.

You might try his terrine de ris de veau et de morilles, garnie avec sa salade de mâche, or the boudin de foie gras frais avec sa macédoine de légumes à l'huile de noisettes, or the escalope de barbue en feuilleté garni au crabe et au gingembre, au beurre blanc. The main courses are priced to include a starter, and you can choose the superb rognons de veau au lard, sauce madère, or maybe filet de boeuf persillé aux truffes or the suprème de canard aux échalotes, sauce vin rouge. For dessert there's a tarte aux poires, sauce framboise, a parfait moka, sauce orange, or a marquise au chocolat.

The dining room hasn't changed dramatically since Philip Britten took over, although it's a little larger, and the bright new décor and bold checks stand out against a white background. The staff out front are as young and helpful as the ones in the kitchen. A fantastic team - may they go from strength to strength.

L'Arlequin   SW8

123 Queenstown Road SW8 3RH
01-622 0555

*— the enlarged restaurant ♣ £50
still retains
its charm, even the
kitchen has a
little more room.*

Closed: Sat + Sun; Bank Holidays
Last
Orders: lunch (2.00pm); dinner (10.30pm)

Christian and Geneviève Delteil run a well-organised small restaurant just down Queenstown Road over Battersea Bridge, with simple décor in shades of brown and beige, a few pictures of Harlequin, and crisp linen on the neat tables.

An excellent salade paysanne contains foie gras, sweetbreads and pigeon on a well dressed variety of leaves. The assiette des poissons has salmon, turbot, sole and monkfish, lightly cooked on a perfect beurre blanc with chives, and properly cooked vegetables. The miroir au cassis has a good texture and flavour and this lunch-time selection only costs about £13.00! I can't understand why there is no queue - does the bridge pose such a problem at lunch time? If so, the barrier disappears in the evening when the restaurant is busy, despite the fact that you then pay higher prices. Service is discreet and efficient from smart young staff under Geneviève's supervision, and the wine list has a good selection from major French regions.

L'Arlequin has a serious yet friendly atmosphere, and some of London's most competent and consistent cooking.

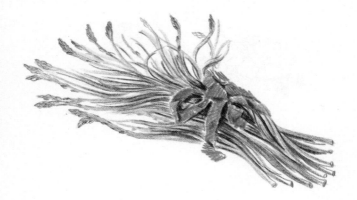

Le Suquet **SW3**

104 Draycott Avenue SW3 3AE
01-581 1785

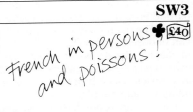

Closed: Christmas
Last
Orders: dinner (11.30pm)

Pierre Martin has done amazing things with his small provençale-style restaurants. In various ways, all bear his stamp, the one linking factor being the excellent quality and range of seafood, as good as you would get anywhere in Great Britain or, for that matter, in many parts of France. The general atmosphere is amplified by a staff brimming with confidence in what they serve. Pierre puts tremendous effort into obtaining good raw produce and feels passionately about his supplies of fish and their availability, even providing the passer-by with a street side view, à la Paris, of the shellfish being prepared. Huge platters of seafood including whole crab, various oysters, whelks and cockles, and quite simply prepared grilled sea bass, prove the point that when the raw material is of quality, the most simple way of cooking is more often than not the best.

Meat dishes are also available. A master-stroke by the Caterer and Hotelkeeper (the magazine for restaurant and hotel people) was to make him Restaurateur of the Year in their 1986 awards.

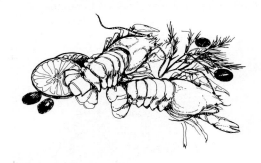

Hilaire   SW7

68 Old Brompton Road SW7 3LQ
01-584 8993

—accomplished cooking with flair ♣ £45

Closed: lunch (Sat + Sun); dinner (Sun);
        Bank Holidays; 1 week Christmas
Last
Orders: lunch (2.30pm); dinner (11.30pm)

I make no excuses for rating Hilaire as highly as I do, since after all I was instrumental in recruiting Simon Hopkinson to open it. I believe that he is one of the generation of young British chefs who will rise to the top of the profession. His cooking is uncluttered, even with some of the more esoteric dishes, and the depth of flavour of the sauces, coupled with the simplicity of presentation make this restaurant a 'must'. It would be wrong not to mention the young, charming front of house staff ably led by Joel Kissin. The décor is simple and unobtrusive, and a suitably sympathetic canvas for Simon's dishes. It's a place for excellent food, good service and a relaxed atmosphere.

From the fixed price dinner menu, which is approximately £20.00 a head, you might like to try the excellent game terrine with onion chutney, or the herring and gravadlax with a dill and horseradish mousse, the delightful watercress mousse with lemon dressing, or the terrine of fresh foie gras which carries a supplement. Main courses might be a breast of pheasant and fresh cèpes, roast best end of lamb with whole garlics or a grilled fillet of salmon with virgin olive oil and roasted pimento. There's an excellent lemon tart or a chocolate marquise to finish. A good range of wines includes an excellent choice of half bottles.

Rue St Jacques   **W1**

5 Charlotte Street W1P 1HD
01-637 0222   *—stylish, the best in the street* ♣ £60

Closed: Sat + Sun; Bank Holidays; Christmas; Easter
Last
Orders: lunch (2.30pm); dinner (11.15pm)

It is only a couple of years since Rue St Jacques opened its doors
in Charlotte Street, and since then a lot of other restaurants have
opened, and improved, to make this one of the most exciting
areas to eat in London. Gunther Schlender, a quiet, modest man,
delivers some exciting and different dishes to tempt some of the
ad-men's jaded palates and give this very individually designed
restaurant the edge over some of its rivals. In the slick, modern,
mirrored ground floor room, there is a brisk, busy atmosphere at
lunch time when they realise that some people have to get back
to work, but in the evening, when some of the London and
international smarter set meet, there's a more leisurely atmosphere.

   Maybe choose a creamy gâteau of smoked haddock served on
a bed of fennel jelly, ravioli filled with crayfish and lobster on a
light tomato sauce, or sweetbreads and veal kidneys simmered
in champagne and served in a brioche pastry to start your meal.
The pavé de saumon sauvage (a slice of salmon filled with
scallops and mushrooms on a delicate red wine sauce) is
outstanding, as is the elaborate squab poached in its own jus
with foie gras and truffles. Desserts are in the modern French
style, as is the rest of the menu. Vincent Calcerano runs the front
of house with care and attention. The wine list is expensive, but
there are some good value wines to be found. This restaurant
has established itself very quickly on the London scene and
deserves to go on for a long time.

Inigo Jones Restaurant WC2

14 Garrick Street WC2E 9BJ
01-836 6456/3223

genteel surroundings nouvelle food

♣ £55

Closed: lunch (Sat + Sun); dinner (Sun); Christmas Day to 4 Jan
Last
Orders: lunch (2.30pm); dinner (11.30pm)

Denis Flouvat runs the front of house very competently with Paul Gayler in the kitchen serving some exciting dishes in the nouvelle cuisine style. He is a dedicated man who works hard at providing the right combination of sauces to garnish his extensive selection of fish, game and meat dishes. The menu changes quarterly, and might consist for starters of a confit of quail with hazelnut oil, quails' eggs and croûtons, warm mousseline of wild salmon with caviar and two sauces, a puff pastry case of fresh snails with young nettles, artichokes and champagne sauce. For main course, you could possibly try glazed saddle of rabbit with oyster mushrooms and madeira sauce, roast milk-fed pigeon with a red wine and blackcurrant sauce or maybe steamed roulade of chicken with vegetables and foie gras soufflé. There is also a cuisine bourgeois which changes every 2 months with a set dish of the day from Monday to Friday plus à la carte for lunch and pre-theatre dinners.

Paul Gayler has a large number of staff in his kitchen and with a menu like this, he needs it. If art on a plate is what you're after with some very delicately flavoured sauces and garnishes, then this might be the place for you.

The 1864 building, once a studio-workshop for the design of stained glass panels, had William Morris teaching here for a time. Apparently it was empty from 1940 until 1968 when Peter Ward, partner of Jean-Jacques Kaeser, purchased and designed this restaurant which has remained faithful to their style ever since.

IJ

Menu Potager

La Poule au Pot   **SW1**

231 Ebury Street SW1
01-730 7763   *exuberant bistro with entertaining staff*

Closed: lunch (Sat + Sun); dinner (Sun); Bank Holidays
Last
Orders: lunch (2.30pm); dinner (11.15pm)

A little bit of France in London. The exterior view with the
entrance to the apartments and the Boucherie Lamartine next
door (excellent choice in cuts from the Roux Brothers) is a
delight to look at, and by the time Marc Faillat greets you and
shows you to your table draped with brown paper slips over the
white tablecloths, you are already convinced that you are going
to enjoy yourself. Some of the bench seating in the centre of the
room is a little awkward but you soon forget this as the whole
place has an atmosphere of fun and enjoyment. The actual dish,
la poule au pot, is worth eating as are the many other bourgeois
French dishes; sizeable portions could come with housewine by
the magnum charged as to what you consume. (After a magnum,
you'll find it even harder to believe you are in London!)

The wine list also provides a good choice. This place, which I
have very rarely seen advertised, always seems to be full with
locals who create their own relaxed and intimate atmosphere:
choose it for its romantic setting or just as a place for a fun table.

Kalamaras
W2

76-78 Inverness Mews W2
01-727 9122

Closed: lunch (daily)
Last
Orders: dinner (midnight)

I wish Greek had more restaurants like this

My friendship with Stelios Platonos goes back many years, and I was first introduced to him in his old premises situated at the top of Queensway. I was taken there by Greek friends who at the time were opposed to the Greek junta and used to gather in little groups to discuss tactics. But as in the manner of some of these things, once everyone arrived at Stelios', the relaxed atmosphere, the always pretty girls and the delightful array of Greek starters, which would quickly appear, turned the conversation to other matters. Stelios has now moved around the corner to Inverness Mews, the Kalamaras Micro carries on as ever at number 66 - a

tiny little restaurant where you take your own wine. It serves perhaps less ambitious dishes than Kalamaras Mega at number 76, the very end of the mews.

This is one of the few really Greek restaurants in London, and however well you might know your Greek dishes, I suspect you will definitely need one of the attractive young ladies to explain what the specials of the day are. There's a great selection of seafood, excellent fresh crab when available, a very good lamb stew with spinach, or straight grilled lamb served with spring onions and garlic. Try some baby suckling pig from the grill, accompanied by a generous portion of Greek salad with good feta, and some sensibly priced resinated and non-resinated Greek wines. On a warm summer night Stelios sometimes sets a table or two in the courtyard outside, and the overwhelming feeling of this place is that of the hospitality and character of Greece.

In the past 20 years I have sent many people to Kalamaras, including several budding young managers or restaurateurs, to watch this true professional at work. He always seems relaxed, always unhurried and very rarely fails to greet or say goodbye to everyone that enters or leaves the premises. He is a charming, informative and lovely man. Even when he is away on one of his trips to his beautiful island of Paros, his spirit remains in the place and his son, as always, keeps a watchful eye on the technical side of the business. Long may this Greek institution continue.

'Carnation' 'Coffee-Mate' and
'Tea-Mate' in liquid mini pots for
creamier tasting coffee and delicious
tasting tea.

THE NESTLÉ COMPANY LTD. St. George's House, Croydon, Surrey CR9 1NR. 01-686 3333.

Carnation, Coffee-Mate and Tea-Mate are trade marks.

Langan's Brasserie

W1

Stratton Street W1X 5FD
01-491 8822

— see you there! ♣ £35

Closed: lunch (Sat + Sun); dinner (Sun); Bank Holidays
Last
Orders: lunch (2.45pm); dinner (11.45pm; 12.45am Sat)

I am a friend of Richard Shepherd, and an admirer of his style and his honesty. He is forthright and outspoken about the value of food and some of the more recherché of the new wave of restaurants. He is without doubt the driving force behind this incredibly busy restaurant and yet still finds time to charge around the country inspiring and judging young students of food in various competitions throughout the year. I am also an admirer of Michael Caine, another of the partners of Langan's, whom fame doesn't seem to have affected at all: he remains a pleasant, interesting and entertaining person.

Peter Langan completes the trio, and it is his name that the restaurant bears and his style is undoubtedly stamped on this place. I have met him many times, but very rarely conversed with him. Between them, they have created a restaurant which, if not the busiest, is one of the busiest in the country, with an atmosphere which buzzes from the time it opens to the time it closes. A dedicated following of regulars is supplemented by people from all over the world, some of whom, one suspects, arrive expecting to see Peter Langan falling over, but go away marvelling at the selection and the competence of the cooking, the number of famous faces, plus the general bonhomie which accompanies both lunch and dinner at Langan's.

Hors d'oeuvres range from the famous soufflé of spinach with anchovy sauce, pike mousse with fresh dill sauce, or samphire and cucumber salad, to a simple and good assiette de charcuterie. Plats du jour might be black pudding with apple and onions (some of the best I've had), or a massive jambonneau aux haricots mange tout. There are 4 or 5 specialities of the day, an excellent selection of vegetables - including my favourite, bubble and squeak - a choice of over 25 puddings or half a dozen cheeses. The wine list is small and well chosen and the prices throughout are very reasonable, especially considering the success of this place.

31

The atmosphere is eclectic and stylish, it's a place to see and be seen. In fact, the place is unique. Peter Langan has tried to emulate this formula with different partners in other parts of London without the same success, and the Coq d'Or, whose premises these were formerly, had been through its best years when Langan took over; so perhaps it isn't the location, but a combination of talent, style, dedication - and the luck of the Irish!

La Croisette   SW10

168 Ifield Road SW10
01-373 3694

very, very French £45

Closed: lunch (Tue); dinner (Mon + Tue)
Last
Orders: lunch (3.00pm); dinner (11.30pm)

Probably more French than most restaurants in France, La Croisette has been dispensing superb fish for some 11 years in this restaurant set in a row of terraced houses near the Brompton cemetery. A more unlikely spot you can't imagine, though having rung the doorbell and been admitted you are completely unaware of the exterior surroundings, and with a little imagination are whisked to the South of France. The walls are cream, abounding with cheerful paintings of southern France, while the tables are close together with cane chairs. When the restaurant is full - and it usually is - the temperature also resembles the Mediterranean! The menu consists of fish served in many ways - oysters may be natures or chaudes au champagne, au curry or au safran; moules can be ordered marinières, farcies or à la crême; and coquilles St Jacques in no less than 5 sauces, as desired. There are daily poissons selon l'arrivage, turbot aux deux sauces, lotte aux herbes, rouget sauce Mireille and so on.

Pierre Martin, the proprietor, also brought the plateau aux fruits de mer to London and this wonderful array of shellfish is still a firm favourite. A fixed price of £20.00 includes everything except service, and while on that subject, the staff find the atmosphere so like home that they forget to speak English until prompted. The wine list is small, mostly white, rosé or Champagne - drink the Bellet to maintain the ambience. The produce is excellent, the cooking is good and the atmosphere is, well, French. You're the customer, you're paying the bill, you're in France - relax and enjoy it!

Grand Hotels

The Dorchester W1

Park Lane W1A 2HJ
01-629 8888

Closed: The Terrace: lunch (daily); dinner (Sun)
Last
Orders: The Terrace: dinner (11.00pm)

This is a very special 205-bedroom hotel, fit for a king, (or a sultan) with marvellous marbled halls, polished floors, mirrored ceilings - opulence everywhere. Everything and then a little more that you look for in a luxury hotel can be found at The Dorchester. You almost expect the staff to break into a Busby Berkeley routine, but they resist any such temptation. To the grand and less grand alike they give courteous and attentive service. At the risk of repeating my comments about other grand hotels, it's no mean feat being Maître Chef of kitchens this size, and with such diverse responsibilities as the very fine, light food in the bar, the room service facility, and the private reception rooms, including the excellent Penthouse Suite with its tiny little garden overlooking London. All that's before you talk about catering for a whole army of staff, and the two main restaurants, The Terrace and The Grill Room.

The man at the centre of all this creative food activity is, of course, Anton Mosimann, once again a man who has contributed immeasurably to the advance of British gastronomy. In moving around the country, I have encountered many of his former chefs and apprentices, who have now found their own niches either in

33

other hotels or in restaurants of their own. Like Michel Bourdin from The Connaught, and the Roux brothers, he is an honest, reliable teacher of the craft of cookery. The talented ones who have trained with him should not fail, provided they use the in-depth knowledge they have gained in the kitchens here as a base from which to build their individual interpretations.

It seems a bit silly, but sometimes when you are asked where to recommend good English food in London, one of the first places that springs to mind is The Grill Room at The Dorchester, and some of the English dishes provided here can indeed be superb - some of the best Lancashire Hot Pot you are likely to taste, or a delicious knuckle of veal or maybe some straightforward British, rare roast ribs of beef. Of the no-nonsense puddings, the bread and butter variety is outstanding. The service is professional and slick, though in my case they always seem to get the delightful varieties of home-made bread and rolls on the table just too quickly and I eat 2 or 3 before even starting the first course! I also like The Grill Room breakfast for those early morning meetings, and although normally I can only manage some brioche with some of their excellent, thick cut marmalade, and coffee, at many a meeting I have seen people wade their way through some of the best British breakfasts in London.

The Terrace Restaurant is altogether a very different thing, and gives great credibility to the versatility of Anton Mosimann and his team. One of the first to introduce the Menu Surprise, the chances of your not enjoying the 6-course extravaganza are very slim, that is unless there are particular foods you don't enjoy, in which case it's worth checking with the head waiter beforehand. Dinner comes at around £35.00 per person and in the summer months can comprise, for example, a delicious summer salad - a selection of various types of lettuce leaves, beautifully dressed, and served with asparagus, perhaps followed by strips of wild salmon and sorrel glazed with white wine sauce, then by breast of corn-fed chicken steamed in its own juice and flavoured with ginger and black mushrooms - a dish which signifies Anton Mosimann's famed Cuisine Naturelle, but more about that later. Finish with the cinnamon parfait and a compôte of fruits. Coffee and petits fours are included, and they are well worth having.

If you're choosing from the main à la carte menu, you might opt for the feuilleté de ris de veau aux écrevisses - calves' sweetbreads with crayfish in puff pastry - or another Cuisine Naturelle dish, saumon d'Ecosse mariné. If it's on the chilly side, maybe the beef consommé with marrow dumplings will suit, and if it's fish you're after, from one of the 5 choices why not try the loup de mer cuit à la vapeur orientale. This is Cuisine Naturelle at its best - steamed sea bass with strips of pork, dried Chinese mushrooms, ginger and spring onions. For main courses you might like the pan-roasted guineafowl on a bed of chicory mixed with cream, or a delicious duck breast roasted and served with glazed apples. If you're eating Cuisine Naturelle then you'll probably miss the selection of good cheeses they offer, including a goats' cheese with chicory, and opt instead for a symphony of natural flavoured sherberts. Or how about this for a Cuisine Naturelle dish that won't make you feel too guilty but will give some sweetness to the end of your meal: a composition of citrus fruits with an orange sorbet and sauce flavoured with tarragon - unusual, but quite delicious. Or if you don't have a weight or a heart problem, you can have a tranche from the delicious pastries they have on offer.

The Terrace is a hotel dining room, and it caters for hotel guests as well as members of the general public who are fortunate enough to eat here; and as a hotel dining room, it has to provide all the things that one expects in a luxury hotel. A trio plays in the later part of the evening, but if this is not your sort of thing, eat earlier when there is just a pianist in attendance, helping Peter Buderath and his staff glide around the room in their normal, efficient manner of service.

The wine list is large and without doubt at the top end of the price bracket. Among the Bordeaux reds you have to go to the Fronsacs to get anything remotely like a reasonably priced claret, or to the Beaujolais, if it's a Burgundy you're after.

Anton Mosimann's skill is in achieving perfection and simplicity. He is a person who worries about sustaining the natural flavours through to the final product, and his final touches in its presentation have made him one of the best known chefs in the world. In his book *Cuisine Naturelle* he explains the basis for his style by denying any contradiction between eating well and eating healthily - use the freshest, most perfect ingredients, and prepare them in the way best suited to bring out the flavour, colour, succulence and goodness; and if you totally exclude butter, cream, oil, and alcohol, and cut down on the amount of salt and sugar used, you can reduce significantly the calorific value of many dishes. That is not to say that Anton does not use these ingredients, plus more, in some of his classic dishes! The basis for his cuisine naturelle is, as I've said, simplicity, and it's explained very adequately in this interesting book with its famous black plate photography.

Hyde Park Hotel SW1

Knightsbridge SW1
01-235 2000

Last
Orders: Park Room: 11.00pm
        Grill Room: lunch (2.30pm; 2.00pm Sun)
                 dinner (11.00pm; 10.30pm Sun)

An elegant and dignified hotel, the Hyde Park has an established clientele who treat this Edwardian institution as their London home. It has one of the most elegant entrances of any London hotel, with its lovely staircase surrounded by exquisite marble, high moulded ceilings and crystal chandeliers. Bedrooms are tastefully furnished with antiques, and the suites have magnificent views across Hyde Park.

There are 2 dining rooms, the Park Room which is a favourite venue for breakfast meetings or a buffet lunch, and the Grill Room for dinner. The Park Room overlooks Rotten Row in the park itself and is beautifully spacious with pink and blue décor. Oak panelling creates a warm club ambience in the Grill Room where Jean-Michel Bonnin's menu combines classic and modern cuisine.

The Savoy WC2

Strand WC2R 0EU
01-836 4343

Closed: Grill Room: lunch (Sat + Sun); dinner (Sun);
          3 weeks Aug
Last
Orders: Grill Room & River Room: lunch (2.30pm); dinner (11.30pm)

"The Savoy Restaurant was opened in 1889 and was the first restaurant de luxe in London. The great Mr Ritz was in charge and Escoffier was his chef. Of course the restaurant was hailed with joy by social London and was an immediate success.

"The Savoy Hotel as it is to-day is immensely enlarged from the edifice of 1889. It stands now, a gigantic pile, abutting on the Strand and uprearing itself from the steep ground running down to the Embankment.

"It takes its name from the Palace of Savoy built in 1245 by Peter, Earl of Savoy and Richmond, which stood on the river bank where now the huge hotel holds sway. Stow wrote of it as 'the fairest palace in all England'. It was at that time the home of John of Gaunt. The spot is full of historical association, but the

only remnant of the old days standing is the little Savoy Chapel Royal which is like a tiny grey thing crouched beside the towering white walls of the giant hotel.

"Spectacularly it is a wonderful position. One turns out of the noisy jostling Strand into the courtyard of the Savoy. Then in through the revolving door and the hall, bright with colour, lies within, and ahead stretches a long, long vista to where the waters of the Thames show through the Embankment trees. One descends from the hall lounge by a dozen shallow steps to a big restaurant foyer, and lengthways beside this is the restaurant with wide windows giving on to the Embankment gardens and the river.

"The riverside views of the Savoy are wonderful, and, of course, upstairs even more so. Very near on the left are the lovely arches of Waterloo Bridge, and just beyond it Somerset House.

"Everyone must notice the flowers at the Savoy. They are about the best in any London restaurant. There are graceful-shaped china vases of varying colours. A few good flowers are placed in each. They look as if they had been put there as a decoration, and not like the plated vases, two-thirds filled with greenery and one-third with mediocre flowers, which stand in a perfunctory way on the tables of practically all our expensive restaurants.

"As a matter of fact the Savoy prides itself on its flowers. Buttonholes are more often than not presented to its women clients, and flowers are apparently very much to the fore in the hotel suites.

"The foyer was fairly recently re-decorated. Its predominating colour is green, and there are some very decorative lalique wall mirrors - coloured glass designs overlaid on the mirrors.

"Looking riverwards, like the restaurant, are four smaller rooms for private parties. They are called after four of the Savoy operas, Pinafore, Patience, Iolanthe and Princess Ida.

"The Pinafore room is the largest and has recently been re-decorated by Mr Ionides, the decorator of Claridge's restaurant. The result in this small room is excellent; the walls are panelled in cedar, and great attention has been given to detail, the fireplace, the window blinds, etc.

"Then there is the Savoy Grill. It is very apparent, and rather Continental looking, as one enters the main courtyard. It is a big place with large glass windows down to the ground and forming one side of the courtyard. These are edged by a window box of flowers and ferns.

"The Savoy kitchens are necessarily huge places, for, apart from the everyday work of restaurants, grill and hotel, there are great banqueting rooms. The chef is M. François Latry, a young man for his big position. He considers that one of his specialities is faisan doré Savoy and poire commis ginette.

"The first is a pheasant stuffed with fresh truffles and heart of celery and cooked in a casserole with Devonshire butter. A glass of port and a glass of cream are poured over it, and a sprinkling of lemon juice is added just as it turns to gold.

"The Savoy Hotel will go down in history as 'The Grand Babylon Hotel' of Arnold Bennett's famous novel."

The Restaurants of London, Eileen Hooton-Smith, 1928

Willy Bauer now runs this stately ship with a firm hand on the rudder. This hotel should be visited for its overall professionalism, both at the front of house and in the kitchen under the expert eye of Anton Edelmann who produces some excellent food, both in the restaurants and in the beautiful private suites. I remember one meal in particular, when I was the guest of the Benedicts Dining Club - it was exemplary both in presentation and content. The excellent new kitchens installed in The Savoy are well justified, given the extent and range of dishes they produce.

The Grill Room, another clubby restaurant of London, has its own dedicated following and with a different set of dishes for every day of the week. On Mondays it's farmhouse sausages with creamed potatoes and fried onions, then boiled leg of lamb with spinach dumplings on Tuesdays, or steak and kidney pie. On Thursdays try the rolled chicken and bacon pie, or roast rib of beef and Yorkshire pudding. There are good straightforward grills and roasts, and of course omelette Arnold Bennett. There is also fish if you prefer. In the evening they also have a fixed daily special, changing according to the day, but different from the lunch-time one. You might be offered a sugarbaked ham served with creamed spinach, or perhaps roast Norfolk duck with almonds and apples.

The Savoy River Room has again been redecorated in the same style and colours as the original dining room, and offers a different style in eating from a well-thought out à la carte menu with a good selection of game in season. A selection of 6 or so fish courses includes the exceptionally good médallion de loup de mer grillé aux huîtres. You can choose from 2 set dinners, le dîner au choix at around £22.00 or le dîner des gourmets at around £30.00 a head.

The Connaught   **W1**

Carlos Place W1Y 6AL
01-499 7070

Closed: Grill Room: Sat + Sun; Bank Holidays; Christmas; Easter
Last
Orders: Grill Room: lunch (2.30pm); dinner (10.30pm)
         The Restaurant: lunch (2.00pm); dinner (10.30pm)

The Connaught is more like a club in many ways, and the
atmosphere and style of this beautiful hotel will envelop you as
soon as you enter the front door. The hotel has infinite style, the
furnishings are well chosen and very English in a clubby way. It's
always a treat to eat in either the Grill Room or the Restaurant, the
latter distinguished by its panelling and feeling of warmth, and the
former by its fresh green décor. Chef Michel Bourdin has class,
and is a firm believer in traditional cooking, and many of his
former associates and apprentices seem to appear throughout the
country either in their own restaurants or as chefs in some of the
larger establishments. I can think of few better places to be
trained than here. In the restaurant, choose from classic dishes
like the freshly prepared foie gras, fine consommés, poached
turbot with a mousseline sauce, roast pheasant, grouse or
partridge. At Friday lunch the coulibiac of salmon recalls Maxim's
de Paris where Michel spent 10 years prior to taking over The
Connaught kitchens.

More modern touches appear in some of the fish dishes, such as the rendezvous de pêcheur, sauce légère à la crème de poireaux à la nage, and blanc de barbue soufflé "Tout Paris". His large menu offers infinite variety to please all tastes - there are oysters, caviar or smoked salmon for rich purists and there are sausages and kidneys with bacon for very late risers.

It is a tribute to Michel's skill that he maintains such high standards within the constraints imposed by The Connaught's clientele and that he has introduced true style to this English institution. Michel is highly respected by British and French chefs for his determination to establish the English Filiale de l'Académie Culinaire de France, of which he is president. Under his guidance, and with the help of his contemporaries, l'Académie is instrumental in furthering the training of young chefs and enhancing the standing of gastronomy.

The style of the bedrooms matches that of the public rooms in grandeur, and the suites are outstanding. Guests lucky enough to get a booking here are rarely disappointed.

Claridge's   W1

Brook Street W1A 2JQ   £70
01-629 8860

CLARIDGE'S

Last
Orders: dinner (11.45pm)

"*Claridge's stands in Brook Street, in the heart of Mayfair and, as Charles, its famous restaurateur remarked, 'It is necessary to make coming to Claridge's a function, for, owing to its position, one does not drop into Claridges's accidentally.'*

"*This has been successfully accomplished. Claridge's is a most delightful and sought-after hotel - and restaurant.*

"*More than a hundred years ago a Frenchman by the name of Milvart opened a hotel in Brook Street and called it Milvart's Royal Hotel; shortly afterwards it was bought by Mr Claridge.*

"*Very many of the world's famous people have stayed at Claridge's during its hundred years of life. The Empress Eugenie was there twice in 1860: the first time she drove up in an ordinary cab, strictly incognito owing to the death of her sister, the Duchess of Alba. On her second visit she received a call from Queen Victoria, and it is said to have been the only occasion on record of the British Queen calling at an hotel. The visit was noteworthy for another reason, the Empress Eugenie was wearing one of the hooped skirts, the fashion for which she had re-introduced into France, and Queen Victoria saw and approved.*

"*Two days later the French Empress left for Paris, but before doing so she leant out of her railway carriage window and thanked Mr Claridge for the 'comfortable privacy she had enjoyed under his roof*

"*Claridge's did not occupy the area it does to-day, at one time it was just two houses; it gradually grew, and the building of the present day edifice took place between 1894-1898. It is red brick, now toned to a becoming dark shade by London soot, and one is certain on looking at it that it is the taste of the late Victorian or early Edwardian period.*

"*The main entrance is inset and under cover of the first floor; there is another, lesser, entrance in Davis Street.*

"Once inside the building everything is modern and sump-tuous. On a winter day one is pleasantly greeted by a great coal fire in the outer hall. There is a view through glass doors to the lounge, and on, through more glass doors, to one of the reception rooms beyond. At one time it was said that Claridge's had an air of solemn grandeur, as if an archduke's body was lying in state up stairs. That feeling has all disappeared now.

"A very large sum of money was spent on the re-decoration in 1926. The lounge is now most beautifully furnished and adorned. It is a big square place with another big square part adjacent on the left which contains a second fireplace. The ceiling is low, as hotel and restaurant ceilings are counted, and the same applies to the restaurant and to the suite of reception rooms.

"The lounge is of no distinct colour, and is set out with a large number of chairs for the most part diverse in pattern and charming in design, the best type of modern furniture, which in reality is merely a copy of the antique. The whole lounge has an air of modern Parisian taste, more especially the amber chandeliers. The walls on the left hand portion of the lounge are painted.

"The restaurant lies to the right of the lounge and is divided from it by fourteen-feet tall wrought iron and glass doors which were part of the scheme of restaurant re-decoration designed by Mr Basil Ionides rather more than a year ago. Within the room gives a low-browed impression, especially so on account of a series of wide arches and pillars which intersect it.

"The decoration is very unusual. The walls and pillars are coloured a kind of 'terra-cotta-elephant', and the walls have on them a series of mirrors engraved in the eighteenth century style from the design of Mr Ionides and by the artist Mr W B E Ranken; the subjects are classic landscapes.

"The light and colour scheme are supposed to be very becoming to women lunchers and diners, as Charles remarked, 'They ensure that a woman of sixty will never feel more than forty while here'.

The Restaurants of London, Eileen Hooton-Smith, 1928

To follow the image established more than 150 years ago is a daunting task, but Marjan Lesnik is an adventurous young chef who spent a few years with Michel Bourdin at The Connaught, which must have been good grounding. He has to combine tradition with fashion, to please young and old, to be adventurous with restraint. His menu does just that. There is a joint to be carved from the trolley for lunch and dinner; at lunch he might offer a quarter of lamb with herbes de Provence and at night a roast sirloin of beef with Yorkshire pudding. On Saturday the lunch-time crepinettes of loin of veal with fennel make way for a simple roast duck in the evening. There are exciting modern dishes too, a chiffonade of vegetables and shellfish with fresh truffles, a terrine of scallops and salmon with aniseed, which vie for favour with a cocktail of lobster, langoustines or crayfish, or beluga caviar (1¼ ozs not the usual 1 oz - this is Claridge's).

The ambience is as of a world that stopped some years ago: staff glide and somehow appear when needed, gypsy musicians play in the lounge and the décor is rich, to say the least.

The legendary Charles' remark: "It is necessary to make coming to Claridge's a function... one does not drop into Claridge's accidentally," still holds good 6 decades later.

41

The Ritz   **W1**

150 Piccadilly W1V 9DG
01-493 8181

£70

Last
Orders: lunch (2.30pm); dinner (11.00pm)

"*Going in at the hotel entrance in Arlington Street the lounge stretches ahead with its lovely handwoven carpet, a copy of one at Versailles. It is like a long gallery of some great French chateau and ends with the restaurant. Now, this is a particularly fortunate room, for its windows look right across the Green Park, and it is one of the very few restaurants in London which can entirely dispense with electric light in the daytime. On a spring or summer day at lunch time it is full of sunlight.*

"*The name 'Ritz' carries weight with it to a particular degree, as befits the name-child of the inventor of the luxury hotel. This is very beneficial in its way, but the authorities have also to bear in mind that that very name is apt to strike terror into the hearts of some would-be patrons on the score of price.*

"*As a matter of fact the prices of London's half-dozen luxury hotels are very much of a muchness. It stands to reason that they must be.*

"*The Ritz has been built for twenty-two years; it rose up in the stead of Walsingham House; for, though that was a nearly new building then, Mr. Ritz would not be content with conversion. He wished to construct a hotel which would be the very last word in luxury, and though many hôtels de luxe have sprung up about the world in the intervening years Mr Ritz's edifice has not been surpassed. It is still the model, and every year architectural students are taken over it. Apart from the design of the building and the general correctness to period it contains every detail for comfort and service, and those which were not invented when it was built have been added as the years went by.*

"*But to return to the beautiful restaurant overlooking the park. It has a deep pink-red flowered carpet, chairs covered with pale green embossed velvet, and lovely old gold brocade curtains.*

"*To serve two hundred customers à la carte, a brigade of forty cooks is necessary', says M. Herberdeau, the chef. 'Amongst these cooks there are experienced specialists, capable of preparing all known specialities. A large restaurant does not only prepare a few specialities, but all those that a customer may desire.'*

"*Next to the restaurant is the charming Marie Antoinette Room, which, by the way, has a signed clock on its mantelpiece worth two or three hundred pounds. This room is used for large or small private luncheons and dinners. Sometimes, however, a great dinner is given in the Palm Court section of the lounge.*

"*The Aga Khan for one has given several magnificent dinner parties in the Palm Court, attended by Ambassadors, important social figures and political celebrities, ranging from Lord Balfour to Mr. J.H. Thomas, the ex-Labour Minister.*

"*On these occasions the Palm Court is screened off from the lounge by a bank of flowers and palms.*

"*Princess Victoria, the King's sister, lunches there most days on which she drives up to town from her house in Iver in Bucks. She just saunters in. The Princess Royal and Prince George are also frequent clients.*

"Of the habitués of the restaurant, many desire to sit at the tables just inside the door to be seen and to see everyone entering or exiting, rather than over by the windows with their beautiful view.

"In a quiet corner is the table always used by Royalty, the Prince of Wales when he dines there, or the Duke and Duchess of York, and many times by the King and Queen of Spain. Most of London's famous people have eaten in the Ritz restaurant."

The Restaurants of London, Eileen Hooton-Smith, 1928

The Ritz is an institution, and has quite a history to live up to. But under the leadership of Michael Duffell, the managing director, it is not afraid to use the best of a past era, yet move forward with some imaginatively arranged evenings, including cabaret performances in the restaurant on Wednesday, Thursday and Friday evenings, which are excellent value.

The décor is grand - the marble work, the furnishings and the magnificent fittings are all carefully and lovingly maintained. The staff are pleased to see you and the dining room, with its little terrace, is still one of the prettiest rooms in London. A well-chosen wine list is comprehensive in its selection, and on chef David Miller's special menu at about £27.00, you get some interesting and original combinations. It's one of the few restaurants in London where you can still get Scotch woodcock or devils on horseback as savouries, and the daily lunch-time roast Scotch beef from the trolley is good value at £13.50.

I like The Ritz - the history of it, the overwhelming feeling of luxury and the sense of occasion.

Other London Hotel Restaurants

Le Soufflé   W1

Hotel Inter-Continental London, 1 Hamilton Place,   £50
Hyde Park Corner W1V 0QY
01-409 3131

Closed: lunch (Sat)
Last
Orders: lunch (2.30pm); dinner (11.30pm)

The Hotel Inter-Continental is renowned for its luxurious
accommodation and the excellent overall standard of food
which is maintained in all its various departments. Graham
Jeffrey's hand guides this 500-room Park Lane favourite, and
Peter Kromberg, the Executive Chef, oversees the food throughout. This includes the coffee-house restaurant, room service,
some exceptional food served in the private rooms, and of
course the much-fêted Le Soufflé Restaurant, which offers a
menu of the day at under £20.00 or the chef's choice - a 7
courses including a sorbet for under £30.00.

As you would expect from a restaurant called Le Soufflé,
when you order one, they are exceptional. A starter of boneless
slip sole filled with a lobster soufflé, served with a fennel and
saffron sauce, is excellent, as is roast rack of lamb glazed with a
wild mushroom mousse, or suprême of duck filled with goose
liver baked in a puff pastry lattice, served on a leaf spinach and
calvados sauce. Or maybe you would prefer a French blue
cheese soufflé with walnuts and celery served with a port sauce,
or - a particular favourite - aubergine mousse flavoured with
cumin, on a capsicum and tomato vinaigrette, wrapped in
courgettes and served with sautéed langoustines. Another excellent dish is poached scallops with young root vegetables in a
light lemon sauce with hazelnut oil. There is, of course, a choice
of soufflés for dessert also. Peter Kromberg is an exceptional
chef and has been here since the opening in 1975, following in
his father's footsteps, for Kromberg Senior was an outstanding
chef pâtissier, and Peter received his early training in the hotel
where his father worked.

There is an excellent wine list in Le Soufflé Restaurant, and
the soft candlelit Art Déco restaurant, though very much in
harmony with the hotel, attracts many besides its residents.

90 Park Lane   W1

Grosvenor House Hotel, 90 Park Lane W1A 3AA   £70
01-499 6363
                          Stephen Goodlad
Closed: lunch (Sat + Sun); dinner (Sun)   has now taken
Last
Orders: dinner (11.00pm)   over as Chef de
                                             Cuisine

The décor and the restaurant are very different from Louis
Outhier's La Napoule in the South of France, but full marks to

THF for importing Louis to this side of the channel to help advise and create some interesting dishes with Vaughan Archer, the resident chef. The restaurant, which seats 85, is sumptuous, and the staff are attentive and alert, as one would expect in this type of establishment and for the price. The interior is cleverly designed to give a warm ambience overall, and yet a feeling of privacy wherever you are seated.

The marbled terrine of fresh goose liver with green peppercorn aspiç was first class, as were the warm medallions of lobster with finely diced vegetables and lobster vinaigrette. The loup de mer en croûte in the style of Louis Outhier was sensational. Alternatively, you can choose from 2 set menus, the Menu Oasis at £29.00 per head, or the Menu Gourmet at £36.00 per head. An incredibly comprehensive wine list has some amazing wines in the top bracket - both in choice and price. It is interesting to see that other hotels in the capital and elsewhere in Great Britain are importing famous French chefs; and if they are as fortunate in combining this strategy with the local talent already available, as at 90 Park Lane, it can only be for the best.

The Chelsea Room   SW1

Hyatt Carlton Tower, 2 Cadogan Place SW1X 9PY
01-235 5411

Last
Orders: lunch (2.45pm); dinner (11.00pm; Sun 10.15pm)

Jean Quero heads this competently run dining room whilst Mr Bernard Gaume is the wizard who runs the kitchens, not just for this dining room but for room service and the other outlets in the hotel. Bernard Gaume, a respected member of the Académie Culinaire, is a quiet, modest man who expresses himself with some exquisite combinations and elaborate interpretations of dishes. The fresh goose liver tossed in butter with fresh grapes, and the leaves of salmon and scallops on a bed of spring salad are two of my favourite starters, out of a choice of some 12 or so. From the excellent choice of fish dishes, fillets of sea bass and red mullet in a light butter sauce, or fresh salmon baked in foil with shredded vegetables are 2 of the best in this section. Choose from around 11 main courses which might include Bresse chicken with red pimentoes, cream sauce and noodles, a finely sliced breast of duck with cider vinegar and honey sauce, or 2 fillets of veal with a ginger sauce. A choice of vegetables which are as well cooked as you would expect, comes with the excellent main courses. There is a good choice of English and French farmhouse cheeses followed by the charmingly named pudding renversé à l'anglaise coulis de fraise (upside down cherry trifle) or the amazing chocolate cake with coffee sauce - these from about 6 or 7 possibilities from the kitchen; and the pastries and fruits on the trolley.

They offer you a short selection of wines on the menu card itself, including an excellent Moulin à Vent, Domaine de la Tour de Bief 1985, or a Hermitage La Chappelle, Paul Jaboulet Aîné 1982. Alternatively you can choose from the more expensive wine list which has more than enough variety for anyone, with Bordeaux ranging back to 1926 Château Margaux, and a good selection of younger Burgundies.

The Capital Hotel   SW3

22-24 Basil Street SW3 1AT
01-589 5171

Last
Orders: lunch (2.30pm); dinner (10.30pm)

The restaurant at The Capital has undergone a few changes since Brian Turner left the kitchen to open his own restaurant, but standards have not declined, as the hotel is too well controlled by David Levin and team for that to happen. It has one of the smallest hotel dining rooms in London, which perhaps explains why such high standards are maintained. The room is elegant with large crystal chandeliers, plush brown and beige drapes, floral paintings, large comfortable carver chairs and Limoges china.

A well-composed à la carte menu has some lavish combinations, like a mousseline of scallops with a cream of oursins, terrine of rabbit with pistachios, brandade of sole with endives or cream of mussels. To follow, try sweetbreads with tomato and garlic, duck breasts with lemon and honey, assorted butcher's meats with whole grain mustard sauce, or charcoal grilled fish or meats for simpler tastes. The cooking is very skilful. Puddings are a delight, for example a perfect biscuit glacé with hazelnuts, a petit pot au chocolate with orange, or a mousse of crème brûlée with passion fruit.

The service is well organised and supervised by Dieter Schuldt, and the staff are friendly but discreet. Wines leave nothing to be desired except perhaps a small inheritance so as to be able to afford them!

NO OTHER WATER SPRINGS TO MIND SO NATURALLY

'Ashbourne' Water is the sparkling choice wherever good food and drink are served.

It rises from a source high in the Derbyshire hills.

It's pure and crystal clear – with nothing added but the sparkle.

Naturally, 'Ashbourne' Water is simply superb on its own – and it mixes marvellously with fruit juice, wines and spirits.

That's why it's such a sparkling success with everyone, everywhere, everytime.

Sparkling 'Ashbourne' Natural Water – the perfect complement to fine food.

THE NESTLÉ COMPANY LTD. St. George's House, Croydon, Surrey CR9 1NR. 01-686 3333.

LONDON POSTAL DISTRICTS

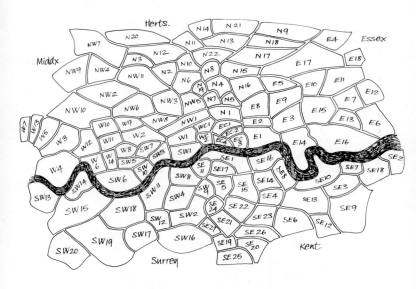

E1 Stepney	N1 Islington
E2 Bethnal Green	N2 East Finchley
E3 Bow	N3 Finchley
E4 Chingford	N4 Finsbury Park
E5 Clapton	N5 Highbury
E6 East Ham	N6 Highgate
E7 Forest Gate	N7 Holloway
E8 Hackney	N8 Hornsey
E9 Homerton	N9 Lower Edmonton
E10 Leyton	N10 Muswell Hill
E11 Leytonstone	N11 New Southgate
E12 Manor Park	N12 North Finchley
E13 Plaistow	N13 Palmers Green
E14 Poplar	N14 Southgate
E15 Stratford	N15 South Tottenham
E16 North Woolwich	N16 Stoke Newington
E17 Walthamstow	N17 Tottenham
E18 Woodford	N18 Upper Edmonton
	N19 Upper Holloway
EC1-4 City	N20 Whetstone
	N21 Winchmore Hill
	N22 Wood Green

NW1   Camden Town
NW2   Cricklewood
NW3   Hampstead
NW4   Hendon
NW5   Kentish Town
NW6   Kilburn
NW7   Mill Hill
NW8   St John's Wood
NW9   The Hyde
NW10   Willesden
NW11   Golders Green

SE1   Southwark
SE2   Abbey Wood
SE3   Blackheath
SE4   Brockley
SE5   Camberwell
SE6   Catford
SE7   Charlton
SE8   Deptford
SE9   Eltham
SE10   Greenwich
SE11   Kennington
SE12   Lee
SE13   Lewisham
SE14   New Cross
SE15   Peckham
SE16   Rotherhithe
SE17   Walworth
SE18   Woolwich
SE19   Norwood
SE20   Anerley
SE21   Dulwich
SE22   East Dulwich
SE23   Forest Hill
SE24   Herne Hill
SE25   South Norwood
SE26   Sydenham
SE27   West Norwood
SE28   Thamesmead

SW1   Westminster
SW2   Brixton
SW3   Chelsea
SW4   Clapham
SW5   Earls Court
SW6   Fulham
SW7   South Kensington
SW8   South Lambeth
SW9   Stockwell
SW10   West Brompton
SW11   Battersea
SW12   Balham
SW13   Barnes
SW14   Mortlake
SW15   Putney
SW16   Streatham
SW17   Tooting
SW18   Wandsworth
SW19   Wimbledon
SW20   West Wimbledon

W1   Marble Arch
W2   Paddington
W3   Acton
W4   Chiswick
W5   Ealing
W6   Hammersmith
W7   Hanwell
W8   Kensington
W9   Maida Vale
W10   North Kensington
W11   Notting Hill
W12   Shepherds Bush
W13   West Ealing
W14   West Kensington

WC1-4   City/West Central

Blooms   E1

90 Whitechapel High Street E1
01-247 6001

Closed: Sat
Last
Orders: 9.30pm; Fri: sunset

Situated in Whitechapel High Street, Blooms is London's best-known
and most firmly established Jewish restaurant. You can have a salt beef
sandwich with lemon tea in the busy bar at the front of the restaurant,
or eat traditional kosher dishes in the large well-ordered dining room. It
is an experience rather than a gastronomic revelation, with some
colourful - if somewhat abrupt - characters for waiters, who don't like to
see anything left on your plate, and wouldn't hesitate to tell you so!

City Limits Restaurant & Wine Bar   E1

16-18 Brushfield Street E1 6AN
01-377 9877

Closed: dinner (daily - restaurant); Sat + Sun; Bank
        Holidays
Last
Orders: lunch (2.45pm); dinner (10.00pm - wine bar)

Situated just off Bishopsgate, City Limits is a wine bar on the ground
floor level with a restaurant in the basement. Simply decorated, with
timber-clad walls, high stools and a small bar, the wine bar offers a
small range of dishes such as steak sandwiches, lasagna or chilli con
carne. The cosy restaurant specialises in char-grilled Scotch steaks,
gravadlax, Danish herrings and Michael Nadell's cakes. Should you
ponder the relevance of the latter speciality, all will be revealed when I
tell you that Mr Nadell is a cousin of David Hughes, the owner of City
Limits!

   The world-wide wine list has some good selections, and the majority
are priced at well below £10.00 a bottle.

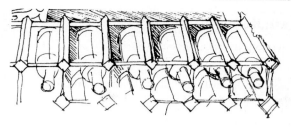

Bubb's
EC1

329 Central Markets EC1A 9BN
01-236 2435

£35

Closed: Sat + Sun; Bank Holidays; 2 weeks Summer
Last
Orders: lunch (2.00pm); dinner (9.30pm)

In the shadow of Holborn Viaduct, this green painted corner site at the side of Smithfield market houses a truly French restaurant. It's earthy in style, and the food and service remind you of places which you were lucky enough to find while driving through France. The menu changes every 3 months to feature seasonal specialities, and the cooking is robust and filling.

Dark red, timber-clad walls, lace curtains and well-worn chairs give an established feel to the restaurant, which is on 2 floors with an iron spiral staircase leading from one to the other. Madame Bubb, who is French, greets customers, and her staff are French too.

Book in advance as the tables fill rapidly once lunchtime draws near.

Café Rouge   EC1

2C Cherry Tree Walk, Whitecross Street EC1
01-588 0710

Closed: Sat + Sun; Bank Holidays; Christmas/New Year;
             first 2 weeks Aug
Last
Orders: lunch (2.30pm); dinner (11.30pm)

Large tubs of plants adorn the outside of this café, which is really
rather more of a restaurant. On the shopping precinct side there is
a patio for tables and chairs to be set outside, and inside the décor
leaves little doubt as to the ethnic origin of the cuisine. Bright red,
white and blue is conspicuous, from the exterior through to the
small mezzanine. Chef Bryan Webb is, however, from this side of
La Manche, and he offers a good à la carte menu with plats du
jour, and a fixed price menu at around £13.00 for 3 courses and
coffee. Fish features strongly, and is brought in fresh daily from
Billingsgate. Wines are all from France and have been well
chosen, with a few slightly unusual selections available.

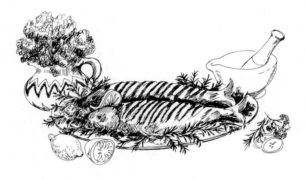

Café St Pierre   EC1

29 Clerkenwell Green EC1
01-251 6606

Closed: Sat + Sun; Bank Holidays; Christmas/New Year
Last
Orders: 11.00pm

A fair way to describe this cheerful corner place, just off the
Clerkenwell Road, would be as a café-like brasserie with a
restaurant. Open for breakfast from 7.30am, it offers freshly
squeezed orange juice and espresso coffee with either continental or English breakfast, next progressing through lunch to a
pre-theatre dinner menu and then dinner itself. Will Thompson's
menu changes daily in the ground floor brasserie, and weekly in
his pink, first-floor dining room.
     The interesting wine list even gives you the opportunity of a
'vertical tasting' - wine trade jargon meaning tasting the wines of
one producer or château from different vintages - of Château
Lynch Bages, at which they offer 5 wines from the 1970s, but you
would need a few friends and slightly over £200 to try it!

Rudland & Stubbs   EC1

35-37 Greenhill Rents EC1
01-258 0148

£30

Closed: lunch (Sat); dinner (Sun)
Last
Orders: lunch (3.00pm); dinner (11.30pm)

This unpretentious straightforward restaurant features mainly seafood, although there are one or two meat alternatives. The grilled fish is best, or shrimps, cockles and mussels from the long bar. Oysters in season are good. This is a useful place for a quick lunch if you are in the area.

Bill Bentley's   EC2

Swedeland Court, 202 Bishopsgate EC2
01-283 1763

£40

Closed: dinner (daily); Sat + Sun; Bank Holidays
Last
Orders: 1.45pm

Down a clean-painted courtyard at the side of Dirty Dick's pub, a Union Jack heralds the entrance to Bill Bentley's. The ground floor oyster bar has a long counter with stools set along it, and a few tables on the opposite wall. The basement houses the restaurant, which has comfortable high-backed settles, giving the atmosphere of an old city dining room where traditional English food should be eaten, washed down with claret or white Burgundy.

The menu combines traditional items such as oysters, eggs Benedict, smoked salmon or lobster thermidor, with more modern innovations like the scallops with shredded endives, gravadlax, or supreme of salmon with sorrel sauce. Meats are also included on the menu, with grilled cutlets and tournedos, roast rack of lamb, escalope of veal, and duck breast.

There are the good clarets and white Burgundies that you expect on the list, together with other popular selections, all at sensible prices.

Corney and Barrow   EC2

118 Moorgate EC2M 6UR   £45
01-628 2898/9

Closed: Sat + Sun
Last
Orders: lunch (3.00pm); dinner (8.30pm)

A stylish, well-designed restaurant catering to the City market
and achieving good standards of food and service with a
memorable wine list, all at an unforgettable price. Well-composed
menus change weekly and feature first courses such as a brioche
served hot with bone marrow and port wine sauce, potted
duckling with Cumberland sauce, or cream of mussel and
vegetable soup. Follow this with steamed brill on a coriander and
ginger butter sauce, grilled fillet of lamb with tomato and basil or,
for simpler tastes, calves' liver and bacon. Puddings from a
separate menu might be fresh fig mousse with a strawberry
coulis, a pithiviers served hot with rum sauce, alternatively one of
those and a selection of cheese for a mere £3.55 (plus of course
12.5% for serving it to you). Main dishes with vegetables or salad
are around the £12.00 mark, and first courses between £2.25 and
£6.00, so I should make this your first stopping point after hearing
that Uncle George has left you the business.

Please see the General Listings at the back of the book for other
branches of Corney and Barrow.

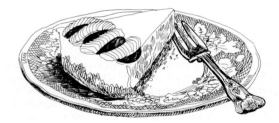

Langan's Bar & Grill   EC3

Plantation House, Mincing Lane EC3M 3DX   £35
01-220 7094

Closed: Sat + Sun; Bank Holidays
Last
Orders: lunch (3.00pm); dinner (8.00pm)

Located in the basement of a vast office complex in the City, this
restaurant has plain walls (hung with hundreds of paintings), a
timber floor, and a large central bar which divides the dining
areas. Obviously, owing to its location, lunch is a busy, bustling
time where much wine is consumed and presumably much
business done across the white-clad tables. A changing menu
offers a good range of dishes as diverse as lobster soup and
Cumberland sausages with onion sauce and mashed potatoes
(up-market bangers and mash).

Excellent turbot cooked with thyme and limes is served with
good vegetables, and the crème brûlée is properly made. The wine

list is fairly small and the wines one would choose to drink are fairly expensive, but then the City is a difficult place in which to operate with such limited opening hours.

Shares   EC3

12-13 Lime Street EC3
01-623 1843

Closed: dinner (daily); lunch Sat + Sun; Bank Holidays
Last
Orders: lunch (2.30pm)

Situated on the ground floor of a large office block, Shares is a popular City venue. Blue curtains screen the large windows overlooking Lime Street, and the material for the rest of the interior is in the serious colours of brown and blue, with comfortable armchairs and attractive wall lighting.

Fixed price menus for 3 or 4 courses offer simply cooked dishes, and the wine list features conventional choices of mainly claret and Burgundy. The restaurant has an earnest ambience and is a good place to strike a deal.

Le Gamin   EC4

32 Old Bailey EC4M 7HS
01-236 7931

Closed: dinner (daily); Sat + Sun; Bank Holidays
Last
Orders: 2.30pm

The recent excursions of the Roux brothers into the world of food for the masses ('sous-vide') may have been inspired by their conspicuous success at Le Gamin. In a brightly lit, loudly tiled, noisy and bustling basement they have brought basic French eating to the City. Speed is of the essence - as you sit down they bring you a kir and a menu, which has a reasonable choice for the set lunch. It might include a boudin noir aux pommes and a pavé de saumon à l'oseille. Some dishes may utilise their 'sous-vide' technique, whilst others are prepared in great quantity behind the scenes. In any event it will be quickly set before you, equally quickly eaten and by 2.15pm you may well be sitting on your own.

Le Gamin

The City's habit of everyone having to eat at 1.00pm is bound to cramp the chef's style somewhat, but the food is honest and straightfoward, and it is good value, as is the reasonably priced wine list.

Le Poulbot   EC4

45 Cheapside EC4
01-236 4379

Closed: dinner (daily); Sat + Sun; Bank Holidays; Christmas/New Year
Last
Orders: 3.00pm

Le Poulbot

It is hard to believe that Le Poulbot has existed for 17 years, it being the second restaurant opened by the Roux brothers following the success of Le Gavroche in its original Chelsea setting. On the ground floor is Le Poulbot Pub, which is a typical French brasserie, catering for breakfast and informal lunches. But it is the basement restaurant which has established its real reputation. When you enter the dining room it is easy to imagine what vast sums of money change hands between the business-men who frequent the restaurant for a working lunch. High backed, buttoned banquette seats fill the centre of the room to prevent conversations being overheard. Red walls and carpet provide a luxurious feel and give you confidence as you enter. Staff are impeccable, and under the guidance of Monsieur Cottard the service is unobtrusive and efficient.

Rowley Leigh is the chef, and his fixed price menu changes daily to offer a variety of well-produced dishes. Chicken con-sommé with lettuce, langoustines with new potatoes and aïoli, a warm salad of sweetbreads with lime, or a terrine of chicken with foie gras and fennel are possible starters. Main courses might include a loin of venison with redcurrants and white pepper, fillet steak in pancakes, red mullet in a cream sauce flavoured with rosemary, or an escalope of salmon with chervil and wild rice. Try some young leeks layered in a terrine and served with a light chive sauce, and then follow it with a delicious chartreuse of partridge, which would be served in a modern rather than a classic way. Finish with a marquise of dark and light chocolate, light in texture and full of flavour. There are a few recommended wines on the menu, or you can choose à la carte from around 30 other wines.

Although it is not cheap, Le Poulbot is very good value, especially compared with other expensive city restaurants.

Sweetings   EC4

£30

39 Queen Victoria Street EC4
01-248 3062

Closed: dinner (by arrangement only); Sat + Sun
Last
Orders: 3.00pm

It seems difficult to accept that Graham Needham hasn't been here almost as long as Sweetings itself, although that's doing

him a bit of an injustice, since this particular establishment has been open for 98 years! Graham is certainly very much part of the atmosphere; an unusual establishment, it's old English in every sense. You can't book a table, so it means you have to get there early - and people do. It's also one of the few places that refuses to take plastic money, but this does not seem to deter the hungry hordes at lunch time either.

Fresh crab, smoked salmon, and smoked eel fillets are among the hors d'oeuvres, there are 6 or so soups to choose from, and all manner of fish - Dover sole, halibut, fresh haddock, Scotch salmon, skate fried or poached with black butter, and Needham's famous salmon fish cakes. The cold table offers crab salad, ox tongue, ham on the bone and roast ribs of beef. Good old British puddings are of steamed syrup, bread and butter, or baked jam roll. There's an excellent selection of wines and Champagne by the glass or the bottle, all at extremely reasonable prices. It's a super place for an evening reception, which Graham Needham would be delighted to arrange for you.

Anna's Place   N1

90 Mildmay Park N1 4PR
01-249 9379

Closed: Sun + Mon; 2 weeks Christmas; 2 weeks Easter; Aug

Last
Orders: lunch (2.30pm); dinner (10.15pm)

Situated next to the Nobody Inn (it's true, just ring them), Anna's Place occupies a converted house, and is best described as a Swedish bistro. It's certainly one of the most welcoming and busiest restaurants in Islington. Pretty flowers outside, plenty of plants inside and a small garden at the rear create a cheerful ambience. Polished pine floors, bright tablecloths, wooden chairs, and colourful posters and prints on the walls add to it. The menu provides dishes such as gravadlax, smoked reindeer, marinated herrings, or tapenade followed by lax pudding (cured salmon layered with potatoes, onions and dill, then baked), gravad mackerel (marinated mackerel grilled with creamed spinach and potatoes), Swedish meatballs and var kyckling (roast spring chicken with lemon and coriander sauce). A small but adequate list of wines at reasonable prices makes Anna's an affordable pleasure.

Frederick's   N1

Camden Passage N1   £30
01-359 2888

Closed: Sun; Bank Holidays
Last
Orders: lunch (2.30pm); dinner (11.30pm)

Amidst the antique dealers of Camden Passage, Louis Segal's well-established restaurant is a popular venue for lunch and dinner alike. The main feature of the restaurant is a large conservatory area with an attractive patio outside for warmer days. Greenery abounds, giving a delightfully fresh atmosphere, and a touch of the country in North One!

Jean-Louis Pollet, the chef, produces an à la carte menu with a good selection of dishes for vegetarians, and the option of low calorie cuisine minceur dishes. For those of us not torn by pangs of conscience, there are dishes such as a veal chop garnished with Parma ham and mozzarella cheese in a port sauce, rabbit simmered gently with mushrooms and herbs, or a duck breast marinaded in honey and then served in a redcurrant sauce with whole redcurrants. Profiteroles with hazelnut cream and coffee sauce, iced soufflé with Grand Marnier, or rich chocolate cake flavoured with peppermint liqueur and served with a vanilla sauce are amongst the tempting puddings which are most definitely not minceur!

A feature of Frederick's is the tantalising display of fine wines and magnums from the patron's cellar, but there is plenty of choice on the list to satisfy most tastes, and prices are reasonable.

M'sieur Frog Restaurant   N1

31 Essex Road N1   £30
01-226 3495

Closed: lunch (daily); 1 week Christmas; 1 week Aug
Last
Orders: dinner (11.15pm)

A true bistro atmosphere can be found here, with timber-clad walls, red and white tablecloths, bentwood chairs and a black-

M'SIEUR FROG

board menu for specialities. Dishes are drawn from bourgeois cooking with some nouvelle influences, and service is friendly. A good wine list has reasonable prices.

Varnom's   N1

2 Greenman Street N1 8SB
01-359 6707

Closed: lunch (Sat + Mon); dinner (Sun + Mon); 2 weeks Jan
Last
Orders: dinner (11.30pm)

John Varnom is one of the growing number of self-taught chefs though his background is more unusual than most, as he claims to have produced an album for the Sex Pistols! Some of his cooking is as fashionable but not as controversial as his previous job, and dishes may include teal and mallard with bilberry and elderberry sauce, or a mousse of celery and black truffles with a warm salad of crisp parsley and glazed baby onions.

The restaurant, in increasingly fashionable Islington, is sleekly furnished with some striking pictures and the wine list, as you might expect, combines the obvious with the more recherché.

Sunday lunch is quite an event when the centre-piece of a no-choice menu can be something like couscous or bouillabaisse.

Le Bistroquet   NW1

273-275 Camden High Street NW1
01-485 9607

Closed: 3 days Christmas
Last
Orders: 11.30pm

A bright, cheerful bar and restaurant just alongside Camden Lock where you can have a glass of wine, a light meal in the bar or eat in the more serious restaurant area - the choice is yours.

The bar menu has dishes like salade chèvre et concombre, rillettes, bratwurst with puréed potatoes, steak sandwich and assiette of charcuterie. In the restaurant there is a fairly large menu with a mixture of nouvelle dishes such as paupiettes of whiting with smoked salmon mousse in cucumber sauce which contrasts sharply with the traditional pot au feu of chicken. The menus change every couple of months and the cooking is of a good standard with some original ideas, crisp vegetables and salads and excellent sweets.

A well-conceived wine list with plenty of regional wines under £10.00 and very good housewines.

Café Delancey   NW1

3 Delancey Street NW1 7NN
01-387 1985

Closed: Sun
Last
Orders: 11.30pm

An open-all-day brasserie, this offers a variety of dishes from
croque monsieur with salad to a rack of lamb with herbs, from
rösti potatoes with a couple of fried eggs to a feuilleté of
mushrooms. If you just want an espresso coffee or a citron pressé
that's all right too, and the waitresses smile, which is a bonus.

The décor is basic café style, with a timber floor, bentwood
chairs and a few marble topped tables. It's also good for
breakfast, providing you don't rise before 9.30am!

Camden Brasserie   NW1

216 Camden High Street NW1
01-482 2114

Closed: 24 Dec - 1 Jan
Last
Orders: lunch (3.00pm); dinner (11.30pm)

There are several brasseries/bistros in Camden but this is one of
my favourites because it is well run and simple, yet sincere in its
cooking and service. The décor is cheerful with polished wooden
floor, white walls with interesting photographs of some of the
local habitués, and red gingham tablecloths. The staff are friendly
and helpful, which can be a rare bonus in London bistros, and they
have obviously been trained to do the job - an even rarer
occurrence! The menu is small with a few first courses such as
grilled sardines, merguez (a spicy lamb sausage with horseradish)
or spicy chicken wings. There is a pasta dish of the day as starter
or main course and a couple of salads which can also be taken to
start or follow. The speciality is charcoal grilled meats and fish:
lamb brochette, steak brochette teriyaki, a rib of beef for two and
fish of the day, any of which comes with a huge wooden bowl of
pommes frites.

The salade niçoise was well made with very fresh ingredients, correctly dressed and enormous, the starter size being almost a meal in itself. Pasta is properly cooked and sauces with it are full of flavour; and the brochette of monkfish was excellent.

Odette's   NW1

130 Regent's Park Road NW1 8XL
01-586 5486/8766

Closed: lunch (Sat + Sun); dinner (Sun); Bank Holidays;
         1 week Christmas
Last
Orders: lunch (2.30pm); dinner (11.00pm)

Long established as a favourite eating place of North West London media types, Odette's buzzes with the latest gossip from TV AM or the BBC. The upstairs room has a distinctly Victorian feel to it with lots of greenery, arched mirrors, and bric-à-brac. The mirrors are popular with some of the customers who, when not looking at each other, like to look at themselves.

They will, however, definitely be distracted by the interesting dishes prepared by chef John Armstrong, who continues the tradition of modern, basically French, dishes such as guineafowl and sweetbread terrine with kumquats, medallions of veal with a red pepper purée and limes, parfait of scallops with cod's roe sauce, fillet of lamb with a tian, or casserole of vegetables; or from the daily specials, maybe a steamed breast of chicken filled with vegetable mousse.

The basement wine bar serves simpler dishes, maybe frank-furters, a tuna bake, or some well-made soups, and you can even just drop in for a glass of wine. The wine bar consists of a series of connecting rooms, making it ideal for a secret assignation - provided you don't really mind being spotted! Waiters are theatrical, and the wine list has some interesting bargains as well as the more obvious choices.

Simone Green, the owner, writes a lovely letter, and I hope this place goes from strength to strength, and that the builders of the smart new extension have now, finally, moved out!

Quincy's '84 NW2

675 Finchley Road NW2 2JP
01-794 8499

Closed: lunch (Mon - Sat); dinner (Mon);
      last week in Aug; 24 Dec for 3 weeks
Last
Orders: Sunday lunch (2.00pm); dinner (10.30pm)

Cricklewood is not an area renowned for its gastronomic delights and this restaurant has seen several changes of owner. The current team however, are from varying backgrounds including the excellent Hintlesham and Hambleton Halls, and the quality of everything shines through. The basic surroundings have a country feel to them and so does some of the food. The excellent chilled beetroot soup was perfectly seasoned, and topped with a swirl of sour cream.

    Menus and wine lists are well thought out and reasonably priced. A lot of attention is paid to detail; Muscat de Beaumes de Venise is by Paul Jaboulet Ainé and you won't get better than that. This is a particularly good place for Sunday lunch and there is always a good choice; on a sunny day you will not even be too aware that you are sitting on the busy A41 out of London.

La Cage Imaginaire NW3

16 Flask Walk NW3
01-794 6674

Closed: Mon
Last
Orders: lunch (2.30pm); dinner (11.00pm)

At the end of Flask Walk, a popular passage off Hampstead High Street, this tiny restaurant comes into its own, especially in the summer when tables are spread outside. Friendly waiters dispense fairly typical bistro food in decent portions, and there is a reasonable wine list to choose from. Inside is usually busy too with a loud buzz of conversation as the Hampstead clientele discuss the issues of the day.

Keats Restaurant NW3

3A-4A Downshire Hill NW3 1NR
01-435 3544

Closed: lunch (daily); dinner (Sun)
Last
Orders: dinner (11.00pm)

This panelled, library-like dining room is relaxed and informal, and has for some 20 years been a favourite with the Hampstead literati, particularly those from North America. Under the present ownership of Aron Misan, wines are imported direct from France and can be bought by the case to take home.

Prices definitely reflect the serious intention of a restaurant that offers dishes like petits soufflés au Gruyère or noisettes d'agneau gousse d'ail. They still have the flambée trolley. But full marks to Keats for a vegetarian menu that changes daily, and they also run some interesting special evenings during their 'Festival Gastronomique'.

Peacheys Restaurant   NW3

205 Haverstock Hill NW3 4QG
01-435 6744

Closed: lunch (Sat + Sun); dinner (Sun); Bank Holidays;
        10 days Christmas
Last
Orders: lunch (2.30pm); dinner (11.30pm)

On rare occasions when the sun shines on Belsize Park, tables spread themselves over the pavement and it seems that all of North West London wants to eat at Peacheys. This is not surprising as the food is freshly prepared and alongside some good examples of bistro dishes like steak frites - a simple thing but not easy to find done well in London - you will find some interesting dishes like grilled prawns with sea salt and fresh chillies.

Cheeses, like staff, are imported from France and service is swift (though you may occasionally experience a language problem). You will certainly need to book on sunny days and also evenings, as it is very popular before and after shows at the neighbouring Screen on the Hill.

Beau Rivage NW6

228 Belsize Road NW6 4BT
01-328 9992

Closed: lunch (Sat); first 2 weeks Aug
Last
Orders: lunch (2.30pm); dinner (11.30pm)

Owner George Ng-Yu-Tin has moved his unique fish restaurant, basically French but with overtones of his native Mauritius, about 4 doors down the road from its previous address. The array of fresh fish and seafood is now set in a comfortable bar on the ground floor, while downstairs is the well-furnished dining room, with its sumptuous banquettes and gentle lighting.

The food is still superb - the freshest fish in generous portions, cooked in some classic and some different ways: an authentic bouillabaisse, for example, turbot with horseradish, 2 types of sea bass, and genuinely 16oz Dover soles.

A serving from the wonderful display of exotic fruits on crushed ice is probably all you'll be able to manage after that, but the crêpes are tempting! Wines are well chosen: most Burgundies come from Louis Jadot.

On the site of the former Beau Rivage, at 248 Belsize Road, George has opened a lively brasserie with the emphasis on meat: boeuf bourgignon en croûte, brisket, and the like. Again, cooking is consistent and the service provided by members of the family, friendly.

Peter's Restaurant NW6

65 Fairfax Road NW6 4EE
01-624 5804

Closed: lunch (Sat); dinner (Sun); 1-5 Jan
Last
Orders: dinner (11.30pm)

Neighbourhood bistro where the simpler dishes, like their rack of lamb, are probably the best buy. Service is exuberant and regular customers are greeted like long lost sons.

Viareggio NW6

332 West End Lane NW6 1RJ
01-794 1444

Closed: lunch (Sun)
Last
Orders: lunch (2.30pm); dinner (11.30pm)

Giancarlo used to be at the Arethusa during its heyday in the 1960s, and he brought to the Hampstead/West Hampstead border the style and pzazz that he learnt there.

The menu is fairly standard Italian, but a little more care is taken: the grilled spring chicken is cooked to order, the pasta is fresh and cleverly sauced, and the recently extended dining room is cool and stylish with a loyal, regular clientele.

Au Bois St Jean NW8

122 St John's Wood High Street NW8 7SG
01-722 0400

Closed: lunch (Sat); Easter; Christmas
Last
Orders: lunch (2.30pm); dinner (11.30pm)

Very 1960s, dark, basement bistro, but with a style of cooking that places it firmly in the 1980s. Poulet aux huîtres was an interesting dish. Service is full of enthusiasm.

Wines from Joseph Berkmann are well chosen and fairly priced.

L'Aventure NW8

3 Blenheim Terrace NW8 0EH
01-624 6232

Closed: lunch (Sat); Bank Holidays; 1 week Christmas
Last
Orders: lunch (2.00pm); dinner (11.00pm)

Madame Catherine Parisot has chosen a quiet corner of St John's Wood in which to establish a real 'restaurant du quartier'. Wines, cheese and staff are imported from France, as are the majority of dishes on the menu. They may flirt occasionally with modern cooking, but the emphasis is on honest and straightforward dishes using good quality meat and fish, and are all pleasantly served.

To start try salad of calves' sweetbreads with crunchy broccoli and French beans on a bed of various lettuce leaves or garlicky snails in puff pastry with a butter sauce. Main courses might be pink-roasted rack of lamb with cloves of garlic, confit of duck on a potato galette, fillet of turbot with cucumber sauce or escalope of salmon in chive sauce with a selection of vegetables or a salad with pine nuts. Sorbets and the parfait aux noisettes have excellent texture and flavour, or choose from the good selection of French cheeses.

The small wine list offers a reasonable selection of a few well-known items and one or two regional bottles.

The room itself is busy and informal in French rustic style, and there is a delightful courtyard where you can enjoy lunch when the sun is shining.

Don Pepe   NW8

99 Frampton Street NW8 8NA
01-723 9749/262 3834

Last
Orders: lunch (2.15pm); dinner (12.15am)

In my opinion this is the most authentic Spanish restaurant in London for atmosphere, noise (including a TV in the bar) and typical cooking from the north west of Spain. There is a small bar at the front of the restaurant which is always full of Spanish people sipping copas with tapas or coffee, the copa probably being sherry if taken with olives or chorizo, or of Spanish brandy or anis if taken with coffee.

You can make a meal of the variety of bits and pieces which are displayed on the bar. They vary, but might be clams cooked in white wine, grilled sardines, mushrooms cooked in oil with garlic and chilli, real Spanish omelette or fried peppers. Small portions of each can be ordered so that you can taste the whole range; so with a bottle of housewine, you get a delicious meal - reasonably priced, too.

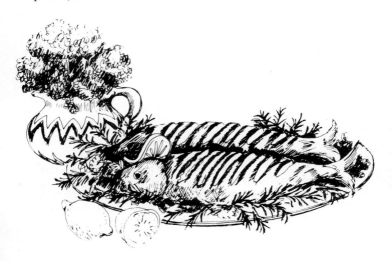

If you want to eat more formally the dining room menu provides a good selection of Spanish dishes - there's paella, of course, but try the parrillada de pescado which is a variety of fish and shellfish grilled with olive oil and finely chopped garlic, or merluza à la Gallega, hake cooked in a casserole as it would be done in Galicia. There is always a good selection of fish, but meats and poultry are also well prepared, and to finish you could try some Manchegan cheese.

In the evening a guitarist plays, and the noisy atmosphere recreates the feeling of warmth and relaxation that is Spain. In fact, surrounded as you will doubtless be by Spanish customers, by the time you're on to the second bottle of Rioja, you'll be convinced that you're actually in Spain!

Rosetti   NW8

23 Queen's Grove NW8 6PR
01-722 7141

Last
Orders: lunch (2.30pm); dinner (11.00pm)

A fairly unusual project this - a sophisticated Italian pub.
Downstairs is very popular with the local drinkers, and the sunny
tiled dining room is up on the first floor. The menu is standard
Italian but with a little more flair than is sometimes found. Try the
cold marinated fillets of anchovies to start, and a nicely piquant
black pepper sauce with a spring chicken to follow. The
conversation level is fairly high and it is not the place to go for a
restful evening. But if lots of smiles and peppermills are your
sort of thing you will enjoy it here. Definitely book for Sunday
lunch when Rosetti seems to be St John's Wood's favourite
meeting place.

Archduke Wine Bar & Restaurant   SE1

Concert Hall Approach, South Bank SE1 8XU
01-928 9370

Closed: lunch (Sat + Sun); dinner (Sun)
Last
Orders: lunch (2.15pm); dinner (11.00pm)

A friendly, unpretentious wine bar. Helpful staff serve simple,
quick food with an interesting selection of sausages from Justin
de Blank. The simple dishes are the best. A piano plays during the
evening, but unfortunately licensing laws mean that just as you
have come from the theatre and are looking forward to some
music, it all stops.

Mabileau   SE1

61 The Cut SE1
01-928 8645

Closed: lunch (Sat + Sun); dinner (Sun); Bank Holidays
Last
Orders: dinner (11.00pm)

The address conjures up memories of Tony Hancock, but this
restaurant near the Old Vic in Waterloo has a serious purpose.
Furnished very much in brasserie style it offers a fixed price
menu at £12.00 plus an à la carte menu on which most of the
nouvelle based dishes include some fruit in their composition.
Loire wines are a speciality, even the house red is from the region,
and prices are reasonable.

Ristorante La Barca · SE1

80/81 Lower Marsh SE1 7AB
01-261 9221/928 2226

Closed: lunch (Sat + Sun); dinner (Sun)
Last
Orders: lunch (2.30pm); dinner (11.30pm)

Situated almost opposite the Old Vic, La Barca is an Italian restaurant in the old tradition. The floor is tiled, walls are cream rendered plaster - though you can hardly see them for photographs of theatre people who call in when working locally - and tables are close together. This is a restaurant for healthy appetites. A first course of tagliatelle alla carbonara seems enough for 4 - until the fritto misto di mare arrives, for that's even larger! You get an overhanging plateful of squid, Mediterranean prawns, North Sea prawns, monkfish, sardines and whitebait cooked in either a light batter or breadcrumbs. A good range of Italian wines complement the food.

I am sure that La Barca is popular with thespians because the huge portions are sufficient to sustain them whilst 'resting'.

RSJ · SE1

13A Coin Street SE1 8YQ
01-928 4554

Closed: lunch (Sat + Sun); dinner (Sun)
Last
Orders: lunch (2.00pm); dinner (11.00pm)

RSJ, situated close to the South Bank complex in a converted cycle warehouse, is a neat, smart restaurant decorated in theatre style, with posters everywhere. There are some interesting and different nouvelle presentations on the menu, like an entrecôte steak with morels, or a nouvelle-style duck breast, followed by a small but good selection of puddings. The wine list is reasonably priced. This is a very useful place before or after the theatre, as it opens in the evening at 6.00pm.

L'Auberge · SE22

44 Forest Hill Road SE22 0RU
01-299 2211

Closed: lunch (Mon - Sat); dinner (Sun + Mon)
Last
Orders: lunch (2.30pm); dinner (10.00pm)

An oasis in the desert of SE22, L'Auberge offers the hospitality you would expect - a warm welcome, a fixed price menu with sound cooking, and a no-nonsense reasonably priced wine list.

The décor is typical of a provincial French auberge with shades of pink and green in the cheerful restaurant, and Mrs Youssef ensures the well-being of diners whilst her husband cooks. Specialities are aiguillettes de foie de veau which are strips of calves' liver sautéed with herbs and garlic, and suprême de poulet orientale (breast of chicken stuffed with crab in a lobster sauce). An unexpected and commendable ambience in East Dulwich.

Auberge de Provence   SW1

St James Court Hotel, Buckingham Gate SW1E 6AF   £40
01-821 1899

Last
Orders: lunch (3.00pm); dinner (11.00pm)

Jean-André Charial has brought to London the cooking of his Provençale restaurant L'Oustau de Baumanière, for which he has 3 Michelin stars. The menu features some classic dishes from the South - a red mullet mousse with a tomato sauce, a fillet of John Dory en bourride, brandade, and of course, fresh pasta au pistou. Monsieur Charial frequently revisits the Auberge from his hotel in France to ensure that his team of chefs in England are maintaining the fine tradition of his family. He also takes a keen interest in the wines, many of which come from his cellars in France.

The service is suitably professional though the room has attracted much comment, as it is not in the style you would expect for the type of food being served. It is an informal setting, reminiscent of a café/shop, and in contrast to the opulence of the Inn of Happiness, another restaurant (Chinese) in this newly and luxuriously refurbished flagship of the Taj group.

Le Caprice   SW1

Arlington House, Arlington Street SW1A 1RT
01-629 2239

Closed: lunch (Sat + Bank Holidays); 1 week Christmas
Last
Orders: lunch (2.30pm; 3.00pm Sun); dinner (midnight)

Christopher Corbin and Jeremy King who run Le Caprice with
their smart little team, work hard and deserve the success they
have achieved in re-establishing this old-time favourite and
increasing its business beyond anything in its long history. The
restaurant, with its designer-cool décor and great élan, seems -
like the majority of its customers - to belong to the 'new world':
there are always interesting people to be seen, but its zippy
atmosphere makes it a place where you can dress up or dress
down (depending on where you begin).

Le Caprice

There's plenty of choice on the menu, ranging from chilled
watercress and mint soup to excellent tabbouleh, or crottin de
chavignol. There are good eggs Benedict, scrambled eggs and
smoked salmon, both served in two different sizes. It's a great
place for Sunday brunch. You can choose the grilled spring
chicken or the grilled veal sausages, or you can try the steamed
monkfish in a warm dressed salad, or the sautéed prawns with
spicy peppers.
    Even their postcode, which is SW1A 1RT, seems to read
'SMART' when you look at it quickly!

Le Casino   SW1

77 Lower Sloane Street SW1
01-730 3313

I was reading the menu outside Peter Ilic's newest restaurant
and was almost dragged in by his enthusiastic and, of course,
attractive young manageress. Le Casino has taken over from The
Windmill in that it proudly boasts that it is open 24 hours a day, 7
days a week, and that in itself is unique! This is the place to eat
after a bad day at the races as it is almost cheaper than eating at
home. There are dishes such as kedgeree at £2.85, cassoulet at
£3.85 and housewine at £4.60. Never mind the quality, feel the
price, especially at breakfast.
    Peter Ilic is determined to offer decent eating at cheap prices.
He began at Lanterns and continues the formula at La Cloche
and Le Pigeon. He is also the person who set up the first
restaurant in London, called Just Around The Corner, where
there are no prices for either food or wine and you simply pay
whatever you think it was worth.

Ciboure

Ciboure	**SW1**

21 Eccleston Street SW1W 9LX
01-730 2505

£40

Closed: lunch (Sat + Sun); dinner (Sun)
Last
Orders: lunch (2.00pm); dinner (11.30pm)

This small, almost clinically designed restaurant has plain walls -
one mirrored - a few prints and paintings, white cloths over a
striped underlay and fresh flowers. Waiters are smart in starched white dress shirts without collar or ties but with crisp
white aprons.

A short à la carte menu changes monthly, and you might be
offered a royale of leeks and mushrooms - a moulded mixture of
the 2 vegetables poached and served with a butter sauce, which
is light but full of flavour. Medallions of pheasant are served
with 2 sauces and well-cooked vegetables. Puddings might be a
poached pear served on a fresh custard sauce with a coulis of
blackberries and a small almond flavoured mousseline.

A small selection of French wines covers the most popular
choices and there are some older clarets listed "at very exceptional prices".

I like Ciboure - it has a good atmosphere, the food is
extremely well prepared and cooked by Richard Price, and
service is friendly.

Dolphin Brasserie	**SW1**

Dolphin Square, Chichester Street SW1V 3LX
01-828 3207

£40

Last
Orders: dinner (10.45pm)

The recently refurbished brasserie is to be found in a large
development along the Embankment. The atmosphere is lively
and none too serious - rather like that of a cruise liner. They
have a pianist during the week, and at the weekend a trio plays
for dancing. The menu, which is ambitious, is in the nouvelle
style. There are some good wines at under £10.00 a bottle.
Breakfast or afternoon tea are also served.

Dukes Hotel   SW1

35 St James's Place SW1A 1NY
01-491 4840

Last
Orders: lunch (2.30pm); dinner (10.00pm)

Dukes Hotel is another of those special, smaller, but elegant London hotels, hidden away right in the middle of St James's, probably thankful not to get passing traffic but to cater instead for guests who return time and time again. This delightful Edwardian Hotel has some 50 rooms, and a feeling of elegance and grandeur of days gone past. It has its own courtyard setting and some lovely Edwardian plasterwork and pillars in the public rooms. The bedrooms have all been modernised and equipped with decent sized beds, smart sofas and fabrics. The clubby atmosphere makes it a nice place to meet for a drink, before having lunch or dinner in the small intimately lit restaurant. There are 2 private rooms, and also the Marlborough Suite which boasts its own entrance. The private rooms are small and can accommodate parties of up to 12.

The restaurant concentrates on English cooking with a modern aspect, and offers a lunch trolley every day with such old favourites as roast rack of lamb with creamed potatoes, and on Fridays, a fresh fish baked in a pastry case. There is a 2 or 3-course table d'hôte luncheon, or from the à la carte menu you might try the salad of spinach leaves with woodland mushrooms and strips of crispy bacon, or perhaps chicory parcels filled with brill, and served on a light red wine sauce. From the 5 or so fish dishes you might like the navarin of sole, turbot and scallops in a dill sauce, or from the 6 meat and poultry dishes perhaps a loin of veal filled with fresh vegetables which is then braised in madeira and served with a butter and chive sauce. There are straightfoward grills if you prefer, and good crisp vegetables. Service is enthusiastic and professional.

Eatons   SW1

49 Elizabeth Street SW1W 9PP
01-730 0074

Closed: Sat + Sun; Bank Holidays
Last
Orders: lunch (2.00pm); dinner (11.15pm)

A straightforward restaurant with good local clientele, and a
short sensible menu which changes weekly. Good-sized portions
of standard favourites, including veal escalope sauté bergère
and lamb with lambs' kidneys sauté provençale. They also serve
trout Colbert with herb butter and apples, their sweet trolley is
full of calorie-packed puddings, and they even urge you to have
more cream from the jug which lurks under the trolley. Young-
ish, helpful staff work hard and seem pleased to see you. A
good local, and most of the locals were drinking the very good
housewine.

Gavvers   SW1

61 Lower Sloane Street SW1
01-730 5983

Closed: lunch (daily); Sun; Bank Holidays
Last
Orders: dinner (11.00pm)

This bustling restaurant has a fixed price menu which includes a
half bottle of housewine in the cost. Choose from 7 starters, then
from 3 fish or 5 other main courses. These might be suprême de
confit de canard, sauté de boeuf arlésienne, or côte d'agneau
landaise. The wines of the house are from Michel Roux's own
vineyard or from the excellent Georges Duboeuf. If you wish to
spend a little more, they will allow you the first £2.50 off any
bottle of wine on the more expensive side of the carte des vins.

The Goring Hotel   SW1

Beeston Place, Grosvenor Gardens SW1W 0JW
01-834 8211

Last
Orders: lunch (2.30pm); dinner (10.00pm)

One of the last of the family-run hotels in London, and very
convenient for Buckingham Palace, this large Edwardian establishment has been in the same family since it was built in 1910. I
believe it was the first hotel in London to have bathrooms with
all its bedrooms, which now total about 90. They take pride in
their family tradition, and in looking after the customer. Window
boxes are always well tended and sparkling, as is the secret
garden at the rear of the hotel.

Green's   SW1

36 Duke Street, St James's SW1 6BR
01-930 4566

Last
Orders: lunch (3.00pm); dinner (10.45pm)

The enterprising Simon Parker Bowles has established Green's
in what seems a short space of time. The restaurant feels as if it
has always been here. It has a rather nice, clubby, West End
atmosphere, and if you are not someone who is going to enjoy
their excellent oysters, Scotch smoked salmon, foie gras de
canard or their quails' eggs, then perhaps you might try some of
the dishes from the menu of the day. This might contain a
vichyssoise or fresh asparagus to start, then traditionally cooked
roast grouse, the less esoteric bangers and mash, or calves' liver
with bacon, onions and mash to follow. Finish with some fresh
blueberry and apple pie with custard, or a summer pudding.
Well, you've got to admit it's a fair choice! Besides the range of
fish which is normally cooked and served simply and with care,
in the evening the menu has a good selection of steaks, chops
and sausages.

If you find the restaurant too crowded, and the bar too full of
excitable people, then try one of the private rooms for a dinner
or lunch party. And since Green's the Wine Merchants have been
around in the City of London since 1787, you can make up your
own mind about the style of the wine list.

Le Mazarin   SW1

30 Winchester Street SW1V 4NZ
01-828 3366/834 4366

Closed: lunch (daily); Sun; Bank Holidays; 1 week Christmas
Last
Orders: dinner (11.30pm)

Set in a bit of a desert for restaurants, Le Mazarin is a smart and
stylish basement restaurant, cool in décor with a clientele to
match. Many customers, like the staff, have been schooled in the
Roux tradition and chef René Bajard used to cook at Le
Gavroche. The service can be a little formal (with echoes of
Upper Brook Street) as is the elaborate presentation of dishes.
From the set menu for dinner which at £16.50 includes service
and VAT, the onglet was excellent.
    The classic wine list you would expect is here and whatever
you order will be served in gleaming glasses with a great
flourish.

Mijanou   SW1

143 Ebury Street SW1W 9QN
01-730 4099

Closed: Sat + Sun; Bank Holidays; 3 weeks Aug;
        2 weeks Christmas; 1 week Easter
Last
Orders: lunch (2.00pm); dinner (11.00pm)

Sonia Blech cooks here in an individual style that has drawn
great praise from many, including Bernard Levin and Paul Levy.
Dishes are always inventive, often complex and have their roots
in classic French techniques. You may find a mousse of wild
mushrooms with wild rice, perhaps a breast of pheasant with
foie gras enclosed in a wholemeal crêpe, and plainly roast
grouse will be served with a marmalade of kumquats. There are
also influences from the more fashionable areas of the Far East,
so that a fish and seafood broth is highlighted with lemon grass.
    Neville Blech runs both small dining rooms, one for smokers
and one for non-smokers. He is always keen to explain the
intricacies of each dish, or the many bargains scattered through
an excellent wine list from France and the New World, which is
particularly thoughtful in its large selection of half bottles.

Motcombs   SW1

26 Motcomb Street SW1X 8JU
01-235 6382

Closed: Sun
Last
Orders: lunch (2.45pm); dinner (11.00pm)

Philip Lawless and Motcombs always seem to have been at the
corner of Motcomb Street where this restaurant and wine bar
has established itself as the local favourite. It's a boisterous and
friendly restaurant where Lawless holds court, and he's normally organising some event or other (the man's even started his
own newspaper!) It buzzes with swift service and has reasonably priced, straightforward dishes. Try the grilled sardines with
mustard sauce, smoked cod's roe, or one of their salad starters,

maybe salade Belgravia, a julienne of livers tossed in butter with bacon, croûtons, and served with assorted salads. Maybe some of their fish dishes appeal - smoked haddock poached in milk with a poached egg on top, wing of skate served with capers and black butter, or sea bass simply grilled with herbes de Provence. There's plenty of choice for meats and grills - calves' liver with bacon, veal cutlets with mushrooms and strips of ham, roast game in season, or chef James Peak's daily suggestion.

Pomegranates   SW1

94 Grosvenor Road SW1
01-828 6560/834 0735

£40

Closed: lunch (Sat + Sun); dinner (Sun)
Last
Orders: lunch (2.15pm); dinner (11.15pm)

Some restaurants need personalities and this restaurant's got one in Patrick Gwynn-Jones, a man who's travelled to most continents and countries and now on his menu shares his interest in the food he's eaten in most of them. Among his specialities to start are lime-pickled raw salmon, Danish pickled herrings with rye bread, burek (feta, spinach and mint in filo pastry) served with Sudanese pepper sauce, beef or chicken satay served with spicy peanut sauce, Lebanese iced yoghurt, cucumber and shrimp soup, and a little closer to home there's potted crab with wholemeal toast, or a cheese pâté with port and cognac. For fish you might be offered har bow bor low (giant prawns, pineapple, chillies and garlic) or for a main course some chicken stir-fried with fresh peaches and almonds, or some roast gigot with rosemary and garlic. Alternatively, how about West Indian curried goat with plantain, or the more straightforward Welsh salt duck, or some canard sauvage.

The cheeses are familiar: a mature farmhouse Cheddar or Stilton, and the meal begins with crudités, aïoli and home-made bread. You can choose from crudités and main course at around £13.00, crudités and 2 courses at around £16.00, or crudités and 3 courses at around £20.00. So if it's a night when you don't know what you want, and you don't know what your guest wants, it's a safe bet that if you are going to find it anywhere, you'll find it at Pomegranates.

The staff is as multi-national as the cuisine and the service attentive and relaxed. There's an excellent choice of housewines which Patrick imports himself, some also available in half bottles, and the wine list is such that if he had rooms there you'd take it to bed to read. This man has fun running his restaurant and does his best to ensure that you'll enjoy it as well.

Santini   SW1

29 Ebury Street SW1
01-730 4094

£45

Closed: Sat + Sun; Bank Holidays
Last
Orders: lunch (2.30pm); dinner (11.30pm)

Santini is one of London's 'new wave' Italian restaurants, with pastel shades on the walls and attractive photographs of the homeland. Good lighting helps to create the ambience, and the tables are usually full of locals or executives entertaining foreign visitors. The menu breaks slightly from the run-of-the-mill Italian dishes, and staff are impeccably dressed in grey pullovers and blue bow-ties.

The wine list is exclusively Italian with some less common selections in addition to the better known generics.

Simply Nico   SW1

48A Rochester Row SW1
01-630 8061

Closed: please ring for details
Last
Orders: please ring for details

The 'enfant' not so 'terrible' of the restaurant world, Nico Ladenis has returned to London and continues to produce some excellent and exciting dishes for a more international audience. At the time of going to press, Nico Ladenis had only just opened this restaurant, but knowing his cooking and ability, we felt able to mention a little of what we believe you will find at Simply Nico. (More on the décor and style in our 6-monthly update.)

Nico's dishes range from a simple Mediterranean-style soupe des rougets to main courses of top quality meat, chosen by Nico personally to his exacting standards, set in powerful, reduced sauces. Up to 8 different vegetables can accompany his main courses, with perhaps a small tart of wild mushrooms or a tiny quiche of leeks. Out of 6 or 7 desserts there might be a soufflé of rum and coffee, or some excellent home-made fruit sorbets which are served with a spectacular array of exotic fruits.

Nico takes to an extreme the preparation of his product, and regards food as more of a science than an art - although I would claim that his dishes very much represent 'art on the plate'. Nico, who is not classically trained, has over a period of 15 years taught himself how to produce a repertoire of many original and beautifully presented dishes, which taste as good as they look.

The Stafford Hotel   SW1

St James's Place SW1A 1NJ
01-493 0111

Last
Orders: lunch (2.30pm); dinner (10.30pm; 10.00pm Sun)

Another one of London's rather special style hotels, this delightful small hotel, tucked away at the bottom end of St James's, used to be one of the London clubs. It now has a well-established clientele and the staff look after you well, with old-fashioned service. Comfortably furnished with sofas, armchairs and antiques, it's still like a club in many ways, particularly the bar, which opens out onto the small hidden mews on warmer days.

The restaurant offers well-prepared dishes, some from the trolley, and an extensive wine list in the middle to upper price bracket. It is a good venue for business meetings, and has its regular following, each with his favourite seat.

The 60-odd bedrooms have good fittings, some reproduction and some antique furniture, and all expected modern facilities.

The Tate Gallery Restaurant   SW1

Millbank SW1
01-834 6754

Closed: lunch (Sun); dinner (daily)
Last
Orders: 3.00pm

Everyone agrees that the thing about The Tate Gallery is the wine, but at the prices they charge, which are, to put it mildly, astonishingly good value, for how much longer can this good thing last? How voluminous are their cellars? Can they possibly replace some of the incredible bargains they have on offer? I think that perhaps the fewer people we tell about this, and the more often we go ourselves before their supplies are exhausted the better, so let's talk about the food instead.

It's necessary to book for lunch, as this 120-seater is always packed. People say that the simpler dishes are best, and I would agree with that. Well, with Rex Whistler on the walls to look at, and being situated in the middle of one of our greatest galleries, it would seem silly to miss the opportunity of lunching here.

The Tent   SW1

15 Eccleston Street SW1W 9LX
01-730 6922

Closed: Sat
Last
Orders: lunch (2.30pm); dinner (11.30pm)

Don't be deterred by the name - you won't be expected to eat on a ground sheet! The Tent is a busy bistro restaurant with tables set close together and a high level of chatter, situated just off Ebury Street. A fixed price menu gives good value with plenty of choices such as an omelette Arnold Bennett, a spinach, dandelion and bacon salad, chicken liver terrine or onion soup to start. Veal escalope with lemon and rosemary, turkey, mushroom and redcurrant pie, halibut meunière, liver lyonnaise or sirloin steak in pepper and brandy sauce are amongst the main courses served with vegetables or salad. A concise list of around 20 wines is pitched at affordable prices.

Le Trou Normand   SW1

27 Motcomb Street SW1X 8JU   £40
01-235 1668

Closed: Sun; 2 weeks Christmas
Last
Orders: lunch (3.00pm); dinner (11.30pm)

True Normand specialities are what characterise this restaurant, set in a fashionable Belgravia street of antiques and restaurants - specialities such as boudin noir aux pommes, tripes à la mode de Caen and a good selection of fruits de mer and poissons. Moules marinières à la normande and a brochette of scallops might be first courses, and somehow even a salade niçoise finds favour on a more northerly oriented menu. There's a small list of French wines to choose from, though vintages are not declared!

A cheerful bistro décor with tiled floor, bentwood chairs and posters of Normandy give an authentic atmosphere. The basement oyster bar is bright, and is a good venue for a light seafood lunch.

Wiltons   SW1

55 Jermyn Street SW1Y 6LX
01-629 9955

Closed: lunch (Sat + Sun); dinner (Sun); Bank Holidays;
        3 weeks Aug; 10 days Christmas
Last
Orders: lunch (2.15pm); dinner (10.15pm)

Wiltons, although it only moved to its present location a couple
of years ago from just around the corner, feels as though it's
always been here. Clever and well-thought-out alterations to
these former café premises give you that secure well-rounded
feeling of Britishness. They are always busy at lunch times in
both the main restaurant and the seafood bar. Traditional
service, traditional style, traditional food, and traditional surroundings all combine in an Edwardian club-like atmosphere.

The Basil Street Hotel Restaurant   SW3

Basil Street SW3 1AH
01-581 3311

Closed: lunch (Sat)
Last
Orders: lunch (1.45pm); dinner (9.45pm)

This old-time favourite is sometimes forgotten amongst the
glamour of the larger or more well-known establishments, but
The Basil Street Hotel has its own following that appreciates the
quiet efficiency of this charming Edwardian hotel, which retains
an intimate atmosphere in its elegant surroundings. It has a
lovely collection of mirrors and paintings, with antique furniture
all down the long corridors and in the little lounges. The
bedrooms, like the well-proportioned public rooms, have their
own individuality, and the ensemble is impeccably run by
Stephen Korany, one of the partners.
  The dining room has some interesting paintings on glass
which depict the four seasons, the elements, and English Royal
families. In the evening you can dine by candlelight and listen to
piano music, which enhances the seductive ambience. The
speciality of the house is roast rib of Aberdeen Angus with
Yorkshire pudding, and this is also offered as a pre-theatre
dinner. The à la carte menu is supplemented with plats du jour
of seasonal produce, and the wine list has some interesting old
clarets at reasonable prices.
  This lovely hotch potch of a building has a very friendly
personal feel to it, and you can never really believe that they
have close on 100 rooms. You'll like The Basil Street Hotel
Restaurant for breakfast, if you happen to be in this part of town.

La Brasserie   SW3

272 Brompton Road SW3
01-584 1668

Closed: Christmas Day + Boxing Day
Last
Orders: midnight

La Brasserie has to be rated since the queues of people most evenings and Saturday lunch times can't all be wrong. Provide your own comments on the food - it does vary but can be very good. The service, which is very 'French' (even if some of the waiters are Spanish!), and the buzz of the place, make even the most timid rise to the occasion and do battle with the Gallic hosts. It's as close to a bright back-street brasserie in Paris as you are likely to find in London. Newspapers are available for lone dining and queuing - it's not possible to book a table.

Beccofino   SW3

100 Draycott Avenue SW3 3AD
01-584 3600

Closed: Sun; Bank Holidays
Last
Orders: lunch (2.30pm); dinner (11.30pm)

Beccofino is a small intimate Italian restaurant with red banquette seating, low ceilings and attractive, bright paintings around the walls.

Pasta is home-made, and there are many other Italian favourites such as seafood salad, risotto, vitello tonnato and their speciality of a veal chop with Gorgonzola cheese sauce.

The atmosphere is good, service is friendly, and the good selection of Italian wines is reasonably priced.

Dan's   SW3

119 Sydney Street SW3 6NR
01-352 2718

Closed: lunch (Sat); dinner (Sun; Sat + Sun Sep-May)
Last
Orders: lunch (2.30pm); dinner (11.15pm)

This restaurant is always a favourite with the local Chelsea
crowd. A small terraced house opens into a conservatory style
room at the back with a garden area alongside, making an ideal
place for outdoor lunches or early dinners. There is an interesting selection of dishes, cooked competently, with some summer
highlights. If you feel like taking your coffee elsewhere, you can
always wander down to the nearby Chelsea Farmers Market,
and perhaps take advantage of the wonderful selection of
wholefoods from the Neal's Yard people.

Daphne's Restaurant   SW3

110-112 Draycott Avenue SW3 3AE
01-589 4257/584 6883

Closed: Sun; Bank Holidays
Last
Orders: lunch (2.30pm); dinner (midnight)

Daphne's seems something of a trip back in time to the 1960s:
the décor hasn't changed and it still has its regular customers.
The selection could be loosely described as international and
the food does come well cooked, and on the bottom of their
menu they are confident enough to say "the chef will be pleased
to show you around the kitchen to discuss any special dish you
might not find on the menu."

Drakes in Pond Place   SW3

2A Pond Place SW3
01-584 4555/6669

Closed: Bank Holidays
Last
Orders: lunch (2.15pm; 2.45pm Sun);
        dinner (11.00pm; 10.30pm Sun)

Drakes in Pond Place has had a face lift. The bar, which
welcomes you as you arrive down the steps, is newly furnished
with comfortable sofas and chairs reminiscent of a country
house, and makes a pleasant place to have a drink whilst waiting
to order. Knowing that Stephen Moss has interests in the wine
trade as well as in this particular restaurant, you'll understand
why he would like you to order the excellent Belle Epoque Fleur
de Champagne. Another wine he likes and which is, I think,
particularly good value, having all the characteristics of a good
claret but in fact coming from Provence, is the Château Vigne-
laure, Côteaux d'Aix-en-Provence 1980.

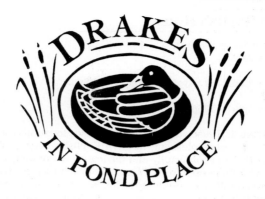

On to the food. This pretty 2-level basement dining room has a nice private feel to it wherever you sit, with a view of the chefs in the kitchen, basting and roasting the food. We plumped for the simpler English style dishes. Try the chilled tomato and cucumber soup which is spiced with cumin seeds, or perhaps the Drakes terrine, which is duck terrine with pistachio nuts, served with a warm herb shortbread. Their half Cornvale duck with brandy and cherry sauce is popular. My own favourite is the leg of English lamb basted with mild mustard and rosemary sauce. They serve good vegetables and a selection of salads with various dressings. For pudding, why not try the date and almond cake, or the fresh fruit water ice?

The English Garden   SW3

10 Lincoln Street SW3 2TS
01-584 7272

Last
Orders: lunch (2.30pm); dinner (11.30pm)

This is another restaurant in the English style. Operated by Malcolm Livingstone, its bright and sunny rooms with tiled floors and lots of greenery have a very 'English Summer' feel to them. The cooking too is light, with dishes like a vegetable terrine, boned and stuffed quails, or steaks of salmon and crayfish with cream and fresh mint. More substantial dishes include a roast rack of English lamb or a grilled rib of beef. Service is polite and informal, and they have a delightful private dining room on the first floor.

The English House   SW3

3 Milner Street SW3 1AQ
01-584 3002

Closed: Christmas Day; Boxing Day; Good Friday
Last
Orders: lunch (2.15pm); dinner (11.30pm)

The English House enjoys a smart Chelsea location and prices to
match. It serves pleasant, modern English cooking. The small
dining room is colourfully and intricately decorated, and seems
popular with people from TV and the fashion world. The service
inspires a rather reverential feeling, and it is one of the London
restaurants that makes a virtue of English cooking. Try the
chicken livers in peppercorn jelly, or the collops of veal with
fresh herbs.

Foxtrot Oscar   SW3

79 Royal Hospital Road SW3 4HN
01-352 7179/351 1667

Closed: Bank Holidays
Last
Orders: lunch (2.30pm); dinner (11.30pm)

This is the place to go when you have an overwhelming desire to
eat sausage and mash, your wife fancies spare ribs and your
guests would like a burger. You'll find all of these on the unusual
menu and lots more dishes suitable for all tastes and combinations. Foxtrot Oscar is a very busy bistro which is popular with
locals and visitors alike. It has a lot of atmosphere, it's not
pretentious, and it offers good cooking at reasonable prices.
Cocktails such as 'Bloody Bull' or 'Tequila Pop' soon get the
party going and the wine list has around 30 choices at sensible
prices.

Restaurant Le Français   SW3

259 Fulham Road SW3 6HY
01-352 4748/3668

Closed: Sun
Last
Orders: lunch (1.30pm); dinner (10.45pm)

This older style French restaurant in the Fulham Road has pine
panelling, a dark interior, and adequate French provincial food
appreciated by a slightly older Chelsea clientele. Carefully run
by owner Bernard Caen and Mr Albert, the restaurant manager,
they offer a weekly regional menu. If there's a region you're
particularly fond of in France they will tell you when in the year
they are featuring it, and you can try it out against your holiday
experiences.

Grill St Quentin SW3

136 Brompton Road SW3 1HY
01-581 8377

Closed: 1 week Christmas
Last
Orders: lunch (3.00; 4.00pm Sat + Sun);
       dinner (midnight; Sun 11.30pm)

The once-famous 'Loose Box' has been converted into a brightly lit, brass-railed restaurant, straight out of Paris, and it's a welcome newcomer that has already built up a good following, situated just opposite Harrods. Staff as well as style are imported and so is some of the food. Eric Garnier, younger brother of Didier from the Restaurant St Quentin across the road, runs this grill with style. Service is brisk and professional, and the odd language problem makes it feel more French.

Confit de canard and foie gras are prepared dishes brought over from Toulouse. The main feature is the charcoal grill with a choice of meats and fish well cooked to order and served with lots of pommes frites. A good place for a simple lunch or dinner, a glass of wine, a baguette to take away, it is one of the places that will really benefit when the licensing laws are relaxed.

Joe's Café SW3

126 Draycott Avenue SW3
01-225 2217

Last
Orders: 11.00pm

The décor is black and white in this stylish bar and dining room just off the Brompton Road, displaying clean lines in the split level dining area behind the bar. Dramatic black linen is offset by white carnations, the black or white china is square or rectangular to emphasise the ordered design, the photographs on the walls are in black and white, and the staff are also dressed in monotone. Hundreds of small bulbs sparkle in the ceiling, and the atmosphere is good with healthy chatter between the tables.

The cooking is as contemporary as the décor, for example consommé with wild mushrooms, angler fish with ginger and lime, and puddings nestling in marbled sauces. Coffee is espresso. There is a small wine list with adequate choice, and housewines are of good quality. The young staff are friendly, attentive and well organised.

Ma Cuisine   SW3

113 Walton Street SW3
01-584 7585

Closed: Sat + Sun; 21 Dec - 5 Jan; 5 days Easter;
         Bank Holidays
Last
Orders: lunch (2.00pm); dinner (11.00pm)

This charming, tiny restaurant, built up with such skill by Guy
Mouilleron, was then run capably by the team of Monsieur et
Madame Aubertin. Guy is now back in the kitchen and recreat-
ing the old magic which we hope will last forever, or at least
until he finds a successor, but do check when you book. If Guy is
there, book a few tables and make the most of it.

Mario   SW3

262 Brompton Road SW3
01-584 1724

Closed: Bank Holidays
Last
Orders: lunch (2.30pm); dinner (10.45pm)

A clean-cut, sophisticated designer restaurant with windows
that open up and tables that spill out onto the pavement in the
summer months, this restaurant is memorable for its delightful
treatment of the trees outside, which are dressed with fairy
lights sparkling away every evening, not just at Christmas. There
are some interesting and varied Italian dishes on Mario Cassan-
dro's menu, and a good buzz in the place, especially in the
evening when Mario is there doing the rounds.

Ménage à Trois   SW3

15 Beauchamp Place SW3 1NQ   £35
01-589 4252/584 9350

Closed: Sun; Christmas Day; Boxing Day
Last
Orders: lunch (3.00pm); dinner (12.15am)

This restaurant is in a simple, white painted brick basement;
wisely, the ceiling has been padded for the protection of those
tall enough to bang their heads! Simple cane chairs and sparkling glassware set on white tablecloths are the perfect setting for
Antony Worrall-Thompson's interestingly different menu. He
uses good raw ingredients and turns simple combinations into
some delightful, excellently presented dishes.

   The menu is quite special and this deserves to be acknowledged. It is expressed both in the innovative style of presentation and in his ability to bring out the flavour of the food he
serves. His dish entitled 'The Ultimate' is a whole truffle set on a
brioche croûton, enclosed with a mousse of spinach and foie
gras, roasted in flaky pastry and served with a truffle sauce. I

don't think I've seen anyone else serve it like that! The list of traditional dishes includes dressed crab, lobster cocktail, or scrambled egg with smoked salmon, then there's something that he describes as 'Cold Taste Teasers', which might include chicken combinations - smoked chicken with chicory and walnut dressing, marinated chicken on wilted spinach with a sesame dressing, and chicken julienne on pickled cucumber with a peanut dressing; or perhaps Josephine's delight - creamed eggs with sevruga caviar, smoked salmon mousse with Scottish smoked salmon, and scallop mousse with diced scallop, all served with toasted brioche soldiers. He offers an amazing array of 'Raw Inspirations' and 'Salads Cold and Warm'. Warm salads might be a selection of French salad leaves served with a choice of one of the following toppings: lobster, scallop, oysters, and fresh crab meat with dill and croûtons; or escalope of duck breast with nuggets of duck foie gras on French beans and shallots; or marinated goats' cheese encrusted in sesame seeds, roasted and served with a pear tartlet, pickled walnut mousse and a pear vinaigrette.

Ménage à Trois

Try one of his Ménage à Trois selections of hot pastry parcels which might contain Camembert and cranberry, Roquefort and leek, or Boursin and spinach; or a seafood version which might have lobster and mange-tout, turbot and leek, or crab and cucumber. Among the fish and shellfish, try the trio of seafood packages, crab with leek, scallops with cabbage, and lobster with spinach, all served on an oyster and caviar sauce. There's meat, poultry and game, for instance boned quail filled with game mousse, red cabbage and a dice of duck wrapped in flaky pastry, roasted and served with a port and orange sauce; or try the roast saddle of rabbit with a compôte of apples, prunes and parsley with an apple and rosemary vinegar sauce. There are also plenty of vegetarian dishes.

The hot and cold puddings are delicious, and might include a hot seasonal berry selection, served over their vanilla ice-cream, Ménage à Trois parcels - pastry parcels with a praline cream, the parcels containing maybe pear and chocolate, bananas and rum, and apple and raspberry. A good summer pudding is served with clotted cream; or try a terrine of oranges, mint and champagne served with bitter chocolate. An amazing wine list contains some unusual choices, and some grand classics.

Antony Worrall-Thompson opened a branch in New York, at Lexington and 4th Street, and I'm pretty sure they'll take to it much quicker than the English have. I hope they don't take to it too well, for it would be a great shame if we lost this talented and unorthodox cook from the London scene.

Le Métro   SW3

28 Basil Street SW3 1AT
01-589 6286/5171

Closed: lunch (Sun); dinner (Sat + Sun)
Last
Orders: dinner (10.30pm)

One of London's most popular wine bars, Le Métro is ideally situated for a break from shopping in Knightsbridge. After descending the stairs from street level, the atmosphere is that of a Parisian brasserie, with tables close together and a high level of noise from busy conversation. You can just have a drink if you wish, though it would be a shame to miss the opportunity to eat. Order a glass of wine from the Cruover machines whilst choosing. In case you're unfamiliar with these machines, they hold opened bottles of wine in an inert atmosphere which prevents oxidisation. This allows quality wines to be served by the glass, and offers a good chance to taste the better stuff before you buy a bottle.

The menu is very brasserie - rillettes, jambon persillé with salade frisée, filets de macquereaux with pommes à l'huile to start, then navarin d'agneau, or saucissons à la Lyonnaise, osso buco or confits de canard aux pommes en robe, which is superb. The cooking is of a high standard not often found in England in this type of establishment, and represents extremely good value for money. Sweets are simple and the coffee is espresso. No less than 100 wines are on the list and most are affordable, but somehow Champagne always seems to be the right thing to drink at Le Métro: it must be the atmosphere!

Monkeys   SW3

1 Cale Street SW3
01-352 4711/5120

Closed: Christmas Day; Boxing Day; 1 week Feb; 1 week Aug
Last
Orders: lunch (2.30pm; 3.00pm Sun); dinner (11.30pm; 10.30pm Sun)

A popular bistro with the locals around Chelsea, Monkeys has a lively ambience and serves an imaginative menu with an impressive wine list. A fixed price menu is offered in the evening where you can choose from soup, a selection of pâtés, hot mousse of salmon, a spinach, calves' liver and straw potato salad or perhaps a ragoût of snails and chervil. Main courses might be a panaché of fish with beurre blanc, sautéed veal sweetbreads, mignons of pork with peppers or a choice of game during the season. Lunch is an à la carte choice reduced from the evening menu, and puddings might be bread and butter pudding, hot treacle tart or summer pudding.

Nineteen   SW3

19 Mossop Street SW3
01-589 4971

Closed: lunch (Sat)
Last
Orders: lunch (3.00pm); dinner (11.45pm)

Little has changed here since my last visit some 6 years ago. As I
opened the door there were others waiting to eat - but don't
book, just turn up; turnover is fast and there are plenty of tables.
Décor is simple: rendered walls above timber panelling with a
few prints of Renoir and Van Gogh. Tables are huddled together
in the separate areas of the dining room and there is a noisy,
friendly atmosphere as the young clientele eat and chatter. This
is a good bistro to frequent if you are alone, as they will steer
you onto a larger table, and as the glasses empty, the conversation flows with other diners.

   Food is simple and sustaining: onion soup, hot mushrooms
with bacon and garlic, smoked trout with mustard and dill sauce.
A whole poussin with spicy sauce, casserole of venison or
delicious calves' liver with bacon come with a choice of
vegetables or salad. Puddings are homely - apple and blackberry
crumble, treacle tart, lemon meringue pie or a light amaretto
soufflé. Wines are all at housewine prices, with even Sancerre at
under £9.00! The actual vin de table is £5.00. Service by
attractive, friendly staff is amazingly fast once you find a table,
and if there is a queue you can always wait in the Admiral
Codrington pub next door.

Poissonnerie de l'Avenue   SW3

82 Sloane Avenue SW3 3DZ
01-589 2457

Closed: Sun; 23 Dec-3 Jan; Bank Holidays
Last
Orders: lunch (3.00pm); dinner (11.30pm)

An old favourite which has a very comfortable and established
feel about it - not that surprising as it is now 23 years since Peter
Rosignoli opened the Poissonnerie. The restaurant has beams
and wall lights, a long bar for eating oysters, and nice touches
such as monogrammed linen, and experienced waiters. The
menu provides a choice of some 15 different dishes with
specialities such as St Jacques aux petits légumes, paupiettes de
saumon à l'oseille, pilaf de lotte au pernod and one or two
non-fishy dishes for those who miss the point of dining here.

   The atmosphere at lunch assumes an urgency and seriousness
owing to the influx of local executives. A concise wine list with
little over £20.00 and not much under £10.00.

Ponte Nuovo   SW3

126 Fulham Road SW3 6HU
01-370 6656/4917

Last
Orders: lunch (3.00pm); dinner (midnight)

This popular 80-seater Italian restaurant has simple, modern décor inside and a few tables spilling onto the pavement patio screened from the road by a trellis that's flower-bedecked in summer. The menu features the usual range of pasta and it is well prepared, and the fish is always fresh and properly cooked. Friendly staff maintain a light-hearted ambience amongst the closely packed tables. An impressive list of quality Italian wines is available, and their espresso coffee is very good.

It's nice to see Walter Mariti firmly established in this restaurant just across the road from his previous venture at the Meridiana.

San Frediano   SW3

62 Fulham Road SW3
01-584 8375

Closed: Sun
Last
Orders: lunch (2.30pm); dinner (11.15pm)

No guide to London would be complete without a mention of San Frediano. This old faithful steams on, still packs them in, and remains reverentially Italian. Saturday lunch times are still a real scrum but they always make you feel like a long-lost customer when you arrive, and manage to get the dishes out in super-fast time. Simple, original, trat-style décor, and everyone's been going so long that they are prepared to forgive any oversights. For atmosphere and pzazz it still beats some of the newer Italian editions.

San Lorenzo   SW3

22 Beauchamp Place SW3 1NH
01-584 1074

Closed: Sun
Last
Orders: lunch (2.45pm); dinner (11.30pm)

Still as popular, still as difficult to get into, you now have to contend with the international brigade as well as its faithful London following. The greenhouse style atmosphere is charming, the place buzzes with exciting conversation, and there are lots of interesting and unusual dishes on the menu, as well as the old-time Italian and regional favourites. With a reasonably priced wine list, this can be a fun place to be.

NESCAFÉ ®
instant coffee
The best start to the day.

Nestlé ®

St Quentin SW3

243 Brompton Road SW3 2EP
01-589 8005/581 5131

Closed: 1 week Christmas
Last
Orders: midnight

The brass-railed bar and the speedy professional French waiters
all combine to give this restaurant a most Parisian feel. It is ever
popular with the Knightsbridge locals and it's essential to book
if you want a table upstairs.

Hugh O'Neill watches over the expanding business, Didier
Garnier is the general manager with chef/directeur Charles
Plumex coming across frequently from the Savoie. The menu is
beginning to feature dishes like steamed turbot with vanilla,
whole veal kidneys with mustard sauce or saddle of rabbit with
a garlic purée. Cooking is basically good and the set lunch is
very good value. Cheeses are from Philippe Olivier and all the
pâtisserie and bread comes from their shop around the corner.
Some wines are imported directly and all are worth trying.

Thierry's SW3

342 King's Road SW3 5UR
01-352 3365

Closed: Sun; Bank Holidays; Christmas; Easter;
last 2 weeks Aug
Last
Orders: lunch (2.30pm); dinner (11.30pm)

Thierry Cabanne's popular King's Road bistro has become a way
of life in Chelsea during the last 17 years, and is one of London's
'really French' restaurants. François Rohlion and Alain Jeannon
cook, and while taped classical music plays, pretty young ladies
serve in the intimate dining room. Tables are close together,
walls are equally crowded with mirrors and paintings, and above
all there is the comforting sound of people enjoying themselves
in this ground floor and basement restaurant. The menu features
a range of well-established dishes which are supplemented with
weekly additions, according to markets. Specialities are soufflés,
a cheese one to start or Grand Marnier for pudding, quenelles of
pike, and magret de canard. Naturally, the wines are French, and
vintages have been carefully chosen with good housewines at
around £6.00.

Toto Restaurant   SW3

Walton House, Walton Street SW3
01-589 2062

Last
Orders: lunch (3.00pm); dinner (11.30pm)

Terraza-tiled floors, a wonderful carved fireplace and photographs of Tina Turner, Ringo Starr, Frank Sinatra and others are features of this trendy Italian restaurant in a mews off Walton Street. Different levels create interest, and there is a mezzanine floor as well as a courtyard for warm weather dining.

Cooking is above the usual Italian level, with good sauces on fish dishes, excellent pasta and a few authentic dishes such as liver veneziana served with polenta.

The busy atmosphere makes this a good restaurant in which to entertain visitors to town, as you tend to feel you're in the right place.

Turner's   SW3

87-89 Walton Street SW3 2HP
01-584 6711

Closed: lunch (Sat + Mon); dinner (Mon); Bank Holidays
Last
Orders: please ring for details

Many talented chefs have failed in their attempts to make the transition from chef to restaurateur, but Brian Turner looks like coping in his customary workmanlike fashion. After eating at Turner's a few weeks after its opening, it was evident that it ought shortly to be amongst London's top restaurants. Those of us who have been familiar with Brian's cooking at The Capital Hotel during the last few years have little doubt as to his skills, but new restaurants usually take time to settle down. Not so at Turner's. It would be difficult to fault a dinner which started with a boned quail which was perfectly cooked, sliced and served on a bed of endive with a nut oil dressing; a navarin of seafood that was superb; a variety of fish with a variety of crunchy vegetables; a tartlet of sliced pear set in frangipane with sauce anglaise, coffee and petits fours completed an excellent meal. The freshly baked bread was good too!

Service is by attractive young ladies, and Brian divides his time between kitchen and dining room in true chef/patron style. The décor is simple - grey walls with colourful prints, a powder blue carpet, and blue and white paisley design underlays beneath white tablecloths.

It will soon be difficult to find a table at Turner's - an American devotee of Brian's cooking was sitting in the restaurant, and had only been in London for 2 hours before managing to track him down!

Waltons   SW3

121 Walton Street SW3
01-584 0204

Closed: Bank Holidays
Last
Orders: lunch (2.30pm; 2.00pm Sun);
        dinner (11.30pm; 10.30pm Sun)

Located on the corner of Walton Street and Draycott Avenue,
this well-patronised restaurant has been established for around
15 years. The primrose and grey silk walls create an elegant
atmosphere, with Louis-style armchairs and lavish drapes. Gary
Jones's menu features a modern range of dishes using ingredients like foie gras, smoked salmon, lobster, crayfish and
asparagus. Sauces contain champagne and chartreuse so that, as
you might appreciate, prices are high, though a set lunch at
around £11.00 is good value, and there is an after-theatre supper
at around £18.00.

   There is a 30-page wine list with a stunning show of clarets,
some rare Burgundies and 20 Champagnes.

Ziani   SW3

45-47 Radnor Walk SW3
01-351 5297/2698

Closed: Christmas Day + Boxing Day
Last
Orders: lunch (2.45pm); dinner (11.30pm)

Cool, clean and elegant with a setting just off the King's Road to
match, this is a place tailor-made for an Italian lunch on a sunny
day. Waiters are friendly and efficient, and good fresh food is
well prepared in generous portions. Gazpacho is properly seasoned and chilled, grilled monkfish tail is really fresh and could
be accompanied by a lightly dressed salad. Ladies feel relaxed
enough to eat here alone - not a common sight in London and
one to be encouraged.

   Wines are well chosen, well priced and all Italian.

Ormes Restaurant   SW4

67-69 Abbeville Road SW4 9JW
01-673 2568

Closed: Christmas Day
Last
Orders: lunch (2.30pm); dinner (11.00pm)

This cheerful bistro and wine bar in Clapham has good atmosphere and reasonable prices. Dishes such as boudin in a blanket
(a black pudding in a pancake served with apple sauce),
mushroom terrine with tomato chutney and smoked eel pâté,
are some of the more unusual first courses. Typical main dishes
are Lancashire hot-pot, sauté of beef, stuffed trout, gnocchi for
vegetarians, and steaks of lamb or beef for traditionalists. There

are good home-made puddings to follow, and the large selection of wines from around the world are mostly well under £10.00 - housewine being £4.50 a bottle.

Lou Pescadou   SW5

241 Old Brompton Road SW5
01-370 1057

Closed: Sun; Aug
Last
Orders: midnight

Lou Pescadou is a fish, pasta and pizza brasserie and if you haven't been to one of these yet I recommend an early visit!

A bistro-style room has cream walls with lots of pictures and models of sailing ships, a quarry tiled floor, a small garden area at the rear and a bar in the basement. A very cheerful and welcoming feel is maintained by the manager and staff who are dressed in striped T-shirts and jeans. Fish is the principal offering on the menu. There are oysters, clams, mussels, winkles and shrimps, fish soup and squid; there is pasta with tomato, basil, fruits de mer or baby clams, ravioli with crab, pizzas with fruit de mer, niçoise or with ham, mushrooms, and cheese... A good variety of salads is offered, and more substantial main courses of skate, monkfish, red mullet and others are available according to the market, and even one or two meats should you wish. In fact, it offers something for everyone, and the informal atmosphere means that you can eat as much or as little as you wish, making it ideal for a larger party with different tastes. The Côtes de Provence housewines are perfect for the food and the coffee is good. A must for a lively evening with friends.

Read's Restaurant SW5

152 Old Brompton Road SW5 0BE
01-373 2445

Closed: dinner (Sun); Bank Holidays
Last
Orders: dinner (11.00pm)

Caroline Read, who cooks at this stylish and fashionable restaurant, has rapidly become, through hard work and creative
skill, one of the top half-dozen professional women chefs whose
skill shows both in the imaginative menu presentation and the
quality of the food cooked. The handling of ingredients and
simplicity of presentation show the true measure of her ability.
Caroline has been influenced by Quentin Crewe's knowledge
and interest in food and has also spent time working with Brian
Turner. The terrine of veal and tongue with redcurrant and
orange sauce was an excellent colour, wonderful flavour and of
a perfect consistency. The main course of lambs' liver, which
was served on a compôte of leeks with a sauce sharpened with
raspberry vinegar was first class, with perfectly cooked French
beans and fennel. There's a good selection of desserts with
extremely fine sauces and some unique dishes. Very pleasant
and caring staff who pay great attention to detail, and a warm,
comfortable feel to the décor make this restaurant very welcoming. The set lunch at £10.50 is remarkable value and the £14.50
Sunday lunch is certainly worth trying.

Since writing this review, Caroline Read has departed for
Antigua, but I decided to leave the review in as a tribute to her.
Let's hope she will return to London some day. The chef is now
Tim Franklin from Hintlesham Hall, and it's good to write that
the standards at Read's have been maintained.

Brasserie Saint Claire SW6

130 Wandsworth Bridge Road SW6
01-731 7835

Closed: lunch (Mon-Fri); Bank Holidays
Last
Orders: lunch (3.00pm Sat; 3.15pm Sun); dinner (11.45pm)

Unusual, an Italian brasserie - I thought they called them
trattorias. A noisy, down-to-earth brasserie with a good atmosphere which is popular with the younger set who are moving
into this up-and-coming area near Parsons Green, this one offers
the usual range of Italian first courses such as prosciutto,
mozzarella salad or grilled sardines, with pasta, fish or meats to
follow. Alternatively you can have a skewer of grilled king
prawns with salad, served at the bar.

Filling Station Bistro SW6

144 Wandsworth Bridge Road SW6
01-736 2418

Closed: lunch (daily); dinner (Sun)
Last
Orders: dinner (11.30pm)

An ideal local bistro with gingham tablecloths, candles at night and an old petrol pump in one corner! The cooking is uncompli-cated but uses good ingredients and doesn't mess about with them. Deep-fried mushrooms with garlic mayonnaise, a grilled rump steak with spring cabbage, and a crème brûlée are excellent. A good atmosphere is created by the young clientele, and for warm evenings there are tables outside.

Le Gastronome SW6

309 New Kings Road SW6
01-731 6993

Closed: lunch (Sat + Sun); dinner (Sun); Bank Holidays
        23 Dec - 2 Jan
Last
Orders: lunch (2.00pm); dinner (11.00pm)

Now called simply Le Gastronome, this popular restaurant has been refurbished, and has changed from its old homely image to a bright, designer-style dining room on ground floor level, with pastel shades, good lighting, grey and white striped chairs and crisp linen. Thierry Aubugeau is still in charge of the kitchens, and his modern style of cooking is as good as ever. An autumn salad with warm crottin cheese and Jerusalem artichokes, a terrine of duck confit, ravioli with wild mushrooms or a tartlet of mussels and courgettes with saffron, shine amongst first courses. To follow, try monkfish with chablis and tarragon, pot au feu of pigeon, grenadin of veal with a vanilla sauce or a fillet of lamb with fricassée niçoise and basil, all well cooked. Puddings are equally well judged and the wine list has a good selection from major French regions. Service is friendly and efficient: Le Gastronome has now come of age.

Hiders   SW6

755 Fulham Road SW6 5UU
01-736 2331

Closed: lunch (Sat + Sun); dinner (Sun)
Last
Orders: dinner (11.30pm)

Hiders really comes to life in the evenings. The menu is imaginative – really quite a high standard to keep up, and they work very hard at it. This very comfortable dining room, with its relaxed atmosphere, is in fact slightly out of place in Fulham Road - the general feeling of the place being perhaps one of an Edwardian lounge. The menu changes every 2 weeks but the prices remain constant at 2 courses for £12.00 and 3 courses for £13.00. Selection might be from an endive parcel filled with light crab mousse served on a pepper sauce, a pastry case filled with a scallop in a fish mousseline, wrapped in a spinach leaf on a watercress sauce. Main courses might include calves' liver, loin of veal, or sliced breast of duck, cooked pink, with apricots and a fennel seed sauce. Wines start from £5.50 with a small but good range up to £57.50 for the most expensive claret.

L'Hippocampe   SW6

131A Munster Road SW6 4DD
01-736 5588

Closed: lunch (Sat); Christmas
Last
Orders: lunch (2.30pm); dinner (11.00pm)

"A fish restaurant specialising in the modern style of cooking but with traditional portions," is the way Pierre Condou describes his bistro in Fulham. A blue and white awning with a bright blue neon sign ensures that potential customers will not fail to locate the small restaurant amongst the houses and shops in Munster Road. Inside there is a small bar, chairs and tables sitting on the blue ceramic floor of what was once a shop, and there is a small conservatory area at the rear.

The chef Philippe Levrey has talent, and the menus show originality and flair for interesting combinations of ingredients. Instead of preparing a fish terrine by making a mousseline, he lays fillets of red mullet in a terrine, cooks them, and lightly presses them so that the texture of the fish is retained. Instead of serving a cream sauce with it he uses vinaigrette, a clever and successful variance. A boudin of crab, a light mousseline of fresh crab, was poached in a sausage skin and served with an excellent sauce of red peppers. The pudding, a tartelette fine chaude aux pommes comprises thin slices of apple baked on superb puff pastry, glazed and accompanied by a light fresh custard sauce. Philippe's other dishes exhibit the same skills: scampi tails and fish quenelles in a light muscadet sauce, poached Dover sole with lobster cream sauce or a slice of salmon stuffed with smoked salmon mousse in a basil sauce.

The small wine selection is all French, mostly white and reasonably priced.

Service is knowledgeable and attentive and L'Hippocampe is a welcome addition to London's choice of fish restaurants with a nouvelle style but sensibly sized portions. The residents of this part of Fulham are fortunate to have this restaurant on their doorstep as the food would cost a great deal more for this standard in a designer restaurant in the West End.

Blakes Hotel Restaurant   SW7

33 Roland Gardens SW7 3PF
01-370 6701

Closed: Christmas Day; Boxing Day
Last
Orders: lunch (2.30pm); dinner (11.30pm)

Anouska Hempel Weinberg's restaurant and hotel must share the honours with David Levin's Capital Hotel for introducing a new style of smaller hotel with added luxury. Although they're very different in design terms, both have managed to establish a following in the restaurant. It certainly proves that if you spend money wisely to start with, you may not continually have to change the style of the place to sustain business. The warm and clever décor in this restaurant still feels welcoming, with veneered and lacquered walls and smart well-informed staff. No-one seems to be overtly in charge of the restaurant but the staff convey a thorough knowledge of their product, and it always maintains an exclusive air.

An interesting selection of music was playing whilst we were there, ranging from "Merry Christmas Mr Lawrence" through to Verdi and Mozart, which was quite appropriate as Dame Kiri Te Kanawa was eating at the next table!

The menu sounds quite exciting in that there's no overall allegiance to any particular country. The dishes might vary from a salad of foie gras served with black truffles and haricots verts, filetto carpaccio con parmigiano, artichoke heart and quails' eggs with a purée of sorrel for starters, via a risotto al pesto or a chicken tikka with a cucumber, mint and chilli raita, to main courses ranging from veal sweetbreads on leaf spinach with capers, to roast rack of English lamb with rosemary, or even a Szechuan duck with roasted salt and peppers. Good crisp vegetables are served, often with a gratin dauphinois, or white or wild rice. To finish there are good puddings, cheese served with walnut bread, or a delicious green salad with Roquefort cheese, bacon and spring onions. The wine list has housewines from £9.50 a bottle.

If I didn't live in London it's certainly a place I would choose to stay. However it isn't cheap to stay, and there are various sizes of bedroom, but they are very well appointed, and you get an overall feeling of luxury and sophistication.

BERINGER CABERNET SAUVIGNON.
This rich, well balanced red wine is produced
at **Beringer** – the oldest continuously
producing winery in California's famous Napa
Valley – <u>the</u> premier Californian appellation.

We are pleased to offer this premium wine for
your dining pleasure.

THE NESTLÉ COMPANY LTD. St. George's House, Croydon, Surrey CR9 1NR. 01-686 3333.

NESCAFÉ®
BLEND 37®
freeze dried instant coffee
Rich, dark and distinctly 'continental.'

Nestlé®

The Chanterelle SW7

119 Old Brompton Road SW7 3RN
01-373 5522/7390

Last
Orders: lunch (2.30pm); dinner (11.30pm)

It's always difficult to get into this very popular and well-established, reasonably priced restaurant. The friendly welcome, efficient service, warm coloured wooden walls, mirrors, and the tightly packed tables create a vibrant atmosphere in which to enjoy some excellent value food.

The 3-course dinner menu at under £12.00 might include, out of a choice of 6 starters, a sorrel soup with anchovy croûtons, a poached egg tart with crab and hollandaise, a warm mousse of sweetbreads with tarragon and cream, or a spinach roulade with mushroom and shrimp stuffing. From 8 main courses you might choose roast rack of lamb with mustard and herb stuffing, or a brochette of scallops on a bed of seaweed. These will be accompanied by good portions of proper vegetables, like little potatoes in their jackets and crisply cooked cabbage. Leave room for puds - a sticky walnut tart, a French apple and raisin tart, strawberry and orange salad, or Atholl Brose. A lunch at around £7.00 with a choice of 3 starters, 4 main courses and 4 puddings is difficult to beat for value. They change their menu every couple of weeks and offer a good range of sensibly priced wines, with some 14 or so half bottles.

It's really nice to see a restaurant that goes from strength to strength, retains its own distinctive style and still offers value for money.

Montpeliano SW7

13 Montpelier Street SW7 1HQ
01-589 0032/2753

Closed: Sun; Bank Holidays
Last
Orders: lunch (3.00pm); dinner (midnight)

This smartly tiled Italian restaurant opposite Harrods, where the clientele seem to be drawn from the cast of Dynasty, may not augur well for the food, but in fact a great deal more care is taken here in the invention and execution of the dishes than is often the case in such places. The lamb arrabiatta, the spaghetti lobster or the Robespierre (finely sliced beef fillet carpaccio-style warmed under the grill with olive oil and fresh herbs) are some interesting dishes served alongside some more substantial Italian food. The service is suitably slick but friendly, and waiters cope very well with children, particularly at weekends.

The wine list is standard Italian and ranges from the medium to the more expensive wines.

Rebato's   SW8

169 South Lambeth Road SW8 1XW
01-735 6388

Closed: lunch (Sat + Sun); dinner (Sun)
Last
Orders: lunch (2.30pm); dinner (11.15pm)

The idea of a Spanish bar and restaurant in Brixton may seem
bizarre, but one visit and you will be convinced that this is an
ideal venue for an enjoyable and reasonably priced evening. The
staff are Spanish, which is reassuring, and the bar has a very
typical Spanish atmosphere. One can eat tapas in the bar, or dine
in the restaurant from the fixed price menu at £9.25. There are
25 varieties of tapas including large prawns, octopus, Spanish
omelette and even tripe, cooked in the Spanish way, of course.
An excellent list of wines from Penedes, Rioja, Galicia, Navarra
and even Jumilla range in price from £4.95 to £14.00, and I
would recommend the Freixenet Cordon Negro at £7.95, which
is a delicious sparkling wine. They make a concession to English
and French dishes on their menu with moules maison and
supreme of chicken Devon but that said, this is a favourite haunt
for a fun evening with a group of friends.

Twenty Trinity Gardens   SW9

20 Trinity Gardens SW9 8DP   £25
01-733 8838

Closed: lunch (Sat + Sun); dinner (Sun); 25 Dec - 1 Jan
Last
Orders: dinner (10:30pm)

There are not that many places to eat in this area of town but
this good value, bistro style restaurant just off Acre Lane is
amongst the better ones. There are two menus at either £8.75 or
£11.75 for 3 courses, or just 2 courses may be had for £1.50 less.
Some of their wines are also fine value, even to a Château Pontet
Canet 1949 for £40.00 on the bin end list.

Bagatelle   SW10

5 Langton Street SW10
01-351 4185/351 9272

Closed: lunch + dinner (Sun); 1 week Christmas;
        Bank Holidays
Last
Orders: lunch (2.00pm); dinner (11.00pm)

A French bistro with a Japanese chef, which explains dishes
such as marinade de filet de boeuf - thin slices of fillet marinated
and served raw - and entrecôte poché which is thin slices of
sirloin "dipped in stock gently". Simple bistro décor and a pretty
patio at the rear which makes this an ideal lunch-time or evening
venue when the sun shines.

Eleven Park Walk   SW10

11 Park Walk SW10 0AJ   £30
01-352 3449/8249

Closed: Bank Holidays; Christmas
Last
Orders: lunch (3.00pm); dinner (midnight)

This sophisticated, tiled Italian restaurant has recently been
revamped, so that cool, hard surfaces, and huge modern paintings now complement good honest Italian food. Risotto di funghi
porcini is delicious and sustaining, and might be followed by an
excellent bollito misto con salsaverdi - a selection of boiled meat
(far more superior than it sounds) with a garlic sauce, thick with
chopped parsley.

    Brisk service and lots of noisy customers produce a very
vibrant atmosphere behind the flat cream façade on Park Walk.

L'Olivier   SW10

116 Finborough Road SW10 9ED   £45
01-370 4199/4183

Closed: lunch (Sun + Mon); dinner (Sun); Christmas
Last
Orders: lunch (2.00pm); dinner (11.30pm)

One of the guides recently paid Pierre Martin a bigger tribute
than they probably realised by describing this little basement
restaurant as being "summery", for Pierre has converted this
zippy, friendly little French restaurant out of a tiny cellar. It's
quite easy to drive past it and not even realise where it is, but it's
well worth a stop. Ring the bell, and you will be answered by a
smiling face and either offered a drink at the small bar on the
ground floor, or taken straight down to your table. It always
seems to be full of people enjoying themselves.

    The menu is presented in the normal Martin manner, but this
time featuring meat rather than fish (although there are 1 or 2
fish dishes you can choose from, including the excellent soupe
au pistou or the marmite de pêcheur). There is a choice of
feuilletés of which you might try asparagus, langoustine, or

fruits de mer. The menu at around £20.00 gives you hors d'oeuvres maison, which is a choice of starters from the menu, followed by a choice of roasts of the day or the plat du jour, both of which include vegetables. The plat du jour might be carré d'agneau, côte de boeuf, poulet fermier, rognons de veau à la moutarde, or sauté de boeuf aux olives. There is also salad, a choice from the cheese board and dessert.

To help you enjoy yourself in this restaurant, full of flower paintings and French bonhomie, choose from the compact but good wine list; its reasonable prices start with the Réserve de l'Olivier, red or white, at around £7.50 a bottle.

Nikita's SW10

65 Ifield Road SW10
01-352 6326

Closed: lunch (daily); dinner (Sun); Bank Holidays;
         last 2 weeks Aug
Last
Orders: dinner (11.15pm)

Nikita's in Ifield Road has been there for longer than I care to remember - it must be over 20 years - and it still has its faithful following. If you're a vodka drinker there is just about everything you could ever wish for. Besides the plain Russian and Polish vodkas, there are flavoured varieties, some 10 in all, including tarragon, and the "if-you've-tasted-it-once-you'll-never-forget-it" red pepper vodka, as well as the liqueur vodkas - try the krupnik, a honey vodka which is served warm. You consume the vodkas either by the carafe, which is presented encased in ice, or by the glass.

There's good sevruga, osetrova and beluga caviar, all served with blinis, and accoutrements of lemon, chopped egg, onion and soured cream. I think that for pure indulgence the best thing is a nice portion of beluga, followed by a bowl of borscht, and if you are so inclined, you can go on to main courses of shashlik - lamb grilled on the sword and served with yòghurt and mint, or goluptzy - parcels of cabbage filled with spiced meats, prunes, mushrooms, and onions. It's still got the same warm atmosphere and the noisy locals, but if you're after something different, then Nikita's is for you.

The Wine Gallery   SW10

47 Hollywood Road SW10
01-352 7572

Last
Orders: lunch (3.00pm); dinner (midnight)

A restaurant which lists its speciality as "sausage, beans and
mash" obviously has no illusions about being an up-market wine
bar, yet the Wine Gallery is just that. Value for money and
bustling atmosphere, where tables are hardly separated nor
empty, are the order of the day. The menu offers a good variety
of dishes other than bangers - there's gazpacho, globe artichokes
and cheese ménage amongst many other starters, and main
courses of fresh fish cakes (that's a relief!) with prawns, lobster
sauce and chips, mozzarella and turkey croquettes with ratatouille, kedgeree, spare ribs etc. Prices are very reasonable, and
there are no less than 24 well-chosen wines for under £10.00.
Service may be erratic, but you can afford another bottle to
drink whilst waiting. Good food is on offer in a relaxed
atmosphere, created by a timber floor, plain walls and a
charming selection of paintings and prints.

La Bouffe   SW11

13 Battersea Rise SW11 1HG
01-228 3384

Closed: lunch (Sat + Sun); dinner (Sun)
Last
Orders: lunch (2.30pm); dinner (11.00pm)

Battersea Rise has in the last few years become an interesting
area for eating and drinking. La Bouffe is situated on the side of
the road that houses the new revitalised Cullens, a wine
merchant, a pizza house, and a hamburger shop as well as an
antique shop and a pub. It's a simple little restaurant with café
curtains, plain cream front, straightforward cream décor inside
and a few wine maps on the walls. They do a set menu at around
£13.00 a head for La Grand Bouffe, and £9.00 for La Bouffe. For
the latter you might be offered a gazpacho, or avocado Roquefort, or a choice of grilled sardines or escalope de boeuf
served with an onion, mushroom and cognac sauce. This would
be followed by a choice of desserts from the buffet, and coffee.
La Grand Bouffe might offer you Mediterranean prawns served
hot with courgettes and ginger, or fillet of beef tartare, and then

for a main course escalope of veal served with apple, cider and cream, or halibut served with 2 sauces - a bisque and a mornay sauce. You also get cheese with salad, followed by a choice of dessert and coffee.

The wine list is good and aimed at the local trade, with house red and white under £5.00, the remainder of the sensible list starting at around £7.00 and remaining in the lower price range. It's a good choice.

Pollyanna's Restaurant SW11

2 Battersea Rise SW11 1ED
01-228 0316

Closed: lunch (Mon to Sat); dinner (Sun)
Last
Orders: lunch (3.00pm); dinner (midnight)

Norman Price's popular restaurant caters for all tastes with its cheerful décor and the possibility of choosing from no less than 2 and sometimes 3 menus. There is a standard à la carte menu, and a blackboard menu brought to each table, when each dish is carefully explained. Every 2 months a third menu might appear offering food representative of different nations as a part of a festival of European cuisine! As if this wasn't enough to think about, a very readable wine list of about 200 chattily described bottles is presented. It is, therefore, advisable to arrive early to make decisions about what one would like to eat and drink.

Eamonn Connolly, the hard-working chef, copes well with his ambitious task but one can't help feeling that they could achieve an even higher standard with slightly fewer dishes. The restaurant is usually full of talkative young executives, which creates a good atmosphere, and if you are dining alone a newspaper will arrive to fill the gaps between courses.

There is a good value Sunday lunch at £8.95 which on rare sunny days may be eaten in the garden.

Sonny's   SW13

94 Church Road SW13 0DQ   £25
01-748 0393

Closed: dinner (Sun)
Last
Orders: lunch (2.30pm); dinner (11.00pm)

This new brasserie amongst a row of shops in Barnes has a
somewhat austere décor, but well-spaced tables and a warm
welcome more than compensate. The small menu has an
interesting choice of dishes such as merguez sausages with hot
potato salad, spinach soufflé with anchovy sauce (shades of
Langan's?), or seafood salad with snow peas. Amongst the main
courses are a bourride of fish and prawns, calves' liver with
beetroot purée, or perhaps hot poached silverside with ravigote
sauce might appeal. Straightforward cooking at reasonable
prices: a 2-course set lunch with coffee is £7.95 and housewine
is £5.00.

Crowthers Restaurant   SW14

481 Upper Richmond Road West SW14 7PU   £40
01-876 6372

Closed: Sun + Mon; 25-30 Dec; 1 week Feb; 2 weeks late Aug-Sep
        Last
        Orders: lunch (2.00pm); dinner (11.00pm)

This is a well-run restaurant amidst a row of shops in East Sheen
where Philip and Shirley Crowther maintain a high standard of
cooking and service. The fixed price menu at £17.50 gives a
choice of 5 dishes for each of the courses and includes good,
freshly made terrines and perhaps an aubergine charlotte with
red pepper sauce, or scallops with leek and vermouth sauce,
followed by salmon en croûte with spring onion or calves' liver
with lemon and port sauce. Good vegetables are served with
main dishes, and with the apéritif an anchovy pastry. It is also
good to see proper petits fours with the coffee rather than the
ubiquitous mints. A well-planned wine list is predominantly
French and reasonably priced, with the excellent Jacquesson
Champagnes at £17.25. Décor is simple but comfortable and the
seriousness of the kitchen is softened by the charming hostess.
It is well worth crossing the river to visit this refreshingly honest
restaurant.

Le Cassis   SW15

30 Putney High Street SW15   £30
01-788 8668

Closed: Sun; Christmas
Last
Orders: lunch (2.00pm); dinner (11.00pm)

New owners and chef are now installed in this friendly bistro just south of Putney Bridge. Le Cassis serves food reminiscent of a French roadside restaurant, Phillipe Herrard's kitchen tending towards fortifying food rather than nouvelle cuisine. His menu says that he produces French onion soup "as in Paris"; the fish soup with rouille is as found in the South of France; and snails come with Roquefort, garlic, pastis, bacon and cream. Main courses such as a côte de boeuf grillée for 2 people, carré d'agneau à l'estragon, and magret de canard au cassis are well prepared and cooked. The menu is small but gives adequate choice and the décor is simple with cane chairs, pink tablecloths and lots of old French film posters to cheer the walls. There are about 20 reasonable wines on the list and housewine is good value at £5.40.

Mr Fish   SW15

393 Upper Richmond Road SW15 5QL
01-876 3083

Closed: lunch (Mon)
Last
Orders: lunch (2.00pm); dinner (10.30pm)

When you have an overwhelming desire to eat fish and chips, Mr Fish is the place to satiate your desire. It has a simple, almost tea-shop décor of beams and rendered plaster with wooden tables and settles; a blackboard announces the day's catch from Billingsgate. If you are really hungry, start with whitebait or crab bisque, and then choose from cod at £2.30 or £3.80 for a monster portion, through a range of prices to sole or scampi at £6.50.

The skate is sensational and almost covers the table let alone the plate! Chips are freshly cooked, as is all the fish, and the batter was light and crisp - I bet your mouth's watering already! Finally, as if one hadn't indulged sufficiently already, there is a large range of ice-creams to choose from.

Drink tea or wine as is your wont, and retire to a quiet place for a siesta.

Hoults   SW17

20 Bellevue Road SW17 7EB
01-767 1858

Closed: one week Christmas
Last
Orders: lunch (2.40pm); dinner (10.40pm)

This busy wine bar and bistro overlooking Wandsworth Common has a small simple menu with fresh food competently cooked and served by pretty young waitresses. The atmosphere is casual, the décor unpretentious, and the small terrace has a few tables outside for warmer days, making Hoults an ideal spot to just drop in for a glass of wine with a snack lunch. Try shelling some prawns and dipping them into garlic mayonnaise on a hot June day. There is a good selection of wines at reasonable prices and plenty of choice for just a glass if you like to change the beverage with the mood.

The Village Restaurant   SW19

8 High Street SW19 5DX
01-947 6477

Closed: lunch (Mon + Sat); dinner (Sun); Bank Holidays;
        last 2 weeks Aug
Last
Orders: lunch (2.30pm); dinner (11.00pm)

'Village' may seem an understatement for the now enlarged and
popular residential suburb of Wimbledon, though it is still
referred to as such by those who live there, and The Village
Restaurant has become very much a part of the local scene. Nick
Rochford, one of the 3 partners, runs the kitchen and offers set
price menus at lunch and dinner with the option of à la carte at
lunch and a few supplementary specialities in the evening.
Cooking is in the modern style without being totally nouvelle -
sole quenelles with lobster and watercress sauce followed by
roast best end of lamb served with an apple and mint coulis are
good, and a highlight is poached pear shortbread with pear
sabayon. Wines are all French and mostly young, with little
under the £10.00 mark. The décor and furnishing are simple and
cosy, the walls covered with an interesting and varied selection
of paintings. Young friendly staff are attentive and anxious to
please.

Alastair Little   W1

49 Frith Street W1
01-734 5183

Closed: Sat + Sun; Bank Holidays
Last
Orders: lunch (2.30pm); dinner (11.00pm)

Alastair Little is one of the media's favourite young English
chefs. He is proud to tell you that his kitchen is bigger than his
restaurant and it probably needs to be, as he changes the menu
twice daily. Magazine editors, publishers, music business executives and hopeful television writers flock there for lunch. Décor
is minimal, and well-informed service is from partners Kirsten
and Mercedes.

 The food mixes some classic favourites with dishes that are as
fashionable and design-conscious as the customers. Try the
ratatouille terrine, or the sashimi of tuna, royal sea bream and
turbot, or a sauté of baby artichokes, fennel and leeks. If it's on
the menu, the chartreuse of partridge is excellent, as are the
steamed baby Dover soles with new season's leeks, or the roast
lobster with basil, tomato and olive oil. To follow, try the
unusual crême brûlée of spiced pumpkin, or perhaps a pavlova
of raspberries and bilberries. Portions are generous, and the

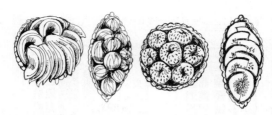

wine list is intelligently chosen, with good wine from France, Italy, California and Australia. Acoustics are inclined to be harsh, and you will pick up several fragments of everyone else's conversation - though this seems to be part of the game.

Anna's Restaurant   W1

34 Charlotte Street W1P 1HJ   £40
01-636 1178/631 1377

Last
Orders: lunch (3.00pm); dinner (11.00pm)

This new restaurant has quickly become fashionable for television and media people. The décor is minimal - clean and functional, with a bright atmosphere and cheerful staff. Paul Grindle cooks some unusual dishes in nouvelle style: scallops marinated in lime and ginger on a bed of salad, snails, bacon and mushrooms in a wine sauce beneath a puff pastry lid, chilled cream of strawberry and cucumber soup with mint. Main courses of duck breast with raspberry vinegar sauce, veal with coarse mustard and blackcurrant sauce, or fillet of lamb with port and honey sauce are interesting. There are around 40 wines from popular regions, and a rogue bottle of non-alcoholic wine. This place really buzzes at lunch time.

The Athenaeum   W1

116 Piccadilly W1   £45
01-499 3464

Last
Orders: lunch (3.00pm); dinner (10.30pm)

The recently refurbished dining room is pleasantly intimate for a large hotel, and service is from suitably professional waiters. The cooking is very much in the modern vein and seasonal dishes feature, usually prepared in a traditional English manner.

  Under the same ownership are the excellent Athenaeum Apartments, about 40 well-decorated luxury apartments in Down Street.

Au Jardin des Gourmets W1

5 Greek Street W1V 6NA
01-437 1816/734 2745

Closed: lunch (Sat, Sun + Bank Holidays); dinner (Sun);
Christmas; Easter
Last
Orders: lunch (2.30pm); dinner (11.30pm)

One of Soho's older restaurants, this was started by the original
chef at the Boulestin, and for many years has been under the
ownership of Joseph Berkmann, the much respected wine
merchant and restaurateur. It is now competently managed by
Franco Zoia with Paul Kaye in the kitchen.

The small and ageless restaurant is on both the ground and
first floors, and I have been fortunate to have had some
memorable meals, particularly in the first floor dining room
which is my favourite. Try the quenelles, light pike dumplings in
white wine sauce with sorrel, or cailles Souvaroff, 2 quails
cooked in a sealed casserole with pâté de foie and truffle, or
maybe the fillets of beef coated with parsley and thyme and then
cooked in red wine with anchovy butter.

There is a 4-course prix fixe menu, plus a sorbet, at £23.50,
and the wine list remains one of the most talked about and
exciting in town. Some amazing value wines can be found at
both ends of the price range, as we have grown to expect from
Joseph Berkmann.

Auntie's Restaurant W1

126 Cleveland Street W1
01-387 1548/3226

Closed: lunch (Sat + Sun); dinner (Sun); Christmas;
2 weeks Aug
Last
Orders: lunch (2.00pm); dinner (10.45pm)

Ian Wild runs the front of house and Shaun Thomson, late of The
Dorchester and Anton Mosimann, runs the kitchen in this small,
neat restaurant situated up the one-way part of Cleveland Street

(somehow I always end up reversing up that street!). This former teashop reminds me of the sort of place you might find in one of the backstreets of Amsterdam, with its intimate atmosphere and tables packed closely together, but the food here is very English and its presentation elegantly designed. A fixed price menu for around £13.00, changing every couple of months, includes a lovely basket of crudités to start you off. You might be offered a fresh iced soup in summer, or a selection of Auntie's summer salads, or some Cornish spiced and buttered crab served with toast, or an Arley oak-smoked chicken salad, from the choice of 6 or so first courses. For Principal Dishes, as they call them, you might get Auntie's bangers with spiced cabbage - superior Cumberland sausages, served with spiced cabbage and mustard sauce. They serve the catch of the day freshly baked in a paper parcel, and steak and mushroom pie or a grilled Barnsley lamb chop with plum and mint sauce. For puddings try tipsy fruit trifle, traditional Bakewell tart, a portion of designer bread and butter pudding or traditional farmhouse cheese. A simple but adequate wine list has a good smattering of English wines. All in all this is a calm oasis for anyone working in that area.

La Bastide   W1

50 Greek Street W1
01-734 3300

Closed: lunch (Sat + Sun); dinner (Sun)
Last
Orders: lunch (2.30pm); dinner (11.30pm)

Psychologist turned chef Nicholas Blacklock is certainly his own man, having taken a listed Georgian building and designed it himself, and even taken control of the kitchen. The feature here is a regional menu which changes every month, and offers some interesting variations on French dishes not usually found in London. The à la carte menu follows a more conventional modern path with occasional variations like a breast of guineafowl with chorizo and wild rice alongside an escalope of salmon with sorrel sauce. There is also an alternative selection of dishes - moules marinières, grilled Dover sole or a steak - for the less adventurously inclined.

There is a list of more than 200 wines from classic clarets to unknown regions of France and in the back room there is a lethal selection of Armagnacs, all bought from small farms, which ensure a happy ending to the evening. Sue Warwick, Nick's partner, runs the restaurant with charm and ease.

Bracewells W1

The Park Lane Hotel, Piccadilly W1Y 8BX
01-499 6321

Closed: Sat + Sun
Last
Orders: lunch (2.30pm); dinner (10.30pm)

It is worth going to Bracewells just to be greeted by Oscar
Bassam, the epitome of what a restaurant manager should be.
He stands at the entrance to the elegant dining room, impeccably dressed, with starched collar and just the right amount of
cuff showing from the sleeves of his well-pressed morning suit, a
monocle casually resting on his waistcoat. You get the immediate impression that you will eat well in his dining room; it would
surely be inconceivable that he'd be connected with anything
less than perfection. His young staff are also smart and efficient,
and show respect for their customers.

Ian Whittock is the chef, and though his training has been in
classic kitchens his menus are very much up-to-date and imaginative in concept. Scallops with a chervil sauce, black and
white truffle and strips of vegetables, a terrine of sweetbreads
with foie gras, or a consommé topped with a herb and cheese
soufflé are a few typical first courses. Loin of lamb with mint
mousse and port wine sauce, noisettes of venison in a light
sauce with blackberries, or perhaps a lobster with tomato and
basil sauce might follow.

Ian also offers a 5-course menu gastronomique, and the set
price lunch menu at around £15.00 is good value. It always
includes a roast joint carved from the trolley.

The décor is in the style of Louis XIV with beautifully carved
panelling which was originally taken from a French château to
embellish the London house of Pierport Morgan. The bar outside
the dining room , which is essentially a cocktail bar, is decorated
in grey and red with bamboo furniture.

The Park Lane is one of London's old established hotels and
has a secure and comfortable ambience, with 330 rooms and
suites and an Art Deco ballroom.

Braganza W1

56 Frith Street W1
01-734 0980

Closed: Bank Holidays
Last
Orders: 9.00pm

Braganza is very different from what it used to be, and very
different from most of its counterparts in London. Inspired by
some designs from Carlos Virgile of Fitch & Company, a fortune
has been spent on this place. As you come into the entrance hall
and look up through 2 other levels of floor space, you can see
the ceiling painted by Ricardo Cinalli, giving an even lighter and
airier feeling to this large restaurant.

It's divided into 3 sections, the cheapest section being on the
ground floor where some of the very attractive staff, dressed in

their Virgile-designed shirts, offer you a choice of some interesting dishes. You can have their straightforward Braganza New York sandwich, or a French baguette with Bayonne ham, salad and pickles, a plate of fresh sardines with almonds and lime, or a delicious grilled Toulouse sausage with warm potato and chive salad. Their main course salad dishes include one of spinach, crispy bacon, and smoked chicken with mango vinaigrette, and another of French beans and sweet peppers with tuna, basil and walnut dressing, and for vegetarian main courses, try the goats' cheese, tomato and leeks in a pastry drum served with a yoghurt and mint sauce, or an imaginative coulibiac of garden vegetables served with a Cajun sauce. They encourage you to have just 1 or 2 courses or, if you prefer, simply a bottle of wine. The place is certainly taking on a zippy, exciting feel.

The décor throughout is cool, modern and stylish with some unusual surfaces, and although the concept for the whole of Braganza is as a restaurant with art, it is displayed differently at each level. In the brasserie, the art is on the floor; on the first floor it's on the walls; and at second floor level it's the ceiling that's the thing. Each level also has its own lighting effects, colour scheme and furniture.

The first and second floors are more restaurant-inspired, the second with its rather clubby atmosphere has great views down to the ground floor, if you're lucky enough to get a table overlooking it. The first floor has some interesting paintings around the walls, almost forming a screen to draw you in and make you pay attention to the eclectic array of dishes from which to choose. The 8 or so starters might include an assiette of oak-smoked fish with horseradish cream and fresh pineapple, or a salad of Bayonne ham, smoked goose and snow peas. Main courses could be the unusual calves' liver with onion and red wine marmalade, or the very good pan-roasted duck with red cabbage and chestnuts. There's a paillard of veal with tarragon butter, or pan-fried scallops and sole with garlic, tomatoes and herbs. The desserts are the same on all 3 floors, with a very good fresh fruit tart, or petits pots au chocolate. It is interesting to see a wine list where the French don't just take second place but maybe even third or fourth, with some excellent value offered in the Californian and Australian departments.

Brown's Hotel   W1

Albermarle Street W1A 4SW
01-493 6020

Last
Orders: lunch (2.30pm); dinner (10.00pm; 9.30pm Sun)

Brown's Hotel is rather special. It runs from Albermarle Street right through to Dover Street and is a collection of Victorian houses carefully integrated over the years, its original owner being a former butler to Lord Byron. The exterior, which is a neat collection of buildings, well anticipates the interior with little rooms and lounges everywhere, full of lovely pieces of furniture and antiques and good paintings. From the moment you enter the reception area, and make your reservation at one of the little desks that are there for that purpose, you are whisked into a world which has old-fashioned standards of service and luxury.

Brown's is rather like a private club with regular visitors returning time and time again. Perhaps the best way for an outsider to sample it would be to try a traditional afternoon tea, when they serve the scones hot, along with cakes, pastries, sandwiches and thinly sliced brown bread and butter. It really gives you a feel of one of London's special hotels.

Café Italien Des Amis Du Vin   W1

19 Charlotte Street W1
01-636 4174

Closed: Sun
Last
Orders: lunch (3.00pm); dinner (11.30pm)

This café gives a new dimension to the Charlotte Street cuisine. The one-time Bertorelli's now has a brisk, smart café atmosphere, and the décor of cream walls, interesting prints, wooden floors and brasserie-style chairs provides a lively and zippy atmosphere for the Italian style menu, which has more imaginative dishes than most. Try their mistero della casa (spinach and ricotta cheese gnocchi) with cream and tomato sauce, or the eggplant stuffed with onions and fresh mint. Live jazz in the evenings and windows opening on to Charlotte Street provide the final touches for this very popular café-restaurant.

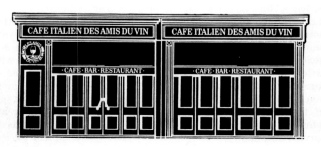

The Café Royal **W1**

68 Regent Street W1R 6EL
01-437 9090

Closed: lunch (Sat + Sun); Bank Holidays
Last
Orders: lunch (2.30pm); dinner (10.45pm)

"About sixty years ago three foreign waiters came to London, not together; they each made a fortune and a famous name. They were Philippe of the Cavour, Nicol of the Café Royal, and Romano.

"The career of each man was a romance. Apart from the personal aspect, surely it is a romance for a peasant from a foreign country to go to the greatest city in the world and to influence its daily life. Nicol, (and his wife), did that in London.

"They started a small café in Paris, but were not successful, so came to London, where they opened an unpretentious café in Glasshouse Street, at the back of the present Café Royal. The little café was, from the first, called the Café Royal. That was in 1863; two years later they started another café in Regent Street itself and joined the two.

"It was the Commune of 1871 which made his fortune. His café was crowded with French refugees, it was so full that it was a difficulty to get a table. But even from the earliest days it has been a cosmopolitan rendezvous, and it continued to be so all through the life of its famous owner, as well as a favourite resort of Bohemians - artists, writers, poets, sculptors, artists' models, beauties, prize fighters, and goodness knows who else.

"The entrance hall of the new Café Royal is architecturally excellent, there is beautiful Carrara marble and a quite startling austerity. The ironwork too is good, and has for its central design the familiar 'N' which instinctively raises a picture of Napoleon, but on second thoughts reminds the in-coming patron that this is still the Café Royal of the Nicols - though very grand.

"The renowned café room still remains open day and night, and has the red velvet benches on which artists, from Aubrey Beardsley to Augustus John and Epstein, have sat superior to the world at large. But the café is new and very large, it is on the left hand of the building with an entrance from the hall or from Glasshouse Street. It is a square room with a wide balcony. The decoration is plain, the walls are painted a yellow buff with touches of strong red and green. The whole place is set with red velvet settees, the old Café Royal chairs, and with marble topped tables. An old fashioned carafe of water stands on every table.

"The balcony is more luxurious, it is carpeted and the tables have cloths.

"In the centre of the ceiling is a large painting reminiscent of the old building.

"Occupying the place of the old café room, though smaller, is the present grill.

"Upstairs there are two restaurants, one very large and over the new café, has music, the other, smaller and overlooking Regent Street, has no music.

"The powers-that-be, headed by Mr Daniel Picache, the grandson of the Nicols, saw that destruction did not overtake the two hundred and fifty ceiling pictures which bedecked the old building. Some are in the present grill room, and others have found a place in other ceilings, notably in that of the smaller restaurant.

"There are large banqueting rooms.

"The Café Royal was always known as a place where the gourmet can spend pounds on his dinner and an artists' model can order a glass of sweetened water (in the café)."

The Restaurants of London, Eileen Hooton-Smith, 1928

Great efforts have been made in The Café Royal to try and regain some of the opulence that has perhaps been eroded in recent years. Robert Burness will proudly show you the recent renovation work which is being carried out on the ceiling in one of the banqueting rooms; and also the other improvements and renovations which are being made to some of the other rooms. They certainly are trying to recreate some of the style and character of a by-gone era, even through recent Beardsley-esque advertisements that were intended to give an overall fin-de-siècle feel. They have opened an intimate little cocktail bar where there is jazz in the evening, and the Grill Room itself remains as splendid as ever. Renewed efforts are being made with the food which hopefully will return the Café Royal to its place as one of the grandest restaurants in the capital.

Champagne Exchange   W1

17C Curzon Street W1Y 7FE
01-493 4490/491 2139

Closed: lunch (Sat + Sun); dinner (Sun)
Last
Orders: lunch (3.00pm); dinner (midnight)

If as a restaurateur you are going to specialise in smoked fish, caviar and Champagne, then Mayfair is the place to do it. Most other international capitals seem to have this type of restaurant, so this is a welcome addition to London's range. Champagne is offered by the glass, half bottle, bottle and magnum, from £3.50 for the first up to £53.00 for a magnum of Special Cuvée Bollinger, and there's plenty of choice in between. Amongst the many houses represented are Bollinger, Veuve Clicquot, Krug, Tattinger, Perrier-Jouet and Louis Roederer. You can also try the still wines of Champagne, including the red Bouzy Barancourt, or some good Champagne cocktails.

Amongst the choices of caviar they have beluga and sevruga which you can accompany with blinis and cream, or baked potato and cream. There's gravadlax, smoked sturgeon, perhaps a terrine of fresh scallops or maybe you'll settle for some French charcuterie. There is a good choice of soft French cheeses which you can have as a cheese course or as a main course with salad. Simple but good puddings, and all this is served in a sharp, shades-of-grey, designer restaurant, with a piano to listen to in the evening.

Le Château Restaurant   W1

May Fair Hotel, Stratton Street W1A 2AN   £30
01-629 7777

Closed: lunch (Sat)
Last
Orders: lunch (2.30pm); dinner (10.30pm)

Chef Michael Coker, whose pedigree includes time spent as
sous-chef for Anton Mosimann and Peter Kromberg, has introduced life into this established and popular hotel restaurant. The
menu is in the modern French style but there is always a
substantial dish of the day on the trolley, an impressive array on
the hors d'oeuvres table and a good value set lunch. Service is
classically correct and polite, and the occasional food festivals
that are on at the May Fair are good examples of this type of
event. I especially remember the Hungarian Festival with the
amazing variety of interesting dishes they produced.

The wine list is extensive, in the middle to upper bracket.

Chez Gerard   W1

8 Charlotte Street W1P 1HD   £25
01-636 4975

Closed: lunch (Sat); Bank Holidays
Last
Orders: dinner (11.30pm)

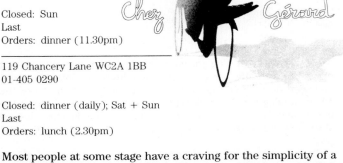

31 Dover Street W1X 3RA
01-499 8171

Closed: Sun
Last
Orders: dinner (11.30pm)

119 Chancery Lane WC2A 1BB
01-405 0290

Closed: dinner (daily); Sat + Sun
Last
Orders: lunch (2.30pm)

Most people at some stage have a craving for the simplicity of a
well-grilled steak, decent chips and a properly dressed salad.
This is the basis of the success of Monsieur Goujon's Chez
Gerard. Service is young and French, and the daily specials,
including a fish dish and possibly a fish soup or a simple salad,
are written on a blackboard. Look through to the grilled meat
main courses and you will find good value and decent meat,
cooked properly to order. The atmosphere from restaurant to
restaurant does change but is generally fairly good natured and
informal with a warm bistro feeling. My favourite is the one in
Charlotte Street.

Chicago Pizza Pie Factory   W1

17 Hanover Square W1
01-629 2669

Last
Orders: 11.00pm

In this basement off Hanover Square, you could easily believe that you have been instantly transported to America. The large room is bedecked with memorabilia from Chicago - street signs, posters, photographs, videos of the Bears playing football running on a screen in the bar while you wait for a table and drink Chicago Old Gold beer. When the table is ready your name is called, you are escorted to the table and the waitress says, "Hi!"

Have some stuffed mushrooms and garlic bread while you wait for the pizza to cook and listen to the pop music. Suddenly a loud bell might ring, silence is called for and a candlelit ice-cream cake will appear, carried aloft by a waitress, for someone's birthday. The pizzas themselves are large but light, with fillings of cheese with mushrooms, sausage and pepperoni, and they are served straight from their cooking pans. If you have any room left, you could have a slice of carrot cake or cheesecake, or one of their unusual and delicious ice-creams. It's a great place for eating out with the children, or simply for lovers of American-style pizzas and atmosphere.

Christys   W1

122-126 Wardour Street W1V 3LA
01-434 4468

Closed: Sun; Bank Holidays
Last
Orders: 11.30pm

"A New World of Vegetarian Eating" - their description, not mine, but I totally agree. Clean, clear lines, uncluttered walls, and tiled floors give this restaurant an image very much of the 1980s: a bright white look with black furniture. Girls (and the occasional boy) serve, wearing white, three-quarter sleeved shirts and black trousers; music is by the Modern Jazz Quartet (tape).

There are more than 100 seats on the ground floor plus a basement bar/café operation and a bake shop which sparkles with a selection of excellent wholemeal bread pizzas, cheese baked cobs, warm walnut cakes, and fresh fruit salads to take away. The vegetables and fruits are organically produced wherever possible; they use 100% wholemeal stone ground flour, free-range eggs and excellent cheeses. We tried a daily suggestion which consisted of broccoli and oat rissole with tomato mayonnaise - it sounds pretty awful but it tasted absolutely wonderful. There are, additionally, some very good pasta dishes with tomato, mushrooms and basil, and an excellent selection of desserts. Their wholemeal bread with poppy seed is first class and their own brown garlic bread is excellent.

The restaurant is open all day from breakfast time at 8.00am to 11.30pm. They have a good wine list, and don't be put off by the vegetarian tag: you won't miss the meat, I promise. Excellent selection from the daily menu, pleasant and helpful staff, this place really deserves to succeed. Go there!

Criterion Brasserie W1

222 Piccadilly W1
01-839 7133

Closed: Sun; Bank Holidays
Last
Orders: lunch (3.00pm); dinner (11.00pm)

"The Criterion is doing huge business, and it is an extremely large restaurant, or rather collection of restaurants, all housed in the one building in Piccadilly Circus.

"Mr Victor Rena, and his wife, had already great triumphs to their name. He had made outstanding successes of half a dozen restaurants in London and the provinces.

"On the day of his arrival at the Criterion in 1923 thirty-four luncheons had been served. Now four figure luncheons are served daily - and dinners too, to say nothing of a prodigious number of private parties and banquets.

"The prices are popular and the food good. The luncheon price is 3s.6d.; dinner 5s.; banqueting is from 7s.6d. a head. The charges are the same in each of the big restaurants.

"They have such a good class of customer at the Criterion, people from town, from abroad, and from the country. They flock.

"And even with such huge business individual wants are carefully attended to. The writer knew an invalid home from Ceylon, he always got his diet at the Criterion. Vegetarians can eat in comfort, and there are two lunches on a Friday, maigre and ordinary; many who are not bothered by religious scruples like a fish meal.

"Mr Rena always specialises in asparagus. He has it special-ly grown for him at San Remo, and is able to include it in a 5s. dinner at Christmas time - surely a triumph."

> *The Restaurants of London*, Eileen Hooton-Smith, 1928

Well, Mr Rena has sadly passed on, as has the 5s. dinner at Christmas time, but you will be offered a plat du jour, an adequate selection of some 13 hors d'oeuvres, a cassoulet bretonne, a tranche de gigot d'agneau grilled with herbs, or the simple calves' liver and bacon. Different styles of potatoes and market vegetables are available, and standard puddings follow.

The fact is, you'll probably end up with a stiff neck after visiting this place, as without doubt the ceiling is the highlight of the neo-Byzantine décor in this beautiful marble hall that's over 100 years old. Full marks to owners THF for developing and renovating this superb room.

The Criterion has to benefit ultimately if a hoped-for relaxa-tion of the licensing laws allows it to trade as a brasserie all day. In any case, the general improvement of the Piccadilly area must encourage the management to develop the true style of a brasserie.

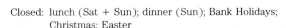

L'Escargot   **W1**

48 Greek Street W1V 5LQ
01-437 2679/439 7474

Closed: lunch (Sat + Sun); dinner (Sun); Bank Holidays;
         Christmas; Easter
Last
Orders: lunch (2.30pm); dinner (11.15pm)

Some unusual, exciting and affordable wines from £6.50 to
£20.00 accompany some good and imaginative brasserie-style
dishes from Martin Lam's kitchen. You can eat in one of the 3
different restaurants on different floors, all with their own style
and character. You might have a radicchio, pear and walnut
salad with Gorgonzola to start, or an assiette of duck terrine
with walnut and pepper salamis, followed by spinach fettucine
with a fresh tomato and basil coulis and fresh parmesan cheese,
or a steamed chicken leg stuffed with mushrooms and herbs,
served with a creamy lemon sauce. In the Brasserie you can
have a selection of cheeses served with a hot baguette, chutneys,
celery and apple, again at affordable prices. Even the more
elaborate dishes served in the restaurant are still good value.

Being the in-place for advertising, showbiz and literary clientele makes this operation really buzz. Everyone has their
favourite room, whether it's with Elena Salvoni or Grahame
Edwards keeping the staff on their toes. The menu changes
every 6 weeks to accommodate dishes that are in season. I hope
Godfrey Smith, who wrote a sad little piece in the *Times* some 5
years ago on the end of an era, when L'Escargot was sold, has
been back, because Nick Lander has certainly started another
era. Long may it succeed.

The Four Seasons Restaurant   **W1**

The Inn on the Park, Hamilton Place, Park Lane W1A 1AZ   £55
01-499 0888

Last
Orders: lunch (3.00pm); dinner (midnight)

The Inn on the Park, under Ramon Pajares, has become one of
London's leading hotels in a comparatively short time. The Four
Seasons on the first floor, with a tinkling piano and its own
cocktail bar, offers eating at the luxury end of the market. Chef
Eric Deblonde has been brought over from France, and creates
some interesting dishes like creamy fish soup garnished with
ravioli of smoked salmon, lobster and coriander, or roast
monkfish in red wine sauce, or fillets of veal with sage and
celery butter. The style of cooking is distinctive and makes the
restaurant interesting for the food alone; the wine list is
extensive and in the top bracket; and the service is headed by

Vinicio Paolini. The décor of the room itself is full: faux marble pillars, lots of mirrors and crisp napery, and views over Park Lane.

The other restaurant at the Inn on the Park is called Lanes. It is essential to book at this bustling restaurant which offers a series of set menus for lunch and dinner. Some menus will include unlimited wine and most give the opportunity to select your starter or main course from a lavish buffet which dominates the room. Many courses will be simple - grills or sauced dishes come from the kitchen, and there is always an impressive roast for the more traditional visitors.

Frith's   W1

14 Frith Street W1V 5TS
01-439 3370

Closed: lunch (Sat + Sun); dinner (Sun)
Last
Orders: lunch (2.00pm); dinner (11.30pm)

This simple, unassuming ground floor restaurant has a small yard at the rear which is used on sunny days. The menu makes imaginative use of ingredients, such as baked bream served with pickled lemons, or layers of aubergine and smoked cheese served with a tomato and parsley sauce. There are interesting starters of spinach and potato charlotte with glazed greens. A good range of British farm cheese shares the board with regional French ones.

The Gay Hussar   W1

2 Greek Street W1V 6NB
01-437 0973

Closed: Sun
Last
Orders: lunch (2.00pm); dinner (10.30pm)

Although some may argue the Magyar ancestry of Victor Sassie, many expatriates claim this is the finest Hungarian restaurant outside of Budapest. This view is certainly shared by the leading lights of the Labour Party, who crowd with their publishers into the intimate downstairs dining room. It's sometimes nice to visit a restaurant where some of the waiters seem to have served since the days of Atlee, and to find a menu that does not change very often either. Standard specialities and old favourites include cold cherry soup and cabbage stuffed with minced veal, brawn or smoked goose. The mid-European tradition of pâtisserie is well represented as well. An interesting wine list includes the full-bodied Hungarians, as well as some old Tokajis from 1963, 1920 and 1889, and very wisely, Victor Sassie writes above these "non-returnable" - the bottle or the wine?! It is essential to book and, consequently, worth noting that no credit cards are accepted.

At the bottom of his menu Victor proclaims, "Jol enni (Eat well), jol inni (drink well), jol elni (live well)."

The Greenhouse   W1

27A Hays Mews W1X 7RJ
01-499 3331

Closed: lunch (Sat + Sun); dinner (Sun); Bank Holidays;
        Christmas; New Year
Last
Orders: lunch (2.30pm); dinner (11.00pm)

Situated just off Hays Mews, the restaurant is approached via a
canopied pathway, and the dining room itself has a country
house feel to it, right in the heart of Mayfair. The menu consists
of a good basic selection, with such dishes as home-made
noodles with cream and parmesan, a Mediterranean salad of
king prawns and mussels, or a smoked goose breast salad with
gooseberry chutney for starters. These could be followed by
sautéed salmon with wild mushrooms, roast rack of English
lamb with rosemary, pot au feu of beef fillet with vegetables or
calves' liver with sautéed onions from the charcoal grill. For
dessert, try their chocolate brandy cream, or an almond apple
tart with blackcurrant coulis.

A good English-style presentation with a limited wine selection, and overall The Greenhouse provides excellent value for
central London. It's a good bet for lunch or dinner, especially if
you are unsure of your companions' tastes in food, as most
dishes are straightforward and appear just as they are described
on the menu.

The Guinea Grill   W1

26-28 Bruton Place W1
01-629 5613

Closed: lunch (Sat + Sun); dinner (Sun)
Last
Orders: lunch (2.30pm); dinner (11.00pm)

Crowds flock to the Guinea Grill for one reason, probably the
finest grilled meat in London. You will have to book, and when
you arrive, you choose your meal from the lavish display by the
front door. No menu is offered, but you discuss your choice with
the maître d'hôtel. To start with try smoked salmon, asparagus
or an artichoke, then spring chicken, or perhaps some lamb, but
the main emphasis is on the superb Scotch beef. Steaks are cut
close to New York size and are faultlessly cooked.

Service is brisk and professional in the long, narrow dining
room and wines, mainly French, are well chosen and priced to
match. Best buys are in the Beaujolais section.

This is a good example of how a restaurant can move
premises, if only just to next door, and keep a firm grip on its
traditional local and international following.

The Heal's Restaurant W1

The Heal's Building, 196 Tottenham Court Road W1
01-636 1666

Closed: lunch (Sun); dinner (daily); Bank Holidays
Last
Orders: 5.15pm; (6.15pm Thu; 5.00pm Sat)

Lorna Wing, an imaginative and very contemporary restaurateur, has been brought in to this revitalised department store. She has created a menu of eclectic dishes, from corned beef hash with Boston baked beans and fried onions, to braised scallops in the shell, or a Szechuan duck with roasted salt and pepper. They also serve breakfast in the morning, and afternoon tea.

The wine list, like the menu and the cooking, is well above the standard that sadly we have come to expect in a department store.

Kettner's Restaurant W1

29 Romilly Street W1
01-437 6437/734 6112

Last
Orders: midnight

"Kettner's is in Soho, but not of Soho. It is a place with a very distinct atmosphere, which it has changed through the years but one has always existed.

"It was opened in 1869 and was patronised by men of fashion. King Edward, then, of course, Prince of Wales, was a customer. As the years went on it became less fashionable until, during the war years, when the writer first knew it, it was a queer mixture. It still looked essentially Victorian, but for the bright pink silk lamp shades on every table. The food was good enough and not especially cheap and the actual restaurant rooms were only sparsely filled.

"Then a great change came over Kettner's. It was bought, and Arthur Giordano, from the Savoy, became its energetic managing director.

"The block of old-fashioned houses just behind the Palace Theatre had a fresh coat of paint outside, but otherwise they kept their nice old-world look. A portico was added.

"But within a revolution took place. Everything was redecorated and reorganised. Kettner's again became smart, and a very charming restaurant it is at the present time, and an efficient one.

"The food is good. And they make a speciality of having some Italian dishes on their menu. There is always one Italian dish among the plats du jour, for example, gnocchi à la Romaine. While every Sunday they have as a speciality Cannelloni Charlotte Kettner's, which contains the national macaroni, made of rather a lighter paste than usual and in a larger form, vaguely like an omelet and also something like a giant ravioli."

The Restaurants of London, Eileen Hooton-Smith, 1928

Arthur Giordan has gone, Peter Boizot is here. This exuberant character who runs the Pizza Express chain and who has done as much to promote live jazz as anyone in this country, runs an interesting, if somewhat different Kettner's to the one described above, although it's certainly moving more and more towards the Italian. He has retained the atmosphere and added some nice touches. There's good pasta and pizza, fun stylish service, the Champagne bar works well on the ground floor and is a good place to meet people and to enjoy a glass, half bottle or bottle in a vibrant but relaxed atmosphere. Who knows, after reading this Peter Boizot might even put "Cannelloni Charlotte Kettner's" back on the menu again!

Langan's Bistro   W1

26 Devonshire Street W1N 1RJ
01-935 4531

Closed: lunch (Sat); Bank Holidays
Last
Orders: lunch (2.30pm); dinner (11.30pm)

This is where it all began. Every conceivable area of wall carries a picture, perfectly chosen and perfectly placed, interrupted only by large antique mirrors which, along with the careful lighting, give a feeling of fun and luxury. This is not, however, reflected in the menu's very reasonable prices. These days Peter Langan is a less frequent visitor, but his portrait by Patrick Proctor still graces the menu, and he has left the restaurant in capable hands.

There are 7 or 8 choices for each course; and you might like to try the goats' cheese with pickled pear salad, the grilled lemon sole with parsley butter, or the loin of pork with prunes and brandy. Sauces are straightforward, and this is a pleasant place for lunch and dinner.

The Lindsay House   W1

21 Romilly Street W1
01-439 0450

Last
Orders: lunch (2.30pm); dinner (11.45pm)

The latest of the stylish English restaurants from the Livingstone brothers, whose small group includes The English House and Waltons, this Soho town house was evidently established in the 16th Century by an early Scottish emigré. He would probably not recognise it now, in its present shades of deep green and red. The bar downstairs, with its comfortable sofas and substantial plants, is ideal for a drink, while the upstairs restaurant is elegant and luxurious as you would expect, its polite and correct waiters ensuring that everything runs smoothly.

Chef Liam Barr has brought with him his menu from The English House, and you can enjoy a cold tomato soup with fresh mint, a large fillet of beef with a Guinness sauce, or a rich fish pie topped with mashed potato.

The revival of the rich English pudding continues here with a junket of rum and ginger, or rich pots of chocolate further enhanced with whipped cream. As with the other Livingstone restaurants, the wine list is strongly French.

Maxim's de Paris   W1

32 Panton Street W1
01-839 4809

Closed: lunch (daily); dinner (Sun + Mon); Christmas
Last
Orders: dinner (11.30pm)

Maxim's has graduated to the first floor of its premises in Panton Street and into what is to my mind a much nicer room, the former Garden Room, and the bar now gives off a much cosier, more intimate feeling. The waiters are as they were downstairs, and they glide around in their tail coats in an efficient and attentive way. The room is still all Art Nouveau swirls, with mirrors of that age - a trio plays at weekends, and the wine list is of classic proportions. The food emulates its Paris counterpart well, with a good use of game in season and classic Maxim's dishes, including salade tiède de foie gras et coquilles aux légumes du jardin, croustade d'huître et langoustines aux courgettes basilic to start with, or perhaps a tournedos Rue Royale - the Rue Royale bit being the truffle and brandy sauce - or the excellent délice de canard avec son foie gras et champignons sauvages from the 12 or so main courses.

Café Maxim's

Closed: Sun; Christmas
Last
Orders: lunch (2.30pm); dinner (11.30pm)

Café Maxim's is altogether something different. A designer restaurant by Fitch & Company in hard black and white, its atmosphere makes a good café/brasserie where you can drop in for one or more courses, as the mood takes you. There are some interesting dishes on the menu - try the salade de crevettes et moules au lardons, a salad of prawns, mussels, and crispy pieces of bacon, topped with a sherry vinaigrette, or the grilled spicy Toulouse sausage with braised red cabbage, or the Scottish salmon en croûte with a lemon sauce from the plats du jour. Alternatively from their main list try a prawn and spinach quiche served with crisp vegetables and a spicy avocado dip, or wild mushrooms and courgettes in a white wine and cream sauce served in a pastry case. Some 12 or so well cooked main courses range from rib steak, grilled and topped with herb butter, to a deep fried assortment of fish and shellfish served with tomato

127

and basil sauce. There are also good vegetarian main courses and some decent desserts. It's a much younger and cheaper outlook than upstairs, but still with some good quality products. Service is formal, by boys and girls in long white aprons, and the wine list is affordable, starting at around £6.00 per bottle. It's worth a visit when you don't feel like going the whole hog with the restaurant upstairs, or perhaps when you're with the younger set.

Le Meridien Piccadilly   W1

Piccadilly W1V 0BH   £55
01-734 8000

Last
Orders: lunch (2.00pm); dinner (11.00pm)

Michel Lorain, the latest chef in France to win a third Michelin star, is now a consultant to the Oak Room Restaurant, though for most of the time dishes are prepared by head chef David Chambers. This combination produces some imaginative top

quality French food with dishes like le gaspacho langoustine à la crème de courgette, or l'aile de caneton aux lentilles et aux oignons blancs.

The dining room itself is very grand, with the original oak panelling having been lined and bleached, giving a pale background to the vast crystal chandeliers. Service is suitably professional, and most of the food is presented on the plate, with the dishes impeccably finished. There is an extensive wine list with good examples from California as well as more obvious ones from France.

The second floor terrace has been transformed into a light, airy conservatory style restaurant, offering a good value set lunch in a pleasant garden-like setting, with lots of trees, hanging baskets and greenery.

There are 290 rooms in this totally refurbished hotel which sparkles from the front entrance through to the Health Club.

Le Muscadet   W1

25 Paddington Street W1M 3RF
01-935 2883

Closed: lunch (Sat + Sun); dinner (Sun); Bank Holidays;
        last 3 weeks Aug; 2 weeks Christmas
Last
Orders: lunch (2.45pm); dinner (11.00pm)

Rather a dead area this - north of Oxford Street - and the
restaurant itself is set in a somewhat anonymous line of shops.
Once inside however, you will encounter the true spirit of
provincial France, largely in the form of M Bessonard, who used
to run the now defunct Michelin-starred restaurant Le Bresson.
His sights are now set on a bistro with honest and straightforward food in fairly large portions. Enjoy a plate covered with
thick slices of hot, lean ham with a not too sweet honey sauce,
and a choice of crisp vegetables and good salads.

They will always make an effort to fit you in but it is probably
worth booking as the locals have taken to Le Muscadet with
great enthusiasm.

Odins Restaurant   W1

27 Devonshire Street W1N 1RJ
01-935 7296

Closed: lunch (Sat); Bank Holidays
Last
Orders: lunch (2.30pm); dinner (11.30pm)

A restaurant full of atmosphere, normally packed with locals.
The place buzzes, and the menu reads well, set lunch at £12.50,
housewines from £6.95.

The Old Budapest   W1

6 Greek Street W1V 5LA
01-437 2006

Closed: Sun
Last
Orders: lunch (3.00pm); dinner (11.00pm)

The Old Budapest, which has opened next door to the Gay
Hussar, may be said to be bold or even impertinent, but The Old
Budapest has quickly built a following with lovers of Hungarian
food. It is substantial stuff, but the presentation is neat and tidy,
and the usual Hungarian dishes of chicken paprika, smoked
goose or roast duck are well represented here.

There is a good list of Hungarian wines and a pretty lethal
spirit called barack. This should be taken in small quantities, and
only in the company of those you know well.

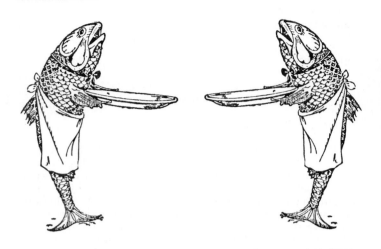

Scott's Restaurant   **W1**

20 Mount Street W1   £60
01-629 5248

Closed: lunch (Sun); Christmas; Bank Holidays
Last
Orders: lunch (2.45pm); dinner (10.45pm)

"First and foremost Scott's is famous for lobsters and oysters.

"In the late nineties and the early years of this century it was known all over England as the haunt of celebrities of the sporting world and the stage. It always figured prominently on Boat Race nights. Mr Malcolm Sinclair, who owned and controlled it for over forty years, died in 1927: he was a rich man. It has now been purchased by a company.

"Scott's really has connections which take it back to Dickens' days. It used to be a little oyster shop which sold chops and such like to keep it going when oysters were out of season.

"One enters rather as into a shop and finds that there is a counter on either hand, they are buffets where all and sundry of the well-to-do can stand and eat. Scott's is by no means a cheap place. White clad attendants behind the counters serve out snacks all day and evening long. Often men and women in evening dress can be seen eating a hasty dinner standing, for there is no room for chairs, they have probably been late dressing for a theatre. Scott's buffet used also to be a favourite place for food after a theatre, but in these days of supper and dancing there are fewer customers for them.

"All the rooms are furnished alike, red carpets, square tables and rather squat-looking chairs. Space, of course, has always been a consideration at Scott's, no room for new fangled notions, but still, the management seems to have been wise in allowing the famous restaurant to remain itself and not bedecking it in ultra-modern guise.

"Everything on the menu is à la carte, and, as has been remarked, it is not inexpensive. The food is very good. To begin with there are the lobsters, the great big ones in the window and smaller ones, in large numbers. Then, during the oyster months, there are first class oysters. Crab salad is another

speciality, 'crab meat' as the many American customers in-
variably call it. By the way, the manager of Scott's, Mr Joseph,
says that he has never known an American customer order
Lobster American, they seem to like best broiled lobster; it is
Japanese customers who appear specially addicted to Lobster
American.

"Scott's is a favourite place with visitors to London of all
nationalities and the attachés of the various Embassies seem
also to appreciate its good fare. Very magnificent is the lobster
salad, that costs six shillings, and is pretty well a meal in
itself."

The Restaurants of London, Eileen Hooton-Smith, 1928

Scott's has changed its position since this first review was
written, from the hubub of Piccadilly to the quieter backwaters
of Mayfair and I must remember to ask Nicky Kerman, the MD of
Scott's, next time I see him, if the American customers still
prefer broiled lobster and Japanese customers ask for lobster
American. According to his counterpart in Wheeler's it would
seem to be exactly the same. Scott's has its own particular style
and its own particular following, and to use the phrase from the
earlier review, it is not inexpensive but the seafood and service
you get are first class. They carry on their tradition with pride in
this smart, clubby restaurant, looking after visitors from all
nationalities and still serving personnel from the various embassies in the area. It is a stylish, well-managed restaurant.

Soho Brasserie   W1

23-25 Old Compton Street W1
01-439 9301

Closed: Sun; Bank Holidays
Last
Orders: 11.30pm

Situated at the Tottenham Court Road end of this ever-changing
thoroughfare of Soho, the Soho Brasserie is a place in which to
meet friends for a mid-morning coffee through to a near-
midnight snack.

In good weather - in true brasserie style - they slide open the
blue and white front doors to give access to the bar where light
snacks are served; the restaurant is at the rear, separated from
the bar by glass partitions. Décor is 1930s stark, apart from
banquette seating and an amusing mural. The menu offers a
good selection of salads, fresh fish, and sausages and mash
(which appear on the menu as home-made herb sausages with a
potato purée), and menus change daily. A few well-chosen wines
have restaurant price tags, as does the food, but forget the cost
and look at the fashion.

131

Tiberio   **W1**

22 Queen Street W1
01-629 3561

Closed: lunch (Sat + Sun); dinner (Sun)
Last
Orders: lunch (2.30pm); dinner (1.00am)

This is like a stepping into a 1960s time warp - no bad thing, for
Basilio De Colle and his team run this Italian restaurant with
professionalism, enthusiasm and flair. They offer very good veal
and seafood dishes, and excellent spaghetti alle vongole. There
is an Italian band to dance to in the evenings, in a simple white
cellar with Italian effects, and everything conspires with the
clientele - showbiz Italian, a smattering of transatlantica, and
neighbouring Mayfair residents - to make this restaurant buzz.

Wheeler's   **W1**

19 Old Compton Street W1V 5PJ   £35
01-437 2706

Closed: Christmas Day, New Year's Day
Last
Orders: lunch (2.30pm); dinner (11.30pm)

Wheeler's, established in 1856, opened its Old Compton Street
branch just after the First World War as an oyster bar and
wholesale fish merchant delivering fish to restaurants and hotels
in London. The wholesale side of the business still exists in an
expanded form but at different premises, and the collection of
small intimate dining rooms, which is a distinguishing feature of
the Old Compton Street branch, still packs in its regular
clientele. It seems to act as a sort of unofficial club to some of
London's wine merchants, and Francis Bacon, amongst other
artists, is a lunch time habitué. Good oysters come from their
farm, and grilled Dover sole and scallop dishes are served in this
traditional and long-established English fish restaurant.

Please see the General Listings at the back of the book for
other branches of Wheeler's.

The White Tower

W1

1 Percy Street W1P 0ET
01-636 8142

Closed: Sat + Sun; Bank Holidays; 3 weeks Aug; 1 week Christmas
Last
Orders: lunch (2.30pm); dinner (10.30pm)

The White Tower is the kind of place you could take anyone, from an elderly aunt to the Chairman of a large company, the Prime Minister or Madonna, and have a fair chance of pleasing them. The restaurant has been going for 48 years, long before charter flights gave the Greek Islands to the masses, and the menu is what Mr Stais decided, in 1938, the English should accept as his native cooking. The menu is à la carte with huge portions of good honest food. It is rare to see such a long-established brigade at work and quite a refreshing experience.

Madame Stais and her lovely Irish matronly niece run the restaurant, or perhaps after 48 years it runs them. Like an old clock that has been cared for, it never misses a beat. I suspect many of the regulars visited this restaurant with their fathers when at home from school, and still maintain their allegiance. A pleasant, unimposing building faces some of the trendier restaurants in Charlotte Street, and is curiously split between ground and first floors. Walls are covered in old plates and older prints. A rickety old staircase links dining rooms which radiate lasting warmth and a feeling of security. There is silver service, and a menu which has to be read to be believed. Nouvelle cuisine certainly passed this place by, for here are starters of courgettes stuffed with rice and lamb, kebab of turbot, tomatoes, mushrooms and blanched onions which are char-grilled and served on a bed of rice, and many more Greek dishes amongst a few French and English specials such as roast poussin, stuffed Aylesbury duck and chop Alexis Soyer.

Le Chef

W2

41 Connaught Street W2 2BB
01-262 5945

Closed: lunch (Sat, Sun + Mon); dinner (Sun + Mon)
Last
Orders: lunch (2.30pm); dinner (11.30pm)

Rather a period piece this, set firmly in the 1960s when tablecloths had red checks, candles were compulsory and nouvelle cuisine had not yet reached W2. Le Chef is a typical local bistro with good honest portions, for example home-made tomato soup from a help-yourself tureen, then veal chop with fresh coriander. It is friendly, full and reasonably priced. It is authentically French in that the housewines are very drinkable - and if you take a pretty girl with you it helps service no end!

Etty's   W2

43 Hereford Road W2
01-221 9192

Closed: Sun
Last
Orders: 11.00pm

The sort of food and prices often said to be unavailable in
London appear in this gleaming café/brasserie which opens onto
the street. Casseroles, grills and properly garnished fish dishes
are honestly and well made. The service is friendly and informal,
and the limited range of wines is fairly priced. For good value
bistro food, follow the locals!

Surinder's   W2

109 Westbourne Park Road W2
01-229 8968

Closed: lunch (Sat, Sun + Mon); dinner (Sun)
Last
Orders: lunch (2.00pm); dinner (11.00pm)

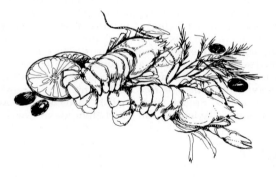

Mr Surinder certainly believes in a 'hands-on' operation. He
chooses and buys all the food, devises and cooks the menu, and
still manages to impress his presence on the dining room!

Menus change daily and are good value - the lobster thermidor
only incurs a supplement of £1.00. Most of the dishes are
French, for example carré d'agneau or lotte dieppoise, though
there are also dishes from other parts of the world from time to
time.

The room is plainly lit with some discreet Art Deco up-
lighting, and decorated with a few pictures. Young waiting staff
are enthusiastic and friendly. This is both a popular meeting
place for the locals and worth making a detour to find.

La Dordogne W4

5 Devonshire Road W4
01-747 1836

Closed: lunch (Sat + Sun); dinner (Sun); Christmas Day;
        Boxing Day; 1 week Jan
Last
Orders: lunch (2.3Opm); dinner (11.00pm)

A large old-fashioned maroon blind makes La Dordogne stand out from amongst some rather dull shops in this street off Chiswick High Road. In the summer a few tables invite diners to eat outside the restaurant, whilst the interior has a comforting ambience, its green walls covered with prints, low level lighting and an attractive small bar. Cooking and wines are French provincial - try the fish terrine with a good coulis of tomato, and an unusual civet of lamb with mint. Vegetables are properly cooked, and the parfait of hazelnuts and caramel is excellent. An unusual list of wines from Jurançon and Cahors are imported direct and are well worth trying. A quiet place for lunch; it is very busy in the evening.

The Ark Restaurant W8

122 Palace Gardens W8
01-229 4024

Closed: lunch (Sun + Bank Holidays); 4 days Christmas
Last
Orders: lunch (3.00pm); dinner (11.15pm)

If you wonder why on earth anyone should call a restaurant The Ark, one visit will reveal all: its location next to the Unitarian Church and The First Church of Christ Scientist may have some significance, but I rather think that its timber construction and shape were the deciding factors. The Ark must be one of London's oldest established bistros, having been in operation for no less than 24 years. Timber walls with black and white photos of some of London's colourful characters, parquet floors and polished wood tables with wicker place mats create the ambience. Tables are close together and usually full - an American couple at the next table who visit London every summer told me that they never miss eating at least one meal at The Ark, and that over the many years they reckon each time it has improved. Praise indeed!

A small menu offers simple uncomplicated food: mushrooms baked with garlic butter were piping hot and needed plenty of crusty bread to absorb the juices, and half a roast guineafowl in lemon sauce with sauté potatoes and a well-dressed salad were very good. A near-impregnable crème brûlée, which once penetrated was lovely, and good filter coffee completed the meal, all for under £10.00. There are a few wines at reasonable prices but the very adequate housewine seems right. The Ark is a certainty when the stomach is empty and the pocket light, for youngsters on first dates and older ones on budgets.

Clarke's W8

124 Kensington Church Street W8 4BH
01-221 9225

Closed: Sat + Sun; Easter; Christmas; 3 weeks Aug/Sep
Last
Orders: lunch (2.00pm); dinner (10.00pm); supper (11.00pm)

Lots of local trade makes Sally Clarke's restaurant always buzz.
You don't have to think too much because the fixed price menu
at £19.00 is a no-choice menu; at lunch time there's a small
choice at £14.00. No choice is no problem when the starter is a
selection of very good salad leaves tossed in walnut oil with
parmesan cheese and Parma ham, followed by salmon served on
home-made noodles and a dessert of sorbets with peach and
banana. Good-sized portions and good quality raw products
make it special, as do very pleasant staff whom you suspect
might also sometimes be customers. Sally Clarke very much
oversees the procedure. On one of the visits the table we had
booked was still being cleared so we were offered a glass of
Champagne at the bar while we waited. Downstairs is interesting with its open kitchen, and the general background of the
place is neutral, leaving the excitement to come from customers,
the pleasant staff and the competent cooking.

Launceston Place W8

1A Launceston Place W8 5RL
01-937 6912

Closed: lunch (Sat); dinner (Sun)
Last
Orders: lunch (2.30pm); dinner (11.00pm)

In a quiet, South Kensington backwater Nick Smallwood and
Simon Slater combine their experience of various fashionable
London venues to create a stylish country house décor with
Edwardian paintings in this English restaurant, aimed at the
young and successful. Booking is essential - you may otherwise
be turned away, though only as far as the pub from whence you
are recalled to eat dishes like simple grills of liver, or sole, or
terrine of pigeon with Cumberland sauce, pan fried scallops with
a champagne sauce or roast saddle of lamb with mint jelly from

the à la carte menu, which are well prepared. The set menu at around £10.00 for 3 courses also offers good value.

Sunday lunch is quite an event and seems to go on for most of the day. The roast beef is good and the company is always interesting. Wines have been well chosen and are sensibly priced from around £6.00 a bottle.

Michel Restaurant   W8

343 Kensington High Street W8 6NW
01-603 3613

Last
Orders: lunch (2.30pm); dinner (11.00pm)

This small cheerful French restaurant has white rendered walls covered with Pito watercolours of attractive French scenes. A combination of wicker chairs and banquette seating is set around the pink clothed tables on a ceramic floor. Michel Ferret is the chef patron, and his menu has modern interpretations of classically based dishes, such as game consommé with madeira, scrambled eggs with wild mushrooms, or a cassolette of snails with herbs and garlic, which might precede steamed fish, either salmon with beurre blanc or halibut with coriander sauce, breast of pheasant with a sauce of pine kernels, or a fillet of pork in puff pastry with a honey sauce. A concise wine list has the staple selection plus a few regional options.

Le Quai St Pierre   W8

7 Stratford Road W8
01-937 6388

Closed: Sun; Christmas
Last
Orders: lunch (2.30pm); dinner (11.30pm)

Alain Patrat cooks competently the normal Pierre Martin selection of fish dishes in this restaurant which has been open since 1981, with Michel Grondin ensuring that the front of house staff remain as French as possible. The décor is very French, and what we've come to expect of Pierre Martin - very inviting and very Mediterranean. There is the normal, small but adequate selection of wines, the majority of which offer excellent value. There is a variety of huîtres, moules, langoustines, coquilles St Jacques, and feuilletés plus a selection of fish available on the day which might include turbot, sea bass, sole and lobster charged for by the kilogramme. There's also a choice for meat-eaters of a contrefilet of beef, making this is a very enjoyable place for an evening out.

137

The Lace Plate W9

Opposite 60 Blomfield Road W9
01-286 3428

Last
Orders: All bookings by arrangement

An excellent way of having a lunch or dinner party - or perhaps both - for 10 or 12 people, is to hire The Lace Plate, a traditional narrow boat, well equipped to give you comfort with some unusual character. The boat glides between Little Venice and Camden Lock along the Regent's Canal, giving you some unusual views of Regent's Park and the zoo, and it's a great opportunity to catch some rarely seen sights of London from its waterways.

A good standard of food is served on this canal boat and you have a set menu - for obvious reasons - which you choose beforehand. However, the choice is not limited and you can pick from at least 10 starters including pears with stilton pâté and walnuts, mushrooms in French tartlets or with garlic butter, or even Javanese steak satays. Main courses include beef Welling-ton, rack of lamb with fresh herbs, or York ham with tarragon cream sauce, amongst the 10 or so choices. The desserts are good and the hazlenut torte with raspberries and cream is exceptional. If you want to suggest some other special dishes they are only too pleased to help you with them. I was lucky enough to share this boating experience with some very good company, including 3 of London's top chefs and their wives at a lunch given by a film director in the summer of 1986 and can thoroughly recommend it for lunch or dinner with a difference.

192 W11

192 Kensington Park Road W11 2JF
01-229 0482

Closed: dinner (Sun); some Bank Holidays; 1 week Christmas
Last
Orders: dinner (11.30pm)

Stars of the show here are the staff and the customers who compete with each other for the most exotic hair cut or the best name to drop into conversation. At times there are enough famous people in 192 to fill every gossip column in the country, but they are safe here because king of the paparrazzi - Richard Young - leaves his camera at home when he comes for dinner. Although Alastair Little has left, his style remains; the menu changes twice daily and is as contemporary as next year's Filofax. You will find raw marinated beef, a salad of quail and asparagus, interesting fish dishes and excellent roasts on Sun-day. You can eat one course upstairs in the wine bar or go down the staircase for a full meal in the restaurant.

The wine list has some real bargains and varies from the classic to the recherché, all at fairly decent prices. It's advisable to book, you'll enjoy the food, and you might collect some style tips!

L'Artiste Assoiffé W11

122 Kensington Park Road W11
01-727 4714

Closed: lunch (Sun - Fri); dinner (Sun)
Last
Orders: lunch (2.45pm); dinner (11.30pm)

Since this place is situated just around the corner from Portobello market, you will definitely need to book for Saturday lunch, which sees the long-established bistro packed with regulars. Evenings are similar, and although there are concessions to the new cuisine, the basis of the food is good plain French cooking, like the veal in a wild mushroom sauce. Interesting accompaniments include a salad of white beans with green olive oil, or latkes, or a tranche d'agneau marinated in oil, herbs and garlic.

The pleasant atmosphere is reminiscent of a rather fading fairground with a Victorian carousel as the centre-piece, giving a well-worn but comfortable feel. Service is brisk and efficient, and you can take an apéritif on the outside terrace during the summer. I like this place at that time of year with its Saturday bustle and its interesting collection of people; or in the winter on a quieter, early evening when the open fires give a warm glow throughout the dining rooms.

Chez Moi W11

1 Addison Avenue W11 4QS
01-603 8267

Closed: lunch (daily); dinner (Sun); Bank Holidays;
       2 weeks Aug; 2 weeks Christmas
Last
Orders: dinner (11.30pm)

Chez Moi is still in Addison Avenue and nothing seems to have changed much for several years - it has its faithful, regular customers who speak highly of it. Bourgeois classical style with occasional excursions into the 1980s.

Julie's   W11

135 Portland Road W11
01-229 8331/727 4585

Closed: Christmas; Easter; Bank Holidays
Last
Orders: lunch (2.15pm); dinner (11.15pm; 10.15pm Sun)

Still going strong after 17 years, this collection of small rooms off a wine bar has palm trees, sofas, soft cushions and newspapers everywhere. A range of simple dishes is available in the downstairs restaurant - grills, salads, rack of lamb with minted garlic purée, or Kent duck with cassis. On a sunny day it's an excellent idea to eat lunch in the courtyard garden, covered with honeysuckle, or in the conservatory which adjoins it.

Leith's Restaurant   W11

92 Kensington Park Road W11 2PN
01-229 4481

Closed: lunch (daily); Bank Holidays; 4 days Christmas
Last
Orders: midnight

Prue Leith is a one-woman industry, and has managed to achieve in 20 or so years what it can take most people a lifetime to accomplish. She runs a cookery school and an ever-expanding outside catering company, writes articles and books, almost froze to death with me on a film set in Penshurst Place, still finds time for her family *and* she has Leith's Restaurant in Kensington Park Road. This amazing lady puts tremendous effort and enthusiasm into everything she does.

She sensibly leaves to Jean Reynaud the running of this all-time favourite, with its late 1960s design, mirrors and thick carpets, and unusual chairs complete with casters so that you can gradually glide closer to your dinner companion or scoot across the floor to inspect the hors d'oeuvres trolley, which Jean keeps fresh and beautifully set (a far cry from the awful old seaside hotel hors d'oeuvres trolley you used to encounter!).

All the old favourites are back on the menu, and some new ones too, with good treatments of fish and pigeon. Menus change with the seasons and are priced according to the choice of main course. Try the duckling with almonds and celery, or St Clement's soufflé, which is made with oranges and lemons. The wine list has a large showing of clarets from good vintages, and housewines are well chosen at more modest prices.

I particularly enjoy the sense of occasion at Leith's. The lighting is kind, the staff are pleasant, and there is a very relaxed atmosphere to the whole place.

Monsieur Thompsons   W11

29 Kensington Park Road W11
01-727 9957

Closed: Sun; Christmas
Last
Orders: lunch (2.30pm); dinner (11.45pm)

This is an attractive and comfortable restaurant located in the fashionable Kensington Park Road. The ebullient host, Dominique Rocher, runs the restaurant with capable staff, and creates a good ambience. The dining rooms are on 2 levels: the ground floor has prints and mirrors on hessian walls; and the basement has a cosy country kitchen atmosphere with lots of pine furniture and checked tablecloths.

Menus are a combination of classic and modern style dishes, so that you might start with a mousse of ham with pistachio nuts, followed by more traditional hake baked in fresh tomato sauce. There are set menus offering good value as well as the à la carte, and the extensive list of French wines has some interesting selections in the middle to upper bracket.

Brasserie du Coin   WC1

54 Lambs Conduit Street WC1
01-405 1717

Closed: Sat + Sun
Last
Orders: lunch (3.00pm); dinner (10.00pm)

The 'coin' is the corner where Lambs Conduit Street meets Theobalds Road, and the brasserie is a typical French bistro style restaurant. Soupe à l'oignon, soupe de poissons, pâté maison, and avocado with prawns are precursors to duck with orange sauce, goujons of lemon sole, escalopes of veal or the plats du jour. Décor is simple with wheelback chairs at clothed tables, and one or two of the tables might even be on the pavement, giving the hustle and bustle a truly continental flavour.

Porte de la Cité WC1

65 Theobald's Road WC1
01-242 1154

Closed: Sat + Sun; Bank Holidays
Last
Orders: lunch (2.30); dinner (11.15pm)

Good news for existing customers of this popular French restaurant is that it is now open in the evening, and offers a choice of 3 set price menus instead of 2. The new petit menu gives a main course with vegetables or salads, a glass of wine and coffee for around £12.00, which is good value.

The dining room is bright and clean in shades of grey and white, the tables are close together and the atmosphere is lively. Dishes are imaginative and well prepared - try the mushroom mousse with sorrel sauce or the sètoise fish soup, followed by the brochette of beef, lamb and veal with red wine sauce, or the sauté of duck with prunes and Beaujolais.

The menu also has plainer dishes such as terrine of duck, grilled Dover sole, roast rack of lamb or fillet steak, and fish dishes rely on the market. Good cheeses are offered, and puddings like petit pot au chocolat, crème brûlée, fruit tartlets and mousse of chestnuts.

A short list of no-nonsense wines and friendly service make this one of the most reasonable of the City restaurants.

Boulestin WC2

1A Henrietta Street WC2E 8PX
01-836 7061

Closed: lunch (Sat + Sun); dinner (Sun); Christmas;
        Bank Holidays; last 3 weeks Aug
Last
Orders: lunch (2.30pm); dinner (11.15pm)

"The Boulestin is a Restaurant Français, that is, a place of good food. It is in Southampton Street, Covent Garden, rather an unusual situation for a restaurant, though it followed another in the occupation of its present quarters; Sherry's used to be there. The premises are scarcely recognisable as re-decorated by M. Marcel Boulestin.

"Before its advent to larger quarters in Covent Garden the Boulestin used to occupy the little restaurant in Leicester Square which is now the Maison Dorée; it was there for about two years and made a big name for its cuisine.

"There is always something very attractive about Covent Garden, it is the most continental scene in London. The Boulestin is in a large modern building just on the edge of the market.

"Below is the restaurant, an 'L' shaped room; the short foot of the 'L' being used as a lounge. The whole place is painted a rich pleasant yellow. There are very large, and extremely modern, mural paintings in the lounge. They are reproductions of the little circus pictures upstairs. Equally outstanding, but much smaller, are two other mural paintings, figures, by Marie Laurencin.

BOULE∫TIN
re∫t aurant françai∫

"The Boulestin is a modern Parisian restaurant in decoration and a luxurious one at that. The carpet is wine colour, the curtains are of patterned yellow brocade; over the mantelpiece is a painting of a dinner table. By the way, the lounge portion of the room is illuminated and decorated by a square of hanging silk balloon lights. In a prominent place is an immense bottle of 1869 liqueur brandy de la maison, a graceful reminder that the place studies drink equally with meat.

"Everything is à la carte at the Boulestin, and the prices are those of the other luxury restaurants in London. One can have a simple meal or a diverse one.

"On a little pink card lying on the tables, with a very modern illustration, are enumerated the spécialités de la maison.:

"Marcel Boulestin is himself generally to be seen at lunch and dinner time, and has, as his major-domo, one Bally."

The Restaurants of London, Eileen Hooton-Smith, 1928

To my mind, the Boulestin is still one of the prettiest dining rooms in London. There is a relaxed but professional attitude towards the service and the food. Kevin Kennedy has now taken over from Marcel Boulestin, and walks the tightrope between control of the front of house and running the kitchen with great aplomb. In the kitchen Ken Whitehead turns out some exciting dishes - amongst a good selection of first courses, a salade Boulestin parfumée aux truffes noires. There's a choice of vegetarian dishes too, and a feuilleté de ris de veau à l'oseille is one of the 10 or so meat dishes. There's a good selection of desserts, and excellent cheeses from Pierre Androuët.

To revert briefly to the past, I like this story from the early days of the restaurant: Marcel Boulestin, who was enjoying a season of Wagner being performed at The Royal Opera House, arranged that towards the end of dinner (taken in the German fashion after the first act) a trumpeter from the orchestra should visit the Boulestin and play a theme from the opera 10 minutes before the curtain went up. I am sure that Marcel Boulestin would be pleased that the atmosphere and spirit live on.

You may notice that the present postal address differs from that of the 1928 text but the restaurant has not moved - it is still on the corner of Henrietta Street and Southampton Street.

Café des Amis du Vin   WC2

11-14 Hanover Place WC2
01-379 3444

Closed; Sun; 3 days Christmas
Last
Orders: lunch (3.00pm); dinner (11.15pm)

It's a bustling café-brasserie, with tables packed together, and simple café décor at the hub of Covent Garden, and it spills out on to Hanover Place on warm days. There's always someone or something to look at. Good plats du jour are offered. There's brisk service, a zippy atmosphere and a good wine list available in either the café or the salon on the first floor, plus an ever-popular wine bar in the basement. It's also very handy for drinks in the interval if you can't get served in the Opera House.

Frère Jacques   WC2

38 Long Acre WC2E 9JT
01-836 7639/7823

Closed: Christmas Day; Boxing Day
Last
Orders: lunch (3.00pm; Sun 2.30pm); dinner (11.30pm)

This brasserie-style fish restaurant in Covent Garden, with several meat dishes also available, has a light airy décor and a guitarist in the evening.

Grimes   WC2

6 Garrick Street WC2
01-836 7008

Closed: 1 week Christmas
Last
Orders: 11.30pm

This bright, friendly restaurant on 2 floors, set in the heart of Covent Garden, is a fun place for lunch or dinner. Described as a "cold fish café", there is quite a cabin-like feel to the small upstairs room with its wooden floor, and a few pictures on the pale yellow walls, all of fish or sea-scenes. On entering the restaurant you are first aware of a pleasant (though not over-powering) smell of seafood - try to get a table upstairs if possible.

The dishes of the day are especially good, and may include English and Irish oysters in season, some good red mullet, skate or fresh tuna cooked in some interesting ways. They do serve hot fish as well - try the mélange des poissons - strips of seasonal fresh fish steamed and served with a butter sauce. Young enthusiastic staff are a feature of the restaurant, being informal and helpful. The wine list is well suited to fish.

Interlude Restaurant   WC2

7-8 Bow Street WC2E 7AH
01-379 6473

Closed: lunch (Sat + Sun); dinner (Sun)
Last
Orders: dinner (11.00pm)

Though no longer part of the Roux empire, the new owners have chosen to continue the theme of modern French food. Plates are large, presentation is a priority, and cooking is adequate. Game is heavily featured in season - perhaps venison, grouse or woodcock - and en supplément to the basic menu. Service is professional and surroundings are sleek and expensive. The tables are close together so if your conversation lags you might pick up some interesting Covent Garden gossip, as the Interlude is just opposite the Opera House. Classic wines feature on the list but you have to search for bargains.

The Ivy   WC2

1-5 West Street WC2
01-836 4751/2

Closed: lunch (Sat+Sun); dinner (Sun); Bank Holidays
Last
Orders: lunch (2.15pm): dinner (11.15pm)

It is nearly 70 years since The Ivy opened. Though now a Wheeler's restaurant serving the range of seafood for which they have become recognized (plus some meat and poultry dishes as well as good grills), The Ivy preserves historical elements of its appeal with its irregular shaped dining room and regular follow-ing of writers, actors, and other theatricals.

Joe Allen   WC2

13 Exeter Street WC2E 7DT
01-836 0651

Last
Orders: 12.45am; 11.45 pm Sun

Virtually a canteen for the theatre in the evening, this restaurant
has developed a classless appeal to actors, theatre-goers and
even critics. The bar turns out decent cocktails, although you do
have to eat here to get one, and the food is a fair replica of the
New York original. Salads are generous and the pecan pie is very
popular. Hamburgers are highly praised, and you have to know
about them as they are not written on the menu. Stars of the
show are the waiters, for whom working at Joe Allen is the
equivalent of opening in a West End show. They may point this
out to you from time to time but are normally slick and efficient.

Magno's   WC2

65A Long Acre WC2E 9JH
01-836 6077

Closed: lunch (Sat + Sun); dinner (Sun)
Last
Orders: lunch (2.30pm); dinner (11.30pm)

A firm favourite in Covent Garden, this bustling restaurant offers
a good selection of modern French dishes. Alongside these are
the more substantial dishes such as mixed grill. There are lots of
daily choices and the pre-theatre supper is a real bargain. There
is a good selection of well chosen wines at reasonable prices,
and the staff are smart and efficient. Magno's is popular in the
evenings for business meetings, which probably accounts for the
good selection of digestifs.

Manzi's   WC2

1 Leicester Street WC2
01-734 0224

Closed: lunch (Sun); Christmas
Last
Orders: lunch (2.30pm); dinner (11.30pm)

Try to get a table downstairs, as the red-checked tablecloths of
the seafood bar itself make for a lively but less hectic atmosphere than that on the first floor. Little has changed on the menu
which offers sole, plaice, turbot and a few dishes which reflect
the changing times - smoked scallops for example, or raw
marinated anchovies, or even a brochette of monkfish. The
traditional accompaniment is some of the best chips in London,
and there is a small selection of green vegetables and some
typical English salads.
  Waiters are brisk and professional so you can eat a substantial
lunch and be out within the hour.

Mélange   WC2

59 Endell Street WC2   £20
01-240 8077

Closed: Sun
Last
Orders: lunch (2.30pm); (dinner (11.30pm)

This small, unassuming restaurant in the heart of Covent Garden
is run with great warmth and enthusiasm, and serves some
genuinely good food at basement prices. Dishes like a leek
mousse with raw salmon and lemon sauce, warm turkey livers
on spinach leaves, supreme of pigeon on baked potato cakes, or
chicken cooked in wine on a bed of shredded cabbage are
imaginatively conceived and carefully executed.

It seems to combine the atmosphere of a bistro and an artist's
studio, with posters scattered around and a feeling of genuine
concern that you should enjoy your meal. It's light-hearted and
fun, and serves very good food at very good prices.

There is a limited selection of wine which, like the food, is
very reasonably priced.

Mon Plaisir   WC2

21 Monmouth Street WC2   £30
01-836 7243

Closed: Bank Holidays
Last
Orders: lunch (2.15pm); dinner (11.15pm)

With some 40 years as one of London's most popular bistros
under its belt, Mon Plaisir has decided to trade up a little, now
that Alain Lhermitte has returned to look after the business
himself. The atmopshere is the same - it would be hard to find a
more typical French restaurant outside France. Tables are close
together and are usually full at lunch time with businessmen,
and in the evening with pre- and post-theatre, as well as their
regular diners. There are frogs' legs, or snails, stuffed duck's leg
poached in port, and good soups amongst the starters. Main
courses might be breast of Bresse chicken with wild
mushrooms, coq au vin, tournedos with Roquefort, escalope of
porc normande, and the blackboard lists the specialities.

A new Menu Parisien provides a choice of snails or gratinée à
l'oignon, followed by a steak with frites and salad, cheese or
crême brûlée, then coffee with a half bottle of wine for around
£18.00. In addition to the very drinkable housewine, there are
plenty of good regional wines.

"Mon Plaisir sera toujours Mon Plaisir," as Alain proudly
boasts - with the best pommes allumettes and cheeseboard this
side of the Channel.

147

Neal Street Restaurant WC2

26 Neal Street WC2H 9PS
01-836 8368

Closed: lunch (Sat + Sun); dinner (Sun); Bank Holidays;
        1 week Christmas to New Year
Last
Orders: lunch (2.00pm); dinner (11.00pm)

Terence Conran has some very ambitious restaurant plans for the former Michelin building in South Kensington. However, the Neal Street restaurant in Covent Garden, one of his ventures in this field, is guided by the safe hand of Antonio Carluccio. The room is stylishly designed and at lunch time, particularly, the customers all seem able to tell their Paul Smith from their Giorgio Armani.

As you would expect, food is modern and drawn from France and Italy, with medallions of veal in walnut sauce, pasta dishes, calves' liver plus some standard dishes. Wild mushrooms are a speciality of the restaurant and a large basket of them will be on show when you arrive. They are worth trying.

Orso Restaurant WC2

27 Wellington Street WC2E 7DA
01-240 5269

Last
Orders: midnight

The décor of this new Italian restaurant is simple: a long bar, plain walls with lots of photographs of yesterday's film stars, and tables often occupied by newer film stars. The menu breaks slightly from the normal Italian fare with lighter dishes such as cucumber, red onion and anchovy salad or grilled baby squid with herbs to start, followed perhaps by the pasta: rigatoni with broccoli, Parma ham, onions, olives and capers. Main courses might include baked sea bass, baked tuna with tomato and white wine or grilled chicken with rosemary, olives and tomatoes, good vegetables and simple sweets, and a totally Italian list of some unusual and quite expensive wines. Service tends to be casual but if you wish to eat Italian 'après théâtre' Orso's has a good zippy atmosphere.

Il Passetto

WC2

230 Shaftesbury Avenue WC2H 8EG
01-836 9391

Closed: lunch (Sat)
Last
Orders: lunch (3.00pm); dinner (11.30pm)

Standard Italian trattoria cooking is served with much flair amid a constant buzz of conversation from the media people who use it like a café, whether entertaining their clients or their girl-friends. There's an informal atmosphere, created by prints and paintings by Italian artists on the walls. Occasionally there's a display of fresh fish alongside the hors d'oeuvres trolley and, of course, there's a sweet trolley. Italian wines at good prices help make this a busy bustling restaurant.

Café Pélican

WC2

45 St Martin's Lane WC2N 4EJ
01-379 0309/0259

Closed: Christmas Day; Boxing Day
Last
Orders: 12.30am; snacks 2.00am

London still craves its first real brasserie where you can linger all day over a glass of wine while developing a new political thesis, or writing your latest play. However, the licensing laws make this rather tricky, so the front area of Café Pélican is filled most of the day with coffee drinkers. Snacks and sandwiches are also served here, while the large dining room at the back offers several menus. Their foray into nouvelle cuisine continues, but regulars enjoy large bowls of fish soup, steak frites and other dishes from the simple bistro-style traditional menus.

Service is brisk and French, and this is a place where the housewine can be seriously recommended, as can other wines at reasonable prices. Décor is brasserie-style with some good posters, about 20 or 30 of them, adorning the walls.

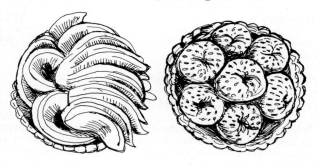

Rules Restaurant   WC2

35 Maiden Lane WC2E 7LB
01-836 5314

Closed: Sun; Christmas; New Year
Last
Orders: midnight

This restaurant, which has been established since 1798, has had
its ups and downs in the past, but now in the capable hands of
the present owners, John Mayhew and Jeremy Mogford, it has
returned to its former glory. The atmosphere is unique and it's
very much a part of London life. They've got the place really
buzzing, with a good regular following and some interesting
dishes. You can start with smoked eel and creamed horseradish,
Loch Fyne oysters, matured Cumberland ham and melon, or
maybe some cock-a-leekie soup. Main courses include steak,
kidney and mushroom pie, steak and kidney pudding, good roast
beef and Yorkshire pudding, steaks if you prefer, most kinds of
game in season, Aylesbury duckling with orange sauce, calves'
sweetbreads with bacon and mushrooms, or jugged hare. You
can still get your Welsh rarebit or devils on horseback as
savouries, and good puddings - Eton mess, burnt cream with
ginger, or good treacle sponge pudding with custard. They offer
a set price menu at around £12.00 a head, and a choice of wines
at reasonable prices. They are now open to a later hour in the
evening, so you can eat after the theatre. It really is good to see
this old London favourite blooming once again. If it's Englishness you want, or a touch of London life, I thoroughly recommend it.

Sheekey's   WC2

28 St Martin's Court, Charing Cross Road WC2N 4AL
01-240 2565

Closed: lunch (Sat + Sun); dinner (Sun)
Last
Orders: lunch (2.45pm); dinner (11.15pm)

A favourite restaurant with theatre goers, the walls are covered
with signed pictures of famous customers and the décor has
been preserved although spruced up, giving a traditional feel to
the place. Everyone comes for the fish and the seafood, with
traditional dishes like fish cakes or even half a dozen oysters

having the edge over more modern creations. The atmosphere is informal and service is brisk.

Please see the General Listing (p414) for Overton's, part of this group.

Simpson's-In-The-Strand   WC2

The Strand WC2R 0EW
01-836 9112

Closed: Sun
Last
Orders: lunch (2.45pm); dinner (9.45pm)

"At Simpson's in the Strand every joint is roasted on the jack.

"Simpson's has always been famous for real English cooking and has been strong minded enough not to include any other kind on its menu. Above all it prides itself on roast saddle of Southdown mutton. The three joints which are always on the menu are, the said saddle of mutton, roast sirloin of Scotch beef and boiled silver side of beef, with carrots and turnips. There are three restaurants in Simpson's (the fare is the same), and in each there are trollies, one to each joint, being wheeled about by white-clad waiters, who carve the required joint beside the customer's table.

"There is also one other meat dish on the menu each day; on Thursdays in the winter it is always beef steak, kidney and mushroom pudding; another day it is venison, another leg of pork, another boiled fowl, and so on. There are, of course, such things as chops, and steaks and any other English dishes if ordered, and there is always turbot, the huge fish each having a trolley.

"Mr Willis, the head chef, is an interesting personality. It is unusual to meet an English head chef in London, but all the staff at Simpson's are English, like the fare.

"Mr Willis wears the usual chef's dress, and looks most handsome in it, but on his head he has a small black velvet cap, the shape that the old 'prentices of London used to wear. This cap is rather traditional at Simpson's, the chef's predecessor also wore one; the sous-chefs wear the ordinary white caps.

SIMPSON'S
IN·THE·STRAND

"There are three restaurants at this particular restaurant. The finest and largest of these is on the ground floor, right opposite to the entrance - it is for men only. Americans are very, very fond of Simpson's and when they enter it they naturally advance straight ahead and then, if there are women in the party, they are told that 'ladies are not allowed in that room'. The American women are dumbfounded. It certainly seems tiresome, for it is the best room and beautifully panelled

151

in oak. Down each side of the room are the 'boxes' which are to be found in each of the restaurants, namely tables with high backed seats on either side; in the case of Simpson's they are upholstered in dark green leather. Over the mantelpiece of the Gentlemen's Dining Room is an amusing and decorative picture let into the panelling; it represents a mediaeval king and queen, seated at a dining table and surrounded by their court, while before them is a pie contained four-and-twenty black birds, very lively ones. Beneath is distinctly inscribed, 'Was it not a Dainty Dish to set before a King?'

"The two 'mixed' dining rooms upstairs are quite nice, with a certain amount of box seats in them. All the waiters at Simpson's are dressed in white, and the carvers, who wheel the trollies, have on chef's caps as well.

"The place a century ago was a Cigar Divan. It was known as the Grand (or Reiss's) Cigar Divan in the Strand, that was before Mr Simpson had it."

The Restaurants of London, Eileen-Hooton-Smith, 1928

Not much has changed in the 50 or so years since this review was written. Simpson's is still in The Strand and deserves a place in this guide for its history alone! Service is formal in both dining rooms, the ground floor seemingly still very much for gentlemen. There's a choice of some typically English dishes; but most people seem to opt for the roast sirloin of beef with Yorkshire pudding from the trolley, the roast saddle of lamb, or roast half Aylesbury duck.

According to the menu notes, prior to 1940 Simpson's daily consumption was 35 saddles of mutton and 15 sirloins of beef. Today they now average 25 sirloins of beef and 25 saddles of lamb. Does this mean that lamb is not as popular as mutton was, or that the roast beef of England has regained its rightful place? The large wine list has some bargains, especially amongst the magnums of château-bottled Bordeaux.

Terrazza-Est   WC2

125 Chancery Lane WC2
01-242 2601

Closed: Sat; Sun; Bank Holidays
Last
Orders: lunch (2.45pm); dinner (11.30pm)

Luigi Destro has run this old favourite for 20-odd years. The brisk, lively atmosphere at lunch time is supplemented by

spaghetti opera in the evening as young opera singers perform popular arias amidst the plates of antipasti and pasta, plus some of Luigi's specials which wing their way around the restaurant. This is an evening with a difference, at a very good price.

Best Restaurants in the British Isles

The restaurants in this section vary in style and type of food but all fulfil the criteria I have set, in that each in their own individual style provides the best in food and service whether it be the brilliant and complex cuisine of Raymond Blanc at Le Manoir aux Quat'Saisons, and Michel Roux at The Waterside, or the simple surroundings and excellent food at The Walnut Tree Inn.

Le Manoir aux Quat'Saisons   Great Milton

Great Milton, Oxfordshire OX9 7PD
(084 46) 8881/2/3

— quite simply, one of the very best.

♣ £80

Closed: lunch (Mon + Tue); dinner (Sun + Mon) Last
Orders: lunch (2.30pm); dinner (10.30pm)

I very much admire and respect Raymond Blanc and have known him for some years, but for those of you who have yet to meet the man, eat his food or enjoy the beauty of Le Manoir, I will try to be objective. The style of his food and presentation is comparable to the majority of the most highly rated restaurants in France. The energy that goes into it, and the artistic creation that emerges from his excellently designed kitchen, are exemplary. A dedicated cook, Raymond is not afraid to experiment with combinations of dishes and ways of presentation that are based on a changing pattern of available produce and supplies.

Le Manoir aux Quat'Saisons

There is a Menu Gourmand of 6 courses, and the à la carte menu boasts a choice of 10 or so starters that might include Scottish langoustines simply roasted, a julienne of courgettes,

154

garnished with ravioli and served with an orange oil dressing; a pâté of aubergines and sweet peppers, veined with fillets of milk-fed lamb set in a tomato coulis and served with a herb scented dressing; or a superb chicken bouillon garnished with raviolis and parcels of foie gras. These might be followed by a maize and corn fed Norfolk squab baked in a salt crust to enhance its unique flavour, served with its juices, potatoes Maxime and a golden sliver of foie gras; saddle of local rabbit roasted, served with seed mustard sauce, and its legs braised in tarragon juice; fillet of matured cross Charollais/Aberdeen Angus beef lightly smoked over cherry tree chips, pan fried, served with a Givry red wine sauce garnished with bone marrow; a small slice of foie gras placed on rösti potatoes, pan fried veal kidneys, pigs' trotters filled with sweetbreads, lambs' tongues, served with the braising juices spiked with morels. The desserts are amazing, especially the hot caramel soufflé served with a prune and armagnac ice-cream.

The comprehensive wine list is in keeping with an establishment of this class, and has a good choice of some wines not normally featured, including some from Cahors, Savoie and the Jura. There are good half bottles, and an amazing selection of clarets in the middle to upper price bracket. The vintages of bas armagnac go back to 1930, and there's also a large choice of eaux-de-vie and marcs.

Le Manoir is stylishly designed with 10 bedrooms, all en suite, and all sumptuously decorated to a luxury standard. The reception rooms and entrance hall are what I expect of an English manor house, and the dining room is run with French charm and élan by the higly regarded Alain Desenclos. The gardens of Le Manoir are beautifully laid out, and the vegetable and herb gardens are given lavish attention, often by Raymond himself.

To young chefs based in this country and in France, Raymond must be an inspiration, in that 6 or 7 years ago he had one small restaurant in Summertown, Oxford; and now, in that short space of time, he has established himself as one of the brightest lights on the culinary scene of Great Britain.

Without doubt, this is the best place to stay if you are in the area, and very convenient if you are simply visiting Oxford or the Colleges. If you are in Oxford, take advantage of it by buying some of the excellent pâtisseries and breads available at the traditional bakery Raymond owns, Maison Blanc, at 3 Woodstock Road.

The Waterside Inn   Bray-on-Thames

Ferry Road, Bray-on-Thames, Berkshire SL6 2AT
(0628) 20691/22941

— leave room for jui
desserts.

♣ £70

Closed: lunch (Mon + Tue); dinner (Mon; + Sun in winter);
        Bank Holidays; Boxing Day for 7 weeks

Last
Orders: lunch (2.00pm; 2.45pm Sun); dinner (10.00pm)

The Waterside Inn
Menu Exceptionnel

Crabe des Iles
ou
Rondeau de Poisson à la Guillaume Tirel

Les Deux Petites Assiettes de Poissons
(Le Filet de Sole en Habit Vert)
(Dos de Saumon d'Ecosse sur Beurre de Tomate
et Basilic)

Cornette de Sorbet au Champagne Rosé

Canon d'Agneau Germain
ou
Aiguillettes de Caneton Juliette
(2 personnes)

Les Fromages Affinés de Maître Olivier
ou
Tarte Citron et Délice Cassis
ou
Soufflée Chaud aux Framboises
(2 personnes)

Café et Petits Fours Secs

Here we find Michel Roux, who, with his brother Albert, has without doubt been one of the main influences in changing the very bleak outlook for food in this country over the past 20 years, into the high standards that are now being reached not only in London, but in England as a whole.

Michel has great talent in all departments of the kitchen, but perhaps excels in the section traditionally regarded as one of the most difficult, that of the pâtissier. In 1976 he was awarded the Paris Meilleur Ouvrier de France, which entitles the holder to teach at the highest technical level; and anyone having the opportunity to be taught by Michel Roux can only benefit from his vast range of knowledge, and the technical ability that the man has in this craft. For those of you who have not had this opportunity, I recommend Michel and Albert's new book simply entitled *The Roux Brothers on Pâtisserie*, from which you will get some idea of the depth of their combined talent. It's a well designed book which describes, for instance, brioche, some excellent bread recipes, some delicious fruit coulis and jellies, a mouthwatering display of tarts, cold desserts, sweets, home-made ice-creams and sorbets, ending up with a delicious chapter on caramels and petits fours.

Enough of the pâtisserie, what about The Waterside and the rest of the menu? It has a delightful setting on the banks of the Thames, and a lovely terrace on the side of the river. Originally an inn, it has been sympathetically and carefully changed into the luxury restaurant it is now. Sitting in the bar for an apéritif

you are surrounded by a myriad of paintings around the walls, and comfortable seats in which to lounge back. The restaurant itself with its trellis work gives the feeling that the outside is coming in to meet you. Sparkling accoutrements, beautiful white napery and attentive alert staff are guided by Olivier Ferretjans, with Michel Roux, Michel Perraud and team in the kitchen. As with Le Gavroche there are specialities of the day, which give the brigade the opportunity of airing some interesting and original dishes; and again the Menu Exceptionnel at around £35.00 per person will give you the best opportunity to try the amazing variation the kitchen can produce.

From the à la carte menu you might try as a starter the feuilleté de saumon à la vinaigrette de citron, or the exceptional soupe de poissons de roche et sa rouille. From the crustacés, try the excellent ravioles de homard tièdes truffées, sauce vierge. There are normally 5 or 6 fish courses on the menu, from which you might like to try the filet de turbot au pamplemousse, sauce Noilly. From the 9 or so entrées the more unusual include escalopes de ris de veau dorées, aux pointes d'asperges.

Although based in haute cuisine, the dishes are in fact very much a new interpretation. In many cases original dishes are presented not only to appeal to the eye (which they certainly do) but also great attention is paid to retaining the flavour within the product, to the depth of the saucing, and to the avoidance of any unnecessary use of garnishing, other than that which is required to complement the dish.

Unless I were into a really good bottle of Burgundy I would probably miss the cheese, although it's excellent and by Maître Olivier, and go on to the part of the menu which makes everyone smile with anticipation. You can actually see faces around the room light up as people hear the explanations of the various desserts: the hot soufflé aux framboises is sensational, the tarte citron et délice cassis has that beautiful lemon tang to it, without being too zesty; and even if you don't drink coffee it's worth ordering some just to get the excellent petits fours.

The wine list is comprehensive and in the top price bracket, but with some more unusual wines at the lower end of the scale. A perfect place for lunch or dinner, especially in the summer.

The Old Woolhouse   Northleach

Northleach, Gloucestershire GL54 3EE
(045 16) 366

beautiful cooking well worth a long drive ♣ £40

Closed: Sun + Mon
Last
Orders: by arrangement

Jacques and Jenny Astic run The Old Woolhouse and have done for some 13 years. I was lucky enough to eat there the first week they opened and really couldn't believe the standard and the quality of their food, especially given the time and location. I made a rule at the beginning of this book that I would compare only like with like and it is pointless comparing a restaurant like The Old Woolhouse, which has the advantage of only seating 18, with a much larger establishment with its attendant difficulties. All I can say is that I find this one of the most memorable places I have ever visited, both in this country and abroad. There are not many frills about the place save the care which is taken with the freshly laundered napkins and the beautiful crockery - all washed by hand. And the softly lit dining room creates as good an atmosphere as any for Jacques to weave his spells from the kitchen, and Jenny - with her charm - to organise the service.

His food is exceptional. You can wait and have a drink in their small lounge where Jenny will recite the daily menu to you. The starters may consist of 2 or 3 fishy dishes, and the main courses are almost always cooked to order.

The kitchen could not be simpler: no fancy gadgets, a double gas stove, a couple of prep tables and a sink. From it, to my mind, comes magic! I'm not going to go into details about the food, or tell you any more - Jacques may even ban me for writing about the place, for his long-standing dislike of guide books in general is well-known. I hope he will forgive me and allow me to return, because some of my most outstanding meals have been eaten in this tiny little restaurant in Northleach.

Hintlesham Hall   Hintlesham

Hintlesham, Near Ipswich, Suffolk IP8 3NS
(047 387) 268

♣ £50

worth staying overnight

Closed: lunch (Sat); 2 weeks Jan/Feb
Last
Orders: lunch (1.30pm); dinner (9.15pm)

Without a doubt the approach to the Hall is dazzling - the beautifully kept gardens and the twin pools leading to the front door, and the cool, tiled hall from which you go into the other reception rooms. As we drew up to the Hall, it took all of 15 seconds before the young porter and Tim Sunderland, the general manager, were on their way to offer us a hand with our cases. Two bedrooms have been refurbished and 4 others are planned. They are landscaping the gardens at the back of the house, and have completely replaced the herb garden.

Ruth and David Watson take the orders in the superb room they use as a bar, and the young, very competent English team are headed by the extremely diligent and hard-working Tim Sunderland, who seems to be everywhere at once. The dining room is elegant and candlelit, with full blue drapes, subdued carpeting and a relaxed atmosphere.

Robert Mabey in the kitchen served us a splendid warm salad of scallops and crab on a bed of salad leaves with summer herbs, and something they describe as a little dish from Japan - rare beef, piquant ginger, soya, sesame and shallot relish - followed by a farmed rabbit served on a bed of spinach with 3 mustard sauces, or a sauté of veal sweetbreads, or a loin of lamb in madeira sauce with home-made pasta, served with hot home-made bread. Excellent cheeses come from the cheese shop in Oulton Broad.

For breakfast the marmalade and jams are home-made. As we left in the morning they were just setting up for a wedding reception, and I can't think of a nicer place than this for such an occasion. Everyone works very hard at Hintlesham, and is determined to get to the very top of the league. A newsletter gives information about coming events and special dinners, and it's worth phoning for a copy.

An excellent wine list has particularly strong emphasis on the Burgundy and claret sections, at affordable prices. They have a house menu at £13.50, a menu gastronomique at £21.50 and a good, short, imaginative à la carte menu.

Altnaharrie Inn   Ullapool

Ullapool, Ross-shire, Scotland IV26 2SS
(085 483) 230

don't miss this experience ♣ £50

Closed: lunch (except to residents); winter
Last
Orders: dinner (one sitting at 7.45pm)

The Altnaharrie is not just a hotel nor is it just a restaurant, as
these descriptions demean its objectives. I can only describe it
as an experience and one that should not be missed. One
Saturday, standing on a small jetty at Ullapool in pouring rain
with 2 cases and an umbrella to afford what little protection it
could, I waited for a boat to take me to the Inn which lies just
across the loch, quite convinced that total insanity had finally set
in. How on earth could this be worth spending one night and
having dinner? 24 hours later I would have been happy to swim
across to repeat the experience, such is the unique atmosphere
created by Fred and Gunn in their remote house.

Fred was originally a metallurgist who decided to become a
vet, then ran a yacht charter business from what is now the Inn;
Gunn was an artist who wished to cook; and the result is the
Altnaharrie Inn. As I stepped off the launch I was helped with
luggage by Fred, who then showed me to my impeccable
bedroom and the rest of the Inn. I felt more like a house guest
than a hotel visitor. A log fire was burning in the sitting room
and by now the rain had eased off. There are no roads to
Altnaharrie: over the water or a walk across the hills behind are
the only means of access, and so obviously it is not everyone's
idea of a hotel. There are only 4 bedrooms - some with a lovely
view back across the water to Ullapool.

Prior to dinner, drinks are served in the sitting room and you
meet the other guests; again the feeling is one of a private dinner
party, although there are separate tables in the dining room.
There is no choice of menu - for so few people this would be
impracticable, and with Gunn's menu a choice is unnecessary.
Fred serves dinner himself, having ensured that wines are all in
place, and his enthusiasm and sense of humour stimulate
conversation between tables.

The first course was a soup of hawthorn and cucumber which
was light but full of flavour, with the slight bitterness of the
hawthorn giving a refreshingly new taste. Following this was a

small whole lobster which had been lightly cooked, taken from its shell and laid on 2 sauces - delicious! Venison was the main dish, medallions cooked and served with a creamed sauce flavoured with juniper, which was perfect, and the vegetables were stir-fried and crunchy. A choice of 3 sweets was then offered or cheese, before or afterwards as preferred. The first sweet was a Norwegian speciality of a tuile biscuit filled with cloudberries and cream, the second a hazelnut meringue filled with wild raspberries, and finally fresh peaches halved, filled with frangipane and baked. I could only manage the latter but you can have all 3 if space permits. I wished it had.

Cooking of this standard is rare. It showed a complete understanding of the raw product and how to achieve its maximum flavour, complementing it rather than overpowering it with other ingredients or sauces.

Bread was freshly made for each meal, and lovely home-made croissants and jams appeared at breakfast which was equally well prepared and cooked.

Guests become regular visitors to the Inn, except for one gentleman who, as Fred explained, couldn't understand why there was no ice machine in his bedroom! The problem was quickly solved: it was suggested that he should stay elsewhere. I wonder if he realises what he missed?

Shipdham Place   Shipdham

Shipdham, Near Thetford, Norfolk IP25 7LX   £40
(0362) 820303

Closed: lunch (except by arrangement); dinner (Tue);
         Christmas; mid-week Jan + Feb
Last
Orders: by arrangement   *check, as the de Blanks are moving*

Shipdham Place is an old 17th-Century rectory with an elegant frontage and additions from 1800. It stands close to the church at Shipdham which, so we were reliably informed by a local one evening (it's the sort of place that inspires you to get involved!), was a wool church, built by prosperous wool merchants in the 15th Century. It has, amongst, other things, an extraordinary cupola, and stands out even amongst the vast number of churches we seemed to encounter in Norfolk, as one that shouldn't be missed.

The de Blanks' house was a very special treat. They were away on our visit but it is a great tribute to them and their staff that the whole place ran immaculately in their absence. The interior has been sympathetically preserved and renovated with beautiful pine panelling, and the dining room has split dark cane

161

covered walls, polished floors and a homely selection of tables, some set with white cloths, some polished and set with wicker mats. There's an assortment of dining chairs, and a delightful candlelit atmosphere.

The food consists of a set price menu, different each day, at £18.00, and we ate an excellent green vegetable timbale, delicate yet full of flavour. Some fillet of beef in a mushroom and tarragon sauce came with spinach tarts, broad beans, peas and carrots, all from the garden and all tasting as if they had been picked an hour before, which they had. I've talked about the

carrots ever since, and would make a journey there just for a plate of them - well, perhaps some broad beans as well... There's an excellent garden salad and cheeseboard, and an excellent wine list too with some interesting half bottles. We tried a 1972 Château La Lagune and a 1967 Châteaux Margaux. You help yourself to drinks before dinner from a trolley in the hall next to one of the 2 homely drawing rooms, and you just write down what you have.

The drinks trolley reminded me of a man called Dudley who ran a pub/restaurant just outside Oxford, some years ago, known locally as 'Dirty Dudley's'. His habit was never to take money at the bar for drinks before dinner, but he expected his guests to remember what they had drunk. He recited the dinner menu which usually consisted of fish and game simply cooked, and called you when the dishes were ready. Then you ordered your wine, which was also not written down. At the end of the meal you were expected to remember everything that you had eaten and drunk! I'm sure some errors were made, but there must be something in this method of running an establishment! One thing that did happen concerned a man known as 'Mr John' (Dudley always referred to his customers as Mr 'Christian name') who had a dinner party for 10 guests and forgot to declare upwards of 15 bottles of wine. Dudley conveyed to the vast majority of Oxford undergraduates his displeasure, not by rebuking him but simply by explaining in Dudley's firm voice - the next time Mr John visited with a girlfriend - that Mr John was not welcome in Dudley's establishment. A lesson to us all!

Back at Shipdham, the de Blanks have carefully planned and planted a beautiful flower and vegetable garden, and Kathy who looks after the vegetable garden was full of praise for the new varieties of lettuce introduced by Justin, while Frank Cox, the flower man, kindly gave us a root of one of Melanie's plants.

Looking around the next morning we decided it would be an ideal place in which to take all the rooms with a party of friends for a festive holiday.

One sad note is that some local told us that there were now only 2 pubs instead of 5 in the village, that the butcher's was closing and the baker's had closed already. Perhaps Justin de Blank might be persuaded to retail some of his excellent food there, just as he does in London.

This is a restaurant with rooms in the country house style which you would be delighted to find in rural France, let alone in Norfolk. The attention to detail and casual charm of the bedroom service - doors propped open by books - combine to make this one of my favourite places.

The Seafood Restaurant   Padstow

Riverside, Padstow, Cornwall PZ28 8BY
(0841) 532485

exuberant atmosphere and excellent fish.

Closed: lunch (daily); dinner (Sun)
Last
Orders: dinner (9.30pm)

Without a doubt this is the place in Cornwall to eat fish, and even if you're not in Cornwall it's worth driving to. The restaurant is in a lovely setting which overlooks the harbour, and the fishing boats alongside help to create an atmosphere that seems to endorse the freshness of the fish. It is an attractive stone-built house and deceptively large. The restaurant is bright and spacious with lots of plants, prints on the white walls and wicker armchairs at the neatly laid tables. There is a small bar at the front of the room for an apéritif or simply to wait for your table.

163

The
Seafood Restaurant

There seem to be almost as many staff as customers, and they speed about the room with the same enthusiasm to serve the fish as a fishing fleet might have to catch it. The menu is such that one could stick a pin anywhere in it yet be quite sure that the right choice had been made. I certainly could have tried everything on the menu.

A 3-course dinner is offered for £11.95 with an excellent selection of 3 main dishes from which to choose. Alternatively you can order à la carte and perhaps try mussels in a saffron and leek soup, fried squid with skorthalia, scallops baked in their shells with a julienne of vegetables and vouvray sealed with puff pastry. Main courses on the July menu included cassoulet of monkfish, lemon sole and scallops with the flavours of lobster, crab, tarragon and cream; lobster with a vanilla sauce, or a traditional fruits de mer platter served French style. My grillade of seafood comprised lobster, monkfish, John Dory and grey mullet was charcoal grilled and served with an excellent chive and fennel dressing which complemented the perfectly cooked fish. This followed a well-made fish soup with rouille, and a light apple tart with yoghurt-soured cream to finish.

The wine list is obviously an affair of love for Richard Stein who has compiled an impressive array of wines concentrating naturally on white but with some well-chosen reds for those who prefer it. As he says of the Château Latour 1966, "at this price something of a snip": £105.00. Don't let that frighten you however, there are lots of excellent alternatives for well under £10.00 which are also snips.

Good news for those of us who wish to eat our way through the menu is that the Steins have now opened 8 bedrooms with bath or shower rooms and all with views over the harbour. Next trip I shall wake at 8.00am and have a half lobster with a bottle of Krug and look out of the window to see what the boats are landing for dinner, the ultimate indulgence.

The Walnut Tree Inn Llandewi Skirrid

Llandewi Skirrid, Abergavenny, Gwent, Wales NP7 8AW ♣ £40
(0873) 2797

warm, friendly restaurant vvvy good food

Closed: 4 days Christmas; 2 weeks Feb
Last
Orders: lunch (2.30pm); dinner (10.30pm)

I started off by writing that the food we ate at The Walnut Tree was exceptional for Wales, but as I wrote it I realised it was exceptional for *anywhere* in Great Britain. In a crowded dining room with everyone jostling together, the occasion was an absolute delight.

To judge from the exterior, this whitewashed building is like any country inn, but from the moment you enter, you appreciate the difference. If you can imagine a cross between an Italian seaside bistro and a traditional English pub you're getting somewhere close to it. Service by well-informed friendly ladies makes you feel instantly at home.

For anyone who loves food and is interested in everything on the menu, it's a marvellous place to be for the simple reason that you cannot fail to see quite clearly what everyone next to you is eating. And more often than not, as in our case, you get into conversation with the tables on either side, a conversation which invariably turns to the food on your own plates, the food on the plates of your neighbours, and other good places to eat in the area (invaluable to us as we picked up 2 good tips).

The seafood terrine in three pale colours interwoven with a layer of prawns, and a layer of chopped green vegetables and herbs was quite delicious, light and full of flavour. Fine threads of pasta, served with pesto sauce and heaped with parmesan cheese, was beautifully presented and tasted equally as good. Main courses included a fish stew which contained 6 types of fish plus prawns and écrevisses, served in a large earthenware pot with a tomato and onion based sauce - something that one can only normally taste on the Continent. It was absolutely delightful. The sea bass served with ginger, pepper and cream sauce was beautifully cooked and full of flavour. The plateau de fruits de mer was as large as I have ever seen with a tremendous range of fresh seafood equalling Pierre Martin's. Despite its length, the menu has no padding, and every dish you read about you want to taste. It's obvious that over the years the owners - the Jaruschio family - have developed their own special dishes which are added to as the ingredients become seasonally available. People at the tables on either side of us had been going there for 18 to 20 years, and agreed that although the place has always been excellent, it has improved and progressed immensely over the years, and that it is now at the height of its development.

165

Peacock Vane   Isle of Wight

Bonchurch, Isle of Wight PO38 1RG
(0983) 852 019

Closed: lunch (Mon + Tue); Sun - Thu in Nov - Mar
Last
Orders: lunch (2.00pm); dinner (9.15pm)

Peacock Vane is a way of life, both for the Wolfenden family in their second generation, and their guests; for once you have visited them you will almost certainly return. The relaxed and friendly home is a perfect setting for a weekend away. Even better, a party of you can book the whole hotel. Almost everyone who has been there claims to have found it first; in fact I was taken there many years ago by friends, to whom I will always be grateful. Their introduction, which was that Peacock Vane was "rather different from most hotels and a bit special", is as true today as it was 10 years ago. Drinks are served from a grand piano that doubles as a bar, in a beautifully appointed room of Georgian proportions with windows overlooking the lovely gardens. The house itself is charming, set in its own grounds with an outdoor swimming pool and lovely views.

   Food is straightforward and unfussy with a touch of home-quality cooking, and some excellent local fish dishes are accompanied by bread baked in their kitchen. If you do get bored between meals, you can buy one of Mrs Wolfenden Senior's own handwritten cookery books which make interesting reading.

- now sold but we left this one in for those of you not lucky enough to have experienced it

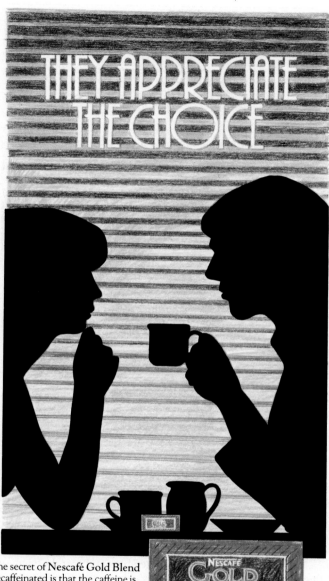

THEY APPRECIATE THE CHOICE

The secret of **Nescafé Gold Blend** decaffeinated is that the caffeine is extracted naturally <u>before</u> the beans are golden roasted – no more than 0.3% caffeine remains.
The coffee is then ground, filtered and freeze dried, just the rich taste and aromas of our selection of the finest coffees including superb mild arabicas are left to be enjoyed. Available in 500g resealable catering cans, 100g jars and individual one cup sachets.

Nestlé ®

THE NESTLÉ COMPANY LTD. St. George's House, Croydon, Surrey CR9 1NR. 01-686 3333.

The Carved Angel   Dartmouth

2 South Embankment, Dartmouth, Devon TQ6 9BH   ♣ £55
(080 43) 2465

goes from strength, to strength.

Closed: lunch (Mon); dinner (Sun + Mon); Jan
Last
Orders: lunch (1.45pm); dinner (9.30pm)

Joyce Molyneux was originally a partner of George Perry-Smith when he founded the Hole in the Wall in Bath back in the 1950s. Subsequently, in 1974, she moved to The Carved Angel with the same partners, and has kept The Carved Angel on a steady path over the last 12 years. If anything, it gets better. The faces have changed at front of house, but certainly with no detrimental effect. The reason is simple: she enjoys doing what she does, and she does it extremely well. Her cooking is inspired by the ingredients which she seeks, and her respect for the seasons, coupled with a determination to purchase only the best produce, make the restaurant what it is. She cannot understand why the local greengrocer has imported mangoes when the country is full of soft fruit; she doesn't want to eat apples all year round, only in November when they are at their best. On the day of my visit someone had called her during the afternoon to see if she would like some fresh chanterelles found locally. Of course she would, it was merely a question of cost.

The fixed price menu is substantial, a watercress and almond soup or a provençal fish soup, basil noodles with cream and smoked ham, or a crab soufflé, a terrine of chicken, ham and tongue with pistachios *and* chanterelles (a deal had been struck). Main dishes might be Porbeagle shark cooked with butter, lemon and parsley, Dart salmon with samphire and champagne, bass wrapped in lettuce with shallots and vermouth, a casserole of young goat with vegetables and sorrel cream, or guineafowl with apples and calvados. The busy kitchen operates only half-screened by a few plants from the simply decorated restaurant, which gives diners the opportunity to see the quiet efficiency of the kitchen.

The restaurant itself is a simple and pleasant room set within a black and white framed building. Meriel Boydon supervises the service and her fleet of well-trained and pretty young ladies serve efficiently and effortlessly. There are about 200 wines to choose from, over 40 of them in half bottles, and I think it would be fairly safe to say that none of them are there for padding; each one has been exceptionally well chosen.

The Carved Angel has the right balance of all the ingredients to make a successful restaurant. Its harbour-side setting, lively ambience, excellent food and wines and, above all, people who care, make this restaurant something special.

Michael's Nook   Grasmere

Grasmere, Ambleside, Cumbria LA22 9RP ♣ £55
(096 65) 496

Closed: lunch (Sat)
Last
Orders: see text

quiet, genteel atmosphere — good, well-prepared food

With a name like Michael's Nook one is not quite sure what to
expect, but Reg Gifford will be quick to upbraid you and point
out that Michael's Nook is in fact the name of the humble
dwelling of the shepherd in Wordsworth's poem. Apparently this
Michael's Nook was once a summer house for a family of
Lancashire industrialists, and a splendid house it is. Reg Gifford
is an antique dealer as well as a hotelier, and his taste shows
throughout the interior. There is a lovely collection of English
prints, rugs, furniture and porcelain, not only in the public rooms
but also in the well-equipped bedrooms including 2 excellent
suites which have been carefully and tastefully built on.

Some of the finest food in the Lake District is served here and
each dish is well described. The portions are not over-elaborate
and leave you looking forward to the next taste to come from
the kitchen. The dinner menu includes home-made ravioli filled
with ratatouille served on a bed of vegetable spaghetti, feuilleté
of lambs' tongues scented with juniper, guineafowl and leek
terrine, or possibly a mousseline of fresh Scottish scallops with
saffron. The soups might be cream of parsnip and apple, or
lentil, to be followed by strips of fresh halibut and loch trout,
poached in fish stock and vermouth and served in a light cream
sauce made from the reduction, a breast of wild mallard with a
sauce of champagne and pink peppercorns or a breast of
chicken filled with veal forcemeat, poached in chicken stock,
finished with a fresh sage sauce made from the chicken glaze.
After these and excellent fresh vegetables, you still seem to be
able to manage one of the delicious desserts. It might be hot
feuilleté of apple with cinnamon sauce, or an individual praline
flan with pears.

The dining room is beautifully appointed with some very nice
touches, and the red walls give off a really warm feeling with the
candlelit tables. Reg Gifford and his charming staff are always
around to help and advise about choosing from the excellent
wine list. Dinner orders are usually taken at 7.30pm for 8.00pm,
but in high season there are two sittings: 7.00pm for 7.30pm; and
9.00pm for 9.15pm.

169

East Anglia

East Anglia - for our purposes Lincolnshire, Norfolk, Suffolk, Cambridgeshire and Essex - is a largely flat landscape, whipped by easterly winds that have encountered no hills since departing the Urals. Dominated again by the sea, as is so much of our island, a great deal of East Anglia has been painstakingly retrieved from Neptune over the centuries, and the diet still pays him allegiance.

The fishing industry is not, however, so firmly entrenched here as it was before the herring shoals marked by East Anglia's donation to the vocabulary of the herring - 'bloater' - were fished out. What particularly distinguishes bloaters from other varieties of preserved herring is that they are cured gut in, giving the finished article a rather gamey taste. Its milder cousin is the red herring, but although it still exists, it's no longer that easy to find. Try the H S Fishing Company Ltd, at Sutton Road, Great Yarmouth (0943 858119).

Crabs, on the other hand, are still available, and are as juicy and tasty as they ever were. Cockles, mussels and whelks are usually taken in vinegar, but go to Colchester in Essex for your oysters, pure and simple, or to the Butley-Orford Oysterage in Suffolk.

Wales has laver, Norfolk has samphire - who said only the Japanese eat sea vegetables? Samphire is enjoying a revival in our cities, probably to the disdain of the east-coast folk who have never stopped enjoying it. Easier to deal with than laver, when picked young it doesn't require much more than a thorough soaking to reduce the salt to an acceptable level. A brief simmer in boiling water renders it al dente. And as sheep have grazed these salt marshes, samphire can be an unusual accompaniment to roast lamb.

The final yield of the sea is the salt itself: Maldon in Essex is the headquarters which refines the salt ready for the cook.

Amongst condiments, there's Colman's of Norwich, the mustard giants. A waving field of yellow mustard is a childhood memory, replaced largely nowadays by yellow rape seed, grown for its oil. The Mustard Shop is at 3 Bridewell Alley, Norwich (0603 627889), established to mark the 150th anniversary of the founding of J & J Colman. It's the place for anything and everything connected with mustard.

Asparagus, some of England's finest, comes from the eastern market gardens, as do Lincolnshire potatoes.

Hare, pheasant and partridge all figure in local recipes like Norfolk Partridge Pot. And if you can't find the game, there's still the pig farmer's trade to rely on. Suffolk sweet pickled hams usually appear around Christmas time, like their Buckinghamshire relatives, the Bradenhams. Essex is the home of the Dunmow Flitch trial - a flitch being a side of bacon, this being the prize awarded annually to a married couple who could prove to the court that they had not had an argument in the previous twelvemonth. Perhaps we could persuade A W Curtis & Sons, bacon curers, of Long Leys Road, Lincoln (0522 27212) to revive the practice!

East Anglia's sweetness comes mainly from fruit, preserved at Tiptree, and by Elsenham's, but names occur in a few other local recipes - although perhaps not so local, most of them are national favourites. There's Ipswich almond pudding, to serve with a compôte of stewed soft fruit, Norfolk treacle tart, and Cambridge burnt cream, as well as Grantham gingerbread.

VINEYARDS

Cambridgeshire
Chilford Hundred Vineyard (18 acres)
Linton, Nr Cambridge

The Isle of Ely (2 acres)
Wilburton

Essex
Nevards (1 acre)
Boxted, Nr Colchester

Norfolk
Elmham Park (7 acres)
Dereham

Heywood (2 acres)
Diss

Lexham Hall (8 acres)
Litcham, Nr Kings Lynn

Pulham (6 acres)
Diss

Suffolk
Brandeston Priory (6 acres)
Woodbridge

Broadwater (3 acres)
Framlingham

Bruisyard (10 acres)
Saxmundham

Cavendish Manor (10 acres)
Sudbury

Chickering (2 acres)
Hoxne, Nr Eye

Willow Grange (1 acre)
Crowfield, Nr Ipswich

HISTORIC HOUSES OPEN TO THE PUBLIC

Cambridgeshire
Anglesey Abbey, Lode
Wimpole Hall, New Wimpole

Lincolnshire
Belton House, Grantham
Doddington Hall, Doddington
Gunby Hall, Burgh-le-Marsh

Norfolk
Blickling Hall, Aylsham
Felbrigg Hall, Cromer
Holkham Hall, Wells
Houghton Hall, Fakenham
Oxburgh Hall, Swaffham

Suffolk
Ickworth, Bury St Edmunds
Melford Hall, Long Melford
Somerleyton Hall, Lowestoft

We have not separated out the Midlands, the Home Counties, the Shires - call them what you will - because although there are great divides, social and economic, there is also a strongly unifying link provided by the pig industry. So since we did this for the North and for the South of England, we're doing it again for the middle, calling it the Heart of England. We can justify this by referring to the village of Whitwell in the now defunct county of Rutland, which, although it only has about 20 houses, is actually twinned with Paris. And you can't get much more heart-like than that!

Pork pies, a hearty feast of meat and pastry, are almost an emblem of this part of England, Melton Mowbray in Leicester-shire still produces some of the finest, the hot water crust still being raised by hand to provide a case for the pure pork filling and clear concentrated jelly. And then of course there are the large commercial concerns based in Wiltshire, producing pies, sausages, bacon, faggots, brawn, black puddings, savaloys, polo-nies and chitterlings. Not all are huge multinationals, however: there's a family concern at H H Collins, of Broadway, Worcester-shire (0386 852374).

Hot pies were a favourite amongst huntsmen when the well-heeled went off at dawn with the Quorn on misty mornings. Hunt servants made do with Quorn bacon roll, roughly chopped cheap cuts of bacon, mixed with onions and boiled in a suet crust. Similar is the Bedfordshire clanger. Again a suet roll, it has a pastry wall in the middle to separate the meal into 'befores' and 'afters' - meat and onions at one end, jam at the other. This seems to have nurtured both quarrymen and hat factory women, while the better off ate spiced beef.

Other carnivorous treats are of course Aylesbury duck, roast goose (especially at the time of Nottingham's Michaelmas Fair), and rabbit stew, all of which might benefit from some Worces-tershire sauce!

We're dealing with an almost landlocked bit of England - but not quite. Gloucestershire has the Severn Estuary and to this point from their spawning grounds thousands of miles away in the Sargasso Sea, come elvers, tiny silvery baby eels looking for all the world like shortish spaghetti. Their destiny: to be fried with bacon and vinegar and eaten in competitions on Easter Monday. No such fate awaits the imperious Wye salmon, though.

The rich central pastures have allowed the burgeoning of the cheese industry. From the king of fish to the king of cheese:

Stilton is made again not far from the village of that name. Farmhouse Red Leicester is a delicious find, as is a true pale Derby, uncoloured by sage leaves. Similarly, a lot of what is sold as Double Gloucester is not strictly so (the milk from two milkings, the curds twice-milled for a different texture). You might find a genuine Single Gloucester, a younger cousin. It tastes totally different and is to be valued. In Gloucestershire, when they're not competing eating elvers, they're rolling cheeses down hills. Competitive lot, aren't they? Two winners in the cheese stakes, though, are the Hinton Bank Farm at Whitchurch, Shropshire (0948 2631) and the Wells Stores at Streatley, near Reading, Berkshire (0491 872362).

Cheese goes well with apples, and Herefordshire has a cider industry to rival or even outstrip that of the West Country; and like that region it is not just imbibed but used in cooking.

Staying with fruit but going back briefly to pies, a variation on the Melton Mowbray pork pies was to sweeten the crust and make the filling of gooseberries. A sweet 'toad in the hole' is a Nottingham apple batter pudding, and in Derbyshire the correct name for its almond and jam pastry dessert is Bakewell Pudding. Poor Knights of Windsor, as well as being a 14th-Century order founded by Edward III, are a way of using up stale bread. Dip the slices in sweetened egg and milk, then fry them in butter, and serve hot dusted with sugar and cinnamon, or jam. French toast is another name for a similar thing. Banbury cakes are similar to Eccles cakes, puff pastry around currants with 3 slashes on the top.

The original bread for the Poor Knights might have come from Jordan's. Once a struggling, lone, pioneer roller mill in the path of the Sliced White, it is now the vanguard of all that is good, healthy, brown and unrefined. And they still slowly grind the wheat on stones powered by water. Contact them at Holme Mills, Biggleswade, Bedfordshire (0767 318222).

VINEYARDS

Berkshire
Ascot (3 acres)
Ascot

The Holt (1 acres)
Newbury

Stanlake Park (17 acres)
Twyford

Westbury (12 acres)
Purley, Nr Reading

Buckinghamshire
Wickenden (4 acres)
Taplow

Gloucestershire
St Anne's (2 acres)
Newent

Tapestry Wines (3 acres)
Apperley

Three Choirs (20 acres)
Newent

Herefordshire
Broadfield (10 acres)
Bodenham

Croft Castle (½ acre)
Nr Leominster

Hertfordshire
Frithsden (2 acres)
Nr Hemel Hempstead

Rowney (3 acres)
Sawbridgeworth

Nottinghamshire
Eglantine (3 acres)
Costock

173

Oxfordshire
Bothy Vineyard (3 acres)
Frilford Heath, Nr Abingdon

Chiltern Valley (3 acres)
Hambleden, Nr Henley

Wiltshire
Chalkhill (6 acres)
Bowerchalke, Nr Salisbury

Stitchcombe (5 acres)
Nr Marlborough

Elms Cross (3 acres)
Bradford on Avon

Tytherley (1 acre)
West Tytherley, Nr Salisbury

Fonthill (6 acres)
Fonthill Gifford, Nr Tisbury

Worcestershire
Astley (4 acres)
Stourport-on-Severn

Sherston Earl (3 acres)
Sherston, Nr Malmesbury

HISTORIC HOUSES OPEN TO THE PUBLIC

Bedfordshire
Luton Hoo, Luton
Woburn Abbey, Woburn

Berkshire
Basildon Park, Pangbourne

Buckinghamshire
Ascott, Leighton Buzzard
Chichely Hall, Newport Pagnell
Claydon House, Middle Claydon
Hughenden Manor, High Wycombe
Waddesdon Manor, Waddesdon
West Wycombe Park, West Wycombe

Derbyshire
Chatsworth, Bakewell
Haddon Hall, Bakewell
Hardwick Hall, Mansfield
Kedleston Hall, Derby
Melbourne Hall, Derby
Sudbury Hall, Sudbury

Hereford & Worcester
Croft Castle, Leominster
Eastnor Castle, Ledbury

Hertfordshire
Gorhambury House, St Albans
Hatfield House, Hatfield
Knebworth House, Knebworth

Leicestershire
Belvoir Castle, Nr Grantham
Quenby Hall, Nr Leicester
Stanford Hall, Nr Rugby

Northamptonshire
Althorp, Northampton
Burghley House, Stamford
Hinwick House, Rushden
Lamport Hall, Northampton
Rockingham Castle, Corby

Oxfordshire
Blenheim Palace, Woodstock
Broughton Castle, Banbury
Buscot Park, Faringdon
Mapledurham House, Nr Reading
Milton Manor House, Milton
Rousham Park, Steeple Aston
Stonor Park, Nr Henley-on-Thames

Shropshire
Attingham Park, Atcham
Benthall Hall, Much Wenlock
Weston Park, Shifnal (see review)

Staffordshire
Shugborough, Nr Stafford

Warwickshire
Arbury Hall, Nuneaton
Charlecote Park, Nr Stratford-upon-Avon
Coughton Court, Alcester
Packwood House, Hockley Heath
Ragley Hall, Alcester
Upton House, Edge Hall
Warwick Castle, Warwick

West Midlands
Hagley Hall, Nr Birmingham
Wightwick Manor,
   Nr Wolverhampton

Wiltshire
Bowood Gardens, Calne
Corsham Court, Corsham
Lacock Abbey, Lacock
Longleat House, Warminster
Stourhead, Stourton
Wilton House, Wilton

BERINGER CHARDONNAY
Classically complex, this full bodied white wine
is produced at the **Beringer** vineyards in the
Napa Valley – California's prestige
appellation. **Beringer** has been producing
premier wines continuously since 1876.

Enjoy this crisp white wine with
seafood or shellfish.

North England

It's rather unfair to lump all of northern England together, for it comprises at least 2 distinct tribes, those honouring the white rose and those the red, divided forever by the ridge of the Pennines. Yet, despite the ferocious differences, they have much in common. Life in the North was - some would say, still is - hard. Both sides owe a great deal to textiles, cotton on the west, wool to the east; and such prosperity came from the upheavals of the Industrial Revolution. Agriculture provided work also, and of course, food. And both sides have coastlines with fishing industries.

Kippering was born up here, and they still make some of the finest at Craster in Northumberland, and on the Isle of Man. They pot shrimps in Lancashire's Morecambe Bay and at Yorkshire's Whitby. Great fishing fleets are harboured on both coasts, so it's hardly surprising that up North, they make the country's best fish and chips. The real maestro appears to be Harry Ramsden's, just outside Leeds, where several hundred portions are served daily. People come in coach loads, literally. The secret appears to be quite simple: use the best and freshest possible ingredients, and consume the finished product as quickly as possible once it's cooked. Mushy peas, bread and butter, and plenty of strong tea don't go amiss either. The freshwater lakes of Cumbria are home to the char, a relative of salmon and trout which can be cooked in roughly similar ways.

In an area given over to hard manual labour, the man of the house needed his protein, and the North is still a stronghold of devoted meat eaters. However, with true economy, very little of the beast is wasted. The northern butcher is able to sell to the housewife: tripe to go with home-grown onions, cow heel to thicken up the gravy of a pie, brains, sweetbreads, hearts, elder (which is cow's udder, pressed and sliced like tongue), lambs' fry, pigs' fry, pigs' trotters, chitterlings, black puddings, white puddings and faggots. Lancashire hot pot uses scrag end of mutton, as does Liverpool lobscouse. The most acceptable of these cooked meat shop specialities, and therefore the one most likely to be sold in its southern equivalent, the delicatessen, (continental influence never did have much sway north of Watford!) is the Cumberland sausage, pure meat, herbs and seasoning which, instead of being sold in links, is sold by length. Yorkshire's contribution to this export drive would be the York ham, prized especially at Christmas, though Cumberland ham ranks alongside. Order the latter from Richard Woodall, Lane End, Waberthwaite, Near Millom (065 77 237). Yorkshire prizes fat on its ham and bacon, for lean rhymes with mean, and fatness is equated with generosity. In Durham, they eat squab pie - young pigeons in pastry.

There would rarely be enough meat to satisfy the hunger without some padding, so whereas the hot pot supplemented it with plenty of potatoes (as did Northumberland's pan haggerty), in Yorkshire was born one of the most famous of English dishes, the Yorkshire pudding. This light batter is baked in a roasting tin in one big piece, not little individual ones, placed underneath the roasting meat so that the juices from it drip into the pudding. Each family member was given a slice including the light crisp puffed-up edge, and some of the centre, moistened by meat juices. It was served before the meat, with gravy, to take the edge off the appetite and to disguise the smallness of the portion of meat.

Also from the North comes a traditional Monday dinner, using up Sunday's joint: shepherd's pie if made from mutton alone, or cottager's pie if other meat was also used, the meat minced and mixed with onions and gravy beneath a crust of creamy mashed potatoes, a sprinkling of grated Lancashire or Wensleydale cheese on top, and popped under the grill to bubble and brown.

The dairy herds are strong and numerous. Cheshire, rare blue Cheshire, salty Lancashire, crumbly Wensleydale - 3 of England's great 9 come from the North. Wensleydale is sometimes baked into a pastry crust of an apple pie or eaten alongside in a chunk. Newer cheeses are also appearing, or reappearing, like Cotherstone and Botton.

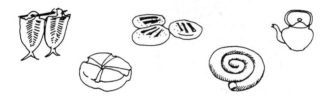

Leftover bits of cheese are just right for cakes, like Yorkshire curd tarts. Let's stick with Yorkshire for a while, and try some parkin (an oatmeal gingerbread with some several hundred different recipes); teacakes (flat sweet dough cakes with currants, split, toasted, buttered and eaten hot); pikelets and crumpets, brandy snaps, Brontë cake with mead, secret cake (with fruit again). Further north you'll find singin' hinny, another flat sweet currant cake, but this time cooked on a girdle or griddle, previously smeared with butter which when heated causes the currants to swell and hiss, or 'sing'.

Bread itself has different names up here: the standard bread roll is flatter and floured, like a Scottish bap. In Lancashire it's a barmcake, in Yorkshire a breadcake (as opposed to a teacake); in Northumberland a stottie cake.

You can't leave Yorkshire without some Pontefract cakes, which aren't cakes at all, but are liquorice sweets. Harrogate toffee is toffee, though. Over the Pennines to Cumbria there's Kendal mint cake, which is also a sweet, though claims of its being the staff of life, owing to its instant energy-giving properties, have been made by climbers who reckon that a piece has given them the extra energy needed to reach the summit. Needlesss to say, Lancashire parkin tastes and looks very different to the Yorkshire version, but is equally delicious.

Cumberland figures a lot in recipes - we've had the ham, which doesn't have to be from a pig. You can also get lambs' ham from the hardy Herdwick sheep, or is it mutton bacon? The end result is smoked 'macon', and it's available from Ashdown Smokers, Skilleran Farm, Corney (065 78 324). Try these with Cumberland sauce, a redcurrant, port and orange sauce which also brings out the best in game. There's Cumberland Rum Butter for your Christmas pudding, available from Calthwaite Dairy Products, Penrith (070 885 292/3). And if you've a really sweet tooth, try Cumberland Rum Nicky. The rum must have come to the region via trade with the West Indies, for it figures largely in local cooking. Nicky is a sweet, sticky pie of dates, sugar, rum butter and ginger baked in a short crust, with more rum poured over the hot pie when serving. From dates to figs, and in Lancashire, fig pie is still a tradition for Mothering Sunday, except in Bury where they offer simnel cake. Also sweet, sticky and fruity are Eccles cakes, round puff pastry pockets of fruit with 3 slashes on the top and a shiny sugar crust. Grasmere's gingerbread is reckoned to have been some of the first produced and sold, at Sarah Nelson's shop, still there today.

Local drinks include Lindisfarne mead, and beers aplenty.

VINEYARDS

South Yorkshire
Graiselound (1 acre)
Haxey, Nr Doncaster

HISTORIC HOUSES OPEN TO THE PUBLIC

Cheshire
Capesthorne, Congleton
Dunham Massey, Altrincham
Peover Hall, Knutsford
Tatton Park, Knutsford

Cumbria
Holker Hall, Cark
Levens Hall, Kendal
Muncaster Castle, Ravenglass
Sizergh Castle, Kendal

Humberside
Burton Agnes Hall, Burton Agnes
Burton Constable, Burton Constable
Sledmere House, Great Driffield

Lancashire
Hoghton Tower, Preston

Northumberland
Alnwick Castle, Alnwick
Bamburgh Castle, Nr Alnwick
Callaly Castle, Whittingham
Cragside House, Rothbury
Wallington Hall, Nr Morpeth

North Yorkshire
Beningbrough Hall, Nr York
Carlton Towers, Goole
Castle Howard, Nr York
Newby Hall, Nr Ripon

West Yorkshire
Bramham Park, Nr Wetherby
Harewood House, Nr Harrogate
Nostell Priory, Nr Wakefield
Temple Newsam, Nr Leeds

South of England

Just as we have dealt with the North in one block so it seems fair to do the same with the South, thus encompassing the Isle of Wight, Hampshire, Surrey, East & West Sussex and Kent. Here is a land of gently rolling hills, downs and weald, rich pasture lands altogether softer and warmer than the Celtic regions. However, we still have the sea and its riches, and Whitstable rivals Colchester in Essex for its reputation with oysters. Kent has Dover, Dover has soles; and all manner of crustaceans are put into a Whitstable Dredgerman's breakfast. I wonder if this is for the same chap who wields a plough by lunch time?

Rich pasture means good meat, and spring lamb from a beast that has grazed on the salty Romney Marshes is quite delicious. Firm and fat, too, are the pigs that have fed on acorns or windfall apples; and haslet, a kind of faggot mixture of chopped-up pork offal, seasoning and crumbs, baked in a loaf shape and then sliced, is said by some to have originated in Hampshire. The New Forest has herds of deer, mostly fallow and roe but occasionally imported red deer from Exmoor or the Japanese sika, so it's a good place to go for local venison.

However, the produce for which the area is mostly famous is that from the Garden of England, or should we say market garden, and it is particularly in warm and sheltered Kent that fruit flourishes. Several varieties of cherry, for example, from the ultra sweet to the mouth-puckeringly sour, are still grown, and it is one area where to eat roast duck with a cherry sauce seems quite acceptable. Cherries also go into a batter pudding not unlike the clafoutis of the French Limousin; and into cherry brandy. So rich is the soil that most hard and soft fruits do well here, and the area is littered with 'pick your own' signs. Cobnuts and filberts herald the onset of autumn, and it is in September that the great Kentish hop harvest begins and the oast houses, which make the landscape so distinctive, come into their own.

From the oast houses too come oastcakes, small, flat currant cakes, fried and served hot. Huffkins, small yeasted buns, were traditionally made for the conclusion of the hop harvest; and at the same time would be eaten sticky gingerbread, now made at Michelham Priory in Sussex. Another cake that's a variation on a countrywide theme is flead cake, flead being a lardy by-product of the pig butchery trade, so that the end result is, to all intents and purposes, a lardy cake. And they also seem to go for really heavy puddings with plenty of suet, either savoury (Ashdown Patridge Pudding, Kentish Chicken Pudding) or sweet, as in the Sussex Pond Pudding, which is a suet encasement for plenty of butter and sugar and a whole well-pricked lemon. Steamed in the usual way, when it is cut open out flows a pond of buttery, sugary lemony delight.

In contrast, though, imagine a delicate, light, chilled watercress soup; for Hampshire is home to several acres of watercress, grown in man-made stone beds alongside the River Test,

179

and fed by artesian springs from it. It's now available all the year round but its sharp taste is still most appreciated in the summer.

Nowadays, however, a serious contender for southern acreage is the vine. There are nearly a thousand vineyards in the UK now, of which about a hundred open their doors to the public. Not surprisingly, a good proportion of these are in the warmer, gentler South; and a selection of them is given below.

VINEYARDS

East Sussex

Berwick Glebe (2 acres)
Nr Polgate

Breaky Bottom (4 acres)
Northease, Nr Lewes

Carr Taylor (21 acres)
Westfield, Nr Hastings

English Wine Centre (1 acre)
Drusillas Corner, Alfriston

Five Chimneys (5 acres)
Hadlow Down, Uckfield

Flexerne (5 acres)
Newick

Nortons Farm (½ acre)
Sedlescombe, Nr Battle

Pine Ridge & Organic Wine Centre
 (7 acres)
Staplecross, Robertsbridge
St George's (20 acres)
Waldron, Heathfield

Swiftsden House (3 acres)
Hurst Green

Hampshire

Aldermoor Vineyards (5 acres)
Picket Hill, Ringwood

Beaulieu (6 acres)

Biddenden (18 acres)
Nr Ashford

Chiddingstone (6 acres)
Nr Edenbridge

Conghurst (½ acre)
Hawkhurst

Elham Valley (3 acres)
Breach, Nr Barham

Harbledown & Chaucer Vineyards
(2 acres)
Nr Canterbury

Harbourne (2 acres)
High Halden, Nr Tenterden

Ightham (3 acres)
Ivy Hatch, Nr Sevenoaks

Lamberhurst (48 acres)
Nr Tunbridge Wells

Leeds Castle (2 acres)
Maidstone

Penshurst (12 acres)
Penshurst

St Nicholas of Ash (2 acres)
Ash, Nr Canterbury

Staple (7 acres)
Nr Canterbury

Tenterden (12 acres)
Small Hythe, Tenterden

Three Corners (1 acre)
Woodnesborough

West Sussex

Bookers (5 acres)
Bolney

Chanctonbury Vineyard (3 acres)
Steyning

Chilsdown (10 acres)
Singleton, Nr Chichester

Ditchling (5 acres)
Hassocks

Downers (7 acres)
Fulking, Henfield

Hooksway (3 acres)
Midhurst

Lyminster (1 acres)
Nr Arundel

Nutbourne Manor (14 acres)
Nr Pulborough

Rock Lodge (4 acres) Scaynes Hill

Seymours (2 acres)
Horsham

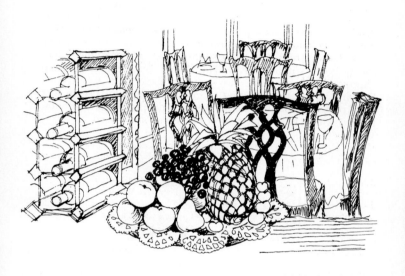

HISTORIC HOUSES OPEN TO THE PUBLIC

East Sussex
Bateman's, Burwash
Firle Place, Lewes
Glynde Place, Lewes
Great Dixter, Northam

Hampshire
Beaulieu Abbey & Palace House, Beaulieu
Broadlands, Romsey
Mottisfont Abbey, Romsey
Stratfield Saye House, Nr Basingstoke
The Vyne, Nr Basingstoke

Kent
Hever Castle, Nr Edenbridge
Knole, Sevenoaks
Ightham Mote, Ivy Hatch
Leeds Castle, Nr Maidstone
Penshurst Place, Penhurst
Quebec House, Nr Edenbridge
Squerryes Court, Nr Westerham

Surrey
Clandon Park, West Clandon
Polesden Lacy, Nr Dorking

West Sussex
Arundel Castle, Arundel
Goodwood House, Chichester
Parham, Nr Pulborough
Petworth House, Petworth
Uppark, Nr Petersfield

181

South West

The South West, a peninsula comprising Cornwall, Devon, Somerset, Avon and Dorset, thrives on agriculture and tourism; and if one can be sold to the other, then so much the better. Indeed, the often-favoured holiday county of Cornwall is almost an island in itself, thanks to the River Tamar being a natural boundary to Devon. You'd be hard pressed to get into the Duchy at all other than by crossing water!

The West is a land of contrasts, stark moorlands of granite or sandstone, soft coastal plains, market towns, valleys sweeping down to wetlands. But common denominators are water (salt or fresh) to nurture fish, and grass to provide (via cows) the cream for everyone's holiday treat, The Cream Tea. Cream Teas can happen anywhere now, but surely originated in this toe of England where the clowting or clotting of surplus cream lent itself perfectly to being piled on top of meltingly warm scones, topped with a glistening gem of preserved strawberry.

Take the fundament of it all: a scone. Plain scone for preference, those with raisins "bain't proper". In fact, even the humble scone can be called into question, some saying it only belongs in Scotland. In Cornwall, the true bun is called a split; in Devon, a chudleigh, but in either place it's a small yeasted bun, gently pulled apart to allow for loading. Regular scones, by contrast, are of course raised with soda and buttermilk, not yeast.

There's even a controversy about the order in which you assemble your tea: either opt for cream next to the bun with the fruity jam on top, or vice versa.

Once you've recovered from tea, which will be supplemented in Bath by Sally Lunns and Bath buns; in Dorset by apple cake and Dorset knobs - buy these from the Goldencap Biscuit Bakery, Morecomblelake, Bridport (029 789 253); in Cornwall by fairings - biscuits - and saffron cake, most people will think of fish, and indeed this industry does much to keep the economy of the area afloat.

Nothing can beat mackerel, fresh from the boat, best served with a sauce of gooseberries to cut the oiliness of the fish. In fact, it's so essential to eat mackerel as fresh as possible that at one time it was the only fish permitted to be sold on the streets of London on a Sunday, for fear it would not keep another day till Monday's trading. The alternative is to smoke them either by a cold or a hot process. Simply served with mustard or horserad-ish - just like a good roast of beef - and plenty of coarse brown bread, these fish take some beating. Buy your mackerel at the Cornish Smoked Fish Company, Charlestown, St Austell (0726 72356).

Cousins of mackerel, the pilchards, find their way into another Cornish offering, Stargazey Pie. In this fish pie, whole fish stand tail to tail in a circular pie dish, their heads sticking upwards and outwards through the pastry, gazing at the stars. Or is it that the whole dish resembles a star? Take your pick! An oil sac located behind the fish's head gradually releases its goodness down-wards when heated, keeping the pie's filling moist and juicy. Others worth taking advantage of before they go to the city markets are crab and red mullet.

You can't leave Cornwall without the ultimate pastry offering - the pasty. Pronounced "Parstee" by some, "Tiggy Oggy" by others, it originated as a mixture of meat, potatoes and other root vegetables, encased in pastry, seam up or on the side; and the point of the pastry was merely to keep the filling clean. Hot pasties were taken down tin mines, and held by unwashed hands while being eaten at noon. The owner's initials would be baked in to one corner of the pastry parcel. He would start eating at the opposite corner and if he had to put his meal down, this ensured he picked up the right one.

Somerset's culinary claims to fame include being the source of Cheddar cheese, and producing tremendous apple harvests. The little village of Cheddar has caved in under the pressure from its competitors, and is no longer the best place to buy Cheddar cheese, but not far away is the Chewton Cheese Dairy, at Priory Farm, Chewton Mendip, near Bath (076 121 666). Another good source is Grant's of Somerset, who are keeping alive the tradition of the distinctive tang of a well-matured wheel or truckle.

The cider maker's art has long been recognised, and true scrumpy is a million times removed from the fizzy stuff you get in supermarkets. The potency is deceptive in this innocent-tasting quencher. And of course, you don't only get cider in a mug. If your pig has fed in the orchard on windfalls, what better medium in which to poach him than cider gravy? Derivatives of cider are coming along nicely, too. There's something called Tarka made in Devon's Otter Valley, an intensified cider drunk like a liqueur, but in the race to produce a British version of calvados, it's rumoured that Bulmer's of Herefordshire are in the lead. The Dartington Cider Press Centre is at Shinners Bridge, Dartington (0803 864171). And we'd better not forget Plymouth Dry Gin, nor that great wine shipper, Harvey's of Bristol. The monks of Buckfast Abbey still keep bees and thus produce mead as well as tonic wine; and there's another Honey Farm at South Molton in Devon.

In Dorset, the culinary trail leads to a rare Blue Vinny, or blue veined cheese. A naturally occurring mould is preferable to an injected culture, but it takes a real expert to tell Blue Vinny from Dorset Blue. The experts are to be found in Winterbourne Abbas. As well as a great cheese, the South West has a great biscuit to support it in the form of Bath Olivers, named after Dr Oliver from Bath.

If you need a walk to get some exercise after all this eating, try Exmoor. But I bet you'll simply work up another appetite! And then it's down to the southernmost entrance to the national park, to the village of Dulverton, where at Balsom's in Bank Square you can buy Exmoor fudge and Dulverton heavy cake, a fruity cake lighter than the name implies, just as a change from cream teas!

VINEYARDS

Avon
Avonwood (1 acre)
Seawalls Road, Sneyd Park, Bristol

Devon
Beenleigh Manor (1 acre)
Harbertonford, Totnes

Capton (½ acre)
Nr Dartmouth

Highfield (1 acre)
Long Drag, Tiverton

Loddiswell (4 acres)
Kingsbridge, Devon

Whitmore House (2 acres)
Ashill, Cullompton

Whitstone (1 acre)
Bovey Tracey, Nr Newton Abbot

Yearlstone (2 acres)
Chilton, Bickleigh, Nr Tiverton

Dorset
Kings Green (2 acres)
Bourton, Gillingham

Somerset

Brympton d'Evercy (1 acre)
Yeovil

Castle Cary (4 acres)
Honeywick House, Castle Cary

Coxley (4 acres)
Church Farm, Coxley, Nr Wells

HRH Vineyard (8 acres)
Curload, Stoke St Gregory, Nr
Taunton

Pilton Manor (6 acres)
Shepton Mallet

Spring Farm (12 acres)
Moorlynch, Bridgwater

Staplecombe (4 acres)
Staplegrove, Nr Taunton

Whatley (4 acres)
Nr Frome

Wootton (6 acres)
North Wootton, Shepton Mallet

Wraxall (5 acres)
Shepton Mallet

HISTORIC HOUSES OPEN TO THE PUBLIC

Avon
Badminton House, Badminton
Clevedon Court, Clevedon
Dodington House, Nr Chipping
Sodbury
Dyrham Park, Nr Bath

Cornwall
Antony House, Torpoint
Cotehele House, Nr Calstock
Lanhydrock, Nr Bodmin
St Michael's Mount, Nr Marazion
Trerice, Nr Newquay
Trewithen, Nr Probus

Devon
Bradley Manor, Nr Newton Abbot
Castle Drogo, Nr Chagford
Compton Castle, Nr Paignton
Knightshayes Court, Tiverton
Powderham Castle, Nr Exeter
Saltram House, Nr Plympton
Ugbrooke, Nr Exeter

Dorset
Forde Abbey, Nr Chard
Sherborne Castle, Sherborne

Somerset
Brympton d'Evercy, Nr Yeovil
Dunster Castle, Dunster
Hatch Court, Nr Taunton
Lytes Cary Manor, Nr Ilchester
Montacute House, Montacute

■■■■■■■■■ AVON ■■■■■

Clos du Roy   Bath

7 Edgar Buildings, George Street, Bath BA1 2EH   £40
(0225) 64356

worth a visit for the creativity and dedication

Closed: Sun + Mon; 2 weeks Jan/Feb; 1 week Aug
Last
Orders: lunch (2.00pm); dinner by arrangement

Don't be put off by the appearance: the entrance is shared with a
dentist's surgery, but Philippe in his compact kitchen turns his
hand to some exquisitely prepared dishes; and the use of herbs
and flowers including sweet marjoram, purple basil, thyme,
catmint and hyssop is itself worth the visit. A simple room seats
30. The tablecloths are pink, the paintings on the wall are for
sale, and the very simple décor is in French country style. The
surroundings are perhaps simple for the standard of the food,
but the charming service and the art on the plate make this
unimportant.

I am not a 'flowers with everything' man but as Philippe
explains on the front of the menu, they prepare dishes in the way
they feel they should be served - and it really does work,
especially the salads with courgette flowers.

The Hole in the Wall   Bath

16 George Street, Bath BA1 2EN   £50
(0225) 25242/3

Closed: lunch (Sun)
Last
Orders: lunch (2.00pm); dinner (10.00pm)

John and Christine Cunliffe with their young team are determined to build up The Hole in the Wall in their own style, and
have considerable changes in hand at the present time which
should come to fruition by the summer of 1987. Knowing John
Cunliffe's capabilities in a different type of catering, I feel sure
that The Hole in the Wall is going to be well worth a visit.

Oakhill House   **Bath**

Oakhill, Bath BA3 5AQ
(0749) 840180

Closed: lunch (Sat + Mon); dinner (Sun + Mon)
Last
Orders: lunch (1.45pm); dinner (10.00pm)

Oakhill House is run by the Long family, late of the Count House
in Cornwall. Ian bustles around at the front of house, Ann
competently cooks in the kitchen and Suzanne works between
the two. They call themselves a residential restaurant; at the
moment there are only 4 rooms, but they are hoping to add some
more. Simply decorated and all with bathroom, these manage to
create a farmhouse atmosphere in this Georgian building situated in some 4 acres of parkland.

The menus offer the best of home/farmhouse cooking. You
might, on the excellently priced £7.25-a-head luncheon menu, be
offered a parsnip and gooseberry soup followed by home-spiced
salt beef cooked in red wine, or a sautéed escalope of veal
glazed with a clear redcurrant sauce. A good selection of
vegetables, excellent desserts from the sideboard, and coffee are
all included. Other à la carte dinner menus could have carrot and
coriander soup, some sliced salmon with a strawberry dressing
followed by roast quails flavoured with herbs and served with
spiced plums, or a trimmed boned best end of English lamb
cooked in a pastry parcel and served with red and yellow pepper
purées. Again, good sticky puds for desserts might include
home-made trifle, a rich chocolate mousse served on a bed of
chopped pineapple, or a raspberry meringue tart. The housewine, of good quaility, is £4.45 a bottle, and the whole family
does its utmost to make sure you have an enjoyable stay.

I wish them lots of luck with their new venture.

Popjoy's Restaurant   Bath

Sawclose, Bath BA1 1EU
(0225) 60494

Closed: lunch (daily); dinner (Sun + Mon)
Last
Orders: dinner (10.30pm)

check, this may have changed hands

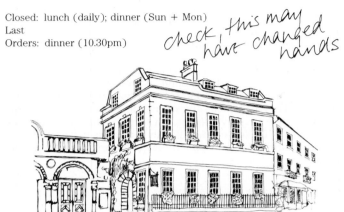

From the time you ring the doorbell you feel as if you're entering someone's home and indeed in a way you are. Popjoy's is situated in a beautiful Georgian house next to the Theatre Royal in Bath, and was built for Beau Nash and his mistress, Juliana Popjoy, in 1720. Chef patron Alison Golden, the current owner, has restored the house to its original colours. Alison offers exceptional value at around £15.00 for a set menu of 3 courses. Try the miniature steak tartare on a garlic croûte with mustard mayonnaise and a quail's egg, or if you're there in the summer maybe a summer mosaic of aubergine, sweet peppers and fennel set in a tomato coulis with a dill dressing. She selects the fish daily and will tell you what they have available on the day of your visit. You might try a fillet of Welsh lamb cooked pink and served in a sherry, honey and thyme scented gravy, or perhaps a fillet of Scotch beef with a duxelles of mushrooms and bone marrow on a madeira sauce. These come with good crisp vegetables. An interesting Lapsang Souchong sorbet, or a wild strawberry ice-cream are available out of 6 or 7 dessert choices. Unpasteurised English farm cheese from Hinton Bank farm at Whitchurch is served, of course, with Bath Olivers. Housewines, by E. Loron et Fils, are very good value at £6.50 a bottle, and I like the idea of classifying wines, as on Popjoy's list, by their taste, so that you know if a wine is going to be dry; dry and ripe; dry and full-bodied; classic; fruity, flowery and aromatic etc.

The beautifully decorated drawing room where you take your drinks leads to the restaurant itself, where the dining room is a delight with its softly candlelit atmosphere and good accoutrements. The place has style and is worth dressing up for. Dishes may not be exactly the same as I have described, when you visit, but you won't be disappointed with the selection that you're offered.

The Priory   Bath

Weston Road, Bath BA1 2XT   £45
(0225) 331922

Closed: 2 weeks Jan
Last
Orders: lunch (2.00pm); dinner (9.15pm)

The Priory has a wonderful garden at the rear of the building,
and perhaps the view from the garden looking at the back of the
house is rather more pleasant than the somewhat austere
frontage, which to my mind looks rather nicer at night with the
clever lighting that has been installed. Inside there was a
friendly, warm welcome from reception, and Jack the porter,
who pops up everywhere, showed us all the gadgets in the
well-appointed and spacious bedroom, as well as helping us with
our cases.

There are two dining rooms, both candlelit, and we were lucky
enough to be eating in the first one which has polished tables
and simple white lace covers, and is served by waitresses in long
skirts. The décor is unpretentious, with good furniture and
antiques but still uncluttered and not over-flowery, giving the
house a warm, homely feel, but with a quiet professional air
permeating the whole occasion. Competently cooked food was
presented in the English country house style. In all, a very
enjoyable experience in a country house on the edge of town.

The Royal Crescent Hotel   Bath

16 Royal Crescent, Bath BA1 2LS   £60
(0225) 319090

Last
Orders: lunch (2.00pm); dinner (9.30pm)

This superb hotel is always a joy to visit. Situated in the middle
of the Royal Crescent, it has some exceptionally well-designed,
even unique rooms and suites, as well as elegant public rooms
and hallways. Great care has been taken everywhere to transport one back to the time of opulence that was Bath in its
heyday. John Tamm of The Royal Crescent has been able to
restore sympathetically, as well as add some very clever extensions to this now world-famous hotel. If 'extensions' sounds
modern I must apologise, for the Pavilion, which is situated at
the rear of the hotel in the garden, is a very clever conversion of

a beautiful Georgian house. There is an exceptionally good conference facility at the Dower House, again situated in the gardens, which can take conferences for up to 60 delegates and feed them in a self-contained building.

The restaurant in The Royal Crescent has been well thought out in sympathy with the rest of the hotel, and the furnishings are elegant and antique. You might try rabbit and leek boudin, baby leek terrine accompanied by a rabbit sausage and served with a sabayon sauce, or a light mousseline of sole filled with ragoût of shellfish in a lobster butter sauce. To follow, perhaps try slivers of sea bass steamed in white wine with a crisp julienne of spring vegetables, or wild roast pigeon with turnips and mushrooms in a wine sauce. One of their specialities is a daily changing soufflé, and, as they explain on the menu, it's inevitable that there will be some delay whilst this is cooked, so while you wait why not try their excellent selection of cheeses or a warm goats' cheese salad. Keen and well-informed young staff in the restaurant, as in the rest of the hotel, make this a very special place.

THE ROYAL CRESCENT HOTEL

Bistro Twenty One   Bristol

21 Cotham Road South, Kingsdown, Bristol BS6 5TZ   £25
(0272) 421744

Closed: lunch (daily); dinner (Sun + Mon); Aug;
              10 days Christmas; 10 days Easter
Last
Orders: dinner (10.30-ish)

This small, always busy bistro which has been around for about 6 years is situated in a row of shops housing, amongst others, the Cotham Porter Stores. It's right in the heart of university and bedsit land. An exceptionally reasonably priced menu make it a favourite with university and local people, who know good value when they see it, but also attracts others from further afield. Small rooms with everyone sitting on top of one another, a fantastic buzz, smiling staff - all of which makes for a normal bistro atmosphere! Simple cream walls, posters, mirrors, and candlelit tables add to it. There's an excellent guineafowl and sweetbread terrine, the much recommended provençale fish soup with aïoli and rouille, and a gratin of seafood with monkfish, scallops, crabs and prawns. There is a choice of some 10 main courses, at least 3 or 4 of them fish, including Wye salmon in pastry with currants and ginger, served for 2 people, perhaps some osso buco, or noisettes of pork dijonnaise. They've got Chewton Mendip Cheddar, a good crème brûlée, a walnut and treacle tart, and from a list of some 60 wines they have a selection of around 20 half bottles. Good food, good wine, zippy atmosphere, no need to dress up, and amongst one or two chefs you might find Stephen and Penny Ross from Homewood Park, on a rare night off, enjoying the honesty of the cooking.

Six doors down is another friendly bistro, called Gorney's.

Harvey's Restaurant   Bristol

12 Denmark Street, Bristol BS1 5DQ

(0272) 277665

£40

Closed: lunch (Sat + Sun); dinner (Sun); Bank Holidays

Last

Orders: lunch (2.15pm); dinner (11.15pm)

Harvey's has to go in this guide if only for its wine list! There's something fascinating about eating and drinking in a setting such as this. Set in one of the oldest cellars of this historic city, the site belonged originally to the Monastery of St Augustine. It's interesting to think that some of the wine you are now drinking might have been bottled in these very cellars. You might prefer to stick to simpler grills from the menu and then follow it with the cheese selection, but do indulge yourself in the truly amazing wine list. Whilst Joseph Berkmann won't agree with my fascination with vintages that date back to 1917, it certainly adds interest to a list to have red Burgundies that go back to 1934 with a Chambolle Musigny Les Charmes, domaine bottled. There's a good selection from the Loire, and the Rhône of course, as well as their famed sherries which are still, like the rest of their wines, very reasonably priced.

191

Les Semailles Bristol

9 Druid Hill, Stoke Bishop, Bristol BS9 1EW
(0272) 686456

Closed: Sun + Mon; Bank Holidays;
1 week Christmas/New Year; 2 weeks Jul
Last
Orders: lunch (2.00pm); dinner (10.00pm)

Despite hundreds of eating places, Bristol has very few notable restaurants, and René Gaté stands out for his food in sleepy Stoke Bishop, one of the wealthier suburbs of Bristol. The simple exterior of his restaurant, situated in a row of shops next to Bolloms the cleaners, leaves you wondering slightly what to expect. Even the inside has a minimum of décor. Well, you'll forget all that when the extremely hard-working and competent Mrs Jillian Gaté gives you the menu, and - not unexpectedly - a very French wine list to study.

Excellent little nibbles are offered which might include a boudin blanc and tiny little individual pizzas. The food is in the modern/nouvelle French style and René Gaté turns out some exceptional dishes. He changes his menus with the season, manages to grow his own herbs in a little garden at the rear of the premises, and has a selection of daily specialities which are available according to the market. His symphonie d'été, a colourful array of summer vegetables served on a strawberry coulis, is excellent, as is the trio of miniature salads - crab, asparagus and French beans tossed in a delicate dressing. Main courses are interesting - squab steamed in seaweed to enhance the flavour, with the natural juices laced into a langoustine coulis, or perhaps a rognon de veau en croûte de sel (milk-fed calves' kidneys baked in a salt crust to retain their silky texture) served on a bed of leeks in a port sauce. A particularly unusual pudding is sabayon glacé aux pointes d'asperges confites - a surprising mixture of asparagus and melon served in melon sauce, or perhaps try the dessert which René describes as being "as light as a cloud - a hot orange soufflé sprinkled with Cointreau". This team is dedicated and obviously works exceptionally hard. I hope Bristolians will appreciate the dedication and sheer effort that goes into producing dishes to which a simple written explanation cannot do justice, and that people from further afield who appreciate nouvelle cuisine will make the journey.

Ston Easton Park Ston Easton

Ston Easton, Near Bath BA3 4DF
(076 121) 631

Last
Orders: lunch (2.00pm); dinner (9.30pm; 10.00pm Fri + Sat)

To the mere mortal, Ston Easton Park can be a little daunting. It is a huge, listed, Palladian mansion set in acres of its own parkland, and there are 20 bedrooms, all decorated in 18th-Century style. Some rooms have Heppelwhite or Chippendale 4-posters, although all modern facilities are provided. The lounges and the public rooms are certainly of stately home proportions. The furnishings are equally impressive in these huge rooms, with ornately corniced ceilings, and some splendid paintings and antiques. The room that used to be the old parlour, and is now the dining room - a warmer, smaller room of more homely proportions - is decorated in soft colours.

From the menu, try the hot timbale of pike and prawns with lobster and dill cream, or a fillet of lamb roasted in a pastry crust and served with redcurrants; or an unusual charcoal grilled breast of duckling with apple and sage. Hot pudding might include amaretto soufflé, or perhaps a lemon and lime mousse with home-made shortbread. They offer a good value luncheon at £14.00, with a choice of 5 starters and 5 main courses. Why not pick the mousse of Scotch salmon with caviar and quails' eggs, followed perhaps by the baked supreme of chicken in vine leaves with a tarragon cream, and perhaps finish off with their tulip Ston Easton. A comprehensive wine list has some good housewines by Edward Sheldon, by the bottle, half bottle and glass. If I haven't raved quite as much about this one as I have about some of the other country houses, put it down to its not being my style of architecture, rather than any fault of the friendly and helpful front of house staff.

Thornbury Castle — Thornbury

Thornbury BS12 1HH £55
(0454) 412647/418511

Closed: 23-30 Dec
Last
Orders: lunch (2.00pm); dinner (9.30pm)

Thornbury Castle is a spectacular establishment in anyone's book. Thornbury was built by the ill-fated 3rd Duke of Buckingham in 1510, and later appropriated by Henry VIII who retained it as a Royal Demesne for 33 years, apparently staying there with Anne Boleyn. The larger part of the castle still remains, with well-tended vineyards, pleasant, lawned gardens and a grand, but tranquil, air. There are some lovely views towards the River Severn, and the main apartments have been converted to give 12 excellent bedrooms, all with their own individual style, looking out over the inner courtyard or the walled gardens. If you ever wanted an example of a castle that has been made homely, this is it. The library, with views out onto the walled garden, is a lovely room in which they serve drinks before dinner. They have enlarged the dining room a little by changing its layout, which now consists of an octagonal room under the original towers, and a smaller, more intimate room to its left, as you enter from the hall.

I have visited Thornbury Castle many times over recent years, and I am sure that Kenneth Bell, who was the man responsible for altering the premises and building the reputation of Thornbury Castle, would be pleased to know that the new owners, Maurice and Carol Taylor, have not only built on the reputation which he gained, but are in fact, improving the range of dishes from the kitchen - they must have one of the best selections of British cheeses I have seen available anywhere in the country!

Amongst the 6 or so starters, you might be offered fillet of monkfish grilled with orange and tomato, cream of wild mushroom soup, or a devilled crab. From the 6 or so main courses, try perhaps a Cornish lobster baked in herb butter, breast of partridge cooked with port and tarragon, or a fillet of brill cooked in white wine with Meaux mustard. The daily plats du jour offer a choice of 2 starters, which might include a terrine of calves' liver with pistachio nuts, and for the main course, a paupiette of veal filled with apricot and basil. For desserts there could be a parfait of 2 chocolates, delicious, hot butterscotch pudding, or perhaps a lemon tart with Cornish clotted cream. There is an à la carte menu, a fixed price menu and a special menu for Sundays.

The selection of farmhouse cheese is superb, and ranges from Caerphilly (from the Walnut Tree Farm, Wedmore), to Cashel Blue, a soft, creamy blue cheese from Ireland. There is a Capricorn goat cheese from Crewkerne in Somerset, Single Gloucester from John Crisps Farm, Newent, a Barac from Carrol Neilson's Windyknowe Farm which is in Dumfriesshire, and an excellent Blue Vinny from Kingston Farm in Dorchester.

There are some amazing bargains on the wine list for under £10.00, some excellent dessert wines by the half bottle, and a very good Californian selection. There is also probably the largest range of Spanish wines I've seen in a country house hotel, as well as excellent Bordeaux at the middle to upper end of the market.

The staff is enthusiastic and pleased to serve you, making Thornbury altogether a very splendid place to stay.

■■■■ BEDFORDSHIRE ■■■■

Flitwick Manor   Flitwick

Church Road, Flitwick MK45 1AE
(0525) 712242

Closed: Christmas Day; Boxing Day
Last
Orders: lunch (2.00pm); dinner (9.30pm)

As owner and chef Somerset Moore says, "This rural yet sybaritic peace is only 40 miles north of Hyde Park Corner," and that makes it perfect for an accessible retreat at any time. Mr Moore and his wife have converted this late 17th- to early 18th-Century manor house into a very comfortable small hotel, which by June 1987 should have some 16 charming bedrooms. The rooms themselves are delightful in décor, each individually done with a very natural touch, not over designed, making this a really comfortable and welcoming place to stay.

There are 2 dining rooms, the Brooks Room being in Regency style, while the Garden Room has more the feel of a conservatory, with trellis work and plants against dark green walls.

194

Menus feature fish - there is a seawater tank keeping lobsters, crab, oysters and the like, fresh until ordered. There are 3 set menus available in addition to à la carte items: one features shellfish, one is for vegetarians, and the third is a 'Year of the Tiger' menu with Chinese dishes.

Try the watercress soup, then follow it with some excellent dressed crab, and for pudding a pear tart, which is sliced pear cooked in frangipane on perfect sweet pastry. Service is friendly and attentive and the host, genial and welcoming, is in evidence to ensure his guests' well being, ably assisted by a competent young team.

The 100+ wines are all French with a few under £10.00, and the Loire and Rhône sections have some fine representation.

Somerset Moore delights in showing visitors around his house and its gardens, with herbs and vegetables, a grotto and a lake; and if you're into vintage tractors he's got some interesting ones in the stable block, which you might persuade him to show you.

Paris House   Woburn

Woburn Park MK17 9QP
(052 525) 692   £40

an unusual house in a beautiful setting

Closed: lunch (Mon); dinner (Sun + Mon)
Last
Orders: lunch (2.30pm); dinner (10.00pm)

Paris House is not terribly well signposted, but is to be found 2¼ miles from Woburn on the B528. Drive through the spectacular gates into the park, past herds of grazing deer and some beautiful oak trees, and then approach Paris House which is a delightful black and white copy of an Elizabethan manor house, built in 1910 for the Paris exhibition. The whole house in fact was shipped to Paris and then returned to this country.

The lunch menu is sensibly priced at £14.00. You might choose from feuilleté of smoked salmon served with celeriac, a ragoût de moules aux poivrons, or mousseline de volaille aux oranges. For main course, perhaps pigeonneau beaujolaise, tranche d'agneau aux tomates et basilic, or poussin rôti à la marjolaine.

Certainly few chefs have the advantage of David Chandler's view of the deer park from the windows of his kitchen attached to the main house – it presumably provides him with inspiration!

Having someone cook for you in your own stately home must be quite something, especially if he is a chef of quality; and the next best thing must surely be having a restaurant in the grounds of your home, with a chef like David Chandler to cook for you.

BERKSHIRE

The Bear at Hungerford   Hungerford

Hungerford RG17 0EL
(0488) 82512

Closed: Christmas Eve; Christmas Day; Boxing Day
Last
Orders: lunch (2.00pm); dinner (9.30pm; 10.00pm Fri + Sat)

An old horse-drawn coach at the front of this inn recalls days of
yesteryear, and the interior emphasises the point. Abundant
beams, antique furniture, old prints and log fires create a
comfortable ambience, but the facilities are those of a modern
hotel. The décor in the dining room is warm red, with polished
wooden tables and relaxing armchairs. A talented young team in
the kitchen is headed by Bruce Buchan who produces imaginative dishes in modern style using good seasonal local produce.
Unpasteurised English cheeses are displayed with their own
descriptive menu. The wine list has over 250 items from 12
countries, with an excellent showing from Provence and even a
few Swiss wines. Visiting European chefs organise gastronomic
weekends from time to time and you could combine one of these
with browsing around the local antique shops and galleries.

Ye Olde Bell Hotel   Hurley

High Street, Hurley, Near Maidenhead SL6 5LX
(062 882) 5881/4

Last
Orders: lunch (2.00pm); dinner (9.45pm)

Built in 1135 and reputedly the oldest inn in England, the Bell
was a guest house for the Benedictine monastery close by, the
magnificent Norman entrance being part of the original struc-
ture. It is very much an English inn, added to with care and
sensitivity over the years. The views from its candlelit restaurant, sometimes extended in the summer to the paved garden
area outside, are glimpsed through a rose arbour and a profusion
of country flowers. The authentically restored Mediaeval barn,
with all modern facilities tactfully hidden, provides an excellent
setting for a reception or conference.

A regular haunt for traditional Sunday lunches, the restaurant is also *the* place in the locality to dress up for, and attracts many 'return' visitors who originally visited this romantic first-nighter as honeymoon couples. It is essential to book, especially during Ascot, the Henley Regatta and the Henley Festival of Music and Arts, although it can be difficult to find in the telephone book - look under 'Y' if you're guideless! A short walk past some superb properties in the village of Hurley, including the 12th-Century church with its Norman west door, unusual bell turret and lovely Mediaeval dovecote, and you discover the Thames, just above a lock with busy waterway traffic and more beautiful walks.

The Dundas Arms   Kintbury

Station Road, Kintbury RG15 0UT
(0488) 58263

Closed: Sun + Mon; 1 week Christmas/New Year
Last
Orders: lunch (1.30pm); dinner (9.00pm)

The Dundas Arms is a country pub set in a picturesque location on the side of a canal, which generates its own old-world atmosphere. For the lucky, there are 8 tables outside. It is run by the Pipers with their son David as the chef. His menu includes simply prepared duck and chicken and other essentially British dishes. A keen interest in wine is reflected in the excellent wine list. Customers travel from a large part of the surrounding area to enjoy an ambience for which the British are traditionally famous - family hospitality and good, simple fare, in a beautiful setting. Very much a pub with accommodation, the modern wing holds six rooms each with bath or shower.

Fredrick's   Maidenhead

Shoppenhangers Road, Maidenhead SL6 2PZ   £35
(0628) 24737

Closed: lunch (Sat); Christmas
Last
Orders: lunch (2.00pm); dinner (9.45pm)

This 37-room, red-brick hotel has some very good food. The menu gives some excellent choices cooked from very good basic materials, and Chris Cleveland in the kitchen turns out some competent and well-presented dishes. There are some firm favourites on the menu, and for around £26.00 there is quite a staggering selection. From the 15 or so starters and the 15 main courses, you might perhaps pick a summer salad with hot chicken livers, or herring fillets in dill with cucumber salad, or in season some fresh asparagus. For main courses try a fillet of lamb with wild mushrooms, a casserole of lobster with sole and scallops, or perhaps escalopes of calves' liver normande. If it's available you could choose a medallion of venison served on a potato pancake with wild Berkshire cèpes. Some excellent sweets are served from the trolley; alternatively, there are home-made sorbets or a good selection of English and Continental cheeses to follow.

There are a hundred or so wines in Fredrick's Special Reserve Cellar, with some excellent ones in the middle to upper range. A very professional standard of service and care is overseen by Mr Lösel, the owner. It's a busy and successful hotel, and if you need a break from the M4 around the Maidenhead turn-off, you would have to look hard to find somewhere better.

The Copper Inn   Pangbourne

Church Road, Pangbourne   £35
(073 57) 2244

Closed: 3 days Christmas
Last
Orders: lunch (2.00pm); dinner (9.30pm)

Originally a 19th-Century coaching inn, this carefully converted small hotel has modern facilities, and is a comfortable base from which to explore the Chilterns. Chef Paul Gilmore's bill of fare offers an attractive range of dishes, with clever contrasts between traditional and modern cuisine, for instance a breast of Aylesbury duck with apple and sage mousse, roast loin of lamb with 3 servings of shallots, a poached breast of chicken with leeks, truffle and local Westbury wine, and Paul's own interpretation of steak and kidney pie.

Michel Rosso, the manager, and Paul are members of the Guilde des Fromagers, and are therefore naturally concerned about the quality of their cheeseboard, which features a superb range of English farmhouse cheeses. Try some before the tempting range of puddings.

In the comfort of the attractive dining room, hung with tapestries, you can enjoy a good-value lunch for about £10.00 a head, or have a snack in the village bar with a glass of real ale.

L'Ortolan   Shinfield

The Old Vicarage, Church Lane, Shinfield RG2 9BY   £45
(0734) 883783

Closed: lunch (Sun + Mon); dinner (Mon)
Last
Orders: lunch (2.15pm); dinner (10.15pm)

John Burton-Race has now opened L'Ortolan in the old vicarage that was previously Chez Nico. Just minutes from the M4, between Reading and Basingstoke, the 18th-Century brick built house has an impressive entrance and an attractive garden. The interior is decorated in warm shades of beige, with pale orange furniture, and is large and comfortable. There is a bright conservatory attached to the main dining room, which is a delightful spot at lunch time, and apéritifs are served in the bar.

John's cooking is complex in the modern style - a salade de caille tiède consists of a roast quail dressed on a bed of seasonal salads in a walnut vinaigrette garnished with walnuts, lardons, mushrooms and garlic croûtons topped with an egg. His fricassée de volaille fermière aux morilles is roast breast of farm chicken, the cooking juices deglazed with white wine, scented with Marc de Bourgogne, enriched with cream and spiked with morels. Presentation matches the description, and each item is carefully arranged to please the eye as much as the palate. The Emmental soufflé with Swiss chard and ham has crisp cheese on the outside, a creamy texture, and nestles on a cream sauce with strips of chard and lardons of ham. Slices of veal kidney are arranged around a small mound of fine noodles on a bed of shallot purée, with a sauce of sancerre rouge. Young, properly cooked vegetables come carefully arranged on a side plate. A parfait of chocolate is encased in a brandy snap and almond basket covered with a net of caramelised sugar which sits on a chocolate sauce dusted with chopped nuts. Good espresso coffee and petits fours complete the lunch which costs around £19.00. Dinner is around £26.00.

Christine Burton-Race supervises the dining room, and her well-trained French girls are discreet and efficient. The wine list has some interesting choices of lesser known French districts such as the Savoie and Jurançon, which are good value and worth tasting.

The Burton-Races seem to have settled down quickly in their new home, and we wish them well.

The French Horn Hotel Sonning-on-Thames

Sonning-on-Thames RG4 0TN
(0734) 692204

Last
Orders: lunch (1.30pm); dinner (9.30pm)

The French Horn is a fine 19th-Century building situated just the other side of the famous 18th-Century brick bridge in Sonning. Back across the bridge is the Sonning theatre, converted from the famous watermill. The French Horn itself has some 10 bedrooms, and you can have a drink in the traditional bar area where there are paintings on the walls by contemporary artists.

They roast their ducks over an open fire, and serve other traditional fare in a dining room which is candlelit at night and has some beautiful views out over the floodlit river. In summer they'll serve you lunch on the terrace, which gently slopes down to the river at the bottom of the garden.

199

Oakley Court Hotel   Windsor

Windsor Road, Near Windsor SL4 5NR   £55
(0628) 74141

Last
Orders: lunch (2.00pm); dinner (10.00pm)

Oakley Court is a large Victorian Gothic property, set in grounds
which reach down to the Thames, and has been decorated with
quiet elegance inside. The building and the grounds have been
used many times for various feature films, and I must admit you
feel as if you know the place even on your first visit - perhaps
this is due to the warm greeting extended by the young, friendly
front of house staff.

Murdo MacSween offers an interesting, sometimes unusual
mixture of dishes. You could try a mousse of guineafowl
encased in a Savoy cabbage leaf and served with a port wine
sauce, or piping hot beef consommé with fennel and baby
vegetables topped with a cheese soufflé as a starter. From the 7
or 8 main courses, you could choose fillet of veal topped with
foie gras and wild mushrooms in a sherry sauce, or suprême of
chicken, stuffed with a stilton and apple mousse and served
with a sage butter sauce. There is a 5-course lunch and dinner
menu; and a table d'hôte luncheon at £12.00 a head offers less
esoteric dishes, with a roast joint of the day from the trolley, or
grilled baby poussin served with white grapes and a pepper and
cream sauce. This is a good place for Sunday lunch, with some
100 wines from which to choose. Housewines are from Louis
Lussac: Côtes du Rhône or a Muscadet at £8.85.

■■■■■■■■ BUCKINGHAMSHIRE ■■■■■■■■

The Bell Inn   Aston Clinton

Aston Clinton HP22 5HP   £40
(0296) 630252

Closed: dinner (Sun + Mon); lunch (Mon; Oct - Mar)
Last
Orders: lunch (1.45pm); dinner (9.45pm)

It is rather difficult to regard The Bell Inn as an inn because it's
better known as a restaurant with rooms - 21 in all - and has had
a reputation for serving good food in this area for many years.
Run by the Harris family, the original inn houses only 5 of the 21
bedrooms, the remainder being found in a very pretty courtyard
just across the road.

Its very good wine list contains a large claret section; and the
restaurant serves some classic dishes, including the local duck,
followed by a choice from the excellent sweet trolley. To my
mind the original bar with its flagstoned floor is the nicest part
of this building. The restaurant has some well-designed garden
and floral murals, and high-backed leather settles reminiscent of
a Victorian chop house. You can select wine or a number of food
products from the Gerard Harris wine shop just across the road,
which is part of the hotel, or arrange for a reception in the white
pavilion.

In your room they give you local country walking maps and a
list of places of interest.

Pebbles   Aylesbury

Pebble Lane, Aylesbury HP20 2JH
(0296) 86622

Closed: lunch (Mon); dinner (Sun + Mon); Christmas Day;
         Boxing Day
Last
Orders: lunch (2.00pm); dinner (10.00pm; 10.30pm Fri + Sat)

Pebble Lane, Aylesbury, hides without doubt one of the best
restaurants in the area - Pebbles. Run by David and Susan
Cavalier, both protegés of Anton Mosimann, the food certainly
draws from Anton's wide repertoire of dishes, but David Cavalier is no clone. Some of his dishes are very much his own and
they are served with style, in nouvelle presentation but sizeable
portions and with great care taken over flavour and saucing.

   The vegetable terrine scented with tomato and basil, with a
light olive oil dressing, was perhaps one of the nicest I have ever
tasted, with an unusual but successful selection of vegetables,
surrounded by a variety of green herbs and tiny slivers of peeled
tomato. The tiara of salmon bound with creamed chives which
was served on a bed of sliced cucumber was equally exciting.
Choose from the 4 starters, then a couple of fish dishes which
might include medallions of monkfish served with forest
mushrooms, tomato and herbs, or wild salmon glazed under a
creamed sorrel sauce. There is always a main course vegetarian
dish with seasonal vegetables, and a choice of 4 main courses
which might include a rosette of Angus beef served with red
wine sauce and white port-caramelised shallots; or perhaps a
breast of chicken braised in a lemon and thyme bouillon, fanned
in a small puff pastry case. The cannon of lamb served with fresh
water crayfish and girolle mushrooms is excellent - the pink
meat is sliced on a plate with an arrangement around it of tiny
fresh carrots still with their green stems, a tiny pile of neat
château potatoes, a little pile of broccoli florets and a turnip
mould with a coulis of tomato inside, all served in a delicious
juice with the crayfish and girolles mushrooms mixed in the
sauce; a really first-class dish. You can follow this with a good
selection of French cheese served from a trolley, or maybe a hot
goats' cheese with a chicory and pine nut salad. Of the 4 desserts
to choose from, you might like to try the delicately rich
chocolate slice, served with home-made pistachio ice-cream and
pear sorbet. You could, instead, try the surprise menu of 6
courses at around £23.00.

   A very reasonable wine list has a good selection of half
bottles, and good housewines by the glass including a Scheurebe
1984 Biddenden Dry, an English wine. Most are at very reasonable prices.

   The setting for this experience is a cottage-style restaurant
with grey walls, pink curtains, and neutral coloured carpets, the
feature being a polished old Victorian stove in the chimney
piece, housing some home-made preserves and pears in jars. The
dining room is split in two, one side seating 16 and the other 10.
They offer you a little appetiser whilst you wait - ours was a
quenelle of salmon mousse. The service is by Susan Cavalier
assisted by pleasant waitresses. This is a find, and it's worth
going out of your way to Pebbles either for lunch or dinner.

Cliveden   Taplow

Taplow SL6 0JF
(062 86) 68561

Last
Orders: lunch (1.30pm); dinner (9.30pm)

Set in the most delightful grounds, Cliveden, the former home of the Astor family, is a grand country house. Parks and woodlands lead up to its imposing main frontage, whilst at the rear of the house an impressive terrace looks over formal lawns reaching down to the Thames.

The interior is grand, with a portrait of Nancy Astor overlooking proceedings in the Hall, lots of oversized furniture and antiques adorning the public rooms. The suites and bedrooms are beautifully decorated in the style that you would expect from such a country house. It is no surprise to learn that it is in the same hands as The Royal Crescent Hotel in Bath. Great care has been taken to enhance the building with period fittings and paintings, and the aim has been achieved with good effect. I like the idea of the clubby room next to the gentlemen's cloakroom, with its own snooker table! There are some other elegantly decorated rooms to see, especially the splendid 18th-Century rococo dining room, acquired from the Château d'Asnières near Paris by Lord Astor in 1897. This is now the breakfast room for overnight guests at Cliveden.

The room used for dinner is, by contrast, not overpowering, and a more intimate feeling has been achieved by the use of comfortable high-backed chairs, giving a cool, elegant atmosphere, with views from the windows over the terrace and beyond.

We visited Cliveden quite soon after it opened, and feel that our assessment will not do justice to the potential of the team that are running it. The general manager is The Honourable John Sinclair who, until recently, ran what is to my mind one of the best hotels in Paris - the Hotel Lancaster, and in the kitchen there is John Webber, late of Gidleigh Park and previously from The Dorchester.

CLIVEDEN

━━━ CAMBRIDGESHIRE ━━━

Meadow Farm Restaurant   Elsworth

Broad End, Elsworth CB3 8JD
(095 47) 413

Closed: lunch (by arrangement only); Sun + Mon; Christmas;
　　　 1 week spring; 3 weeks Aug
Last
Orders: dinner (9.00pm)

This pleasant farmhouse in Elsworth has a French style menu with some competent use of fish, game, local meats and vegetables. Nicolas Toke-Nichols and Leonora Cooke offer a menu priced according to your choice of main course, to include starter and dessert. Depending on the time of year, you might be offered a cotriade bretonne - a fish soup with sorrel and cream - or some Loch Fyne oysters to start, followed by fillet or haunch of fallow deer with port and juniper sauce, or their often quoted Norfolk Black turkey with chestnut, French plum and pear stuffing. If you're there in early summer you might be offered delicious spinach, dill and cheese pancakes, or a 4-seasons watercress vichysoisse. For main courses there might be parslied chicken - French corn-fed chicken with a stuffing under the skin of parsley, spices and fromage blanc, served with a sherry vinegar sauce, or perhaps some duck with green peppers on a cognac sauce. You have 5 starters and 5 main courses to choose from, plenty of puddings and a good selection of hand-made French and English farmhouse cheeses. It's remarkable value for money, so it's well worth finding your way to Meadow Farm if you're in the area. Wines are reasonably priced and, warmed by their open fire, you can have a splendid evening.

The Old Fire Engine House   Ely

25 St Mary's Street, Ely CB7 4ER
(0353) 2582

Closed: dinner (Sun); Bank Holidays; 2 weeks Christmas/New Year
Last
Orders: lunch (2.00pm); dinner (9.00pm)

Here is one place which is definitely English and, more specifically, features as many dishes as possible from the local area. You will not actually find a fire engine here now, as it was converted in 1968 from Ely Fire Station into this restaurant and gallery, but you will find paintings for sale.

Helpings are substantial and there are good English farmhouse dishes - eels stewed in white wine, pork and rabbit pie, whole pigeon in a casserole; the ham is of course home cooked, and there are favourite dishes like steak and kidney pie.

The wine list is lengthy and well thought out, and the notes are particularly informative and helpful.

Old Bridge Hotel Huntingdon

High Street, Huntingdon PE18 6TQ
(0480) 52681

Last
Orders: lunch (2.15pm); dinner (10.15pm)

This rather splendid building, which is ivy clad from top to toe, was built in the 18th Century. Inside they have tried to retain the period feeling, except in the 20 or so bedrooms where they have opted for a variety of themes. Pleasant grounds behind the hotel lead down to the river. Both hotel and restaurant are manned by friendly, helpful staff.

You might be offered for starters a winter pea soup flavoured with smoked ham, or quenelles of local pike. You might like to try some sprats for either a first course or a main course, likewise hot Brancaster mussels. Other main courses include their roast sirloin of prime North Norfolk beef which they carve in the dining room, and each evening there's a different joint available. There may also be some boned Lincolnshire duck roasted with fresh sage and onion stuffing and served with Bramley sauce.

A comprehensive wine list includes choices to suit most palates, a good selection of half bottles and a well-thought-out short list with recommendations for the month, bearing simple explanations, such as "dry white", "fruitier white", "soft light reds", or "powerful reds", and ending with "and for a treat".

The Haycock Hotel Wansford-in-England

Wansford-in-England, Near Peterborough
(0780) 782223

Last
Orders: lunch (1.30pm); dinner (9.30pm)

The Poste Hotels have some interesting properties including The Haycock. It's a 17th-Century coaching inn set in some nice grounds, with the river at the rear. There are crackling log fires in the winter, 28 bedrooms, comfortable bars, lounges and a restaurant.

CHANNEL ISLANDS

Le Nautique Restaurant   Guernsey

Quay Steps, St Peter Port, Guernsey
(0481) 21714

Closed: Sun; first 3 weeks Jan
Last
Orders: lunch (2.00pm); dinner (10.00pm)

Situated on the first and second floors of a building overlooking
the harbour, Le Nautique, which has been here for 25 years,
offers a friendly welcome and splendid views of the nautical
activity in this busy port. White walls, ships' wheels and rudders
create the atmosphere, and it will come as little surprise that the
speciality is seafood. Fish and shellfish are competently cooked;
for example the langoustine à l'ail and gratin de crabe au
cayenne are excellent. With the sun shining over the harbour
and a bottle of Provence rosé, you can imagine that you are in
the South of France. Superb lobsters are served cold, thermidor
or grilled; Dover soles meunière, Walewska or grilled; scallops
fried or bonne femme; and there are many more locally caught
items served in various ways. If fish doesn't tempt you there is
plenty of variety on the menu, and Carlo's charming staff will
look after you well.

Hotel L'Horizon   Jersey

St Brelade's Bay, Jersey
(0534) 43101

Last
Orders: lunch (2.45pm); dinner (9.45pm)

A fairly large modern hotel overlooking St Brelade's Bay,
L'Horizon has become well established as one of Jersey's best
hotels. With its excellent facilities and position it is an ideal base
from which to explore the island. All rooms have en suite
bathrooms, and, if the sea is cold, a heated pool, sauna and
solarium are available at the hotel.

There are 2 dining rooms and in the Star Grill you can have a
leisurely lunch of hors d'oeuvres, with plenty of good fresh
prawns, squid and Parma ham. Pink noisettes of lamb are served
with a slightly piquant sauce of fresh redcurrants, and a selection of perfectly cooked vegetables. There is a large choice of
charcoal grilled meats and fish, together with specialities such
as friture de poissons du Golfe or, if you prefer your fish grilled,
an assiette de fruits de mer l'Horizon. Many other dishes feature
poultry and meats. Freshly picked blackberries and rich Jersey
cream might follow, and then you can take coffee out on the
terrace, overlooking the golden beach.

Wines are not neglected - there are about 275 from most of
Europe and the New World, and Clos de la Mare which is
produced on the island. Service is professional and very competent, which is no real surprise in such prestigious surroundings.

Longueville Manor Hotel   Jersey

St Saviour, Jersey
(0534) 25501

Last
Orders: lunch (2.00pm); dinner (9.30pm)

I don't think that it would be unfair to other Jersey hoteliers to
describe Longueville Manor as the most beautiful hotel on the
island since it competes very favourably with virtually any in the
British Isles. It dates from the 13th Century and is impeccably
decorated and furnished with antiques. The bedrooms are
individually designed and offer all amenities. The oak-panelled
dining rooom is exquisite and is the perfect backdrop for the
skills of John Dicken, the talented chef who previously worked
at Hambleton Hall and with the Troisgrois brothers in Roanne.
You can choose from a small à la carte menu, or take the fixed
price menu which offers a couple of choices within courses, and
is extremely good value. The chef's proposed menu or menu
gastronomique is 6 courses and is always a good opportunity to
enjoy a perfectly balanced variety of dishes.

   The style is modern - a mousseline of sole filled with a morel
and cucumber fricassée flavoured with chive and lobster fondue, noisette of lamb crowned with a sautéed courgette and
spinach charlotte perfumed with mint, memories of Troisgros
with a suprême of salmon on a bed of home-grown sorrel. Each
dish has been carefully considered and composed and cooking
is precise.

   John has a container delivered from London once a week, full
of items that Jersey cannot provide. The hotel's garden, however, does supply herbs, fruits and vegetables. Wines are mostly
French, and vintages have been selected with the same care
shown in purchasing food. In these surroundings the prices are
not unreasonable, but having no VAT helps, of course!

   The tranquil air and opulence of Longueville make it a unique
experience and is reason in itself for a visit to Jersey.

Old Court House Inn   Jersey

St Aubin, Jersey   £30
(0534) 46433
Last
Orders: lunch (2.30pm); dinner (11.00pm)

History surrounds this famous old inn located at the harbourside of St Aubin, and more recently, those of you who watch *Bergerac* on television might recognise it as "The Royal Barge" which features in that series. Jonty Sharp with his twin sisters, Vicky and Caroline, run this excellent hostelry with its well-furnished bedrooms, restaurant and bars, all recently refurbished but maintaining the wonderful character of the building. The outside of the hotel is a blaze of colour - bright red window boxes contrast with the white building, and a pretty courtyard with tables and umbrellas overlooks the harbour.

The cocktail bar resembles the inside of a ship and the heavily beamed restaurant has polished tables and comfortable chairs in which to enjoy the superb seafood - mussels, oysters, crab and lobsters, seafood casserole or a bouillabaisse; and the fisherman's platter consisting of all imaginable cold shellfish is a speciality. Crab cocktail followed by lobster grilled with butter is perfect. Puddings are simple but just right - rich chocolate mousse or just plain strawberries. Pretty girls serve in smart pink and grey outfits, and present the menu on a wooden board. There's a good choice of wine, but jugs of sangria make a nice change. A very well run inn which is as popular with the locals as with visitors to the island, and an absolute 'must' if you are nearby. If it's good enough for Bergerac...

Aval du Creux Hotel   Sark

Sark   £25
(0481 83) 2036

Closed: Oct-Mar
Last
Orders: lunch (1.30pm); dinner (8.30pm)

This unspoilt Channel Island with no motor vehicles apart from tractors - the general mode of transport being by bicycle or horse-drawn cart - has a character of its own, reflected in the accommodation and restaurant at Aval du Creux. Run by Peter and Cheryl Tonks, a straightforward small establishment houses a good restaurant. There's good local seafood on the menu, including half a lobster, maybe preceded by half a pint of fresh Guernsey prawns served in their shells with rose mayonnaise or hot with a provençale dip, or fresh Guernsey crab served hot with a glaze of cheese in a coquille shell, which can be taken either as a starter or as a main course. Steaks are served plainly grilled or au poivre, or you can choose from a presentation tray of fresh seafood which will be prepared to your liking. There is a simple set dinner menu at around £11.00 which might include smoked trout served with Dijon mustard cream or a crispy fresh vegetable and salad appetiser, followed by half a Sark lobster dressed on a bed of salad with prawns and rose mayonnaise, or a sirloin steak chasseur. There is a fresh fruit kebab to finish, or a choice from the cheeseboard.

CHESHIRE

Crabwell Manor Hotel   Chester

Parkgate Road, Mollington, Chester CH1 6NE
(0244) 851368

Closed: please ring for details
Last
Orders: please ring for details

David Brockett has been at Chewton Glen for many years and
has done much to inspire and bring that hotel its well-deserved
international repute. He has now taken on this converted manor
house with the aim of making it one of the best in the country. It
is scheduled to open on 1 May 1987 and although at the time of
going to press we have not had the opportunity of viewing it, I
feel sure that the standards that David Brockett sets will prevail
in this establishment. It should have 9 bedrooms and 5 suites,
and the restaurant, which will seat 80, intends to serve traditional English dishes. It would be worth giving David Brockett a call
at Crabwell Manor to find out more about the style and the
opening times for what promises to be an interesting addition to
the country house hotel range.

Rookery Hall   Worleston

Worleston, Near Nantwich CW5 6DQ
(0270) 626866

Closed: 20 Jan - 15 Feb
Last
Orders: lunch (1.30pm); dinner (9.15pm)

The Marks have been at this grand house for a couple of years
now and have recently been joined by chef Clive Howe from The
Dorchester. The Georgian hall set in 28 acres of garden and
woodland looks a little like a small château, with mellowed
sandstone walls and a slate roof complete with tower. The
interior has some good antiques and furnishings and in the
beautiful, panelled dining room with its gleaming silver and
crystal, food is served in the modern English style making full
use of English and local produce. You may find carrot and
orange soup, rack of lamb baked in a salt crust, scallops steamed
in the shell with fresh ginger, all of which are taken from the
6-course menu which offers a good choice at every stage.
Cheshire sausages or lamb with laverbread sauce are also
available.

Peter Marks is particularly proud of a superb selection of English cheeses, served with home-made bread. There is an extensive wine list, and housewines begin at £12.00. Service is formal and coffee can be taken in the large drawing room.

Some of the furnishings are more contemporary than the surroundings and there is a bold green carpet which leads up to the bedrooms. These are large, comfortably and tastefully furnished - besides a hair-dryer and a trouser press you get a quarter bottle of Champagne. Rookery Hall is certainly run in the grand style and priced accordingly.

■■■■■■■ **CORNWALL** ■■■■■■■

The Count House   Botallack

Botallack, St Just TR19 7QQ
(0736) 788588

Closed: lunch (Mon - Sat); dinner (Sun + Mon)
Last
Orders: dinner (9.30pm)

The name is derived from the Accounting House of the Botallack Tin Mine Company, which was next door to the present restaurant, but became derelict long ago. In its heyday the company's Annual General Meeting was held in the Accounting House, and, following the meeting, shareholders were wined and dined in grand style, so that they left not too concerned about the company's previous year's performance! The actual restaurant used to be the carpenter's shop, and is an interesting stone building with a high beamed roof and a vast fireplace dominating one end, giving the atmosphere of an old manor house.

Arrive there early for Sunday lunch and take a walk around the old mine buildings, which have wonderful views of the sea from the most western point of England. Afterwards, back to The Count House with a keen appetite to enjoy a relaxed lunch, simply prepared from a short but varied menu.

Riverside Restaurant   Helford

Helford, Helston TR12 6JU
(032 623) 443

Closed: lunch (daily); Dec - Feb
Last
Orders: dinner (9.30pm)

beautiful & romantic setting

The Riverside at Helford comprises a cluster of picturesque white painted cottages which are rose-clad in summer and not dissimilar to a small version of Portmeirion. They overlook the Helford estuary and can be reached, when the tide is out, by a ford across the muddy waters.

The interior of the main building retains the theme of simplicity with wheel-back wooden carver chairs, coloured tablecloths, plain white walls and a few prints. A shelf over the fireplace at one end of the dining room is laden with a collection of

comforting wine bottles. Service, under the supervision of Heather Crosbie, is by young ladies who are competent and efficient and 'speak when spoken to'. The fixed price dinner menu offers 9 first courses and 9 main courses which revolve around the use of good local produce with fish to the fore - a lobster bisque, a terrine of salmon, lobster, mushrooms and herbs, fresh pasta with cream and garlic, salmon and mushroom cutlets with tartare sauce, broad beans with ham or perhaps a shellfish tart. To follow, try the local lobster with salad, Tamar salmon baked in pastry with currants and ginger, a bourride of monkfish and brill with rouille and aïöli, or sea bass baked in butter with cream and tomato sauce. The cooking is simply executed, for the ingredients are first class and need no over-elaborate treatment. Meat and poultry are similarly prepared: a leg of lamb roasted with rosemary and garlic served with pepperonata and almond potatoes, or calves' liver with avocado and herbs, or a roast Scotch ribsteak à la bretonne. The wine list is well composed with a good selection of regional wines alongside some fine claret and Burgundy.

There are some fine walks around the estuary and you may be lucky enough, as I was, to meet one of the locals who could tell you a few tales about Helston before the Customs Officers became as alert as they are today!

Mr Bistro   Mevagissey

East Quay, Mevagissey PL26 6QH
(0726) 842432

Closed: Nov - Feb
Last
Orders: lunch (2.00pm); dinner (10.00pm)

To find this type of honest, no-nonsense bistro in a tiny fishing village like Mevagissey is rare, and the fact that they can cook almost makes it unique! The bistro is housed in what used to be a bark house, which for the uninitiated is where tree bark and resin were made into a preservative for the cotton fishing nets. Locals apparently still refer to very strong tea as "like bark water". Situated right on the harbour the restaurant is small and unpretentious with wooden settles at polished wood tables with an open servery to the kitchen over which a blackboard proclaims the catch of the day. This is the lunch-time menu which very much depends on the landings by the fishing boats. At my visit there was cod, pollack and shark steak, often the choice includes squid, monkfish and the small queen scallops. To start there are moules marinières, smoked salmon pâté, seafood platter or whole prawns with garlic mayonnaise. The very good crab salad was made with the large claws from ordinary crabs and spider crabs with mayonnaise, and a lobster pick is provided so that no meat is wasted. For pudding don't resist the treacle tart - shades of childhood - which is superb, with a hint of lemon to cut the sweetness and a naughty great blob of Cornish cream...

In the evening the menu becomes slightly more serious with sauces replacing the freshly made chips of lunch time, dishes such as hot lobster grilled with butter and sherry, red mullet scored and rubbed with fennel and the popular shark steak now appearing with prawn sauce.

There is a small, reasonably priced list of wines including good quality housewine, well looked after. What more could you need?

The Abbey   Penzance

Abbey Street, Penzance TR18 4AR
(0736) 66906

Closed: lunch (daily); Jan + Feb
Last
Orders: dinner (8.00pm)

From the outside, the Abbey is a lovely building, and I can promise you that the interior is just as nice. On your left as you enter is the beautifully decorated dining room, where you'll be served simple and well-cooked meals that have made good use of fresh ingredients. You might be offered a soup, or a tapenade topped with a little goats' cheese, then for a main course perhaps a grilled lemon sole, or sole meunière served with baked red peppers, or a delicious chicken, bacon and mushroom pie. There's a choice of simple puds like plum crumble, or brown bread ice-cream or perhaps a chocolate St Emilion.

Nicely designed and comfortable bedrooms, 6 in all, are in individual styles, and there's a beautiful lounge where you can relax in soft, comfy sofas and look out of lovely big windows to the garden behind. The whole atmosphere might remind you a little of the style of Justin de Blank's Shipdham Place in Norfolk. It's a good place to hide away for a couple of days - no telephones in the rooms – useful if you simply want to be left alone to rest and regain your equilibrium, as did Dudley Winterbottom on the evening we were there. He had just finished cycling with Patrick Hughes and team from John O'Groats to Land's End.

Enzo Restaurant   Penzance

Newbridge, Penzance TR20 8QH
(0736) 63777

Closed: lunch (daily); Christmas Day; Boxing Day
Last
Orders: dinner (9.30pm; 10.30 Sat + during summer)

In an old pub-style building on the way to Botallack - or at least
that's where we were going - we found this Italian restaurant,
run by a family. It has a pretty dining room set in a conservatory,
with all manner of citrus fruits growing. It's quite continental in
that you can choose your own fish, which might consist of sea
bass or perhaps trout, which they then char-grill for you to
order. There's good home-made pasta, and Mrs Gill Mayro to
look after you in the front of house, with Vincenzo Mayro
looking after the kitchen. There are plenty of other dishes to
choose from on the all-Italian menu, with a fair range of Italian
wines at reasonable prices.

What a pleasant change to find somewhere different in this
part of the world; and Enzo's is certainly that.

Mill House Inn   Trebarwith

Trebarwith, Tintagel PL3 0HD
(0840) 770200

Closed: restaurant: lunch (daily)
Last
Orders: dinner (9.00pm)

Near the legendary birthplace of King Arthur, The Mill House Inn
is an excellent base for visiting Tintagel Castle and the rugged
north Cornish coast. Once a corn mill, this old slate inn now
offers comfortable accommodation, friendly bars and a popular
restaurant. Beams and flagstone floors remind you of the mill's
former working days, and the trout stream still flows past the
inn, though it no longer drives the old mill wheel. Bar meals are
served at lunch time, and the restaurant is open for dinner,
serving local produce in homely style. Don't miss the Port Isaac
kippers at breakfast.

Boscundle Manor   Tregrehan

Tregrehan, St. Austell PL25 3RL
(072 681) 3557

Closed: lunch; dinner (Sun) mid-Dec - mid-Feb
Last
Orders: dinner (9.30pm)

Andrew and Mary Flint gave up the excitement of an accoun-
tants' office in London for the country life and peace of
Cornwall. They bought a run-down hotel and have worked very
hard for the last 8 years to make Boscundle what it is now. They
describe it as a restaurant with rooms run like a luxurious

country house and I would happily agree with that having enjoyed their hospitality. They possess that all too rare talent of wishing to please their guests. As Mary said, "I can't stand the idea of a kettle in the bedroom - if guests want a cup of tea we make it for them." This attitude shows in everything. The house is tastefully furnished yet still feels lived in; bedrooms have teletext TV and direct dial phones and certain rooms have whirlpool baths for the adventurous. They have just completed a self-contained cottage in the grounds which has a fully equipped kitchen, but typically Mary doesn't wish the guests to have to cook. "If they want to have a cooked breakfast I go in and cook it for them." Mary also cooks for the restaurant, concentrating on local produce which she likes to cook simply without too many sauces to mask flavours. Fish features prominently on the daily menu, with crab and smoked fish amongst the first courses and sea trout, salmon or lobsters when in season. Andrew's wine list is strong in claret with some good vintages of the sixties and seventies with representation from Iberia, Germany, Italy plus the New World for variety.

Boscundle is very much home from home with the facilities of a larger hotel run by friends.

◼◼◼◼ CUMBRIA ◼◼◼◼

Rothay Manor   Ambleside

Rothay Bridge. Ambleside LA22 0EH
(0966) 33605

Closed: New Year - mid-Feb
Last
Orders: lunch (2.00pm; 1.30pm Sun); dinner (9.00pm)

This charming Regency hotel has some comfortably furnished bedrooms, many of which have beautiful views, and a long tradition of real hospitality. The restaurant uses good local produce to make up its mainly English menus, and the buffets at lunch time are fresh and impressive. Dinner consists of 5 courses: look out for the Lancashire cheeses, the sticky puddings and home-made bread, and there is a good range of wines, from some of the more unusual French regions.

Underscar Hotel Applethwaite

Applethwaite, Keswick CA12 4PH
(076 87) 72469

Closed: mid-Dec - mid-Feb
Last
Orders: dinner (8.45pm)

The Lake District abounds with houses built between 1850 and the turn of the century; and this huge house built by one William Oxley in 1860, as a country retreat, is fairly typical. Set amidst 5 acres of grounds, it enjoys a tranquil situation on the lower slopes of Skiddaw.

From the conservatory restaurant window you have magnificent views of Derwent Water and Borrowdale Fells. The public rooms have been lovingly restored in the old manner and a great deal of attention has been paid to the plaster work, and also to the comfortable chairs and sofas which seem to fill every corner. A warm atmosphere pervades the house throughout - the staff are courteous and try very hard (although it is difficult when there are only 2 in a dining room which normally seats about 40.)

The food is in the country house style, and given the opportunity of a willing audience, you feel that this is one of the places that could win through.

Farlam Hall Brampton

Brampton CA8 2NG
(069 76) 234

Closed: lunch (daily); Mon + Tue in Dec + Jan;
        Christmas; Feb; 2 weeks Nov
Last
Orders: dinner (8.00pm)

Being situated just south of Hadrian's Wall makes Farlam Hall the northernmost of the English Relais & Châteaux hotels. It is run by the Quinion family who are caring hosts and who go to great lengths to spoil you during your stay. The Hall is set in an attractive garden with an ornamental lake and fountain, and 4 mallard drakes who plod around the water's edge, as stiff and smart as uniformed sentries. Décor and furnishings are tasteful, and Mrs Quinion's collection of dolls appear in unexpected places - one sits in a cot on the landing! Barry Quinion looks after the kitchen and produces a small daily menu of local produce. Langoustines, guineafowl, quail and halibut are popular items; and the sweet trolley will put paid to any thought of a diet. From this superb location the itinerant guest has the option of exploring the lakes to the south, or making sorties over the border into the delightful Dumfries and Galloway district of Scotland.

Uplands   Cartmel

Haggs Lane, Near Grange Over Sands LA11 6HD
(044 854) 248/9

Closed: lunch (Mon); 6 weeks Jan/Feb
Last
Orders: lunch (1.00pm); dinner (8.00pm)

Tom and Diana Peter worked with John Tovey at Miller Howe for 12 years and have now opened this small country house hotel as his partner "in the Miller Howe manner". There are just 4 double bedrooms which have been prettily decorated and well furnished, and the public rooms are in pastel shades with large colourful Impressionist prints, from the Metropolitan Museum of Art in New York. There is comfortable furniture and superb views of the surrounding countryside and Morecombe Bay.

Fixed price menus are presented at lunch and dinner with the latter having a slightly larger choice. Lunch is served at 1.00pm and dinner at 8.00pm. A loaf of delicious, warm wholemeal bread is served on a board for you to cut from as you wish, and if you order soup it arrives in a steaming tureen which is left on the table for second helpings. The bread and soup are in themselves a substantial lunch! Fish, meat and game in season are well prepared and cooked with a selection of good fresh vegetables. Puddings are in the hard-to-resist category, for example blueberry pie with cream, passion fruit mousse or raspberry coffee meringue. It was a refreshing and enjoyable change to see a New Zealand Chardonnay served as housewine, and there are several other New World wines on the list which are well worth trying.

While Tom slaves over a hot stove, Diana looks after the diners with the help of friendly young waiters, and creates a comfortable and relaxed atmosphere.

White Moss House   Grasmere

Rydal Water, Grasmere LA22 9SE
(096 65) 295

Closed: lunch (daily); dinner (Sun); mid-Nov - mid-Mar
Last
Orders: dinner (8.00pm)

This charming house, built in 1730 and overlooking Rydal Water, was once owned by William Wordsworth, and looking out from the porch where he used to rest, it is easy to see how he was inspired by the local splendours. Nowadays it is a small hotel in which the Dixons and the Butterworths have created one of the best restaurants in the Lake District with a delightful atmosphere.

This is English cooking at its best, with ingredients sought locally and nationally to offer superb 5-course dinner menus. A terrine of wild Tay salmon and Dover sole with a sorrel sauce, a mushroom, marjoram and marsala soup, or a soufflé of undyed smoked haddock and hake might be followed by roast loin of lamb with rosemary and a stuffing of fennel and pistachio nuts, served with an orange, redcurrant and mint sauce, or crisply roasted Lakeland duckling with sage and onion stuffing, served with a plum, port and claret sauce. Vegetables receive the same care - mange-touts stir-fried in walnut oil, grated courgettes marinated in lemon, sweet and sour red cabbage, glazed turnips or carrots with chives.

For pudding there is a choice, but you will probably find that choice difficult - bread and butter pudding with calvados, Mrs Beeton's chocolate pudding with double Jersey cream, cabinet pudding with a sabayon sauce, prune and armagnac ice-cream, or a Sussex pond pudding (you'll have to go there to find out what that is, or turn to the South of England food notes). There is even an English cheese menu which says, "Our cheeses bear so little resemblance to the vacuum packed supermarket variety, that we are sure you will enjoy trying them." Chewton Mendip Cheddar, Cumberland farmhouse, Ribblesdale goats' cheese, Coleford blue (made from ewes' milk), Tynedale and Cornish yarg are just a few that might be offered with White Moss oat biscuits.

The wine list is a match for the food, with carefully chosen wines from good vintages bearing the names of well-known growers and well-loved châteaux. The hotel's size means that a homely atmosphere is retained, and the rooms are comfortably furnished with flowered fabrics and antiques.

The pretty terrace overlooking the lake affords a wonderful opportunity to enjoy a pre-dinner drink, and possibly recall a few lines from *Michael*, which Wordsworth wrote at Town-End, Grasmere:

> *...When day was done,*
> *And from their occupations out of doors*
> *The Son and Father were come home, even then,*
> *Their labour did not cease; unless when all*
> *Turned to the cleanly supper-board, and there,*
> *Each with a mess of pottage and skimmed milk,*
> *Sat round the basket piled with oaten cakes,*
> *And their plain home-made cheese...*

The Wordsworth Hotel   Grasmere

Grasmere, LA22 9SW
(096 65) 592

Last
Orders: dinner (9.00pm; 9.30pm Fri + Sat)

Situated in the middle of the picturesque village of Grasmere, this would make a very good place to stay if you wanted to eat at Michael's Nook but could not get into one of their bedrooms - it's owned by the same people. It has its own indoor heated swimming pool, some pleasantly decorated private rooms, and Champagne from The Ritz, which can't be bad!

The Castle Dairy Restaurant   Kendal

Kendal
(0539) 21170

Closed: lunch (daily); dinner (Sun, Mon + Tue)
Last
Orders: dinner (9.30pm)

It took a fair bit of time to find the Castle Dairy as there is no exterior sign telling you where it is, and it is situated in a one-way street. To give you a clue, it's opposite the fish and chip shop, and 2 doors down from the curry house - but don't let that put you off! It's one of the oldest, habitable, masonry-built Tudor houses in Westmorland and was part of the Kendal Castle Estate. They certainly haven't altered the frontage of the building since 1566, and even if you don't want to eat there, you can go and have a look around. You have to book in advance because the restaurant itself is tiny, with stone-flagged floors, and a huge fireplace in which there are actually a couple of tables set for 2. One other table for 6, or at a push 8, and another for 4, completes the restaurant. With the candles flickering, it's not difficult to imagine yourself back in the days of HenryVIII.

The food is English, there is no choice on the fixed price menu but it's certainly worth a visit if you're in the area. The menu will cost you about £15.00 for 7 courses - when we enquired what the 7 courses consisted of, it was pointed out that one of the courses was coffee and mints! So make up your own mind.

Leeming on Ullswater
Leeming-on-Ullswater

Leeming-on-Ullswater, Watermillock CA11 0JJ   £50
(085 36) 622

Closed: beg-Dec - mid-Mar
Last
Orders: lunch (1.45pm); dinner (8.45pm)

Across the water from the legendary Sharrow Bay, it speaks volumes for the Fitzpatrick family that Leeming has developed its own identity and following. The large, white Georgian house is immaculately furnished with comfortable armchairs, perfect for relaxing after lunch. The elegant dining room has picture windows over the grounds and cheerful, young professional staff.

Food mixes the modern and the classic - one of their starters is an avocado with a properly sharp yoghurt sauce; another might be a salmon and prawn terrine with chive dressing; a third, smoked turkey and pigeon breast with French leaves, oranges, and raspberry vinaigrette. Puddings are quite stunning and there is a large seductive display of them at the end of the dining room. Choose from chocolate brandy slice, Leeming country pie, which is packed full of fruit and served hot with fresh egg custard, strawberry mille feuilles, or lemon and passion fruit mousse.

There is a good selection of wines, properly served, and the bedrooms are spacious and well furnished. Leeming offers a good opportunity to spend a few days taking in the fabulous scenery.

The Blue Bell at Heversham   Milnthorpe

Milnthorpe LA7 7EE   £25
(044 82) 3159

Closed: Christmas Day; Boxing Day
Last
Orders: lunch (2.10pm); dinner (9.10pm)

A pretty little pub/inn slightly off the beaten track as you enter the Lake District from the south, it was formerly a vicarage and is now a useful place to break your journey. It serves adequate food with lots of smiles and enthusiasm from local ladies.

March Bank House Hotel   Scotsdyke

Scotsdyke, Via Longtown, Carlisle CA6 5XP
(0228) 791325

Closed: Nov - Mar
Last
Orders: dinner (8.30pm)

The border of England and Scotland runs right through the garden of the Grants' homely, grey stone hotel. Fellow guests may well be anglers who flock up here for the superb fishing, and after-dinner conversations in the parlour will surprise real townies. Patricia Grant and daughter Louise prepare all the food, including several home-made chutneys and jams to accompany interesting menus prepared from local ingredients, all beautifully cooked. Portions are as enormous as they need to be if you've spent 12 hours on the river, but even if you have been resting all day you will want to finish everything. Lunches are more informal, and it is best to telephone ahead. Rooms are unpretentious and peaceful - no TVs or telephones. When you are leaving, buy one of Louise's fruit cakes that will remind you of what fruit cakes should really taste like.

Bridgefield House   Spark Bridge

Spark Bridge, Near Ulverston LA12 8DA
(022 985) 239

Closed: lunch (daily)
Last
Orders: dinner (7.30pm)

There's just one sitting - 7.30pm for 8.00pm - at David and Rosemary Glister's small hotel in the southern Lake District, but it is a 6-course meal, so plenty of daytime walking is advised! The dishes are well balanced, and Rosemary includes a sorbet halfway through to revitalise the palate. Her cooking is based on good local ingredients, many of them home produced, and she creates some unusual dishes in her daily menus - for example, carrot and coriander soup, smoked Cumberland sausage with quails' eggs and apple and celery mayonnaise, gammon in cider with damson and port sauce, and puddings like soured cream and plum flan, crunchy rhubarb and cinnamon pudding or Cambridge burnt cream and grapes. David's wine list offers well over 100 bottles, more then half of which are also available in half bottles - good sense for those of us who like to vary the choice with the dishes.

This slate-roofed stone-built Victorian hotel is set in heavily wooded grounds, with fields leading down to the River Crake. It is very comfortable, unpretentious, and well located for visiting a lesser known part of the Lakes with many places of interest. A trip on the steam yacht on Coniston Water is essential!

Langdale Chase Hotel   Windermere

Windermere LA23 1LW
(0966) 32201

Closed: lunch (Sat)
Last
Orders: lunch (2.00pm); dinner (8.30pm)

Another huge, industrial magnate's house, overlooking Windermere. Extraordinary décor - a sort of a cross between a Bavarian
hunting lodge and a Victorian set for a Shakespearean play
...heavy wood panelling, carvings and tapestries in abundance.

Miller Howe   Windermere

Rayrigg Road, Windermere LA23 1EY
(096 62) 2536

Closed: lunch (daily); early Dec - mid-Mar
Last
Orders: see text

Set amongst the diplomas and awards around the walls of Miller
Howe is one from the Restaurateurs Association of Great
Britain, signed by Robert Carrier. Certainly John Tovey shares
his flair for the theatrical. Although I have never quite got used
to being audience to the 5-act play put before me, there is no
doubt that he does have a large number of devoted followers.

Dinner is served at 8.30pm except on Saturdays, when there
are sittings at 7.00pm and at 9.30pm. We seemed to have hit the
Lake District in the season of carrot and orange soup, and
followed this with halibut, accompanied by John Tovey's
yoghurt sauce, which is excellent. The main course of the 5 was
a delicious local chicken, full of flavour and surrounded with
many vegetables.

There are lovely views overlooking Lake Windermere and the
interiors of the public rooms are plush and provide a rather
1960s atmosphere in the restaurant. A lovely place to stay, and a
short walk down the hill takes you to the Steamboat Museum on
Windermere, where there are some beautiful vintage craft.

Roger's Restaurant   Windermere

4 High Street, Windermere LA23 1AF   *check as this may have changed* £25
(096 62) 4954   *hands - we'll try & keep*

Closed: lunch (by arrangement only); Sun; Christmas;   *you up to date*
        2 other 2-week periods during the year   *on the whereabouts*
Last   *of this talented*
Orders: lunch (1.30pm); dinner (9.30pm)   *chef.*

Most good dining rooms in the Lake District tend to be within
hotels, but Francis Coulson of Sharrow Bay recommended this
restaurant at the top of the High Street in Windermere. Roger
and Alena Pergl-Wilson bought a café 4 years ago, and have
created an intimate restaurant with extremely good food and

friendly service, in this busy lakeside town.

The small à la carte menu changes according to daily supplies, and Roger cooks in the classic style with a few concessions to the more modern trends. Ingredients are exceptionally good and are used to full advantage. Soups are of the bourgeois type - leek and potato with spinach which had all the vegetables visible, not puréed as is often the case these days. Other menus have French onion soup, or mushroom, and occasionally Roger's own bisque of squat lobsters. Meats are enhanced with complementary herbs or fruits, for example roast rack of lamb with rosemary and garlic, venison with port and cranberries, or breast of duck with blackcurrants. Fish might be sea bream with asparagus and chervil, turbot with prawn sauce, or an Isle of Skye lobster in the classic americaine manner. Puddings are equally tempting and well prepared, the specialities being hot almond and apricot brandy pudding with butterscotch sauce, or St Emilion with a raspberry sauce. The home-made ice-creams and sorbets are also excellent. There are around 50 well-chosen wines with something for all tastes and pockets, and good housewines.

Alena is a charming hostess who looks after her guests well and maintains order in the pretty dining room. Lunch is by prior arrangement only and dinner is busy, so do book well in advance - you'll enjoy the experience.

The Old Vicarage   Witherslack

Witherslack, Near Grange-over-Sands LA11 6RS
(044 852) 381

Closed: lunch (daily); 1 week Christmas
Last
Orders: dinner (8.00pm)

Another hotel in the country run by two couples who have deserted the rat race and entered the hotel business, The Old Vicarage has been converted gradually to develop into a pleasing and unassuming place to stay, where the bedrooms are tidily furnished and comfortable. Mr Reeve cooks the food and Mr Burrington-Brown serves it with some local help.

A set dinner is timed for 8.00pm precisely, and wines may be ordered in advance from a reasonable list. Generous portions of fairly advanced home cooking are served, and the highlight could be a perfect Queen of Puddings, enough on its own but always served with an alternative dessert, and followed by a good range of cheeses.

DERBYSHIRE

Fischer's   Bakewell

Bath Street, Bakewell DE4 1BX   £35
(062 981) 2687

Closed: lunch (Mon); dinner (Sun + Mon); 2 weeks Christmas,
         and New Year; 2 weeks Aug/Sep
Last
Orders: lunch (1.30pm); dinner (9.30pm)   *the best in the area*

There are some restaurants which immediately have a good feel
about them and somehow you are sure that you are in the right
place - Fischer's is one such restaurant. Max and Susan Fischer
bought a café in this pretty Derbyshire town some 6 years ago
and have gradually turned it into the county's best restaurant.
Max is the chef patron and Susan runs the front of house with
efficient charm.

While you sip an apéritif and look at the menu, 2 tiny kebabs
of scallop are offered, which is typical of the innovative nature
of the cooking. At lunch time a small fixed price menu is served.
Choose tomato soup with herbs followed by a seafood platter,
for example. The soup is excellent, light but full of flavour, and
in it are 3 little 'sacks' of freshly made pasta filled with spinach
and herbs - a welcome change from croûtons! The seafood
platter comprises sea bass, salmon, sole, monkfish and scallops
with plenty of small mussels, all lightly cooked with tomato and
seasonings so that each is quite distinct but the juices blend as
an unthickened sauce. It is delicious, and the accompanying
selection of well-cooked vegetables, though hardly needed, will
nevertheless be eaten. Try to leave room for a slice of tarte tartin
with a scoop of Max's home-made vanilla ice-cream - you can't
have too much of a good thing! Considering the quality and the
modest price of £9.50 its amazing that there isn't a queue to get
in.

Evenings are a lot busier and the à la carte menu contains a
larger selection of dishes which demonstrates Max's precise
cooking in terrines, or calves' sweetbreads on young vegetables,
or fresh scallops cooked with Noilly Prat. Main courses include
sea bass on tomato and ginger sauce, breast of chicken with
lobster and wild rice, tenderloin of veal with wild mushrooms or
saddle of lamb gratinée with herbs, and in season, game features
strongly.

Décor is simple, with white walls and a beamed ceiling,
attractive carpet and curtains, peach coloured linen and good
cutlery and glassware. The wine list carries no padding nor high
price tags, the vintages being well chosen and reasonably priced.
Fischer's is a delight, the sort of restaurant you wish you could
find in every town that you pass through at meal times. Perhaps
the Fischers could give lessons?

Cavendish Hotel
Baslow

Baslow, Bakewell DE4 1SP
(024 688) 2311

Last
Orders: lunch (2.00pm); dinner (10.00pm)

Situated on the Chatsworth estate, this attractive old inn has been converted into a well-run hotel by Eric Marsh. Bedrooms and public rooms are comfortably decorated, and the staff are friendly and enthusiastic. Nick Buckingham is the chef, and he produces everything freshly each day in his kitchens. A clear wild mushroom soup with noodles, cheese soufflé or fillet of beef tartare are typical starters, and amongst main courses you can choose from a light Dover sole with 2 sauces, or the more substantial dishes like braised oxtail with dumplings.

Sweets are tempting, as is the selection of cheeses with home-made walnut bread. Over 100 wines come from a good selection of producers.

Nick Buckingham offers a table for 2 actually in the kitchen itself, if you really want to be where the action is!

Riber Hall
Matlock

Matlock DE4 5JU
(0629) 2795

Last
Orders: lunch (1.30pm); dinner (9.30pm)

Salvaged from a fate similar to that of its neighbour, Riber Castle, the Hall is now a comfortable hotel with wonderful views over Derbyshire hills, making it a good starting point for exploring the Peak District. Alex Biggin is the proprietor and he runs an efficient and welcoming hostelry in this stone built Elizabethan manor house. Interesting features of the rooms are the antique 4-poster beds. Each room also has a private bathroom, some even with whirlpool baths. The heavily beamed drawing room and dining room have open fires and are furnished with antiques, while polished dining tables with sparkling silver and glassware and flickering candles revive the atmosphere of the Hall's earlier days.

In addition to the dishes on the à la carte menu, seasonal game is a speciality. Early September provides venison with a peppered sauce or grouse with port wine sauce. Fish soup comes with a vast pastry crust or there is a mousse of avocado with Mediterranean prawns, vol-au-vent of snails with garlic and shallots, or a soufflé of Stilton cheese. For those who don't eat game there are plenty of choices - sea bass flamed in Pernod, a rib of Scotch beef with red wine sauce cooked for two people, duck with champagne sauce or veal with kumquat sauce amongst others. Prices are not cheap, a selection of vegetables costing £5.00, but the quality of the produce is good. A choice of 200 wines starts at £6.85 for house selections, with a large range of Champagnes, clarets and Burgundies for expense account dining.

━━━━━━━━━━ **DEVON** ━━━━━━━━━━

The Country Garden   Ashburton

22 East Street, Ashburton TQ13 7AZ
(0364) 53431

Closed: lunch (daily); dinner (Sun); 2 weeks Oct; 1 week Christmas
Last
Orders: dinner (10.30pm)

The Country Garden would seem more at home in London's
Fulham Road than a small provincial town in Devon. This almost
theatrical restaurant, guarded by its flamboyant owner, is heavily decorated with red washed-silk wallpaper, lots of gilt mirrors
and paintings, and crystal light fittings. Spanish shawls act as
overlays on the bar tables and the rooms have a somewhat
Eastern feel. Pressed linen and lots of fresh flowers frequently
appear which I suppose one would expect in a country garden.

Holne Chase Hotel & Restaurant Ashburton

Ashburton TQ13 7NS
(036 43) 471

Last
Orders: lunch (1.45pm); dinner (9.00pm)

Holne Chase is a comfortable, family run hotel in a romantic
setting on the southern slopes of Dartmoor National Park,
ideally situated for touring around Dartmoor and visiting Torbay. For the more energetic there is salmon and trout fishing,
walking, pony trekking and golf, and after a hard day, rejuvenate
yourself with a glass of wine made by the monks at the nearby
Buckfast Abbey. The hotel menus change daily, and offer freshly
cooked dishes. The wine list is extensive, and has plenty of
bottles at well under £10.00.

Lynwood House Restaurant   Barnstaple

Bishops Tawton Road, Barnstaple EX32 9DZ
(0271) 43695

Closed: lunch (Sat + Sun); dinner (Sun)
Last
Orders: lunch (2.00 pm); dinner (10.00 pm, 9.30 pm in winter)

A family run business in the true sense of the word, John
Roberts and second son Matthew run the restaurant with wife
Ruth and eldest son Adam in the kitchen. If this puts a strain on
the family, it certainly doesn't show in the warm welcome, and
the high standard of food which they serve. Décor and furnishing are ordinary but comfortable, and there are 2 dining
rooms, upstairs opening only in the evening.
    The emphasis is on fish, and great care is taken to purchase
only prime quality produce. The ingredients in the first course of
Greek salad seemed still to be growing, so fresh did they taste,

and the seafood mixed grill is undoubtedly sea fresh. There is salmon, sea trout, halibut, baby hake, a scallop, a langoustine and herring in oatmeal, all perfectly grilled and served with a spicy mayonnaise. The creamiest of cream caramels should not be resisted and it had a wonderful texture - could it be Devon cream in the custard, I wonder?

The restaurant is popular with locals, and John and Ruth plan special evenings with tempting offerings of "Seafood and Champagne" or a "Kate and Sydney Supper". I hope they let me know about that one, it sounds good!

Burgh Island   Bigbury-on-Sea

Bigbury-on-Sea TQ7 4AU
(0548) 810514

Closed: lunch (daily); 15 Jan – 15 Mar
Last
Orders: dinner (8.30pm)

If you are at all a fan of the 1930s, then Burgh Island could be the place for you. When I first saw the brochure in a window in Chelsea, I actually thought it was a photograph of a Caribbean island, showing the water washing up on the sand, and the house white and glistening amongst the grass. In fact, Burgh Island is set off the coast at Plymouth, and when the tide is in, can only be reached by means of a sea tractor provided for that purpose. When the tide is out, it is possible to walk across a strip of sand to the island itself.

The ground floor of the hotel is pure Art Deco. They've not only retained what was originally there, but renovated and enhanced it. The tables are set around the edge of the dining room almost giving one a feeling of being on board ship; the music played is of the period; and Beatrice and Tony Porter do their best to make you feel transported back in time. They have fitted out 13 self-contained suites and for around £13.00 they serve a simple set price menu. This would be a great place to take a party, with everyone wearing 1930s attire. Noel Coward, Agatha Christie and others have written and performed (I'm not sure in which order) at Burgh Island. Apparently Harry Roy and his Mayfair Four played there in days gone by and there are plans to re-introduce musical evenings, amongst many other types. There are maple cocktail cabinets, Lloyd Loom chairs, chrome standard lamps and the curved glass dome in the Palm Court is still being renovated, bit by bit. It's well worth a fun weekend, for they are charming people who do their best to make you feel relaxed. The dining room has some staggering views and just down the road is the Pilchard Inn, which the Porters also own.

Highbullen Hotel   Chittlehamholt

Chittlehamholt, Umberleigh EX37 9HD
(076 94) 561

Closed: lunch (except residents)
Last
Orders: lunch (2.00pm); dinner (9.00pm)

The Neil family have run Highbullen since 1963 and have developed it now into a 35-bedroom hotel set in about 60 acres of beautiful Devon countryside between Exmoor and Dartmoor. The hotel has its own 9-hole golf course, indoor and outdoor swimming pools, squash court, tennis court, and croquet lawn, and represents extremely good value when taking into account all these facilities. The bedrooms are very spacious, one having a dressing room between it and the bathroom, and all rooms have television and direct dial phones.

The dining room serves unpretentious food, which is well cooked and prepared, and there is an exceptional list of wines (especially for claret buffs who can drink their way through good vintages to 1961 - no bad year at which to stop). As an apéritif try the distinctive sherries on offer from Antonio Barbadillo, a rare treat.

Combe House Hotel   Gittisham

Gittisham, Near Honiton EX14 0AD
(0404) 2756

Closed: lunch (Mon - Sat except bar)
Last
Orders: dinner (9.30pm)

Gittisham is a delightful little village with thatched cottages, light stone houses and interesting towered church, and Combe House stands in beautiful rolling countryside, with some fine woodlands around it. The house itself is outstanding, dating from the late 16th and early 17th Centuries. John and Térèse Boswell have taken great care in the conversion of this country house, maintaining all its original features.

Although it's a large house, it still conveys an intimate family atmosphere. The beautiful main hall has some marvellous panelling, open fires, and comfortable sofas in which to relax. The drawing room is another delightful room with an intricate ceiling, and lovely portraits that gaze proprietarily down at you. There is a tiny snug bar next to the smaller of the drawing rooms where again the colours and the tones are soft and welcoming, and the open fire in winter provides much of what you look for in a country house atmosphere. There are 2 dining rooms, one muralled and one with an amazing rococo fireplace and pink panels around the walls. Both are candlelit at night, and give a romantic and relaxed atmosphere.

Térèse Boswell oversees the kitchen with help from some cordon bleu girls. There are some well-cooked dishes on the set menu which is around £17.00. You can get some excellent fresh fish which normally features on the menu, as well as perhaps filet de boeuf moutarde - thin strips of fillet sautéed and served

Combe House Hotel

on a sauce of mustard, brandy and cream, or maybe a pigeon-neau poivrade - a young squab cooked en cocotte, served in its natural juice and accompanied with a pilaff of rice - or a straightforward charcoal grilled fillet or sirloin steak. Good crisp vegetables come with it, and there's a tempting selection of puddings served from a trolley.

The housewines are from Corney and Barrow and are good value at under £6.00 a bottle. The clarets range from £7.50 to £85.00 for a magnum of Château Ducru Beaucaillou 1976. Service is by charming young staff, and the 12 elegant and well-decorated bedrooms make this a superb place to stay if you're visiting this part of the country.

Buckland-Tout-Saints Hotel   Goveton

Goveton, Near Kingsbridge TQ7 2DS   £35
(0548) 3055/6/7

Closed: Jan + 2 weeks Feb
Last
Orders: dinner (9.00pm)

A delightful Queen Anne house standing in its own grounds just north east of Kingsbridge. The hotel is owned and run by the Shephard family who have created a warm atmosphere and a high standard in décor and furnishings. Public rooms and bedrooms are comfortable and there is plenty to do in this beautiful and interesting area of Devon. Alastair Carter, the head chef, joined the hotel in February 1986, and is assisted by Paul Eason. Their menus show good use of local produce without being over fussy. There is always a wide choice on the menu and it's good to see English cheeses featured. They have Devon farmhouse Cheddar and blue cheese, Loddiswell goats' cheese, Sharpham, Ashprington and others as they are in season. Sweets such as an apple frangipane with clotted cream, Capton summer pudding, and perhaps peaches in lemon and brandy are offered. The extensive wine list has extremely detailed tasting notes alongside each wine and there is good value among the less popular regions.

The Horn of Plenty   Gulworthy

Gulworthy, Tavistock PL19 8JD
(0822) 832528

Closed: lunch (Thu + Fri); dinner (Thu); Christmas Day
Last
Orders: lunch (1.30pm); dinner (9.30pm)

We have not yet managed to stay in one of the 6 rooms that have
been added to this beautiful valley-top restaurant. Each of them
has french windows opening on to a balcony, and there are
views which stretch for many miles towards Bodmin. Sonia
Stevenson's menu is broken into starters and fish, meat and
poultry. The former might be a salad of squid and monkfish in a
provençal mixture of tomato and herbs, or Lady Curzon's
chicken soup, hot fish roulade in a rich fresh lobster sauce and
red mullet, roasted, with a crunchy savoury topping, as a starter
or a main course. The latter would include her favourite - lamb
cooked in pastry with mint béarnaise or maybe a dish of cold
slices or Old Spot ham, locally raised and cured, served with hot
potato pancakes and Cumberland sauce. The vegetables are
excellent and the desserts are extensive and simple. There is a
fixed price menu at £12.50 at lunch time, and, as she says at the
bottom of the menu, "And *no* cuisine nouvelle in any of that!" A
good French wine list, and, for the lucky few, 5 tables outside.

   If you really enjoy the experiences at The Horn of Plenty, you
can enroll in one of Sonia's cookery courses which are excellent
value, and might enable you to return home and impress the
family!

The George Hotel Hatherleigh

Market Street, Hatherleigh EX20 3JN
(0837) 810454

Closed: dinner (Sun)
Last
Orders: lunch (2.00pm); dinner (9.30pm)

Originally built in 1450 as a retreat for monks, and subsequently used as a coaching inn, the heavily timbered character of this old inn has been retained. There's a fireplace, 12 bedrooms and a swimming pool in the hotel grounds. Standard dishes on the menu are served in a warm, friendly atmosphere.

Bark House Hotel Oakfordbridge

Oakfordbridge, Near Tiverton EX16 9HZ
(039 85) 236

Closed: lunch (daily); Jan + Feb
Last
Orders: dinner (8.00pm)

The exterior of this old converted and extended bark house is immaculate, with pretty gardens around the hotel on the sloping hillside. From the outside it looks inviting and the interior certainly lives up to one's expectations: nice furnishings, books, prints and paintings all around the walls, and the basic spotless dining room with a combination of settle seating and wooden ladder-back chairs. The welcome you receive immediately makes you feel at home; it's almost a join-the-family job! The bedrooms, of which there are 6, are decorated in a very nice cottage style. Pauline and Douglas West seem to have learnt quite a lot about hospitality from their stay in France, and combine this with an almost North-Country homeliness. They run the restaurant the way they want to, and as Pauline West remarked, she prefers to serve her food with simple sauces so that the flavour of the food can show through. An honest, straightforward style of cooking has excellent vegetables, large portions, and the peach melba was as it should be with a freshly poached peach, ice-cream and fresh purée of raspberries and strawberries.

The fact that there is no formal menu makes no difference - you are given a choice of perhaps 3 starters, a couple of main courses and desserts at a set price of £9.25 including coffee, which is excellent value. And they manage all the cooking with an Aga solid fuel cooker. The housekeeping is really impeccable and the kitchen is as spotless as any we have seen: the linen, which is laundered and ironed on the premises, is crisp and bright and, as one of my colleagues remarked, this could well become a rest-home for reviewers working on the guide! No sauce is too rich, no 300-page wine list (the housewines you are invited to taste before you buy), and very pleasant people to talk to - it's definitely one we want to go back to.

The Lodge   Ottery St Mary

Silver Street, Ottery St Mary   £35
(040 481) 2356

Closed: lunch (Mon); dinner (Sun + Mon) - group bookings by arrange-
        ment
Last
Orders: lunch (2.00pm); dinner (9.30pm)

The black and white painted exterior of this restaurant makes it
easy to find. Once inside, you have the feeling of being in a
private house. There are some fine antiques, the clocks are
noteworthy, and the walls are decorated with water colours and
plates. Polished tables have place mats, fresh flowers, silver
cutlery and cut glass. A typical lunch might start with a spinach
soufflé accompanied by a fresh tomato sauce, Torbay sole in
Pernod sauce with excellent vegetables, and a fruit-filled brandy
snap with raspberry coulis. A small granité of Earl Grey tea
might be served after the first course, and a savoury is always
available as an alternative to pudding.

   The charming host manages to keep an eye out for the local
traffic warden whilst serving lunch. His wine list has some fine
selections with a choice of no less than 8 Madeiras by the glass,
and housewines from the indefatigable Monsieur Duboeuf.

   If you go to The Lodge, allow enough time to visit the
magnificent Church of St Mary, which is almost next door.

Chez Nous   Plymouth

13 Frankfort Gate, Plymouth PL1 1QA   £45
(0752) 266793   *the best in the area*

Closed: Sun + Mon; Bank Holidays; 10 days Feb; 10 days Sep
Last
Orders: lunch (2.00pm); dinner (10.30pm)

The good burghers of Plymouth should take this small bistro,
run by Jacques and Madame Marchal, to their hearts. These
dedicated and honest restaurateurs perhaps do themselves an
injustice in describing the place as a 'bistro'. But the blue
frontage with white louvres, the wooden chairs, coloured tablecloths, tongue and groove boarding decorated with menus from
the Troisgros brothers, photographs and posters, certainly give
it a typical French roadside feeling. Jacques is a genuine and
very capable chef. Working in his tiny kitchen, which was
spotlessly clean even in the middle of service, he turns out some
excellent dishes including panaché of fish with noodles in a light
cream sauce: perfectly fresh, it can only be described as
sensation. There is a good selection of fish, poultry and butcher's meats, followed by some excellent puddings such as a
sorbet served in a freshly made tuile, with a poached pear and
sauce anglaise. The £15.00 set menu is good value and is
supplemented by a blackboard menu endorsing the chef's wish
to offer spontaneous cuisine.

■ DORSET ■

Le Provence   Bournemouth

91 Bellevue Road, Southbourne, Bournemouth
(0202) 424421

Closed: lunch (daily); dinner (Sun);
Last
Orders: dinner (10.00pm)

Pierre Novi has brought to the quiet seaside town of Bournemouth an alternative to hotel dining with his truly French cooking
of genuine quality. Set in simple surroundings, the food is what it's
all about at this restaurant. Fish and seafood, perhaps poached
lobster on turbot with red wine, take their place on the
well-planned menu alongside game in season and other meat
dishes. There is some intricate work, too, with stuffed courgette
flowers and a sometimes dazzling array of vegetables.

Claire Novi runs the dining room with smiling charm and
natural skill, and the wines are soundly chosen.

Innsacre Farmhouse Hotel   Bridport

Shipton Gorge, Bridport DT6 4LJ
(0308) 56137

Last
Orders: dinner (10.00pm)

Finding that it is more profitable to accommodate and feed
humans than rare breeds of pig (the farm's former occupants), Mr
Smith converted the building into a hotel. The pigs have definitely
lost out!

The small, comfortably furnished hotel now has 8 bedrooms, 3
with private bathrooms and all with colour TV - an ideal base for
visiting beautiful west Dorset.

The Smiths run the hotel and make everyone most welcome,
whether staying or just dining in the attractive stone-built
restaurant. The small set menu changes frequently but may
include starters like cheese soufflé with prawns, terrine of rabbit
with hazelnuts and pistachios, or pigeon breast and quails' egg
salad. Imaginative dishes such as guineafowl with honey and
armagnac, escalopes of salmon with mint and vermouth, or
medallions of beef with water chestnuts and oyster sauce
demonstrate the kitchen's innovation and skill. Sweets are not
overlooked - there is an excellent apricot and frangipane tart to
complete the meal and it would be hard to find better value
anywhere for £13.25.

Chedington Court   Chedington

Chedington, Beaminster DT8 3HY
(093 589) 265

Closed: lunch (daily); 3/4 weeks in Jan/Feb
Last
Orders: dinner (9.00pm)

Stunning views across the rolling countryside of Dorset, Somerset and Devon can be enjoyed from this elegant house, built in
1840, and now owned by Philip and Hilary Chapman. The
Jacobean-style mansion is well maintained and very comfortably
furnished, and although I never travelled on the Queen Mary, I can
at least feel some recompense in having slept in a bedroom
equipped with a suite of her furniture!

Hilary Chapman cooks set menus with just a choice of first
courses and sweet. You might be offered a good pasta with whole
grain mustard incorporated into the pasta itself, then a fillet of
Dover sole with mandarine Napoleon sauce, followed by an
excellent sirloin steak in a red wine sauce, accompanied by
perfect vegetables.

Mine host supervises the dining room with the help of young
ladies, and he takes great care in the service of wines, which are
obviously his forte. His list is amazing in both volume and variety,
including 18 rosés, about 30 Italian wines, 12 from Portugal, over
50 from Spain, 51 half bottles of different clarets, 8 red Loire, 11
white Rhône and so on and so on. All that I can add is that the
prices are extremely reasonable, and that when you decide to stay
at Chedington, you should go briefly beforehand, just to choose
your wines!

The gardens are a delight, and there is much to see locally.
Beaminster became 'Emminster' in Thomas Hardy's *Tess of the
d'Urbervilles*, and the chalk giant of Cerne Abbas is well worth
seeing.

Summer Lodge   Evershot

Evershot DT2 0JR
(093 583) 424

Closed: lunch (daily); 1 Dec - 31 Jan
Last
Orders: dinner (8.00pm)

Nigel and Margaret Corbett 'escaped' from London in 1979, bought this house that was the home of the heirs to the Earl of Ilchester, and established a popular country house hotel in Thomas Hardy country. The comfortable bedrooms look out over the gardens or rooftops to Evershot village, and all have private bathrooms. During cooler weather log fires crackle in the large sitting room.

Dinner is a set menu, with perhaps spinach roulade, smoked salmon mousse, dressed crab or a soup to start, then traditional dishes such as roast beef with Yorkshire pudding, steak and kidney pie, fillet of lamb with soubise sauce or local rainbow trout poached in wine. Local cheeses are served (don't miss the excellent Blue Vinny), and then puddings such as sherry trifle or chocolate and black cherry bombe. The smart staff are friendly, and work hard to make your stay enjoyable.

Mansion House Hotel   Poole

Thames Street, Poole BH15 1JN
(0202) 685666

Closed: Christmas Eve - 10 Jan
Last
Orders: lunch (2.00pm); dinner (10.00pm)

A delightful Georgian mansion is the setting for this efficiently run hotel and restaurant, situated close to the quay in Poole. Originally just a members' dining club, the Mansion House has now opened its door to visitors, and I would recommend it either for its hotel facilities or simply for eating within the area. It is comfortably furnished, with 19 well-equipped bedrooms, and hotel guests receive temporary membership of the dining club.

The busy restaurant has extremely pleasant staff who really seem to enjoy their work, and the à la carte or fixed price menus offer good variety at both lunch and dinner.

At lunch time, a 3-course meal with coffee and unlimited housewine for £15.95 is incredible value. Start with a plate of your choice from the hors d'oeuvre table, and the chef's pie of the day is usually well worth trying. A portion of pork with sage pie comes with well cooked vegetables, and only leaves room for fresh fruit salad. In the evening the menu concentrates on more à la carte items whilst the fixed price is £15.50 for 4 courses and coffee.

The Mansion House maintains its club atmosphere and is both very comfortable and very friendly. A long sweeping staircase to the first floor private dining rooms give an impression of how life used to be in days of Georgian elegance.

The Eastbury Hotel   Sherborne

Long Street, Sherborne DT9 3BY
(0935) 813131

Last
Orders: lunch (2.30pm); dinner (9.00pm)

David Lloyd-Jones is a hotelier of many years' experience, although this is his first solo venture. The house, built in 1740 and now a listed Georgian building, has been extensively and tastefully converted, with lots of pale greys and pale pinks. Bedrooms have all the accepted extras and Laura Ashley décor. There is a quiet formality about the well-furnished public areas, and in the dining room, gentlemen are requested to wear a jacket and tie in the evening. The staff have been instilled with a great sense of professionalism.

Chef Jonathan Binns offers à la carte or set menus, with the emphasis placed firmly on modern dishes. Portions are not large, but the set menu runs to 5 courses, and may offer spinach and salmon terrine, or a consommé of duck with herb pancakes, alongside more classic dishes like beef Wellington from the à la carte menu. The wines are well chosen and properly served.

Plumber Manor   Sturminster Newton

Sturminster Newton, DT10 2AF
(0258) 72507

friendly and caring people. £40

Closed: lunch (daily); dinner (Mon in winter)
Last
Orders: dinner (9.30pm)

The Prideaux-Brune family has occupied this Jacobean house for some 300 years. The imposing building, set in extensive lawns with some mature trees, in the midst of Hardy's Dorset, has its own trout stream running through the grounds. The whole setting is one of peace and tranquillity. Richard Prideaux-Brune, who now runs the house, has created an exemplary sense of comfort and hospitality. The accent is firmly on the comfort and enjoyment of the guests, who are joined by various members of the family who, though there to help you enjoy yourself, clearly enjoy what they are doing and enter into it all with great enthusiasm.

The restaurant comprises 3 interconnecting rooms, and Brian Prideaux-Brune cooks very well a menu that varies from well-executed classic dishes, like beef Wellington, or lamb Shrewsbury, to escalopes of salmon or interesting dishes of local game and fish, and the wine list is equally well planned with housewines

from £6.00 a bottle and reasonably priced Burgundies and clarets.

The 6 bedrooms in the main house are traditional and comfortable and there are also 6 in the converted stable, with vast beds to match, decorated in pale contemporary colours, with every conceivable comfort of home and more.

Plumber Manor is a country house which places the emphasis on serving good food in warm, comfortable surroundings.

◼◼◼◼ EAST SUSSEX ◼◼◼◼

The Grand Hotel   Brighton

King's Road, Brighton BN1 1FW   £50
(0273) 21188

Last
Orders: lunch (2.30pm); dinner (10.00pm)

THE
GRAND
BRIGHTON

Welcome back to The Grand Hotel, rebuilt in fine style with a conservatory frontage housing the coffee shop and bar on the left-hand side, and on the right-hand side Kings Restaurant. Modern reproduction furniture has been installed in the well-thought-out lounge and bar area. Overlooking Brighton seafront, the original long bar - staffed by courteous and attentive uniformed attendants - is just the place for afternoon cream tea, or a drink before going into Kings Restaurant - 2 large well-decorated rooms with some nice features.

By seaside hotel standards the menu is carefully considered. The restaurant itself is better at night when it's softly lit, and the newness of it is perhaps not quite so obvious; and although the menu is relatively predictable, the food is well cooked and presented. There's a choice of the cassolette of seafood, Scotch salmon steak, or supreme of turbot poached in Noilly Prat amongst the fish courses, and a brace of quails stuffed with wild rice, or a breast of chicken flamed in calvados for main courses, or perhaps a straightforward grill. They still prepare dishes at your table here including steak Diane and steak tartare.

The hotel has the normal range of reception rooms, a swimming pool, and a gymnasium is planned. At the moment, this certainly is the brightest and best of the Brighton hotels in which to spend some time.

La Marinade　　　　　　　　　Brighton

77 St George's Road, Kemp Town, Brighton BN2 1EF
(0273) 600992

Closed:　lunch (Mon); dinner (Sun + Mon);
　　　　　last 2 weeks Aug; 2 weeks Christmas
Last
Orders:　lunch (1.45pm); dinner (9.45pm)

This little basement restaurant - perhaps more reminiscent of an
oriental or Indian establishment - is worth visiting for the
extremely good value it offers, and although the décor is all swirly
carpets and dark colours, it's spotlessly clean and very welcoming. Try the warm scallop salad, or a good chicken terrine. On
Sundays there's rare roast beef, salmon in a cream and lemon
sauce, and excellent bread and butter pudding - just one of the
simple but good home-made puddings that are on offer. At less
than £9.00 a head, the set menu includes a half bottle of
housewine. The reception is welcoming, and plated service is by
pleasant and attentive staff.

The Twenty-One　　　　　　　Brighton

21 Charlotte Street, Brighton BN2 1AG
(0273) 686450

Closed:　lunch (daily); dinner (Sun + Wed)
Last
Orders:　8.30pm

Charlotte Street is in Kemp Town and this modest, terraced,
bow-fronted Victorian house has some 7 rooms, all of charming
design, and with direct dial telephone, remote control television
etc. There is even a 4-poster room and a garden suite, and in order
to enjoy Simon Ward's cooking you'll have to stay here or be the
guest of someone who is staying. They offer 5 courses which
might consist of carrot soup flavoured with fresh coriander
leaves, followed by a cheese soufflé, then a marmite de poisson
Normandy (salmon, sole, scallops, Dublin Bay prawns and
mussels served in a white wine and vermouth cream sauce) with a
selection of fresh vegetables. Afterwards a cheese platter might
be followed by raspberry and mango mousse served in a tartlet,
with a mango coulis flavoured with raspberry liqueur. Finally you
can enjoy a cafetière of ground coffee and home-made petits
fours. The seafood is excellent, the vegetables are crisp, and the
service is caring and friendly in this tiny seaside hotel.

Sundial Restaurant　　　　　Herstmonceaux

Gardner Street, Herstmonceaux BN27 4LA
(0323) 832217

Closed:　lunch (Mon); dinner (Sun + Mon);
　　　　　mid-Aug - early Sep; Christmas - 20 Jan
Last
Orders:　lunch (2.00pm); dinner (9.30pm)

Twenty or so years of running this restaurant have not diminished Guiseppe and Laurette Bertoli's enthusiasm for their food, service or their customers. The welcome is genuine and they're really concerned that you enjoy your food and that you go away satisfied. Laurette in the front of house is assisted by one or two young local staff who have been trained to be attentive, and even ask if you'd like cream with your coffee instead of the all too frequent, "Black or white, sir?"

The décor is cottage style, and the building is 17th Century in origin, although there have been some later additions including amongst other things a brand new kitchen. Everyone seems to mention Guiseppe's speciality of petite bouillabaisse, and I'm afraid I have to add my comment on it - it *is* exceptionally good. It is served with rouille, the right assortment of fish and a seafood taste that is rich without being overpowering. Quenelles de saumon, darne de saumon gentillesse, and fresh wild salmon trout baked with herbs are just 3 of the fish dishes available on this large menu. Chicken, venison, lamb and duckling provide additional fare in their set lunch or set 3-course dinner. Then, if you still feel able to eat more, even after the generous sized portions and accompanying vegetables, there are the puddings, some displayed in the centre of the room, some served from the kitchen. If you order a sorbet, they automatically give you 4 different flavours in one serving.

Equally memorable are the lovely views around the cottage, the terraces on which to have an apéritif, and above all the welcome and enthusiasm of people who genuinely care.

The Eaton Restaurant   Hove

Eaton Gardens, Hove BN3 3TN
(0273) 738921

Closed: dinner (Sun); Christmas Day; Good Friday
Last
Orders: lunch (2.15pm); dinner (9.45pm)

John Cutress has been running The Eaton for some 25 years and this seaside-style dining room still seems to pack them in. There is straightforward no-nonsense silver service of the set menu for under £10.00, which offers a good choice of fish dishes. You might have fried local dabs, whitebait or soused herring, or a choice from the 6 or 7 non-fish starters, followed perhaps by a straightforward grilled fillet of plaice, trout Colbert, or a very good steak, kidney and mushroom pie. Puddings are true to style with mince tart and custard, lemon syllabub and crème caramel amongst the 7 or so choices, or maybe you'd prefer a savoury of soft roes on toast. Specialities of The Eaton, from their à la carte menu which has all the old-time favourites on it, include tournedos Rossini, entrecôte steak Roquefort, roast duckling Montmorency, veal cordon bleu etc. The Cutress family also run the Courtland Hotel, and are well known in Sussex as bakers and pastry cooks.

The Hungry Monk   Jevington

Jevington, Near Polegate BN26 5QF
(032 12) 2178

Closed: lunch (Mon - Sat); Christmas Eve; Christmas Day; Boxing Day
Last
Orders: lunch (2.00pm); dinner (10.00pm)

A tiny village on the Sussex Downs boasts a Norman church and a
converted row of 14th-Century cottages known as the Hungry
Monk Restaurant. This is a straightforward, no-nonsense or frills
restaurant with log fires burning in the lounges, where you can sit
on a comfortable sofa, enjoy an apéritif and choose from the
menu displayed on a blackboard. First courses of curried parsnip
and apple soup, mousseline of chicken with red pepper sauce,
spiced beef and Gruyère pancake or terrine of duck with
Cumberland sauce might appeal. Then perhaps try a feuilleté of
salmon, squid and mussels, turkey breast stuffed with prunes and
bacon with almond and Madeira sauce, or rare Scotch sirloin with
Yorkshire pudding, all accompanied by good crisp vegetables on
hot side plates.

    Puddings appear on a separate blackboard, and might include
almond, raspberry and kirsch roulade, pear tulipe with mango
sauce or a selection of ices and sorbets.

    The wine list shows prices with and without VAT, as if we had
the choice! But even with the dreaded tax, prices of wines are
reasonable with plenty of bottles at well under £10.00 and a good
showing of half bottles.

Kenwards Restaurant   Lewes

Pipe Passage, 151A High Street, Lewes BN7 1XU
(0273) 472343

Closed: lunch (by arrangement only); dinner (Mon);
          occasional 1 or 2-week closures
Last
Orders: dinner (9.30pm)

This plain, simple, even stark restaurant (with pine tables, young
staff, and owner John Kenward cooking) is situated just off the
High Street in the beautiful town of Lewes. Great care is taken
with the wine list which is in 2 parts, one for the main meal and
another for dessert. They concentrate on fish and game, and
certainly the latter is cooked in some interesting ways. Every
available part is used - the plumper, less sinewy pieces are lightly
grilled, fried or roasted pink, whilst - sensibly - the less tender are
potted or casseroled. Generous portions of well-cooked vegetables are also served. I would suggest that this is a place used
regularly by people from local and surrounding areas, rather than
for an occasional, celebratory night out.

Horsted Place   Little Horsted

Little Horsted, Uckfield TN22 5TS
(0825) 75581

£55

Closed: lunch (by arrangement Mon - Sat)
Last
Orders: lunch (1.30pm); dinner (10.00pm)

A simple sign on white fencing just south of Uckfield tells you that Horsted Place is close by. Up a winding drive you come to a rather grand if somewhat forbidding façade, but go through the oak door and everything comes to life. In winter a blazing log fire greets you with that lovely wood smoke smell, and behind the reception desk there's a very welcoming smile. You turn around and the grand gallery stretches out before you, beautifully decorated, cool, stylish and elegant. There's a stunning staircase, ornately carved, leading up to the suites which are all named after people who've been associated with the house through its history. It was originally built in 1851, a fine example of Gothic revivalist architecture, and in fact it remained in the Barchard family, who built it, right up until 1965 when Lord Rupert Nevill acquired it, and it has only been transformed into an 18-suite luxury hotel in the last year or so. A great deal of care and effort has been put into retaining as many original features as possible during the conversion. Beautifully designed suites in the luxury category have comfortable furniture and lots of fresh flowers.

The charming Guy Rigby, who manages the hotel, is know-ledgeable on his wines and will spend time discussing with you your selection from the very adequate list. The set menu at £25.00 a head might consist of a wild salmon terrine served with a green dill-flecked creamy sauce, salmon set in a delicate mousse encased in a seaweed wrapping, or a pink lamb fillet served with a mint vinaigrette, topped with a spearmint flower and served on a small pile of 4 different salad leaves. Try thinly sliced sirloin with a well-reduced rich madeira sauce, served rare with no unneces-sary garnish other than crisp vegetables, then perhaps a small blackcurrant mousse topped with a sprig of currants like a bunch of grapes, sitting in a dark cassis coulis. Service is discreet and charming in a dining room of soft brown shades. Coffee is served in one of the blue lounges.

Other interesting features are a Gothic library, an indoor pool and an unusual knot garden and fountain outside. The garden walks have rare shrubs and there's even a perfectly circular sunken garden. The tennis court has an all-weather surface. The whole hotel is full of charm and style, and it's a delight to see such a young and willing staff.

The Priory   Rushlake Green

Rushlake Green, Heathfield TN21 9RG
(0435) 830553

Closed: 22 Dec - 16 Jan
Last
Orders: dinner (9.00pm)

£40

check, as this may have changed hands.

First of all, *find* The Priory, which is not easy! The address is
Rushlake Green, but in fact it's almost a mile from Rushlake
Green. You head out on the Wood's Corner/Dallington road, and
where you meet the crossroads for Rushlake Green, Wood's
Corner, Heathfield and Dallington, you'll certainly find it sign-
posted. But then there is about a mile of driveway before you
come to The Priory itself, a most beautiful, original 14th-Century
monastery set in its own massive grounds, which manages to
capture the very Englishness of the countryside and its people.

The owners are charming and make everyone feel at home. The
staff themselves, who are mostly from the local area, are helpful,
attentive and willing. There are huge fireplaces, smouldering
away even in summer, and the whole atmosphere is like that of
being welcomed into someone's home. On the occasion we were
there, the dining room was full of people who had come from all
over the world to taste a real piece of England. And this is it: the
atmosphere in the dining room, as in the rest of the house, is
beautifully English and the bedrooms, with their mullioned
windows, all seem to have lovely views of the surrounding
countryside.

There is talent in the kitchen, but somehow I thought that the
guests in the dining room were really expecting something a bit
more traditionally English at dinner. As it is, it's worth the journey
just to have the well-cooked English breakfast and the magnificent English cheese board and wines from an exemplary list. (I
know it's strange having a Californian red wine as one of your
housewines, in the middle of Sussex, but it *is* from Geoffrey
Roberts Associates.)

The Mermaid Inn Rye

Mermaid Street, Rye TN31 7EY
(0797) 223065

Closed: Mon - Fri in Feb
Last
Orders: lunch (1.45pm); dinner (9.15pm)

Rye itself is a beautiful place and is one of the Cinque Ports. The Mermaid Inn is situated up a little cobbled street. Sitting in one of the interesting bars listening to the locals talk, you can almost imagine smugglers and pirates discussing their spoils, though nowadays you're more likely to hear antique dealers and other tradesmen. With a timbered exterior and interesting bedrooms, some 4-poster, this particular inn is full of atmosphere: apparently there are even secret passages. I like The Mermaid in winter; standing beside its huge fireplace in the bar you have the feeling that you could quite easily turn back the clock a couple of hundred years.

The restaurant serves a good selection of standard inn food. The staff are courteous, friendly and proud of this ancient hostelry. It's not been spoiled over the years and the work that has been done to it has been carried out with a great deal of care and sympathy. Despite the hoards of tourists who invade Rye in the summer, everyone here seems attentive and polite and delighted to take time out to explain the history of the building to you.

Simmons   Rye

68 The Mint, Rye TN01 7EW
(0797) 222026

check –. this may have changed hands.

Closed: lunch (Mon - Sat); dinner (Sun + Mon)
3 weeks Feb; first week Oct
Last
Orders: lunch (2.00pm); dinner (10.00pm)

This friendly and pretty little restaurant is housed behind a shop
front in an ancient building at the bottom of the High Street.
Inside, crisp, clean linen cloths with pink napery adorn the
restaurant, and a spiral staircase leads up to the owners' quarters.
Kenneth and Susan Simmons run this good little establishment
with care and a great deal of hard work, assisted by young local
staff. They're open for dinner only - apart from Sunday lunch
which is amazing value, as is the fixed price dinner menu at £9.50.
You might be offered a chilled cream of sorrel, watercress and
lettuce soup, followed by a baby chicken with lemon and herbs, a
choice of any 2 vegetables from a selection of 6 or 7, and a green
or mixed salad. There's a good selection of international cheeses
and excellent desserts which are displayed on a little table in the
restaurant - indeed, everything that Susan Simmons turns out is
most appealing to the eye. There's also a good à la carte list to
choose from if you're tempted away from the fixed price menu.
The fine wine list represents most of the regions of France, really
safe bets being the Georges Duboeuf table wines. The Simmons
will be delighted to talk to you about your choice. If you're there
in the summer, have a glass in the tiny little terrace at the back of
the restaurant.

▰▰▰ ESSEX ▰▰▰

Whitehall   Broxted

Church End, Broxted CM6 2BZ
(0279) 850603

Closed: 3 weeks Jan
Last
Orders: lunch (1.30pm); dinner (9.30pm)

This 12th-Century manor house has been skilfully and luxuriously converted into a restaurant with rooms. Set in beautiful
gardens, the emphasis is on comfort with large beds, spacious
bedrooms, comfortable bathrooms and even a swimming pool.
The dining room concentrates on very modern French and
English cooking with the accent on presentation.

Le Talbooth & Maison Talbooth   Dedham

Dedham, Near Colchester CO7 6HP
(0206) 322367/323150

Last
Orders: lunch (2.00pm); dinner (9.00pm)

242

Maison Talbooth is situated just outside the beautiful Essex village of Dedham, with its pink and blue washed cottages and fine 17th- and 18th-Century buildings. The village is on the River Stour, and you can get a boat and row yourself up to Flatford Mill, which Constable immortalised. Le Talbooth appears in another of his works, as the jovial owner, Gerald Milsom, will point out to you. If you are staying in Maison Talbooth then St Stephen's Church - also of Constable fame - stands out on the landscape.

The hotel, Maison Talbooth, is a large Victorian house situated in its own grounds. Carefully modernised rooms are filled with antique furniture, and a comfortable lounge complete with grand piano overlooks a croquet lawn. Half a mile down the road is the Dedham Vale Hotel, also owned by the Milsoms, featuring a huge rôtisserie actually in the dining room, and 6 additional bedrooms besides. Another half mile on and you reach Le Talbooth, the restaurant itself, an excellent example of a timber-framed inn, with beautifully kept grounds, terracing at the rear, and its own mooring on the river. Gerald describes himself as an Innkeeper, and he has been keeping inn here for more than 30 years, steadily building up his business and looking forward to his sons joining him, once they have completed their training.

The restaurant currently comes under the guidance of Dick Sawyer, from Michel Bourdin's kitchens at The Connaught and a better pedigree for working in a busy traditional restaurant would be hard to come by. The fare is traditional, with favourites such as steak and kidney pie, whole boned rainbow trout cooked en papillote, or rognonnade of lamb - a whole roast best end of lamb stuffed with kidneys, served with poached pears and redcurrant jelly, and carved in the restaurant. Starters of soufflé Talbooth - poached finnan haddock with mushrooms and white wine, topped with cheese soufflé - or a tartlet of quails' eggs and smoked salmon, might precede.

Red and white housewines start from £6.50 and are from the excellent Georges Duboeuf. Gerald Milsom has chosen a total of 14 wines specifically for quality and value, the most expensive being about £16.00. These start a wine list whose total range is 179, including some good New World selections and some excellently priced magnums and half bottles.

The Starr   Great Dunmow

Great Dunmow   £35
(0371) 4321

Closed: lunch (Sat); dinner (Sun); 3 weeks Aug; 2 weeks
           Christmas/New Year
Last
Orders: lunch (1.30pm); dinner (9.30pm)

There was an inn on this site called The Starr as long ago as the
15th Century, and a few of the beams in today's bar apparently
belong to it. The present pretty white building faces you as you
come down into the market place. Some nice greenery outside
gives it a friendly appeal that is enhanced when you enter. On
the left is a delightful bar, with bottles of Champagne and white
wine cooling in a large container; the restaurant itself, off to the
right, is quietly decorated in shades of green, with large well-
spaced tables and a very civilised atmosphere throughout. The
staff are friendly, smartly dressed and offer professional service,
full of joie de vivre.

This is a popular place to eat in the area and you can see why.
Chef Mark Fisher's changing menu might offer a choice of fresh
scallops with mange-touts, or a terrine of veal with herb jellies
served with hot toast or hot garlic bread, moules marnières
when available, or perhaps a home-made curried apple soup in
winter, or gazpacho in summer. Red mullet, escalope of wild
salmon, and wing of skate feature when available. Some excellent English rack of lamb with herbs and garlic is also served,
though you might prefer their individual steak and kidney pie, or
game in season. Puddings might include baked bananas with
dark rum, cream and brown sugar, or rhubarb crumble served
with custard, or a selection of home-made sorbets; and there's
always a good selection of cheeses. This is a precise style of
cooking with flavours kept intact.

Give youself plenty of time over an apéritif to read the
comprehensive wine list; it has bargains at almost every level,
for under the inn lies a honeycombe of cellars only discovered
during restoration work. They try hard to please and are keen to
do business. On a visit I made some time ago just to check it out
before deciding whether to eat there, the bar was temporarily
unmannned. I took a quick look around and walked back to my
car some 500 yards away, but Mr Jones got there before me,
order book at the ready, to see if I wanted to make a reservation.
They deserve their business.

If you're staying overnight at Great Dunmow, you could try
the Saracen's Head Hotel, a period Essex inn with 24 rooms.

Renouf's Restaurant & Hotel Rochford

Restaurant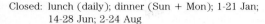

1 South Street, Rochford SS4 3BU
(0702) 544393

Closed: lunch (daily); dinner (Sun + Mon); 1-21 Jan;
        14-28 Jun; 2-24 Aug
Last
Orders: dinner (10.00pm)

Derek Renouf is a larger than life figure whose original restaurant called Renouf's is set in a cosy timbered house, bedecked with his many awards and heraldic shields. It offers
everything on the extensive menu from nouvelle cuisine to
duckling à la presse. The restaurant is now open only in the
evening and, on a closed circuit television screen in the bar, you
can watch the dexterous Monsieur Renouf as he prepares your
dinner.

Hotel

Bradley Way, Rochford
(0702) 541334

Closed: lunch (Sat)
Last
Orders: lunch (2.00pm); dinner (9.00pm)

Derek's son controls the kitchen at the newly opened Hotel
Renouf, and cooks in the family's traditional way. This modern
hotel, situated on the edge of the town car park, is lightly and
comfortably furnished, and from each one of the well-spaced
tables in the dining room you can see a reproduction of the
Bayeux Tapestry, reflecting the Norman ancestry of the Re-
noufs. Bedrooms at the hotel are large, modern and well thought
out; the suites, all reasonably priced, even have videos. Throughout the hotel the young staff are friendly and professional.

Le Champenois Restaurant   West Mersea

Blackwater Hotel, 20-22 Church Road, West Mersea
(020 638) 3338/3038

Closed: 2 weeks Jan
Last
Orders: lunch (1.45pm); dinner (9.45pm)

West Mersea is the home of the native oyster and Le Champenois is set only yards from the sea. It is the quintessential French
bistro, complete with red-checked tablecloths, wooden beams
and copper pots everywhere, plus the warming presence of
Madame Chapleo. It seats 50, with a few extra tables outside on
sunny days. Dishes make good use of local and imported
produce and feature firm favourites like moules farcies, or
rognons au moutarde. Fish dishes feature heavily as well. Try
the casserole of turbot with West Mersea samphire. Wines,
French of course, are well chosen and presented.

Le Champenois is actually a part of the Blackwater Hotel,
originally a Victorian coaching inn, now with 7 bedrooms and a
pretty ivy-clad exterior with hanging flower baskets. It's a
delightful place for a restful and civilised stay. This is a very
honest establishment and offers good value all round, and it is
run by people who care about their guests' comfort.

■■■■■■ GLOUCESTERSHIRE ■■■■■■

Buckland Manor   Buckland

Buckland, Near Broadway WR12 7LY
(0386) 852626

Closed: mid-Jan for 3½ weeks
Last
Orders: lunch (1.45pm); dinner (8.45pm)

This is a rather splendid manor house situated in the village of
Buckland in Gloucestershire, which is not far from Broadway in
Worcestershire. A sympathetic conversion includes some lovely
furnishings, with antiques in the main hall and lounge. There's a
relaxed, comfortable and welcoming feeling about the whole
place under the caring eyes of Barry and Adrienne Berman. The

young, smartly dressed, competent staff are all helpful and smiling.

The dining room seats about 40 and has a few tables outside in the summer. You might try as a starter their mousse of chicken and parsley served with a sauce of fresh tomatoes, or langoustine steamed in a cabbage leaf, garnished and served on a chive butter sauce. From the 8 main courses perhaps try a half duckling, boned and crisply cooked, served with glazed apples in a calvados sauce, or perhaps a veal fillet cooked on a little pile of carrots and onions, sliced and served with a sauternes and grape sauce. The desserts and cheeses are well displayed on the buffet. Housewines are good value at under £6.00 a bottle.

La Ciboulette Cheltenham

24-26 Suffolk Road, Cheltenham GL50 2AQ
(0242) 573449

Closed: Sun + Mon; 1 week Christmas; 1 week Easter; 2 weeks Aug Last
Orders: lunch (2.00pm); dinner (10.30pm)

After sitting in the restaurant for about half an hour you might look through the window and not understand why the traffic is on the wrong side of the road - then you'll remember that you're in England. Such is the warm, French, bistro-style atmosphere of La Ciboulette. It is evocative of a French roadside restaurant: window boxes and lace curtains, cream walls with a few pictures, one or two pot plants, bentwood chairs with wicker seats, crisp white linen, an oversize cover plate and glasses upside down until required.

Blandine Jenkins runs the dining room whilst her husband Kevin cooks, and his cooking is in keeping with the atmosphere created - classically based with nouvelle touches. Lunch sees dishes like moules marinières or hot bacon salad, followed by kidneys dijonnaise or blanquette of veal, whilst the à la carte menu shows the more modern dishes: fish pâté with beurre blanc, puff pastry filled with asparagus in a cream sauce with chives, breast of duck with green peppercorn sauce, or a baby chicken cooked with crayfish and cognac. For pudding try the 'proper' profiteroles, filled with vanilla ice cream and coated with a perfect hot chocolate sauce.

Wines are all French and have been well chosen. The list is well-written, describing characteristics of the wine together with grape varieties, and pricing is sensible.

Cheltenham is lucky to have France so close!

Corse Lawn House Hotel   Corse Lawn

Corse Lawn GL19 4LZ
(045 278) 479

£45

out of the best in Gloncestershire for food

Last
Orders: lunch (2.00pm); dinner (10.00pm)

Both our visits to Corse Lawn have been at night. The house, which was built in 1745 as a coaching inn, is a fine example of Queen Anne style and stands reflected in its own large pond in front of the house. It's more of a restaurant with rooms than a hotel, having only 4 double bedrooms. The meals we have eaten here have been excellent. Mrs Hine cooks in the kitchen and Mr Hine tends to stay a little in the background, leaving his capable staff to run the dining room.

It's so nice, when you sit down to eat, to find something different to taste: in this case, home-made cheese pastries - rather like scones. Their bread is home-made, both brown and white. A fantastic seafood soup and a feuilleté of wild mushrooms, were both delicious. Main courses consisted of poussin, which really tasted of its natural flavour although served in a champagne sauce, and I made the decision, looking around and realizing I might be the only one to do so, to opt for the tongue; it was served hot with a beautifully reduced sauce and crisp vegetables. And there was no disappointment in my choice. The menu provided a good selection of home-made puddings to follow. It was good to experience again the feeling of wanting to try all the starters and main courses because they sounded and looked so delicious.

The dining room itself is fairly plain in décor but comfortable; and candlelit at night, the whole room looks soft and welcoming. If I lived in the country, I would gladly accept living here with such a good restaurant on my doorstep. There are some fine wines on the list and an excellent variety of half bottles: we just missed the last Côte Rôtie '67 and settled for half a Médoc Château La Lagune '76, which was excellent. Good food, good service: good value.

The Greenway   Shurdington

Shurdington, Cheltenham GL51 5UG
(0242) 862352

Closed: lunch (Sat); Bank Holidays; 28 Dec - 10 Jan
Last
Orders: lunch (2.00pm); dinner (9.30pm)

The Greenway, which takes its name from the historic walkway
alongside, is a beautiful 16th-Century Cotswolds manor house
just south of Cheltenham, which has elegant public rooms,
comfortable bedrooms and formal gardens where squirrels
entertain at breakfast time. Tony Elliott has decorated the hotel
tastefully, furnished it with good antiques and maintains a
homely atmosphere, along with his capable staff who make you
feel comfortable and relaxed. Rooms are well proportioned and
spacious - the half-panelled dining room has been extended into
a substantial conservatory that overlooks the garden. At night,
low-level lighting, together with candles, creates an intimate
atmosphere, and an illuminated view of the lily pond and
fountain.

A fixed price 4-course dinner gives a good choice of modern
style dishes - scallops grilled with breadcrumbs and herbs on a
bed of leeks, then a pancake filled with vegetables accompanied
by a sweet and sour sauce, which might be followed by calves'
liver with 2 well-made mustard sauces, and a fresh blackberry
yoghurt mousse served on a blackberry coulis to finish. Bread is
home baked as are the croissants at breakfast, together with
good fresh preserves and marmalade.

Service is extremely good from a young well-trained team
under expert guidance from Azad Khodabaccus.

Oakes   Stroud

169 Slad Road, Stroud
(045 36) 79950

Closed: lunch (Mon); dinner (Sun + Mon); Jan
Last
Orders: lunch (2.00pm); dinner (10.00pm)

Chris Oakes has recently opened his converted house as a
restaurant, and his innate ability demonstrated during 6 years at
The Castle Hotel, Taunton, with Kit Chapman, leaves little doubt
in my mind that I can recommend his new venture, even prior to
having the opportunity to eat there!

His cooking is modern, based on classic technique, and he
offers inclusive fixed price menus at around £14.00, £16.00 or
£18.00, with a choice of dishes at each course.

The dining room, brightly decorated in peach, white and
green, is supervised by Caroline, Chris's wife, with help from
local staff.

There should be more about this one in our 6-monthly update!

Calcot Manor   Tetbury

Near Tetbury GE8 8YJ
(066 689) 355

Closed: dinner (Sun - non residents); first full week Jan
Last
Orders: lunch (2.00pm); dinner (9.30pm)

The name, Calcot Manor, perhaps creates the wrong impression, for this is a very pleasant, large farmhouse near some of the oldest barns and outbuildings in the area. Charming owners, with young and enthusiastic staff - even 2 Labradors give you a welcome when you arrive. There's a pleasant, simple dining room, the food is light and attractive and well presented, and there is an excellent salad menu of lighter courses at lunch time as well as the full menu. The Ball family, who run the establishment, keep this hotel on an informal, family basis, and it works. There is certainly talent in the kitchen and the presentation of the dishes we sampled was imaginative, and they tasted as good as they looked: not over fussy but with a degree of style.

With menus that feature 6 or so starters such as crisp lambs' sweetbreads on toasted brioche served with a basil cream sauce, or a terrine of quail, guineafowl and pigeon served with plums in red wine, possibly followed by a fillet of sea bass wrapped in cabbage and placed on a caviar and chive sauce, breast of corn-fed chicken accompanied by a parcel of leek and chicken liver, or beef fillet with wild mushrooms, goose liver and a port wine sauce, this place will certainly continue to build up its reputation for some of the best food in the area.

◼◼◼◼ GREATER MANCHESTER ◼◼◼◼

The Moss Nook Restaurant   Manchester

Ringway Road, Moss Nook, Manchester M22 5NA
061-437 4778

Closed: lunch (Sat + Sun); dinner (Sun); 2 weeks Christmas
Last
Orders: lunch (1.30pm); dinner (9.30pm)

Situated close to Manchester airport this 1940s house with white shutters, window boxes and hanging baskets has become one of the City's most popular dining venues. Derek and Pauline Harrison's restaurant has been established for 13 years and Pauline's brother Robert Thornton is in charge of the kitchens, from where he produces an ambitious range of menus. In addition to à la carte there is a gastronomique menu of 5 courses, a 4-course vegetarian menu (it's nice to see thought going into this type of menu) and frequently changing specialities from the market.

Cooking is rich in the modern manner, with starters such as Lancashire black pudding and spicy baby black puddings with fried apple and a whole-grain mustard sauce, a pancake filled with fish, shellfish and Welsh laverbread with a light sauce, or a tartlet of wild mushrooms topped with breast of quail. Main courses might be a fillet and kidney of Welsh lamb wrapped in smoky bacon and served with a mint, ginger and Madeira sauce; sea bass, salmon and sole cooked separately and each served with its own sauce, or medallions of veal with a delicate garlic sauce. Puddings are mainly fruit based, exotic fruits with home-made ice-cream, a peach with ice-cream and strawberry coulis or a layered chocolate cake with oranges and Grand Marnier.

The wine list is a large volume with 23 Champagnes (9 of them rosé), almost 40 Burgundies, 30 from Bordeaux, and representation from California, Switzerland, Italy and Germany. A fine wine section includes some desirable bottles for very special occasions.

The dining room seats 50 and has a warm Victorian feel, deep red being the predominant colour for carpets, wall coverings, drapes and seating. Wall clocks, plates and a barometer adorn the walls, and crisp linen, cut glass candle holders and silver brighten the tables. There are even some tables outside for the summer - if it isn't raining!

Service is organised by Mavis Matthews who is extremely friendly and competent, and the dining room runs with the same precision as the clocks on the walls.

■■■ HAMPSHIRE ■■■

Le Poussin   Brockenhurst

57/59 Brookley Road, Brockenhurst SO42 7RB   £35
(0590) 23063

Closed: lunch (Sun + Mon); dinner (Sun)
Last
Orders: lunch (2.00pm); dinner (10.30pm)

Alex Aitken is another of the encouraging group of self-taught English chefs, and this simple but comfortably furnished restaurant in a quiet town in the heart of the New Forest is one of the most popular eating places for miles around. Lunch may be fairly quiet but in addition to a very good value set menu, Alex offers an interesting à la carte menu, made more so by the fact that fish dishes may be taken in half-portions as a starter - for example, a local fillet of turbot wrapped in leek leaves with a light leek sauce. Venison, naturally enough, is available locally, and all the meats are well chosen and in excellent condition.

Presentation is modern, and dishes are brought at their best from the kitchen. Waiters could not be more polite and helpful; and the wide availability of wines by the glass is a good idea. By the bottle there are some bargains too, especially if you make a night of it and stay in one of the comfortable rooms upstairs!

251

Whitewater House   Hook

Hook, Near Basingstoke RG27 9EA
(025 672) 2436

Closed: lunch (Mon); dinner (Sun + Mon); Christmas; 2 weeks Jan
Last
Orders: lunch (2.15pm); dinner (9.30pm)

Whitewater House is a former mill, and has a superb and tranquil
setting by a stream - the River Whitewater actually runs right
underneath the house. Its style is still very much that of
someone's home, and large golden retrievers will greet you if
you arrive during the day. If the weather is fine, you can enjoy a
drink in the several acres of garden whilst reading through the
set menu. Mrs Hoare now has a chef to assist her, and between
them they produce varied and interesting menus, the dinner one
being, understandably, the more complex.

   You may find a salad of quails' eggs with artichokes, spiced
potted prawns in aspic, roasted breast of pigeon with noodles
and black grapes, or a noisette of veal and kidney with a Madeira
sauce. You can choose from a menu of 3 or 4 courses, but in
either case you'll have plenty of choice at each course. Service is
friendly, and the dining room - which seats about 30 - is elegantly
panelled, with large well-spaced tables.

Fifehead Manor   Middle Wallop

Middle Wallop SO20 8EG
(0264) 781565

Closed: 1 week Christmas
Last
Orders: lunch (2.30pm); dinner (9.30pm)

Middle Wallop is a beautiful village near the spot where 3
counties meet, and part of Fifehead Manor has been there for
nearly 1,000 years! The rest of the house in mellow red brick has
been sympathetically and lovingly restored, to give a timeless
feeling from the moment you enter the spacious hall which has a
reception at one end and bar at the other. It has 13 rooms, some
in the more modern stable block.
   A simple, beamed dining room is the setting for a small menu
of modern and traditional dishes, perhaps a salad of scallops and
gravadlax or a carefully stuffed guineafowl with a sharp fresh
lime sauce, from the fixed menu.

Bedrooms are light, spacious and well considered. You could stay here comfortably for a few days to explore south-west England and still be only an hour and a half or so from the centre of London.

The Old Manor House   Romsey

21 Palmerston Street, Romsey
(0794) 517353

Closed: lunch (Mon); dinner (Sun + Mon); 23-30 Dec
Last
Orders: lunch (2.00pm); dinner (9.30pm)

Romsey is a quiet town and The Old Manor House is an impressive Tudor house run by an Italian, Mauro Bregoli, who seems to combine good features from France, Italy and England. Game in season is a main feature, as is trout from the Test. Cheeses are from Philippe Olivier and chocolates are home-made. Mr Bregoli offers a set price dinner with a choice of 6 starters, and 4 main courses. You might try the tartare de saumon, or a brioche with a mousse of chicken and lambs' sweetbreads, or a main course of fillet of venison in puff pastry or an entrecôte cooked with pink peppercorns and pistachio nuts.

Despite Mr Bregoli's ancestry, French patriots beat a path to his door as do the local English. The cooking is confident, consistent and good value. The extensive wine list has an excellent selection of vintage Italian wines, as well as a good selection of clarets and Burgundies, which are competitively priced.

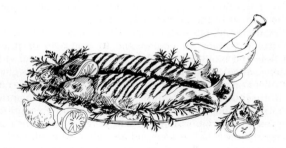

253

The Old House Hotel   Wickham

The Square, Wickham PO17 5JG
(0329) 833049

Closed: lunch (Sun + Mon); dinner (Sun); 10 days Christmas;
         2 weeks Easter; 3 weeks Aug/Sep
Last
Orders: lunch (1.45pm); dinner (9.30pm)

Wickham is a quiet little town, very close to both Southampton and Portsmouth, and The Old House Hotel is therefore very popular with businessmen. It is in fact Georgian, and the careful conversion by Richard Peyton-Skipworth has very much kept its identity as a house. The 10 bedrooms are all carefully furnished, many with antiques, and the small, private dining room is a useful feature.

The restaurant itself specialises in French provincial cooking, with dishes like poulet au vinaigre de vin, or foie de veau aux petits légumes. There may now also be the occasional dish with a more contemporary, oriental flavour. In any event, menus change weekly and all ingredients are fresh. The Old House Hotel conveys a curiously French atmosphere to this Georgian building.

■■■■ HEREFORD & WORCESTER ■■■■
The Bell Inn   Belbroughton

Bell End, Belbroughton DY9 9XU
(0562) 730232

Closed: lunch (Sat + Mon); dinner (Sun + Mon)
         Bank Holdays; first week Jan
Last
Orders: lunch (2.00pm) dinner (9.45pm)

I was one of the 6 or so judges in the competition to find the Young Chef of the Year which the Restaurateurs Association instigated, and in 1985 its first winner was Roger Narbett who was then joint head chef at this popular roadside inn. In 1986 the winner was Idris Caldora, who was the other half of the talented young team who have helped to put modern cuisine on the map in the Midlands. Who says that lightning doesn't strike twice in the same spot? Roger is now chef patron at Sloan's Restaurant in Birmingham but Idris remains at The Bell with John Narbett, Roger's father. The training with Mosimann at The Dorchester and then at the famous La Mère Blanc in Vonnas-sur-Veyle in France is evident in Idris's style of cooking.

The menu is small but well composed. Specialities are saucisson de fruits de mer au champagne (a 'sausage' of prawn, salmon, sole and monkfish which is poached and served with a champagne sauce), filets de lapereau grillés aux marrons glacés (grilled fillets of rabbit with a chestnut and cognac sauce) and omelet Rothschild (a sweet soufflé omelette served with apricot and Cointreau sauce). There is a 5-course 'Menu Exceptional' which gives a good opportunity to taste a variety of dishes, and on Sunday the set lunch is tremendous value, so book early.

The presentation and cooking are of a very high standard,

with sauces made from reductions in the modern way which give real depth of flavour, and a granité is served between courses instead of a sorbet.

The dining room is a new addition to the inn but is in keeping, with beams and a bar reception area where orders are taken. Andrew Alchurch's team of dining room staff take as much pride in serving the food as the kitchen does in preparing it, and are friendly and polite in their work. Housewines are Cuvée Duboeuf and there are around 100 wines to choose from on the list.

Sadly in 1988 the brewery which owns The Bell will take back the site, but by then John Narbett should have found another outlet for Idris, and we look forward to that with interest.

Hunters Lodge   Broadway

High Street, Broadway WR12 7DT
(0386) 853247

Closed: lunch (Mon); dinner (Sun + Mon); first 2 weeks Feb; first 2
          weeks Aug
Last
Orders: lunch (1.45pm); dinner (9.45pm)

This attractive ivy-covered restaurant is situated in the main street of Broadway amongst gracious houses and cottages built of honey-coloured Cotswolds stone. Kurt and Dottie Friedli's Hunters Lodge has become a well-established hostelry sitting amidst the many antique shops. It is a warm and comfortable restaurant with log fires in winter and a pretty garden for the summer months.

Kurt's menu is essentially classic, for example you might be offered a confit of duck, home-made potted shrimps, a quail consommé or quenelles of pike to start. Main courses could include classics such as breast of chicken hongroise or guineafowl normande, together with the lighter fish dishes like poached salmon with dill-flavoured hollandaise, or scallops sautéed and served on a bed of fennel.

A sensible lunch menu is cheaper, giving the chance to eat as much or as little as you like, choosing from such dishes as Arbroath smokies, grilled lemon sole, or lambs' kidneys in madeira sauce. A comprehensive wine list offers good value in all areas, together with a selection of grands vins.

The Lygon Arms   Broadway

Broadway WR12 7DU   £45
(0386) 852255

Last
Orders: lunch (2.00pm); dinner (9.30pm)

Broadway is perhaps one of the prettiest villages in the Cotswolds and the earliest parish records show that The Lygon Arms
has been an inn for well over 400 years, although parts of the
building date from much earlier. The gabled frontage is thought
to have been built by the Trevis family who were landlords in
1620, the year that the Mayflower sailed for the New World,
which perhaps explains why so many Americans have this on
their itinerary! Helpful and well-informed staff do their utmost
to provide every comfort at the hotel, plus advice and sugges-
tions for tours and trips round the local area. The huge dining
room itself is a more modern version of a Mediaeval dining hall.
It will be interesting to see what the Savoy Group change,
bearing in mind the style which it has given to all its other
establishments. The food we tried was good: an imaginatively
prepared mousseline of mange-touts served with slivers of
artichoke and chervil vinaigrette, excellent vichyssoise, very
good summer salad with tiny pieces of lamb in it, a good
selection of various lettuces, a simple steak, grilled well and an
accompanying salad with peeled tomatoes.

The rooms at the Lygon do vary: it's worth checking where
you will be staying because the original rooms are in the hotel
proper, and the extensions at the rear are modern, although
decorated traditionally inside. At the rear of the courtyard there
is a magnificent garden which runs through to a tennis court.
That coupled with the fact that The Lygon also has its own wine
bar, adjacent, might give you the idea that The Lygon Arms is
rather more than a traditional coaching inn. I personally prefer
the original part of the hotel with its smaller rooms and historic
features but over the years everyone has tried hard to blend the
old with the new.

Grafton Manor Bromsgrove

Grafton Lane, Bromsgrove B61 7HA
(0527) 31525

Closed: lunch (Mon - Sat)
Last
Orders: dinner (8.45pm)

Though the present manor house was commissioned in 1567 by Sir Gilbert Talbot, the history of Grafton goes back to before the Norman conquest. It was substantially rebuilt after a fire in 1710, and is now an elegant and interesting old house converted into a comfortable hotel. Six acres of gardens lead to a large lake, and there is a formal herb garden providing essential ingredients for the kitchen. The hotel is owned and run by the Morris family, and John Morris is the chef who creates daily menus using fresh local produce.

The herb garden comes into play with dishes such as mousse of pike with a sage sauce, rabbit cooked with nettles and bay leaves, crab and sorrel tart with cucumber sauce, fillet of beef with a bergamot sauce or Worcestershire lamb roasted with rosemary. Service is informal in the simple, uncomplicated dining room.

Bedrooms are tastefully decorated and furnished with 20th-Century facilities such as television, trouser press and hairdryer, bringing present and past together.

The Feathers Hotel Ledbury

High Street, Ledbury
(0531) 5266

Last
Orders: lunch (2.00pm); dinner (9.30pm)

When Ledbury was a post town in the 16th Century on the Royal Mail routes, The Feathers was a coaching inn, and this atmosphere is still retained in this heavily timbered building in the High Street.

John Masefield, the poet, was born in Ledbury in 1878, and he describes Ledbury as "pleasant to the sight, fair and half timbered, black and white" - little has changed. Ledbury is an old market town with interesting buildings, ancient churches, and narrow cobbled streets; and just across the road from The Feathers is the 17th-Century Market House, built on wooden pillars.

The hotel itself has been modernised, though its characterful interior still has the beams and panelling, there are 37 bedrooms, and the courtyard is now used for parking cars instead of horses.

Hope End Hotel   Ledbury

Ledbury   £35
(0531) 3613

unusual, and one of the best in the area.

Closed: lunch (daily); dinner (Mon + Tue)
Last
Orders: dinner (8.30pm)

This is a favourite country house hotel for several reasons,
firstly because it is very different from the classic country
mansion. Hope End is a listed building and was formerly the
childhood home of Elizabeth Barrett Browning. When the
Hegartys bought the house there was nothing but an empty shell
and so rather than create a sham of what might have been, they
designed a modern Scandinavian-style interior which surprisingly suits the unusual minaretted exterior perfectly. The character
of the house is retained but instead of heavy ornate fireplaces,
logs burn in circular stoves, and paintings are shown to full
advantage on white walls. There are bright rugs on parquet
floors and modern furniture combines well with antiques. This
unusual house is set in 40 acres of fields and woods.

The second and perhaps predominant reason for liking Hope
End is Patricia Hegarty's cooking, which shows a simplicity and
appreciation of fundamental materials similar to that demonstrated by the décor and furnishing of the house. She uses only
the finest produce, and prepares and cooks it with total honesty,
remembering that whatever is added should be secondary to the
natural flavour of the main ingredient. Unpasteurised cheese
from small producers who perhaps only make three or four
cheeses a week, free range chickens and fruit and vegetables
from their own walled garden are the types of material upon
which her cooking is based.

Her menu changes daily, and she provides a choice of first
courses and puddings, whilst the main course is the same for
everyone. There might be sorrel soup, or mussels cooked with
fennel, followed by chicken in a paprika sauce with vegetables.
A salad is served after the main dish and will include unusual
flavourings such as caraway leaves, and perhaps some pine nuts
for texture. Cheese is offered either before or after pudding, but
on no account should it be missed as there might be the local
Cloisters, a Welsh Pant-y-Llyn, a double Berkeley or Shropshire
Blue - cheeses that you won't find on the shelves of your local
supermarket. Puddings again show originality, with gooseberry
and elderflower cream, apple-mint ice-cream with chocolate
sauce, or demerara meringues with strawberry sauce.

Allow plenty of time to choose your wine, for John Hegarty's
list is a fine example of how a list should be. Each wine has been
carefully chosen, the clarets are all from good years and none is
younger than 7 years of age. There are no items of padding, and
the prices are reasonable. Book well in advance when you want
to stay at Hope End, as good news travels quickly!

Le Croque-en-Bouche   Malvern Wells

221 Wells Road, Malvern Wells WR14 4NF
(068 45) 65612

Closed: lunch (daily); dinner (Sun, Mon + Tue); Christmas
Last
Orders: dinner (9.15pm)

Nestling in the side of the Malverns, this large Victorian stone-built house is on the Elgar route, which leads tourists around the hills where Sir Edward used to compose much of his music. Marion Jones is just as competent a composer though her métier is cooking, and with her husband Robin she runs one of Britain's most highly acclaimed provincial restaurants. The ambience is that of a private house rather than a restaurant, and Robin will serve an apéritif in front of the fire in the sitting room bar. On the table is a list of suggested apéritifs, some good olives with a couple of canapés and the menu, presented and explained in detail.

It is a fixed price menu with a choice of dishes at each course except for the soup which starts the meal. The dining room is small with an almost Victorian atmosphere, tables are neatly laid with fresh flowers, and interesting alcoves house cognac and armagnac bottles. Robin's wine list has everything that you could possibly wish for, and it is frustrating to have to choose just one of the wines, leaving you dissatisfied with having had to reject the other 434 equally tempting selections! Every post-war vintage is represented except 1951, there are 16 pre-war vintages for good measure, and no fewer than 24 housewines.

The soup is served in a large tureen from which you help yourself, and subsequent courses are served on dishes which are placed on the tables in family style service. A typical menu might be a fish soup served with rouille, then a choice of local Wye salmon with sorrel and watercress sauce, a pancake filled with crab and spinach, or a globe artichoke with smoked trout and dill mayonnaise. Then main courses could include leg of lamb cooked with ginger, rosemary and soy, wild rabbit with flageolets and Dijon mustard, medallions of beef with orange and green peppercorn sauce, or guineafowl with bacon and thyme.

The cooking is sound and well judged, herbs are used to advantage, and the sauces have depth without overpowering the main ingredients. Instead of a large plate of vegetables, you are perhaps given a few delicious potatoes, and then a good salad with or after the main course. Cheeses are a selection of English and French farmhouse varieties, and puddings such as tarte tatin or a collection of sorbets and ice-creams might be offered.

I like Le Croque-en-Bouche for its lack of pretence, its honest cooking, and its overall high quality, of the sort you so often find in provincial French towns and yet so rarely in England.

259

Suefflé   Bearstead

The Green, Bearstead, Near Maidstone
(0622) 37065

Closed: lunch (Sat + Sun); dinner (Sun + Mon)
Last
Orders: lunch (2.00pm); dinner (9.45pm)

This, small, intimate restaurant overlooks Bearstead's village
green. The dining room is heavily beamed and cheerfully
furnished with a wood-burning stove and baker's oven set into
the wall. At lunch time a small blackboard table d'hôte menu is
offered, and in the evening an à la carte selection. There are a
few unusual wines on the list, and a good choice of unpasteurised cheeses.

Eastwell Manor   Boughton Aluph

Eastwell Park, Boughton Aluph, Near Ashford TN25 4HR
(0233) 35751

Last
Orders: dinner (9.30; 9.00pm Sat)

When you arrive at this beautiful manor house, you get the
impression that it has stood overlooking the lovely Kent countryside for at least 400 years, and it comes as something of a
surprise to learn that the present house was built in 1926! In fact
some 65% of the materials used were from the original building
which explains its style and elegance. Queen Victoria and
Edward Vll were frequent visitors, and a Queen of Rumania was
born in the old house which had origins as far back as 1069.

Now a luxurious hotel amidst formal gardens and 62 acres of
parkland, Eastwell Manor provides a comfortable base for
exploring Kent.

There is an English Fayre luncheon, and in the evening a table
d'hôte menu is available in addition to the à la carte selection of
modern style dishes. A claret and Burgundy lovers' list has some
fine wines with relative price tags.

Restaurant Seventy Four   Canterbury

74 Wincheap, Canterbury CT1 3RS
(0227) 67411

Closed: lunch (Sat + Sun); dinner (Sun); Bank Holidays;
          26-30 Dec; 1 week Easter; 3 weeks Aug/Sep
Last
Orders: lunch (2.00pm); dinner (9.30pm)

This smart, crisp dining room with almost black wood-panelled
walls is set inside a 16th-Century building, and Ian McAndrew
takes the best of the presentation from nouvelle cuisine coupled
with some excellent use of raw materials and sensibly sized

portions, beautifully sauced. You really don't worry too much about the décor, since you're here for the food.

Ian McAndrew enjoys cooking fish, and some of the dishes are quite unusual. Take his sautéed scallops with rhubarb, for instance, or perhaps the roast lobster on a bed of artichokes. It's a precise style of cooking, and a tremendous amount of thought and effort has gone into it. They have an excellently priced lunch menu, 2 courses for around £9.00, and a 3-course lunch for under £11.00, which includes 3 starters plus a soup. There might be a courgette flower filled with mousseline of red mullet, steamed and served on a tomato vinaigrette. From the 4 main courses you might choose a puff pastry case filled with lambs' sweetbreads in port wine, tomato and basil sauce; and then from the 4 or so puddings perhaps you'll be tempted by the glazed orange tartlet with an orange sabayon. The à la carte menu has some original and interesting dishes: among the starters is a terrine of fresh scallops and green peppers with a green pepper vinaigrette, and a mousseline of salmon filled with fresh girolles in a madeira sauce served hot. You could follow either of these by a roast breast of duck served with a confit of spring onions and a sauce made with fresh foie gras, or a sautéed breast of chicken served in a pastry case with a duxelles of mushrooms in a cream sauce. For dessert there are tartlets of fresh local raspberries served with a home-made gooseberry and calvados ice-cream, or a delicious chocolate box filled with an almond cream and poached fresh apricots, served with an apricot purée.

They'll do you a set menu at £21.00 if you're dazzled by this marvellous choice, or for around £26.00 there's a speciality menu where they tell you what they're going to serve and you just leave it to them to bring you 6 or 7 small courses. They promise that these won't be so large that you can't enjoy each course fully, and I believe them. The food we had was first class, and the people of Canterbury and surrounding areas should take advantage of this talented chef.

The service is professional, and the wine list offers a fair choice for most pockets and palates. Try the wines of one of France's leading chefs, Roger Vergé. He sells them at the Moulin de Mougins, and they're good value here at around £8.00 a bottle. Unfortunately we did not get a chance to visit the English brasserie which the McAndrews have opened in St Peter's Street, Canterbury, and which opens from 10.30am through to 10.30pm.

RESTAURANT SEVENTY FOUR.

Waterfield's   Canterbury

5A Best Lane, Canterbury CT1 2JB
(0227) 450276

Closed: lunch (Sun + Mon); dinner (Sun); 25-30 Dec
Last
Orders: lunch (2.00pm); dinner (10.30pm)

This interesting restaurant is tucked away up a little alleyway off
a side street. It is simple in décor, with brick walls, modern
chrome chairs, decoration in shades of pink with lots of
greenery, and it overlooks the river at the back. From the bridge
I noticed a boat at the back door, and I wonder perhaps if that's
the way Michael Waterfield gets to work in the morning, or
maybe he ferries in his supplies by this route.

However they arrive, he makes of them some imaginative and
interesting dishes or accompaniments, for instance rack of lamb
served with spiced damsons and dauphinois potatoes, or maybe
wild duck Queen Victoria, which is served with orange and plum
sauce and a purée of peas. To start with perhaps try some
salmon roe caviar with smoked halibut and chicory, and to finish
perhaps some excellent chocolate St Emilion.

The Gate Inn   Hildenborough

Rings Hill, Hildenborough TN11 8LV
(0732) 832103

Closed: Sun; Bank Holidays; Christmas Day; Boxing Day
Last
Orders: lunch (2.30pm); dinner (11.00pm)

There is nothing fancy about the exterior or the interior of what
is supposed to be a typical pub: some sepia printed photographs
on the wall of cricketing people from about 1913, some advertising signs. It was packed with people, some sitting at the bar
drinking beer and eating smoked salmon, others spread through
the rear restaurant which seats about 30. The only difference
appears to be that you can book in the restaurant, whereas in the
bar you have to take a chance.

For the country there is an amazing selection of foods: stuffed
garlic clams, samphire, two types of oyster, and Greenland
prawns as starters, or just one mixed plateful if you wish; whole
sea bass, dressed crab, John Dory, turbot, langoustine and
crawfish are amongst the choice of main courses. There is an
excellent and dense chocolate mousse for pudding, and a variety
of other sweets; Cheddar cheese comes from Grant's of Somerset - all served across the bar or by local ladies who bring the
food to your table. Simply cooked, simply presented, nothing
'chi chi' about this establishment at all - salad dressing is in beer
bottles with stoppers - excellent value for money and well worth
a visit, though it's wise to arrive early to ensure a table as it's
obviously well used by locals and travellers alike. Good quality
wines range from about £5.00 a bottle.

Stone Green Hall **Mersham**

Mersham, Ashford TN25 7HE
(023 372) 418

Closed: lunch (Mon - Sat); dinner (Sun except residents);
      mid-Feb - end Mar
Last
Orders: lunch (2.00pm); dinner (9.00pm)

Architecturally, Stone Green Hall appeals to me. It is a lovely house - friendly, with a Georgian exterior and a beautifully tiled entrance hall and restaurant. The thoughtfully and cleverly designed conservatory doubles as a breakfast room and a room for drinks in the summer. Some beautifully appointed bedrooms have lovely individual touches to them - marvellous overstuffed chairs and sofas, lots of attractive fabrics, and tables filled with a good range of books to read. There's also a little games room off the main sitting room, filled with every conceivable kind of parlour game. James and Ingrid Kempston are charming, and do their best to make you feel at home, and as you may have gathered, it is a very warm, friendly home. The gardens are everything I think an English garden should be, with a wonderful collection of well-trimmed round and tall topiary and formal gardens. Then just on the other side of the hall, there are fields running off into the distance to the hills with woods and lots of grazing sheep.

From the perfect surroundings which I'm sure you'll enjoy, let's move on to the food. An excellent value fixed price menu at around £15.00 might consist of poached scallops with gingery garlic, home-made elderflower sorbet, followed by a roast loin of Romney Marsh lamb with apple, ginger and mint relish, new potatoes and braised fennel. Ginger pudding Stone Green Hall is a must, and if it's available try the marmalade pudding or the chocolate marquise. The simple but adequate wine list has reasonable prices. I want to go back there in the Winter and take over all 4 rooms with friends, and have a relaxed, pleasant couple of days.

Thackeray's House   Tunbridge Wells

85 London Road TN1 1EA
(0892) 37558

Closed: Sun + Mon; Christmas; Easter; 2 weeks Aug
Last
Orders: dinner (10.00pm)

The attractive green and white exterior of this house, one of the
oldest in Tunbridge Wells, has instant appeal, and the interior is
cosy and welcoming. The ground floor dining room has large
beams, pictures on the walls and an open fireplace, and there are
several old volumes of Thackeray's works on bookshelves
alongside some bottles of old Cognac and Armagnac. Bruce
Wass is the chef patron, and he offers a choice of fixed price or à
la carte menus at lunch and dinner. Try the fresh herb fettucine
with mussels, venison with a red wine sauce accompanied by a
well-dressed salad and perhaps a sorbet to finish - the blueberry
one has an excellent texture and flavour.

Service is friendly and efficient, and when the weather is
warm there is an outside patio on which to have an apéritif. In
the basement is an attractive bistro called Downstairs at Thack-
erays, which has a quarry-tiled floor, gingham cloths and a
reasonably priced menu of country-style dishes.

■■■■■■■■■■ LANCASHIRE ■■■■■■■■■■

The Foxfields   Billington

Whalley Road, Billington, Near Blackburn BB6 9HY
(025 482) 2556

Closed: lunch (Sat + Mon); dinner (Sun); Bank Holidays;
        3-4 days Christmas
Last
Orders: lunch (1.30pm) dinner (9.30pm; 9.00pm Sun)

Situated just outside Blackburn, The Foxfields is a popular restaurant and banqueting suite. The modern building is very comfortably furnished and exceptionally well run by Terence Parkinson and his friendly staff. His long established rapport with Hank van Hellman, the chef, is reflected in the quality of food, using ingredients to good effect.

Menus reflect the seasons, and apart from the main menu, specialities are offered according to market supplies. A fixed price lunch menu offers good value. The wine list is comprehensive with some good choices, plenty of half bottles and a connoisseur's section for special occasions.

High Moor Restaurant   Wrightington

High Moor Lane, Wrightington, Near Wigan WN6 9PS   £35
(025 75) 2364

Closed: lunch (Sat + Mon); dinner (Sun + Mon); 1 week Jan;
      2 weeks Aug
Last
Orders: dinner (9.45pm)

Turn into Robin Hood Lane from the B5239 Southport to Wigan Road, and then left at High Moor Lane, and this restaurant is a little way along on your right. Paolo Rossi is the manager and James Sines the chef patron in this 17th-Century hostelry, where you will find a warm welcome and some of the best cooking in Lancashire. Long beams and divided areas create an intimate old inn atmosphere in the dining room, and leaded windows look out over the hills.

Canapés are served with drinks, crisp home-made rolls are offered at the table, toasted brioche comes with the excellent terrine of duck livers, and all of these are made in the kitchens. The à la carte menu uses good fresh ingredients, like Dublin Bay prawns, or scallops on a bed of leaf spinach and bacon glazed with Emmental cheese. A cassoulet of monkfish and mussels with saffron and winter vegetables, an escalope of salmon with pistachio butter, or a nut of lamb with claret sauce and a small ratatouille are also excellent. Vegetables are also well prepared, for instance a small mousse of brussels sprouts, crisp mange-touts, and pear-shaped duchesse potatoes. The pudding menu has equally tempting dishes, like fresh pineapple charlotte, a basket of strawberries with pink champagne sorbet, or a dark chocolate rum truffle cake.

The wine list is mainly French with a good range to suit all tastes and pockets. Service is lively and efficient, and all the staff seem to enjoy their work - small wonder that the restaurant is so busy with such enthusiastic young management. Jim's sparkling white kitchen was shown with pride, and you go away feeling that Wigan is lucky to have a good rugby side and the High Moor!

■■■ LEICESTERSHIRE ■■■
Restaurant Roger Burdell   Loughborough

The Manor House, Sparrow Hill, Loughborough LE11 1BT   £45
(0589) 231813

Closed: lunch (Sun + Mon); dinner (Sun); Christmas; 1 week Aug
Last
Orders: lunch (2.00pm); dinner (9.45pm)

Roger Burdell's pretty little restaurant is situated in the Old
Manor House at Loughborough, and as he explains to you on his
menu, it once welcomed King Richard II and then on another
occasion King Henry VIII. It is his intention to continue such
hospitality in this rather splendid building, but don't go running
away with the idea that it's full of nooks and crannies and
blackened beams, for certainly on the ground floor it is not like
that at all. The décor is reminiscent of a 1930 s dining room, all
pretty colours and shell lamps, with a pleasant lounge bar in
which to have a drink while you're waiting to order. Staff are
pleasant and attentive, and the waitresses have been taught to
remember the dishes on the menu, and the individual names of
the cheeses and where they come from.

The menu is carefully thought out and varies by the month,
and at a set price of around £20.00, it includes some excellent
choices. If you're there in late summer, you might be offered a
summer vegetable terrine with herb mayonnaise, or a warm
salad of pigeon breast with bacon and croûtons, from a choice of
4 starters. There's a fish course included, which might be a
timbale of monkfish with a crayfish sauce, or a home-made fish
sausage with cockles and mussels, flavoured with bacon and
served on a bed of leeks. From the choice of 4 main courses,
perhaps you might like the stuffed breast of chicken with
mushrooms, chives and cream, or the simpler pan-fried calves'
liver with artichoke hearts and shallots. Cheese is also included
in the price, as are some excellent puddings. Try the iced
gooseberry soufflé with blackcurrant fool, if it is available, or the
traditional English summer pudding. The menu is supplemented
by daily specialities, and there's also a set lunch. There are some
good choices on the sensibly priced wine list. All in all, this
restaurant is quite a find.

Rothley Court   Rothley

Westfield Lane, Rothley LE7 7LG
(0533 37) 4141

Closed: lunch (Sat)
Last
Orders: lunch (1.30pm); dinner (9.30pm)

Situated on the edge of Sherwood Forest, the building dates
from the 13th Century. It has an international-style menu and
can make for a pleasant overnight stay, with some well-
furnished rooms. The bedrooms in the main building are of a
better standard than those in the converted stable block; and the
Macaulay Room is a favourite. Pleasant conference suites can be
hired. Rothley has its own chapel attached to the main court.

Ram Jam Inn   Stretton

Great North Road, Stretton, Near Oakham LE15 7QX
(0780) 81776

Last
Orders: 11.00pm

Here's a tip for those men in the ministry who are responsible
for giving out contracts to build catering outlets and hotels by
the side of motorways; and also for some of the larger con-
glomerates that normally operate this type of place: do yourself
a favour and go up to the Ram Jam on the A1 just above
Stamford. There you'll find a pleasant revolution which, for
people who have travelled extensively in France, will be no
surprise - except for the fact that this is situated in England! The
nearest example I can give for Francophiles is the Motel 16 near
Angoulême.

The style of the place is simplicity itself, in creams and browns.
It opens at 7.00am and there is a little café-bar as you go in
where, amongst other things, you can have coffee, hot chocolate,
croissants and snacks, and where you rub shoulders with a
mixture of truck drivers and businessmen, as well as families
just stopping off. (See the French connection?) Go past the
reception desk, down a couple of steps into the bar area to the
open grill where they char-grill your steaks to order, and into a
simple restaurant, with white tablecloths and pine furniture.
Here you can enjoy a simple, well-cooked and well-presented
meal. The first thing that envelopes you as you come into the
building is the delicious smell of woodsmoke and charcoal.

For first courses you can pick from a warm brioche filled with
mushrooms in a creamy sauce, a Stilton dip with raw vegetables,
a half pint of prawns with fresh bread and mayonnaise, or a
delicious home-made vegetable and sausage soup. You can get
some huge 6-inch sandwiches with fresh salmon and cucumber
(apparently a favourite Ram Jam dish in the 1930s), a steak
sandwich served on a salad of lettuce and avocado, grilled
Rutland sausages with sweet and sour onions, steak and
mushroom pie, all served with Ram Jam Fries - a huge portion of
French fries - or jacket potatoes. Have some Colston Bassett

Stilton to follow. Puddings are treacle and nut tart, blackberry and apple pie, or Ram Jam ices, or you can go really French and have fromage blanc with fresh fruit purée and chopped nuts.

Georges Duboeuf stars again with the housewines, and Geoffrey Roberts creeps in with the Californian reds amongst the 20 or so from which you can choose. If you're a beer drinker there is Ruddles County, Ruddles Best Bitter and Murphy's Stout all the way from Cork, and a Belgian Duvel Red Label. The bedrooms are well laid out with jumbo sized beds, good fittings, well fitted bathrooms, simple in style but all good quality - no fuss, and excellent for one or two nights' stay.

This place is a find and really is a must if you're travelling up or down the A1 or M1, and it's well worth a detour. At the moment it's a one-off, but I would truly love to see a whole chain of these up and down the country for motorway travellers.

Incidentally, the name Ram Jam was adopted by the locals when in the 1920s a previous owner advertised his Ram Jam Brew outside and the name stuck. Apparently something similar happened on the other side of the road when Jackson, Stops & Staff had a 'For Sale' sign outside of a pub for over a year - the name stuck, and since then the pub has been called The Jackson Stops!

■■■■■■■ LINCOLNSHIRE ■■■■■■■

The Bull and Swan   Stamford

St Martins, Stamford
(0780) 63558

Last
Orders: lunch (2.00pm); dinner (10.30pm)

This Melbourn Brewery house has a simple menu with fisherman's platter, home-made soup, sardines provençale, or shell-on prawns with garlic and curry dips. A speciality is devilled whitebait with brown bread, or you can just have a simple ploughman's if you prefer. In the restaurant section you can also get swordfish in prawn and mushroom sauce, whitebait or crab, a choice of grilled meats - fillet, rump, or sirloin, mixed grill and rack of lamb. Waiters in long white aprons sing out your order, and all in all there's a fun, boisterous atmosphere, and it's definitely the place to visit if you're seeking something less elaborate than the full menu at The George.

The George of Stamford   Stamford

71 St Martin's, Stamford
(0780) 55171

Last
Orders: lunch (2.30pm); dinner (9.30pm)

Stamford is a town of much historic interest, and The George is
the type of solid old coaching inn that you always like to find in
the heart of England. Built in the 16th Century, The George has
been carefully modernised and now has 47 bedrooms and a
conference centre.

The large dining room, with its heavy furnishings and large
trolleys laden with roasts of the day or sweets that look
appealing, seems always to be busy, and the staff are polite and
professional.

On the menu there are some genuinely interesting English and
continental dishes: chicken liver pâté is rich and smooth, pork
fillet with kümmel sauce makes an unusual and well-made main
course, or you may prefer a very decent mushroom risotto. For
less formal eating there is a bar and buffet which offers large
roast joints, lots of home-made savoury dishes and good solid
snacks.

The wine list has many bargains and is well worth reading
carefully.

▬▬▬▬▬▬ NORFOLK ▬▬▬▬▬▬

Congham Hall   Grimston

Grimston, King's Lynn PE32 1AH
(0485) 600250

Closed: lunch (Sat); dinner (Sun); Christmas Day - 10 Jan
Last
Orders: lunch (2.00pm); dinner (9.30pm)

An immaculately furnished and well-appointed white Georgian
country house, Congham Hall has its own stables, swimming
pool and even a cricket pitch. They also make good use of the
gardens to produce many herbs and vegetables for the kitchen
and whenever possible use locally caught fish. The cooking is
modern English food in the French style - potted pepper chicken
garnished with a crayfish salad, good quality fillet steak with a
savoury sauce of shallots and anchovies. The extensive dinner
menu is priced on the choice of main course. Young commis
waiters try hard to please.

The wine list is small, but has an interesting selection from
southern France. Comfortable bedrooms are well furnished, and
a proper English breakfast is served in the sunny pink dining
room.

Adlard's Restaurant Wymondham

16 Damgate Street, Wymondham NR18 0BQ
(0953) 603533

Closed: lunch (daily); dinner (Sun + Mon)
Last
Orders: dinner (9.00pm)

In this charming converted butcher's shop - the front still has the original tiles - you'll find a warm welcoming interior more reminiscent of a provincial French village than of Norfolk. Tables are set close together on a flagstone floor; paintings and pictures cover the walls. You'll also find David Adlard, cooking with the type of skill, flair and imagination that reflects his time at The Carved Angel in Dartmouth and at The Connaught. You may be offered a parfait of young pigeon livers with marjoram, a ragoût of monkfish with ginger sauce, or an escalope of wild salmon with a beaujolais sauce. Puddings are all imaginatively and perfectly executed - try perhaps the elderflower fritters with a gooseberry purée.

Mary Adlard runs the dining room with style, and can advise on a very interesting list of wines drawn from all over the world, carefully priced to enable you to experiment.

■■■ NORTHAMPTONSHIRE ■■■

French Partridge Horton

Horton, Northampton NN7 2AP
(0604) 870033

Closed: lunch (daily); dinner (Sun + Mon); 2 weeks Christmas; 2 weeks
Easter; 3 weeks Jul/Aug
Last
Orders: dinner (9.00pm)

The Partridges have run a successful restaurant in their pretty Georgian house for the last 23 years and it is easy to understand why. The chef patron's 4-course menus are consistently good, and very reasonably priced in relation to the type of dishes which are served. The menu changes monthly to use seasonal

produce, and there are sensible choices of classic cook
together with the more modern style of today. On the sam
menu one might find soupe à l'oignon, confit de canard, pear an
Stilton quiche and poulet rôti farci aux filets de gibier. Puddings
show the same variety and there is a choice of a savoury as an
alternative, which has become a rare sight on today's menus.
Mrs Partridge watches over the dining room, and service is by
friendly girls in smart uniforms. She also selects the wines for
the comprehensive list and has over 60 choices at under £8.00 a
bottle, a commendable policy.

The house is elegant with a French style bar full of interesting
prints, and the dark green dining room creates an ideal ambience in which to enjoy the accomplished cooking of David
Partridge.

NORTH YORKSHIRE

The Devonshire Arms — Bolton Abbey

Bolton Abbey, Skipton BD23 6AJ
(075 671) 441

£35

Last
Orders: lunch (2.00pm); dinner (9.30pm)

The nearby ruin of Bolton Abbey and the picture postcard
village are a perfect and tranquil place for a weekend. The
Devonshire Arms has modernised rooms and a pleasant dining
room, offering a mixture of French and English dishes in the
evening, served by young and professional staff. At lunch times
there is a well-presented buffet with lots of roast meats, perhaps
some fresh salmon en croûte and some warm or hot dishes -
perfect after a long walk.

Also attached to the hotel is their own pub, a lively rendezvous for the local cricket team and fell walkers.

271

~~ty~~'s Café & Tea Rooms   Harrogate

~~Pa~~rliament Street, Harrogate HG1 2QU   £10
~~(04~~23) 64659

~~Cl~~osed: Christmas Day; New Year's Day
Last
Orders: 5.30pm (6.00pm Sun)

Betty's is wonderful. Frederick Belmont, a Swiss immigrant, started the business in 1919 and it is now run by his nephew, who still sends their bakers and confectioners to Switzerland to learn their trade. There is a large range of excellent teas and coffees and good Alsace wines from Jean-Jacques Müller available during licensing hours.

At a time when so many of the real English cafés and tea rooms have long since gone, Betty's flourishes, proving that childhood memories are not dreams and can be re-lived in the 1980s. It's the sort of place to which, as a youngster, you were taken by mother for afternoon tea as a special treat. There were waitresses in very smart black and white uniforms with little aprons, and a black and white headband, and trolleys with a vast array of mouthwatering cakes which you couldn't wait to taste. A pianist would play and the room would buzz with conversation and chinking teacups. Sometimes, if you were going to the theatre or the cinema, you might have a high tea of poached eggs on toast, Welsh rarebit, gammon and eggs, or crisp fish and chips; and there was always one of those lavish cakes to finish, or perhaps an ice-cream sundae or melba.

I wear long trousers now but in Harrogate time stands still, and Betty's can still conjure up the magic.

Drum and Monkey   Harrogate

5 Montpellier Gardens, Harrogate HG1 2TF   £30
(0423) 502650

Closed: Sun; Christmas Day to 2 Jan
Last
Orders: lunch (2.30pm); dinner (10.15pm)

Sounding more like a pub than a fish restaurant, this is certainly the place to see and be seen in when in Harrogate. Regulars testify to the quality of the product and judging by a visit on a busy Saturday morning, they are right. The bar on the ground floor is usually packed with people eating and drinking as others wait to, while the first floor is a little more sedate, with slate topped tables and slightly faded décor. Menus vary from lunch to dinner but fish is the thing, and a large selection of fish and shellfish is prepared in a varied number of ways. Good fish soups are substantial starters, whilst there is anything from smoked salmon to prawn cocktail for traditionalists, sweet and sour prawn and fish roulade, to queen scallops with cheese and garlic butter for the more adventurous.

Wines are mainly white and the service is quick and friendly, but do book unless you want to eat late in this bustling, busy atmosphere! John Russell, who gives good value in his carvery restaurant in York, recommended the Drum and Monkey and there's a man who knows value for money!

Cockett's Hotel   Hawes

Market Place, Hawes DL8 3RD
(096 97) 312

Closed: lunch (daily); 15 Nov - 20 Dec; 2 Jan - 10 Mar
Last
Orders: dinner (9.30pm)

Hawes is a small town in Wensleydale, one of the most beautiful of the Yorkshire Dales, and you might discover Cockett's whilst exploring this glorious area of waterfalls and castles. The small stone built hotel dates from the 17th Century, and is located in the market place. Brian and Cherry Guest own and run the hotel themselves, he fronting the operation while Cherry does all the cooking for their busy dining room.

When they bought the property 5 years ago and wanted to build the reputation of the restaurant, they found that their greatest problem was to obtain reliable supplies of good commodities. They have now solved the problem, but have to depend on many different sources from a widespread area. The effort is justified, as the produce is put to very good use in the kitchen. Excellent mussels might be followed by a perfectly cooked grouse, to provide a meal where fingers take precedence over knife and fork! Next comes a plate of local cheeses, white and blue Wensleydale and the more unusual Swaledale, all in perfect condition. It's good to see the increasing use of local English cheeses, showing that we can do just as well in providing a good choice as Messrs Androuet or Olivier from France.

The décor and furnishings are homely and comfortable, there's a 4-poster bedroom for honeymooners or older romantics, and Brian has an enviable collection of paintings and prints which fill every wall. Some are on sale in the adjacent gallery, and he kindly loaned a copy of what must be one of the earliest restaurant guides, entitled *The Restaurants of London* by Eileen Hooton-Smith, published in 1928, some of which we have reproduced in the London section.

Heriot's Hotel and Wine Bar   Hawes

Main Street, Hawes
(096 97) 536

Closed: weekdays in winter (we suggest you check)
Last
Orders: lunch (2.30pm); dinner (9.45pm)

Should you wish to stay in Hawes and Cockett's is full, this
newly renovated hotel is comfortable and well run. All rooms
have shower rooms, and the ground floor wine bar is good value
for a light lunch or to pass a restful evening after walking the
dales.

   The building is of local stone and occupies a prominent corner
site, and most rooms have views over the surrounding hills. The
attractive split-level wine bar has some excellent water colours,
and is comfortably furnished.

Kirkby Fleetham Hall   Kirkby Fleetham

Kirkby Fleetham, Northallerton DL7 0SU   £35
(0609) 748226

Closed: lunch (Mon - Sat)
Last
Orders: lunch (1.30pm); dinner (9.00pm)

Country life goes on all around you at this carefully restored
17th-Century manor house about a mile from the small village.
Young English girls look after reception and wait at table with
lots of smiles and enthusiasm, and the owner is usually on hand
to keep an eye on things! Polished tables and gleaming silver in
the dining room give a true country house feel to the place, and
if you wish you can enjoy the benefits of a really excellent cellar.
Wines are well chosen, very fairly priced and kept in tip-top
condition. It is necessary to give a couple of hours notice if you
want a really great wine properly served, as they are cellar kept.

   Dinner always starts with a soup - chilled lettuce, beef
consommé with sherry, turkey or fish, followed by perhaps an
orange, date and walnut appetiser, garlic mushrooms, duck liver
pâté or fresh scallops in grain mustard sauce. Main courses
might be a sirloin steak in madeira sauce, veal escalope with
apricots and almonds, fillet of brill with avocado and prawns or
lamb cutlets with honey and walnuts.

   Herbs and vegetables are from their own walled garden and
are combined with some top quality local produce; seasoning
and sauces are light; and you can enjoy a pleasant dinner. If you
stay the night in the large and comfortable bedrooms you will
get a substantial breakfast to see you on your way.

Schwallers Restaurant   Knaresborough

6-8 Bond End, Knaresborough HG5 9AQ
(0423) 863899

Closed: lunch (daily); Mon + Tue; Boxing Day; New Year's Day
Last
Orders: dinner (10.00pm)

Caroline Schwaller is the lively hostess and her husband, Martin, the chef patron at this restaurant with a wine bar in downtown Knaresborough. The wine bar décor is startling in black and white, whilst the first floor restaurant has more of a cottage feel with beams, an open fire and cosy tables. A small lounge on the ground floor serves as a bar for pre-dinner drinks.

If you drop in at lunch time, Martin prepares some of his native Swiss specialities such as fondue, schnitzels and veal sausage (würst), with different sauces or potato salad. Don't miss the rösti which is a delicious potato and onion cake. In the evening there are 5-course menus offered at various prices, and the good quality ingredients are carefully cooked. Fish is a speciality, and the puddings endorse the reputation which the Swiss have for pastry. The wine list makes interesting reading, and it's even more fun to drink your way through, with an excellent range of wines at affordable prices. It was a welcome change to see an Alsation Sylvaner as a white housewine, and the gutsy Spanish Jumilla as a red.

Knaresborough is an interesting old town with a superb fishmonger and butcher's shop near the castle.

The Black Bull   Moulton

Moulton, Richmond DL10 6QJ
(032 577) 289

Closed: lunch (Sat other than bar snacks, Sun); dinner (Sun)
Last
Orders: lunch (1.45pm); dinner (10.15pm)

There can be very few pubs in Yorkshire, or anywhere else for that matter, that have a fully equipped Pullman railway carriage in their back garden. If there are, it is unlikely that they take such care with the food as well. Chef Charles Somerville has been here for years, working with enthusiastic owner Harry Pagendham. In the public bar they serve sandwiches and snacks that are exemplary. In the small Victorian-style oyster bar there is simple food at lunch and a wider range of classic dishes in the evening. Modern cooking is served on the train in the evenings only using good, fresh food in some interesting ways. Portions are large even by Yorkshire standards and our starter of prawn provençale would fill up most southerners well before they get to the lemon sole, perfectly cooked and covering the plate.

The wine list has been lovingly collected and compiled, and service at lunch time is by friendly local ladies, and in the evenings by waiters.

McCoys   Staddlebridge

The Tontine, Staddlebridge DL6 3JB
(060 982) 671

one of the best in North Yorkshire for food & ambience £55

Closed: Restaurant: lunch (daily); Sun + Mon; Bank Holidays
Last
Orders: Restaurant: 10.30pm; Bistro: lunch (3.00pm); dinner (11.00pm)

This somewhat austere building at the roadside must have been a welcome sight to the drivers of mail coaches when they drew in to change horses and break their long journeys. The inn is just as welcome a hostelry today as it was then, and the McCoys' hospitality must rival that afforded to travellers of the past. The interior again revives memories of a different era, this time the 1920s, with dramatic décor and just a touch of theatre. Furniture is of the period, and there are lots of fresh flowers and palms amidst the memorabilia, moquette settees, wicker armchairs, Art Deco lights, and Al Bowley's singing.

"We are certainly not a country house hotel," says Peter McCoy, "nor do we think of ourselves as a restaurant with rooms. We are what we are and wish to please customers in our own way." Peter's brothers cook and their style is based on classic principles with modern touches, more substantial than so-called nouvelle cuisine. The dining room is not carpeted, the silvery wallpaper has huge colourful flowers, Chinese parasols serve to lower the ceiling level, the crisp linen is deep pink, and candles flicker on the tables creating a unique, intimate atmosphere. The ambience is so evocative of the 1920s that you wonder whether alcohol might still be prohibited!

Noodles surrounded by huge langoustines and scallops are served on a rich sauce topped with a plump oyster, then try a Bresse pigeon roasted and garnished with baby leeks, truffle and pieces of duck foie gras. Rest awhile, then try the wafer-thin slices of pastry sandwiched with pastry cream and slices of strawberries. Don't miss the McCoy's pastry, either in the tiny mussel tartlets served as an apéritif or in the puddings - it *melts*!

Service is attentive without being overbearing, friendly without being oppressive. All is done without fuss yet nothing is missed. Bedrooms are spacious, tastefully decorated and comfortable with air conditioning, and by staying you will be able to sample the excellent breakfast and also eat in the bistro. As Peter said, he likes to please customers in his unique style and he achieves this objective rather well.

Located in the basement of this much-fêted restaurant, the bistro is packed most of the time. Tables are solid wood, a few wines are written on the blackboard, service is friendly and swift, and American rock music provides the background.

Unsurprisingly, considering the reputation of the McCoy family, the food is the star. Classic, almost clichéd bistro dishes take on new life. The generous portion of coq-au-vin is darkly sauced, and the boeuf bourguignon is as good. You may find a celery and red pepper soup or some plump, pink breasts of pigeon in a well-reduced vintage port sauce. All main courses come with a bowl of new potatoes and a gleaming bowl of salad. Puddings are enormous and prices are at the bargain level.

The Bridge Inn   Stapleton

Stapleton DL2 2QQ
(0325) 50106

Closed: lunch (Mon - Sat); dinner (Sun + Mon)
Last
Orders: lunch (2.00pm); dinner (9.30pm, 10.00pm Sat)

From the outside it looks just like a local pub and there is a distinct effort made to keep the diners and the locals in their separate bars. Once this is understood, though, you can enjoy a drink in the cocktail bar and read the blackboard in the parlour-like room next door.

Owner/chef Nicholas Young changes the menu daily and produces some interesting modern country cooking, stylishly presented. Sunday lunch offers a selection of roasts. The pork with fresh thyme was perfectly cooked and surrounded with roast potatoes and crisp, fresh vegetables.

The evening menu offers some ambitious cooking which is well executed and charmingly served. The wine list is rather limited but will no doubt develop as the restaurant does. This seems a place that will justify the faith that the many followers (including Francis Coulson and Brian Sack of Sharrow Bay) have shown.

277

■■■■■ OXFORDSHIRE ■■■■■

Woods Restaurant   Chesterton

Chesterton OX6 8UE
(0869) 241444

Closed: lunch (Mon); dinner (Sun + Mon)
Last
Orders: lunch (1.45pm); dinner (10.00pm)

In a pretty countryside setting just outside Bicester, David and
Georgina Wood run an attractive restaurant which offers French
nouvelle style cuisine. Set price menus have first courses such
as a warm salad of goats' cheese with walnuts and chives,
smoked goose with avocado in yoghurt and gooseberry dressing,
and main courses of panaché of veal, calves' liver, kidney and
sweetbreads in madeira and citrus sauces, or rack of lamb
scented with sorrel and tarragon. Cooking is competent and
service very attentive, and there is a compact list of 40 mostly
French wines.

La Madonette   Chipping Norton

7 Horsefair, Chipping Norton OX7 5PL
(0680) 2320

Closed: lunch (daily); dinner (Sun + Mon)
Last
Orders: dinner (9.45pm)

La Madonette occupies the corner in a row of similar buildings
in Chipping Norton, built of Cotswolds stone and painted fawn,
although any resemblance with the area stops there. This is very
much provincial France. Mrs Ritter runs the front of house with
Alain Ritter cooking competently. They try and book the tables
15 minutes apart, and once you're in you have your table for the
whole evening. It's incredibly busy, so necessary to book; the
locals seem to have completely adopted this capable French
chef. You might choose from cassoulet of fruits de mer (scallops, monkfish, and John Dory poached in a chablis and cream
sauce), or escalope of salmon with écrevisses in a champagne
sauce. Other courses might include veal fillet cooked with
sweetbreads and served with a wild mushroom and oregano
sauce, lamb noisettes cooked pink with a Dijon mustard and
tarragon sauce, or a small fillet steak cooked with a soft green
peppercorn and brandy sauce. Choose from 5 starters - at least 3
will be fish - plus some excellent desserts, including a light
chocolate mousse flavoured with Cointreau, or a trio of puff
pastry cases filled with soft fruits, warmed with liqueurs. There
are excellent cheeses from Philippe Olivier, and Alain Ritter is
very proud of the fact that even in Chipping Norton he can get
fresh supplies of fish from St Austell, oysters from Loch Fyne,
excellent meat from Newton Meadow of Warwickshire, and
game from the local shoots. Again, here is a man who sets great
store by his raw material. Wines are suitably priced for the
country, with housewines from £5.50 a bottle from his family
firm, and a good selection if you wish to spend a little more.

The White Hart — Dorchester-on-Thames

Dorchester-on-Thames
(0865) 340074

Closed: dinner (Sun)
Last
Orders: lunch (2.00pm); dinner (9.30pm)

Originally a 17th-Century coaching inn on the route between London, Oxford and Stratford-upon-Avon, this charming hotel has been refurbished and now offers a high standard of accommodation. In the 8th-Century Doric, as it was then known, was the Cathedral city of Wessex and Mercia. The famous Abbey remains and is well worth visiting. In the reception area of the hotel is the well which was used to water the horses during their long journeys, and the restaurant was originally a granary. The floor of the loft has been removed to expose superb beams in the roof. Copper pans gleam on the white walls in the dining room, and the polished wooden tables and chairs blend with the profusion of beamed walls and ceilings. Bar snacks such as game pie and lasagna are served in the Abbey room at lunch time, and good fresh produce is used in traditional dishes.

Feldon House — Lower Brailes

Lower Brailes, Near Banbury OX15 5HW

Closed: please ring for details
Last
Orders: dinner (9.00pm)

Situated in the tiny village of Lower Brailes, next to the church, is a small red brick restaurant with rooms run by Allan and Maggie Witherick in a very friendly and homely manner. Newly decorated in a country style, it has comfortable furniture and pretty floral curtains and cushions.

It's ideal if you want to throw a private dinner party for 12 people or less but don't feel up to cooking, because it feels just like home for the evening. Allan Witherick cooks, and Maggie runs the 2 dining rooms. They don't like to mix parties so if you book a table for 2 you'll be on your own for the evening.

All meals have to be ordered in advance as they shop and cook for each party of people. When you make your booking you can specify any particular foods you don't enjoy, and they will cater accordingly. The menu is set - 3 courses for lunch and 4 courses for dinner with coffee and home-made petits fours. A typical lunch could consist of buckling pâté, breast of chicken stuffed with pine kernels and served with hollandaise, followed by strawberry pavlova, all at around £12.00 a head. For dinner there might be chilled lovage soup, gravadlax, collops of beef, and strawberry shortcake.

It's also a good venue if you want to come down from London for the weekend or just a night for a dinner party, and meet up with friends. You can take over the 4 bedrooms and have the place to yourselves. It's pretty and comfortable, and the Withericks do their best to ensure you'll come back. By the way, don't forget to take your own wines - they don't have a licence.

279

The Old Swan Hotel   Minster Lovell

Minster Lovell, Near Witney OX8 5QN
(0993) 75614

Last
Orders: lunch (1.45pm); dinner (9.30pm)

Once or twice I've been privileged to play cricket on the pitch
opposite The Old Swan, which is situated in Minster Lovell, a
beautiful Cotswolds village with the River Windrush winding its
way through. If you position yourself right in the outfield, you
can actually nip across the road for the odd pint of local brew
between overs. A typical English inn, The Swan has flagstone
floors, log fires and a character which is very much part of the
Cotswolds. The restaurant, which is candlelit in the evenings,
has a range of standard dishes, always one a vegetarian.

Browns Restaurant & Bar   Oxford

5,7 & 9 Woodstock Road, Oxford OX2 6HA
(0865) 51195

Closed: Christmas Eve; Christmas Day; Boxing Day
Last
Orders: 11.30pm

This huge brasserie à l'anglaise, set in what used to be a garage
and showrooms, is an Oxford success story. Together with the
pâtisserie and boulangerie of Raymond Blanc next door, this
restaurant provides an attractive frontage on the Woodstock
road. Its large windows give a tempting view of the interior to
the sometimes long queues waiting to get in - not because their
service is slow, but because this is the most popular place in
Oxford.

Inside are potted palms, cream walls, huge mirrors around the
edges of the rooms, lots of green planting, a smart long counter
bar, and some of the prettiest girls and boys in Oxford serving. A
very zippy atmosphere, full of life, and it's been running on the
same successful formula for about 6 years. As they say in
showbiz, looks like it will run forever! I hope it does. They were
the first of their kind in Oxford, and probably one of the first
outside London brave enough to try this now firmly established
formula.

You can eat any of the different types of sauce with spaghetti
or a combination of any two, all served with garlic bread, mixed
salad, and a choice of dressings, for around £3.50; a choice of
salads including avocado, bacon and spinach, or a good Caesar
salad, for under £5.00; a choice of hot sandwiches including
pastrami or a Reuben's sandwich which is salt beef, all for
around the £3.50 mark. Or you can spend a little more and go for
the leg of lamb, char-grilled with rosemary and served with
Oxford sauce; a half-pound Scotch sirloin steak with herb butter;
prime roast ribs; or perhaps steak, mushroom and Guinness pie.
They open from 11.00am to 11.30pm so you can try their desserts
and gâteaux in the afternoon, along with the thick ice-cream
milkshakes. There's a good choice of coffees and teas, and they
still manage to serve the housewines for under £5.00 a bottle,

along with some 20 or so cocktails. No wonder there's a queue outside!

If you've got a few moments while you're waiting for someone, you can idle away your time looking in the pastry shop, or perhaps Mr Taylor's plentiful and well-stocked delicatessen and grocery shop on the corner of Little Clarendon Street; or if you want a change you can choose from one of the pizza or pasta establishments situated in Little Clarendon Street itself.

The Cherwell Boathouse   Oxford

Bardwell Road, Oxford OX2 6SR
(0865) 52746

Closed: lunch (Mon - Sat except by arrangement); Christmas/
        New Year
Last
Orders: lunch (2.00pm); dinner (10.30pm)

The Cherwell Boathouse is a bit of an institution, having been here for 18 or so years. Owned and managed by Anthony Verdin, it's had a whole succession of interesting and attractive Oxford undergraduates and locals working in and enjoying the atmosphere of this converted boathouse, literally on the banks of the River Cherwell. As you go out of town on the Banbury road, there's a turning on the right with a small sign, marked Cherwell Boathouse. You carry on along Bardwell Road, and as the road bends round to the left, you take a turning on the right which is little more than a lane. You follow this for a couple of hundred yards and then go through a pair of white gates. The river's directly in front of you, with the boathouse on the left. You can still hire punts here, a favourite Oxford transport as are bicycles.

The interior décor is minimal - it is after all a boathouse! There are a few pictures scattered around the walls, polished wooden floors, and doors that in summer open up onto the slipway. You can by arrangement have exclusive use of the terrace which overlooks the river, and for around £10.00 or so, you are offered a very good set menu. You might be given a choice at dinner of a cream of mushroom soup, pigeon breast with blackcurrant sauce, roast guineafowl with red wine sauce, or pork normande; followed perhaps by a crème brûlée, or a chocolate and Cointreau mousse. Cheeses are generally English, and fruit and coffee are also included - not a bad deal!

The wine list is extensive for such a small place, with a good range of sensibly priced clarets starting from £6.00. Burgundies are not forgotten, with a representation from Côte de Beaune, Côte de Nuits, and Beaujolais. Whitestone Vineyards in Devon is included in a choice of wines from around the world. On a magical summer evening, many a romantic punting down the river has followed dinner at the Cherwell Boathouse.

Fellows Brasserie   Oxford

37 St Clements, Oxford OX4 1AB
(0865) 241431

Closed: Christmas
Last
Orders: 11.00pm

The St Clements area of Oxford seems to have taken off as far as restaurants are concerned. Though they tend to come and go, Fellows Brasserie seems to have established itself, and deserves to succeed.

The exterior is very inviting with deep French blue paintwork, huge windows and lots of bay trees and hanging baskets outside - a more welcoming exterior you could hardly wish to find. The crisp brasserie style is continued inside, with a wooden bar, wooden floors, plain tables with flowers on each, bentwood chairs, and lots of mirrors. Simple well-presented food ranges from tortellonis, a brochette of king prawns, char-grilled and served with a garlic roll, brioches, and vegetarian salads, to simply cooked steaks, followed by English puddings, or black cherry frangipane. There's an excellent array of teas, coffees and milkshakes on offer, or in the afternoon, scones, buns, and cakes. Waitresses are young and attractive, and there's a good-humoured feeling throughout.

If you fancy a change, try Go Dutch which is 5 doors up, where they have a great range of pancakes both savoury and sweet. With simple plain décor, it's excellent for a quick snack or a full meal. A few doors further down, towards the Oxford city centre, a local brewery has even changed one of its not so attractive pubs into a cocktail bar.

Le Petit Blanc Restaurant   Oxford

61A Banbury Road OX2 7JX
(0865) 53540/58346

Closed: lunch (Tue + Wed); dinner (Tue); last 2 weeks Aug;
         first 2 weeks Jan
Last
Orders: lunch (2.15pm); dinner (10.15pm)

Le Petit Blanc is set in a beautiful conservatory which was formerly a nursery and flower shop, behind white wrought iron gates just off the main Banbury road. There's lots of green planting outside and huge windows with those semi-see-through blinds that seem to tempt you in. Once you've succumbed to those, and more especially the menu outside, you enter a simple dining room with pink tablecloths, lots of greenery, cane chairs, and candles on the tables, backed up by individual spotlights over each one. Sit down and enjoy a glass from the reasonably priced selection of French wines while you relax and choose from a very imaginative menu for this type of establishment.

From the 8 or so starters, try the ravioli de fromage de chèvre served with sauce vierge, or the unusual mille feuille de hadock à la fondue de légumes which is fine layers of pastry, slivers of haddock, and a julienne of vegetables served with its own juice. For the main courses try the excellent sea trout char-grilled, served with a light emulsion butter and spiked with cucumbers, or the equally good saddle of rabbit, roasted and served with a white wine sauce, tomatoes, artichoke hearts and herbs from Provence. There's wild pigeon, roasted and filled with a pheasant mousse served with a red wine sauce, garnished with baby onions, lardons and mushrooms. Green salad or vegetables are served with the main courses, and these range from £8.50 to £10.50. A good selection of English and French cheeses follows. From the 6 or 7 puddings perhaps you might choose the layers of apple baked on to a leaf of puff pastry moistened with calvados butter - delicious, as are the seasonal fruits set in a red wine and cinnamon jelly.

It's nice to see this area of Oxford taking off, food-wise. Just around the corner from Le Petit Blanc, there's La Luna Capresa, Oxford's oldest restaurant serving Italian food like someone's mamma used to make; and a newcomer to the scene, Number 17, North Parade, is trying to establish itself.

Restaurant Elizabeth   Oxford

84 St Aldates, Oxford OX1 1RA
(0865) 242230

Closed: Mon; Good Friday; 24-30 Dec
Last
Orders: lunch (2.30pm); dinner (11.00pm)

Antonio Lopez is a welcoming, hardworking and thoughtful host
who over the last 28 years has fed and watered countless
numbers of the wealthier Oxford graduates; and perhaps on
their return here the most comforting thing about the establishment is that nothing seems to have changed. Señor Lopez
doesn't look any older, and I certainly still recognise quite a few
of the waiting staff. Surely I can't be the only person in the world
who likes to go to a restaurant some 8 to 10 years after my last
visit and find a familiar feeling still present.

The wine list has some amazing choices on it at not unreasonable prices. Particularly good value are the magnums - it makes
you wonder if he's got a deal with a cellarman from one of the
Oxford Colleges! The menu still has all the old favourites on it,
with a heavy French bias, but also some other dishes such as
piperade, a Basque dish of eggs with sweet pimento and tomato,
or prawns with rice and aïoli, or quenelles de saumon, sauce
nantua. Main dishes are from a choice of perhaps 8 or so, and
might include a slice of salmon sautéed in butter, cooked in
white wine and served with hollandaise sauce, or the entrecôte
maison au poivre vert, or their carré d'agneau dauphinois for 2
people. The décor is traditional with beautiful moulded ceilings
and in this candlelit room where there is a vin rouge or vin blanc
de patron at under £5.00 a half litre, Oxford seems a very
pleasant place to be!

La Sorbonne   Oxford

130A High Street, Oxford OX1 4DH
(0865) 241320 or 242883

Closed: Bank Holidays
Last
Orders: lunch (2.00pm); dinner (11.00pm)

André Chavagnon still runs this old Oxford favourite, housed in
a black and white timber-framed building in Wheatsheaf Passage. This building has survived 20 odd years of undergraduates,
lecturers, tourists and André Chavagnon. André, a robust figure,

occasionally takes the limelight with some of his more outrageous caprices...

...He once came along to a football match played between a
French team and an assortment of locals. Much to the delight of
the team I was playing for, he decided to substitute for the
French centre forward. Stripping down to his underpants (and
occasionally accompanied by his large Alsation dog) he suc-
ceeded in single-handedly reducing the game to a farce.

Not so his food. André cooks competently in a classic style,
and has trained and worked with some very capable people,
including Raymond Blanc, now at Le Manoir aux Quat'Saisons,
Alain Desenclos, the restaurant director at Le Manoir, and
Michel Sardonnes who has gone on to open his own bistros in
Oxford.

André's menus offer a wide selection of traditional French
dishes, with many old favourites such as escargots provençales
or à la bourguignonne, quenelles de brochet lyonnaise or
suprême de volaille à l'estragon. His daily specialities normally
include at least 2 fish dishes, or possibly ris de veau. He has a
grand selection of wines, priced in the middle bracket.

The Little Angel   Remenham

Remenham, Henley-on-Thames RG9 2LS
(0491) 574165

Closed: Mon
Last
Orders: lunch (2.00pm); dinner (10.00 pm)

Run with flair and dedication by the hardworking Paul and June
Southwood and their capable staff, this one-time ordinary black
and white pub on the outskirts of Henley-on-Thames has been
transformed by giving the restaurant as much prominence as the
bars themselves. There is an especially good selection of wines,
and excellent seafood (including lobster, crab and seasonal
varieties) and game dishes. During the Henley Regatta and the
Festival, a huge marquee is somehow fixed on to the building
which doubles the size of the existing pub restaurant and is
decorated with imagination. This place really packs them in. The
food is robust, simple and plentiful, and the service is always
friendly, a place you can treat as your local even if you're not.

The Harcourt Arms   Stanton Harcourt

Stanton Harcourt OX8 1RJ
(0865) 882192/881931

Last
Orders: lunch (1.45pm); dinner (9.45pm)

The Harcourt Arms, a pretty 18th-Century inn, is set on the edge of the Cotswolds. Just beside the inn is a 10-bedroomed, individually furnished little hotel and conference centre, and oppposite the Harcourt Arms is the Stanton Harcourt Manor House, which dates from around 1380. They open the Manor House on certain days during the year, and the gardens too, and I'm sure George Dailey would be delighted to tell you precisely when, should you wish to look around. The Harcourt Arms is warm and inviting, and most of Oxfordshire at some time or another seems to have passed under its portals, from undergraduates who found their way there, to the county set. It fairly throbs with life.

The food is reasonably priced - I've eaten some delightful meals there. In season, George is very much into seafood, perhaps a bowl of steaming hot mussels, their famous hot prawns, or deep fried squid might be served as an hors d'oeuvre. Otherwise a good hot terrine of fish and shellfish, good fresh raw spinach salad with hot bacon, honey vinaigrette and croûtons. For main courses try their double skewer of grilled king prawns with garlic bread and mayonnaise, or an excellent traditional steak and kidney pie, to which they add a little port wine. There are plenty of other things to choose from, including excellent grilled calves' liver with back bacon, and steaks, simply grilled, or served with garlic butter. Good home-made puddings to finish; and there's a very reasonable wine list. This is an excellent place for Sunday lunch, if you can get a table.

The Red Lion   Steeple Aston

South Street, Steeple Aston OX5 3RY
(0869) 40225

Closed: lunch (daily)
Last
Orders: dinner (9.15pm)

This extremely popular village pub is run by Colin Mead, a gregarious former rugger player, and his wife Margaret. Dating from the mid-17th Century, it was created out of stabling and accomodation into the actual inn. The small dining room takes a maximum of 20, so booking is essential, and if you get together a party of 12 or more, you can take over the whole room. A regular diner confided that if you ring up and choose your wines, the menu can be created to suit your selection!...which brings us to the wine list. Not the average pub list, as you may have guessed, but as Colin describes it, "a browser's list". There are 26 clarets back to '64, 30 Burgundies with some examples of '76 and '79 and representations from Alsace, Rhône, Loire and Champagne - you can see that regular's point!

Margaret changes the menu frequently, and offers a small range of dishes using good seasonal produce, such as a broad bean and hazelnut soup, rough country liver pâté, or a terrine of grayling with a sorrel mousse. Main dishes might include lobster thermidor, grilled salmon with béarnaise sauce, calves' sweet-breads provençale, or escalope of veal cordon bleu. Puddings could be crème brûlée, summer pudding, or a mousse of fresh limes.

Mallards Wine Bar   Thame

87 High Street, Thame
(0844) 6679

Closed: Christmas Day
Last
Orders: lunch (2.00pm); dinner (10.00pm)

A small well-run wine bar and bistro are to be found in converted cottages in the High Street of Thame. Quarry tiled floor, exposed beams and a large fireplace with clean pine tables and chairs create a cosy atmosphere. Simple dishes are ade-quately cooked, 40 odd European wines at reasonable prices and pretty girls to serve: what more could you want in Thame?

Thatchers Hotel & Restaurant   Thame

29-30 Lower Higher Street, Thame OX9 2AA
(084 421) 2146/3058

Closed: Sun
Last
Orders: lunch (1.45pm); dinner (10.00pm)

A restaurant with rooms can be found housed in a delightful and - not surprisingly - thatched cottage in the main street of this charming Oxfordshire market town. Terry Connor, the patron, buys his meat from three butchers as one cannot be a master of all meats; he has fish and vegetables delivered daily from the London markets, local bread baked daily and the game shot locally, as and when required. Someone must be a good shot! Nigel Marriage is the chef, and his dishes are adventurous in the combinations of ingredients - raw turbot with a lime marinade served with spicy coconut sauce, lambs' sweetbreads, langous-tine and asparagus on seasonal salads, breast of chicken on a coulis of red peppers with orange zest, and for pudding a praline ice-cream lined with passion fruit sorbet and served with apricot sauce. Other dishes are more restrained, for example a warm duck salad followed by escalope of veal with a green peppercorn sauce, and for pudding a white chocolate mousse which has 2 sauces to complement it, one of mint and one of bitter choco-late.

287

The rooms are all beamed and furnished with antiques, and have private bath, and phone and television. Mr Connor is also proud of his two Californian hot tubs with jacuzzi jets, the sauna and the solarium about which he says, "The benefits and pleasures of these facilities are self-evident to anyone who has tried them." That is what *The Sun* reviewer must have meant when he wrote, "We had a good night" - as quoted in Thatcher's brochure!

Brown & Boswell   Wallingford

28 High Street, Wallingford OX10 0BU
(0491) 34078

Closed: lunch (Mon + Tue); dinner (Sun + Mon); 1 week Oct; 2 weeks
        Mar
Last
Orders: lunch (1.30pm); dinner (10.00pm)

Robert Boswell supervises every area of this charming restaurant in this busy market town. The food is imaginative, and may run from a skewer of chicken satay or a Californian basil burger to a more classic veal chop with basil and tomato sauce. Time and trouble are taken over starters, vegetables and, of course, puddings. The wine list merits close attention, as alongside carefully chosen wines from France, you will find good bargains from Italy, California and even the Lebanon. Dinner is generally more sophisticated than lunch but either meal will be interesting and rewarding.

They occasionally run joint evenings with Nick Treadaway of the Lamb Wine Vaults opposite for a tasting and then, as Patricia Boswell explains, you are escorted carefully across the High Street to the restaurant. It's worth giving Patricia Boswell a call to see if there's anything on when you're in the area, as these evenings sound very good value for money as well as informative. As Robert Boswell says, he offers simple but stimulating food and wine in an uninhibiting situation.

The Bear Hotel & Restaurant   Woodstock

Park Street, Woodstock OX7 1SZ
(0993) 811511

Last
Orders: lunch (2.15pm); dinner (9.45pm)

The phrase 'The Bear was old when the Palace was new' puts into perspective this 16th-Century hostelry, situated in the village of Woodstock. The Palace in question is Blenheim, built for the Duke of Marlborough by Vanbrugh, with grounds and lakes by Capability Brown, as a reward for his victory over the French at Blenheim in 1704. The Bear also has reception rooms at the Palace which can be booked by prior arrangement.

I personally like The Bear best in winter with roaring log fires, timbered bars and restaurant, and the comfortable feeling that the place has been around for a very long time. The building itself still sparkles, each room with an individual character and style, and the 4-poster Stewart and Georgian rooms are very romantic. (Several friends can testify to this!) The garden suites and apartments are conveniently private in the courtyard setting at the rear of the hotel, covered in ivy and climbing roses.

Above average food for a country inn is served in traditional surroundings by friendly staff. If you want a change of food, they will book you into Wheeler's restaurant in Woodstock, which also belongs to The Bear. Woodstock itself is steeped in history with some lovely buildings, and it was the birthplace of the Black Prince and Sir Winston Churchill, who was born in Blenheim Palace itself.

The Feathers Hotel   Woodstock

Market Street, Woodstock OX7 1SX
(0993) 812291

Last
Orders: lunch (2.15pm); dinner (9.45pm)

This gentle, calm hotel has some 10 rooms and seats 40 in the
dining room, with a few extra tables outside in summer, and you
can have drinks in the lovely little garden. The bedrooms are all
individually decorated and designed, with some nice pieces of
antique furniture and some good quality materials. The bar and
the lounge are prettily decorated, and furnished with cosy sofas
and chairs, while the calm, crisp dining room has some comfortable velour-upholstered dining chairs.

   The food is in the modern English style, and you might be
offered a set lunch menu of 3 courses plus coffee for around
£10.00. From a dinner menu at around £22.00 you might be
offered a timbale of scallop mousse served on a lobster, butter
and chive sauce and garnished with queen scallops, or The
Feathers salad, which amongst other things includes strips of
smoked goose breast, red cabbage, carrot, cucumber, pine
kernels, and crispy bacon in a honey dressing. The 4 or 5 main
courses might include a medallion of venison with 2 sauces -
rich game sauce, and a cream, sherry and oyster mushroom
sauce - garnished with quenelles of mushrooms, or perhaps a
supreme of salmon, stuffed with a mousse of sole and truffles,
baked inside a light strüdel pastry and served on a watercress
sauce. Good crisp vegetables accompany them. Among the
desserts you might find a hot puff pastry case filled with
frangipane and served with a custard sauce, or ginger shortbread biscuits filled with butterscotch cream and served with
caramelised walnuts.

   A good selecton of wines offers a fair choice of half bottles,
and it's very nice to be offered some 6 or so dessert wines, and
Champagnes by the bottle or the half bottle, and even a number
by the glass. The charming Gordon Campbell-Gray oversees the
young friendly staff. The Feathers is a welcome addition to the
other more traditional restaurants in Woodstock and its surrounding area.

· THE FEATHERS HOTEL ·

■■■ SHROPSHIRE ■■■

Country Friends Restaurant   Dorrington

Dorrington, Shrewsbury SY5 7JD
(0743 73) 707

Closed: lunch (Sun + Mon); dinner (Sun)
Last
Orders: dinner (9.00pm; 9.30pm Sat)

A black and white timbered building at the roadside on the A49
between Shrewsbury and Craven Arms houses the Whittakers'
friendly restaurant. Pauline's cooking is homely and sound. She
uses good raw materials, bakes her own bread and lets the
produce speak for itself rather than over saucing it or using
complex presentation. A small à la carte menu changes with the
seasons, and a fixed priced menu is also available which is good
value. The wine list is also small but offers something for most
tastes. A welcome find in this somewhat barren area!

The Feathers at Ludlow   Ludlow

Bull Ring, Ludlow SY8 1AA   £35
(0584) 5261

Last
Orders: lunch (1.45pm); dinner (9.30pm)

The Feathers Hotel, Ludlow, dates from around 1600 and with its
stunning half-timbered elevation situated in the centre of historic Ludlow, it's a building you really can't miss. The warm and
friendly bars always make me associate The Feathers with
winter and mulled wine and good beer. The restaurant itself
serves traditional British fare. There are 35 rooms, some with
4-poster beds.

Weston Park   Shifnal

Shifnal TF11 8LE   £60
(095 276) 201

Last
Orders: all bookings by arrangement

Weston Park, a stately home set in beautiful parkland, is the seat of Richard, 7th Earl of Bradford and 12th Baronet, and has been in the family for some 300 years. The enterprising Earl has now opened up the house in a number of ways. As well as allowing you to look round, just as you would normally do in a stately home, he regularly holds gourmet dinners in the magnificent dining room, for a minimum party of 15 people. And by booking into the 20 or so bedrooms now available, you can have exclusive use of this beautiful house. As well as the overnight stay you get a champagne reception, a 5-course dinner with wine and full English breakfast, and you will not be short of choice from the house-party dinner menus. Choose beforehand from a selection of some 10 starters which might include cheese and almond beignets, game terrine with Cumberland sauce, or chicken and brandy pâté with diced Sauternes aspic and brioche toast. The 9 fish courses might include a feuilleté of salmon and leeks with a champagne sauce, a mousse of smoked trout and chives with a tomato and basil sauce, and you might like to try one of the home-made sorbets which include grapefruit or gooseberry. Main courses include a spendidly British half duck, roasted with honey and served with a redcurrant sauce, or stuffed chicken breast with madeira sauce. Desserts can be fun with burnt caramel mousse, whisky and hazlenut whip, and coffee comes with home-made petits fours.

If you are looking for a special meal to impress a party of friends, or you have to host a small banquet in this particular part of the country, you could do far worse than telephone Weston Park and check the availability of the splendid rooms. I forgot to mention the orangery and the loggia, if you like more of a knees-up! And if it's sport you're after they can arrange everything from clay pigeon shooting to archery, from fly fishing in season to ballooning. So if you feel like the life of a Lord, this could be for you.

SOMERSET

No. 3 Dining Room   Glastonbury

3 Magdalene Street, Glastonbury BA6 9EW
(0458) 32129

Closed: lunch (except by arrangement); dinner (Mon); Jan
Last
Orders: dinner (9.30pm)

Should you ever decide to visit the ruins of the once magnificent
Glastonbury Abbey, which I would suggest is well worthwhile,
you will no doubt work up an appetite. And the ideal place to
satiate your hunger is just a stone's throw from the Abbey. No 3
is a fine old Georgian house which now houses a restaurant and
also accommodates a few residents should you wish to stay in
the area. The dining room is decorated dramatically with red felt
on the walls, flowered tablecloths to soften the effect, and fresh
flowers and cut glass on the tables. A set menu is offered for
lunch and dinner at £17.00 - perhaps 1 or 2 unusual combinations in some dishes but very good home-made ice-creams and
sorbets - and the wine list offers a good range at various price
levels. Ann Tynan also makes the chocolates served with the
coffee.

Bowlish House   Shepton Mallet

Wells Road, Shepton Mallet BA4 5JD
(0749) 2022

Closed: lunch (daily)
Last
Orders: dinner (10.00pm)

Bowlish House is a restaurant with just 4 bedrooms in an
attractive Georgian house, tucked into a hollow just outside
Shepton Mallet. Its formal entrance leads into a small bar; the
small, elegant, brown and white dining room has a separate
plant-filled conservatory for coffee and smokers.

   Host Brian Jordan has an excellent cellar, and a long-standing
reputation for his wine list. Fixed price menus are offered for
dinner, and cooking is in classic style with nouvelle overtones.
No credit cards are accepted.

The Castle Hotel Taunton

Castle Green, Taunton TA1 1NF
(0823) 72671

Last
Orders: lunch (2.00pm); dinner (9.00pm)

When asked how long The Castle has been open in its present state Mr Chapman replied, "300 years or 6 months depending on your point of view!" It was a perfect response, for whilst retaining the atmosphere of its long history, The Castle has been brought into the 1980s in terms of standards and comfort. Gary Rhodes has taken over from Chris Oakes in the kitchen, and menus include local produce cooked in a lighter style than when The Castle was first built! Courgette flowers stuffed with salmon mousse on a champagne and saffron sauce, summer salad of crisp young vegetables with warm scallops, salmon steamed with coarse sea salt and chives in a butter sauce or breast of corn-fed chicken with glazed apples and toasted almonds on a cider vinegar sauce give an idea of the à la carte menu. The set lunch offers more traditional fare such as roast beef, Yorkshire pudding and roast potatoes.

To describe the wine list as 'comprehensive' would be an injustice, 'amazing' seems inadequate, 'tempting' an understatement. Suffice it to say that it is Kit Chapman's pride and joy, and rightly so. There are 21 housewines under £8.00, 9 English wines, a stunning range of Burgundies and clarets from good vintages and even Rhône wines with bottle age. The wine list notes that "wines have been nursed and served in this building for 800 years" - a tradition that Mr Chapman will clearly maintain.

Langley House Wiveliscombe

Langley Marsh, Wiveliscombe TA4 2UF
(0984) 23318

Closed: lunch (daily)
Last
Orders: dinner (9.30pm)

Peter Wilson cooks in this wonderfully quiet and friendly country house right in the heart of Somerset. He and his wife Anne, who looks after the dining room, have created a civilised atmosphere in which to relax for a couple of days. Though the house goes back to the 16th Century, the comfortable and elegant lounge is more reminiscent of the 18th Century. The dining room is a simple affair, beamed, and candlelit at night, where set menus are served featuring good and where possible local produce. You may find a Clatworthy trout baked in its own juices, or a breast of duck grilled with pink peppercorns, apple and calvados. There is a good selection of wines and an interesting array of port, Cognac and Armagnac. It is worth looking for bin-ends as there are some good bargains here.

The bedrooms, including a 4-poster, are carefully and comfortably furnished with some thoughtful extras like a small bottle of sherry on arrival. One highlight of Langley House is the friendliness of the staff, who soon make you feel totally at home.

■■■ SUFFOLK ■■■

Bradfield House   Bradfield Combust

Bradfield Combust, Bury St Edmunds IP30 0LR
(028 486) 301

Closed: lunch (Mon - Sat); dinner (Mon)
Last
Orders: lunch (2.00pm); dinner (9.30pm)

Mrs Stephenson has elevated home cooking to great heights using mainly local produce, and vegetables and herbs from her garden. Dishes may include a summer soup of broad beans, courgette flowers and lovage, a sauté of local quail with brandy and crushed peppercorns, or at Sunday lunch time superb roast beef with a rich gravy, fresh horseradish and real mustard.

The dining room occupies the ground floor of the house with a small, casual bar where you can choose from a small but interesting wine list, selected by Mr Stephenson who abandoned the insurance business to open the restaurant.

You will be made very welcome, fed well, and it is worth having a walk around the 2-acre garden and vegetable gardens if the weather permits.

Mortimer's   Bury St Edmunds

31 Churchgate Street, Bury St Edmunds IP33 1RG
(0284) 60623

Closed: lunch (Sat); Sun; Bank Holidays + following Tue
Last
Orders: lunch (1.45pm); dinner (9.15pm)

This little seafood resaurant, situated in a row of shops and private houses not far from the market centre of Bury St Edmunds, offers some very good local fish and smoked eels. A full range of seafood includes fresh Scottish langoustines, and Loch Fyne oysters. The 2 ladies at the next table, who have lived there for 40 years - although Mortimer's hasn't been open that long - rated both the restaurant and the off-licence next door as the best in the area. Michael Gooding gets the majority of his fish from Grimsby Fish Market on a daily basis, and therefore the menu varies depending on what he can purchase. Puddings might be Mortimer's lemon chiffon, chocolate pot or possibly a sheep's milk yoghurt (from the Ostler flock) which they serve with honey. A good range of wines is available by the glass, half bottle and bottle. If it's a no-nonsense, straightforward fish night you're looking for, Mortimer's could be for you.

Mr Underhill's   Earl Stonham

Earl Stonham, near Stowmarket IP14 5DW   £45
(0449) 711206

Closed: lunch (except by arrangement); dinner (Sun + Mon)
Last
Orders: dinner (9.00pm)

Chris and Judy Bradley called their restaurant Mr Underhill's
from Lord of the Rings (because it was the travelling name of
Frodo Baggins) but, as they say in their newsletters, that has
nothing to do with the restaurant whatsoever: it was simply the
only Underhill in the phone book at the time they opened some 4
years ago. It seems a good enough reason to me!

This 30-seater restaurant in a private house is always busy.
Customers are well looked after and also kept well informed
about events. An occasional newsletter announces special
evenings such as 'salmon and Chablis' or a 'Pomegranates
evening' - not dedicated to the fruit but to the London restaurant
where Christopher worked. They look after the front of house
capably with local ladies to help, and they even use their
newsletter to advertise for staff.

Christopher Bradley makes good use of local produce,
particularly meats and poultry; they are keen on growing their
own salads and herbs, and the set menu offers you some
splendid choices. Try spiced apple soup, tomato and basil soup,
an hors d'oeuvre of harlequin omelette Roger Vergé, or warm
fillet of beef Japanese style, or a mousseline of turbot with
shellfish sauce. By way of fish you might be offered escalope of
salmon with Pernod, or baked giant prawns with creole sauce.
Amongst poultry and game, you might be given the choice of
chicken Aunt Celestine, with Grand Marnier and apple, and
suprême of duck with green peppercorn sauce. Meat dishes
include a rib of veal with chive sauce, roast sirloin served with
vinters' butter or mustard seed butter, or fillet of pork with
apples and calvados. To follow they have a bitter chocolate
granité, a marjolaine, a prune and armagnac tart, or perhaps a
praline pancake.

They are delighted to cater for private parties of up to 16 in
their additional dining room, and they both take a keen interest
in wine. The list includes some interesting examples from
Australia and California as well as from France. I suppose this
place ought to be entered as a restaurant with accommodation,
but as it has just one letting bedroom we thought we'd leave it as
it is!

The Fox and Goose   Fressingfield

Fressingfield, Eye IP21 5PB   £35
(037 986) 247

the local's favourite story *

Closed: Tue; 21-28 Dec
Last
Orders: lunch (1.30pm); dinner (9.00pm)

The Fox and Goose was built in 1509. The north of the building
fronts into the churchyard, and it was, originally, the Church
House, built by church authorities when, apparently, abuses
of the practice of eating and drinking in the naves of churches
reached a peak in the 16th Century. The Clarke family has been
here since 1967 and Adrian Clarke cooks, with his wife helping,
and his father runs the front of house. Father is a charming old
boy who explains the menu to you, and by all accounts catches
some of the excellent fish you eat here. In fact, when I enquired
why the sign proclaimed "Closed on Tuesdays", I received the
simple explanation: he goes fishing on Tuesdays - which must
endorse the saying 'no fresh fish on Mondays'!

There is no doubt that this is a superb piece of English
eccentricity. You know you are in the country - the whole village
seems friendly, and even the other diners enquire how you
enjoyed your food. We did. Country-sized portions of pike
quenelle were served in a lobster, prawn, cream and brandy
sauce. Home-made vichyssoise was followed by an escalope of
salmon in a sorrel sauce, and chicken Marie-Louise (white wine,
tomatoes, onions, yellow, red and green peppers). In season they
have venison, pheasant, partridge, wild duck, grouse and squab.

If you telephone, they will send you a menu to make your
choice by phone. You then call back with your booking time and
your order, and they will have the meal prepared by the time you
arrive.

Local places to stay include Mrs Willis' lovely Queen Anne
house in the village (037 986 254) and Mr & Mrs Thompson's
farmhouse (037 986 443).

Weavers Restaurant   Hadleigh

25 High Street, Hadleigh IP7 5AG
(0473) 827427

Closed: lunch (daily); dinner (Sun + Mon); 1 week Christmas
Last
Orders: dinner (9.30pm)

This small 38-seater restaurant is situated in some converted
weavers' cottages, and serves some straightforward and well-
cooked dishes in a beamed dining room. Lots of bric-à-brac and
trinkets give the atmosphere, pretty tablecloths are well set with
service by Sally Ghijben, the smiling owner, and the friendly
local girls who help her. Roy Ghijben in the kitchen might offer
you a hot-pot of seafood, or maybe pasta twirls tossed in cream
and parmesan and fresh basil, as one of the 6 or so starters.
Maybe choose a carbonnade flamande - strips of beef cooked in
brown ale into a rich sauce and topped with a mustard croûton -
or rack of lamb roasted and served pink with orange and ginger
sauce, or possibly a nice tranche of salmon cooked in white
wine and served with a green herb mayonnaise from the 7 main
courses. At around £7.00 they offer good value for money, and
include a selection of fresh crisp vegetables. Good interesting
puddings at under £2.00 a portion are made by Sally, and they
are particularly proud of their filet de boeuf dijonnaise.

   Housewines are under £5.00 a bottle, and some bargains can
be found at the lower end of the market.

The Singing Chef   Ipswich

200 St Helen's Street, Ipswich
(0472) 55236

Closed: Mon; Sun (except last Sun of each month for lunch)
Last
Orders: dinner (11.00pm)

We include Mrs Toye's own comments on her restaurant which,
we feel, say it all!
   "We started The Singing Chef 26 years ago in Connaught
Street as a small family concern with Ken in the kitchen and
Cynthia front-of-house. The dishes are from the regions of
France with a change of region every month. Favourites?
Bouillabaisse pêcheur (from fresh fish of the North Sea), carré
d'agneau aux aromâtes, cassoulet de Castelnandry, omelette
soufflée flambeé (Ken's speciality).
   "From September we are starting a bistro-style meal in our
annexe (low prices, £1.50 pâté du chef, £2.00 mayonnaise
pêcheur with wine by the glass £1.00). Bookings for lunch taken
in the restaurant - menu by negotiation.
   "What else can I say? We are a small, friendly family
restaurant - Ken sings French songs on request. We like our
customers and many of them become friends."
   What else can *we* say?

The Swan   Lavenham

High Street, Lavenham, Sudbury CO10 9QA
(0787) 247477

Last
Orders: lunch (2.00pm); dinner (9.00pm)

Lavenham is probably one of the best preserved Mediaeval towns in the country, and walks around its galleries and antique shops are rewarding. The Swan, however, is its focal point. This historic, beamed building goes back to the 14th Century, and many of its bedrooms have beams to match and good solid furnishings. Its heavily timbered bars are popular meeting places, and the restaurant has a high timbered ceiling and an original minstrels' gallery. An international menu is available. The hotel manages to combine 20th-Century facilities with old world charm.

The Black Lion   Long Melford

The Green, Long Melford, Sudbury CO10 9DN
(0787) 312356

Closed: dinner (Sun + Mon)
Last
Orders: lunch (2.00pm); dinner (8.30pm)

Luke and Amelia Brady have carefully restored this 17th-Century inn which sits on the green at Long Melford, just off the High Street (said to boast the highest concentration of antique shops in Europe). The accent at the Black Lion is on comfort, hospitality, good beer, good wines and good food.

The dining room menu may feature a hot onion tart with tomatoes provençale, or a sliced breast of steamed chicken with fresh lime. Cooking is interesting, and concentrates on using local ingredients whenever possible.

The Bradys are shortly to open another bar at the rear of the hotel, behind which you will find the walled garden, ideal for a drink on a summer's day.

Chimneys Restaurant Long Melford

Hall Street, Long Melford CO10 9JR
(0787) 79806

Closed: lunch (Mon); dinner (Sun + Mon)
Last
Orders: lunch (2.00pm); dinner (9.30pm)

Sam Chalmers for many years manned the stove at Maison Talbooth, and has now branched out to open his own place. Set in the centre of the long High Street, Chimneys is easy to find as it is the only pink washed, wooden beamed building in sight.

Inside, the bar and dining room are furnished with well-spaced tables, crisp linen and fresh flowers. The art on the walls is for sale, and varies from the predictable to the quite outrageous. The cooking is more mainstream - set lunch is very good value and, like the à la carte, written clearly in English. You might find ravioli of smoked fish or spiced marinated chicken breast, or even pressed English lambs' tongues with Cumberland sauce.

Some dishes are more intriguing, like perhaps a parfait of poppy seeds, and the cooking is well balanced by the service which is friendly and correct. There is an interesting choice of wines, and very fairly priced housewine starts at £7.00 a bottle.

The Butley-Orford Oysterage Orford

Market Hill, Orford IP12 2HQ
(039 45) 277

Last
Orders: lunch (2.15pm); dinner (8.30pm)

Winding lanes through the Suffolk countryside bring you to the coastal village of Orford. The Oysterage seen at its centre bustles with locals and visitors, its 2 café-like dining rooms are ruled with a rod of iron by Mathilde, more in the manner of a French patronne than an English restaurateur.

The oyster beds now hold Pacifics and these are cheap enough to afford a dozen. Irish salmon is home-smoked on wood and is excellent. In addition there is a daily selection of fish dishes, mainly local with perhaps grilled sole, or a hot coquille of garlic prawns with piped potato. Guinness is a popular alternative to reasonably priced wines.

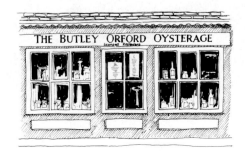

The Crown   Southwold

High Street, Southwold, IP18 6DP   £25
(0502) 722275

Last
Orders: lunch (2.00pm); dinner (10.00pm)

The Crown, situated in the centre of this pleasant Suffolk town, is justly famed for its extensive wine list, and Adnams, the owners, wisely leave a copy to study in your bedroom before dinner. The more you can afford to spend on wines the greater will be the bargain, but there are some excellent selections at the cheaper end too. There is an amazing selection, which changes monthly, of wines by the glass from a Cruover machine.

The dining room, adjoining a bustling local bar serving good fresh food, offers a limited selection of well-prepared dishes, including some good local fish such as a casserole of seafood with anchovies and garlic, or a sauté of brill with spinach and nutmeg.

Bedrooms are in the process of being extensively refurbished, and are simple but perfectly comfortable, so that after a good night's sleep you can enjoy for breakfast a Southwold kipper, or buckwheat pancakes with maple syrup, and some freshly squeezed orange juice.

Seckford Hall Hotel   Woodbridge

Woodbridge   £35
(0394) 385678

Last
Orders: lunch (1.45pm); dinner (9.15pm)

Clearly sign-posted from the A12 rather than in the delightful town of Woodbridge itself, Seckford Hall is a perfect Elizabethan house, surrounded by acres of garden and lake. Many original fittings remain inside with splendid fire places, imposing staircases and numerous antiques.

Rooms are spacious and comfortably furnished in period style. Dinner in the large dining room is a formal affair - jacket and tie required - and menus feature French and English dishes.

SURREY

The Crown Inn Chiddingfold

The Green, Chiddingfold GU8 4TX
(042 879) 2255/6

£30

Closed: dinner (Mon: Elizabethan Restaurant)
Last
Orders: lunch (2.00pm); dinner (9.30pm)

A typical English setting on the edge of the village green, with a welcoming bar full of locals and a burning wood fire in the restaurant in winter. The main Elizabethan restaurant has a good selection of dishes ranging from scallops with endive or pigeon breast salad with toasted pine kernels, to a choice of seafood including John Dory or fillets of turbot with asparagus and chervil butter sauce. There are puddings of summerberry tart and iced lemon biscuits. There is a good choice table d'hôte menu at £12.00, and a cheaper restaurant called The Woodfyre with simple entrées and home-made duck pâté, soup of the day, followed by sirloin steaks, chicken or salmon, barbecued on an open wood fire. On our second visit one evening after we had been to a gastronomic lunch, the restaurant was absolutely packed with 2 large parties, yet they still managed to find a table for 2 and serve us first-class entrecôte steaks perfectly cooked pink, with a plate of good pommes frites and a salad - just what we wanted, plus that warm glow of satisfaction from pleasant surroundings and a Romanée St Vivant les Quatre Journaux 1970.

La Bonne Franquette Egham

5 High Street, Egham TW20 9EA
(0784) 39494

£45

Last
Orders: lunch (2.00pm); dinner (9.30pm)

La Bonne Franquette offers a modern style menu with dishes containing "hints of garlic or curry spices" and "quartets of pink lamb cutlets or sorbets". If you live within 10 miles of La Bonne Franquette, you can have 'Smart' dinner parties, with the prepared dishes from David Smart's kitchen being delivered to your home. They also offer a fixed menu including wines at £20.00 which is a good way of trying this attractive, well run restaurant.

Morels   Haslemere

25-27 Lower Street, Haslemere GU27 2NY
(0428) 51462

Closed: Sun + Mon; Bank Holidays; 3 weeks Jan; 2 weeks Sep
Last
Orders: lunch (2.00pm); dinner (10.00pm)

Jean-Yves and Mary-Anne Morel run this neat, stylish restaurant excellently. Jean-Yves' style of cooking, based on some inspired nouvelle interpretations, is worth a trip to Haslemere. The à la carte menu offers dishes such as a warm salad of duck confit with beetroot, a tartare of salmon with avocado in soured cream flavoured with dill, or smoked salmon with blinis, yoghurt and Danish caviar. Next you could choose boned quail with a parcel of mushrooms, fillet of Scotch beef with a green peppercorn soufflé, fillet of veal stuffed with lobster in sherry sauce or perhaps a fillet of roe deer with caraway seed pancakes in port and juniper sauce. The menu changes monthly, and on Fridays a 7-course menu gastronomique is available. About 100 French wines are reasonabaly priced and vintages have been well chosen.

The Old Lodge   Limpsfield

Limpsfield RH8 0DR
(088 33) 2996

Closed: lunch (Sat + Mon); dinner (Sun + Mon); Good Friday;
        first 2 weeks Jan
Last
Orders: lunch (2.00pm); dinner (9.30pm)

The dark, panelled dining room is in an elegant setting with its highly polished tables, glass and silver. Service too is fairly formal, from young waiters who are smartly dressed. The food is in the modern style and attractively presented. Some dishes are fairly complex, like the rolled fillets of lemon sole stuffed with a salmon mousse and served with a pink peppercorn sauce. The veal in Madeira sauce with truffles is well executed, and vegetables are carefully cooked. At Sunday lunch times the traditional English roast is served alongside dishes similar to those above.

Mainly classic wines feature on the list and are properly served.

Lichfield's   Richmond

Lichfield Court, Sheen Road, Richmond TW9 1AS
01-940 5236

Closed: Sun + Mon; 1 week Christmas; first 2 weeks Sep
Last
Orders: lunch (2.15pm); dinner (10.30pm)

A cheerful restaurant situated in a row of shops in Richmond,
Lichfield's has a serious attitude in its modern style of food. The
dining room is simply decorated in shades of apricot, with black
timber to dado level, and humourous prints and pictures of food
subjects on its walls. It has comfortable modern armchairs and
there are always lots of fresh flowers on the tables to cheer the
diners.
   Stephen Bull's cooking is innovative, and his set price choice
of menus offers a good selection of fresh produce. Quails' eggs,
cooked en cocotte with foie gras and madeira, puff pastry filled
with wild mushrooms and artichokes, or perhaps cheese
terrines with watercress sauce - one of roquefort with hazelnut,
the other of parmesan with leek - might tempt you. Afterwards,
try the sea bass and turbot with pistachio butter and sauternes,
a fricassée of sweetbreads, chicken and lobster with tomato and
ginger, or noisettes of lamb with a chick pea soufflé and a lemon
and parsley sauce. There is a good selection of English
farmhouse cheeses, and excellent puddings - try the mango
soufflé with passion fruit sauce.
   Around 80 wines have been carefully chosen with good
vintages, and several dessert wines are served by the glass.
   We've heard that Stephen Bull is looking for new premises, so
suggest you check, when ringing to book, that he is still there.

Chez Max   Surbiton

85 Maple Road, Surbiton KT6 4AW
01-399 2365

Closed: lunch (Sat); Sun + Mon; 2 weeks Jan; 2 weeks Aug
Last
Orders: lunch (2.00pm); dinner (10.00pm)

Situated in a parade of shops in Surbiton, the décor may not be
as stylish as its food but Chez Max is certainly a find! Large
portions, with good variety, support a menu that changes
frequently but has included petit casserole de lotte with shellfish
sauce; a cold watercress, cucumber and yoghurt soup; and a
goats' cheese salad with walnut dressing. There is a good choice
of desserts, a wine list with 76 choices and housewine from
£7.50. A lunch-time table d'hôte menu is priced at £15.00 plus
service. Max Markarian cooks with style, combining excellent
fresh ingredients to good advantage and presenting them in
exciting ways.

Partners 23 **Sutton**

23 Stonecot Hill, Sutton SM3 9HB
01-644 7743

Closed: lunch (Sat, Sun + Mon); dinner (Sun + Mon)
        2-3 weeks Aug; Christmas Day to 6 Jan
Last
Orders: lunch (2.00pm); dinner (9.30pm)

Its pleasing frontage lifts this restaurant out of its surroundings of a rather mundane row of shops. The décor is cream and peach; it is furnished in chrome, and air conditioned like a provincial French restaurant. The small menu offers a good selection of appealing dishes which can range from terrine of veal and sweetbreads served with a sauce verte, to maybe escalopes of brill and salmon with a lobster sauce. This could be followed by mainly English home-produced cheeses, ably interpreted by a front of house staff who not only understand the differences in the cheeses but are efficient with their service (perhaps they are all partners in Partners 23). Great attention is paid to detail: there is also a selection of home-made bread and petits fours. A set 2-course lunch costs £9.75, 3 courses £12.25 - extremely good value. A good atmosphere with friendly staff who are all English. They even have their own Partners 23 teeshirts for sale and a visitors book. Wines are from an excellent range, mostly French: 6 housewines at £6.95 a bottle.

■■■■■ WARWICKSHIRE ■■■■■
Ettington Park Hotel   Alderminster

Alderminster, Near Stratford-upon-Avon CV37 8BS   £65
(0789) 740740

Last
Orders: lunch (2.00pm); dinner (9.45pm)

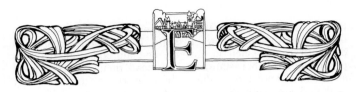

Ettington Park is situated just outside Stratford on the Oxford to
Stratford road and is certainly the place to stay if you're doing
Stratford in the grand manner. The style of the house is
Romantic Gothic, and it was built on the site of an earlier manor
house dating back to 1738. It has some incredibly well preserved
pieces, including an elaborate plasterwork ceiling dating from
1740 in the dining room and, in the drawing room and the
bedroom immediately above it, Venetian windows from 1766.
The house itself is set in 14 acres of land with some beautifully
appointed luxury rooms and suites, a good size pool and a
jacuzzi. The interior of the house is interesting and ranges from
the Italianate conservatory at its entrance, to some quite small
rooms which lead into a grand drawing room and bar, then on
into the restaurant, a smaller room where you can concentrate
on the cuisine of Michael Quinn.

He has developed his own style, and uncomplicated starters
might include seasonal terrine, salmon with crab meat served
with a yoghurt and dill dressing. For main courses try perhaps a
fillet of wild salmon with a sole mousse and champagne sauce,
or a grilled breast of duck with crystallised oranges and
armagnac sauce, or new season's lamb served with scallops and
fresh herbs. A sizeable selection of vegetables might be followed
by bread and butter pudding, lime syllabub, some home-made
water ices or a good selection of English and French cheeses.
The wine list, like the price of the rooms, is at the top end of the
market, but when you're staying in a neo-Gothic castle you
expect to pay accordingly.

If you want to stay in Stratford itself, try the Shakespeare
Hotel, a beautiful black and white timber framed property in the
centre of Stratford, close to the theatre. This lovely 16th-Century
inn, with its gabled frontage, is a splendid example of the
architecture of that period. There are lots of beams inside, open
fires, and generally a traditional feel to this popular 66-room
hotel.

The *Shakespeare*

Mallory Court   Bishops Tachbrook

Harbury Lane, Bishops Tachbrook, Leamington Spa CV33 9QB   £60
(0926) 30214

Closed: 26 Dec - 1 Jan
Last
Orders: lunch (1.45pm); dinner (9.45pm; Sun 8.30pm)

An imposing house in the country with comfortable furnishings
and modern fabrics. The panelled dining room has a real sense
of occasion, and it is worth dressing up and making a real night
of it. The car park shows the calibre of high-powered locals who
will be joining you, whilst wine prices will suit the more
well-heeled. The food is good modern cooking in the French
style; plates are enormous but the substantial portions do not
look lost. Artichoke heart topped with a cheese soufflé, both the
sauce and garnish being powerfully flavoured with crab, was an
example of this type of cooking at its best. Good quality local
produce seems to be used whenever available and this was
evident in the guineafowl. You will need an appropriately sweet
tooth for the puddings, and the service is a clever combination
of French waiters and English waitresses, who seem to work
well together.

There is a real feeling of professionalism here and some
genuinely good cooking. Bedrooms are carefully furnished and
immaculately kept.

Bosquet Restaurant   Kenilworth

97A Warwick Road, Kenilworth CV8 1HP   £25
(0926) 38451

Closed: Sun; Bank Holidays; 2 weeks Jul
Last
Orders: lunch (2.00pm); dinner (10.00pm)

This small converted house with an unimposing frontage belies
the talents of Bernard and Jane Lignier, who run an excellent
French restaurant in Kenilworth's main thoroughfare. The
dining room is small, seating a maximum of 28, comfortably
furnished and with a homely atmosphere.

Bernard is creative in his modern style of cooking and tries
some unusual combinations, so that pigeon and scampi become
partners in a salad, boned oxtail is wrapped in lettuce then
served with a red wine sauce, knuckle of veal is cooked in an

307

orange sauce, and snails with Parma ham and mushrooms are blended with a garlic cream sauce topped with puff pastry.

Whilst he labours to produce his creations, Jane looks after the guests with charm and confidence. The wine list is totally French, with some exceptionally good value in all sections.

Here you will get some of the best food in the area.

Diment Restaurant   Kenilworth

121-123 Warwick Road, Kenilworth CV8 1HP
(0926) 53763

Closed: lunch (Sat, Sun + Mon); dinner (Sun + Mon);
        Bank Holidays; 3 weeks Aug; 1 week Easter
Last
Orders: lunch (2.00pm); dinner (10.00pm)

Tony and Jennifer Martin's popular restaurant and bistro is well situated for visitors to the National Exhibition Centre and the Royal Show site at Stoneleigh. You can enjoy a relaxed meal in the rust and brown ground floor dining room, or have an informal dinner in the cosy basement bistro. In the restaurant try the speciality of côte de boeuf which is a rib of beef cooked to order for 2 people, carved at the table and served with béarnaise sauce. Game is also featured during winter months. Lunch is popular with local businessmen, and at around £6.00 a head for the excellent 3-course table d'hôte menu, it's hardly surprising! Puddings like the hazelnut meringue filled with raspberries, or a pancake with bananas in rum, coated with hot mousseline sauce are hard to resist.

The beamed bistro with its copper-topped bar and checked cloths has a good atmosphere and you will find it full of locals on most evenings. Good fish and meats from Birmingham markets are grilled and served with frites and fresh salads, and 3 courses with wine can be had for around £10.00 a head.

The Butchers Arms   Priors Hardwick

Priors Hardwick, Near Rugby CV23 8SN
(0327) 60504

Closed: lunch (Sat); dinner (Sun)
Last
Orders: lunch (2.45pm); dinner (9.30pm)

My first visit to this charming restaurant was many years ago. It was on a Sunday morning that I drove along winding Warwick-shire lanes leading apparently to nowhere, the only other traffic being the odd chicken scampering across the road. On reaching the sleepy village, you turn a corner and in front of you is a vast car park filled with a selection of machinery that would do credit to a Berkeley Square showroom. This is the Butchers Arms!

Sunday lunch is quite something. Customers drive from miles around to enjoy the traditional food and tremendous atmosphere in Lino Pires' dining room. It is almost like a club, as the same faces can be seen week after week. During the week the menu becomes more classical - basic first courses, good quality meat and fish dishes, many plainly cooked on the grill, and game is a feature in season. Having decided what to eat you will find the choice of wine more difficult, as the list has around 200 tempting selections, predominantly Burgundy and claret but with a strong Portuguese representation. Should you be entertaining in large numbers there is a range of clarets in civilised sized bottles - magnums, double magnums, jereboams and even an imperial!

Originally an old inn dating from 1375, it has been extended and improved over the years, maintaining the old character but creating more modern comforts. The garden is a delight in the summer, and roaring log fires welcome cold travellers in the winter. Friendly staff serve, and time is irrelevant in this cosy hostelry which seems to wrap itself around you.

■■■■ WEST MIDLANDS ■■■■

Sloan's   Birmingham

27-29 Chad Square, Hawthorne Road, Edgbaston B15 3TQ
021-455 6697

Closed: lunch (Sat + Sun); dinner (Sun); Bank Holidays;
         Christmas
Last
Orders: lunch (1.45pm); dinner (9.30pm)

Roger Narbett, RAGB Young Chef of the Year in 1985, has recently moved from The Bell at Belbroughton to become chef patron at this modern restaurant on the outskirts of Birmingham. Whilst we have only had one opportunity to visit this new venture, the signs are good, and once the dust has settled, this could well become one of the second city's premier restaurants. It is located in a shopping development opposite The Dirty Duck public house, which is a popular venue with students from the nearby university. Décor is bright and light in shades of green with a large bar, and a split level divided dining room. Large windows look out on to the parking area through the white painted balustrades, and the bamboo furniture with flowered upholstery retains the almost conservatory feeling.

The à la carte menu is small, with modern dishes like a hot salmon mousse filled with crayfish and salmon in a delicate dill sauce - light and well made, with strips of vegetable for garnish. Canon of lamb is sautéed, sliced and served in a crown with a light tomato and basil sauce. A selection of vegetables is served, or a salad if you prefer. For pudding try the sablée of pears, which is very light, thin layers of sweet pastry, filled with pastry cream and sliced poached pear - delicious!

At lunch time there is a menu rapide, with a choice of 2 dishes for each of the 3 courses, which with coffee comes to about £10.00. Service is by friendly young staff, who are efficient and enthusiastic.

■ WEST SUSSEX ■

Belinda's   Arundel

13 Tarrant Street, Arundel   £10
(0903) 882977

Closed: Mon
Last
Orders: 5.30pm

Belinda's has apparently been on the map since 1560 and was
converted into a tea-room in 1920. There are fantastic cream
teas with home-made scones and cakes, plus shortbread.

Gravetye Manor   East Grinstead

Near East Grinstead RH19 4LJ   £60
(0342) 810567

Last
Orders: lunch (2.00pm); dinner (9.30pm)

Gravetye was originally built in 1598, but its most notable
occupant before Peter Herbert took over here in 1957, was
probably William Robinson, who in the 1880s began work on
embellishing the grounds, designing what is now internationally
known as the English Natural Garden. Certainly the planting and
landscaping of the grounds around Gravetye are some of the
best in the country. While you are going through these beautiful
grounds, the house gives you your first glimpse of this very
English manor. Stone-flagged floors covered with carefully
chosen rugs and carpets, beautiful antique furnishings, soft
chairs to fall back into and later additions to the panelling, some
of which were added in Victorian times, all fit in to give a
comfortable country house atmosphere. There are 14 rooms in
the main house, all decorated in country house style.

  Chef Allan Garth in the restaurant produces Anglo-French
dishes which are generous in portion, making an imaginative use
of fresh local produce. You might have timbale of asparagus
mousse, lightly smoked duck breast served with soured cherries
and celery salad, poached egg with a ragoût of morel
mushrooms served on an artichoke bottom with sauce mousseline as starters, followed perhaps by red and grey mullet à la
nage, baked brill Strindberg (brill covered with mustard and
onion farce, served on a glazed sauce) some noisettes of lamb
served with rösti potato and tarragon sauce, or perhaps a roast
rib of beef for 2 people. Home-made ice-cream and sorbets are
excellent or you could force yourself to have a carrot and
hazelnut cake or one of their chocolate whisky cakes, served

with a coffee sauce. I really think that this is the sort of food that visitors to Great Britain, of whom there were many in the dining room on our last visit, are really looking for.

The wine list is comprehensive with a good selection of wines at the upper end of the market, which you would expect in surroundings such as these. A lovely touch is the Gravetye Manor spring water, which comes from the spring that has served the Manor since 1598. Peter Herbert and his family run this very English of English houses with great capability.

Stane Street Hollow   Pulborough

Codmore Hill, Pulborough RH20 1BG
(079 82) 2819

Closed: lunch (Sun, Mon + Tue); dinner (Sun + Mon);
       2 weeks May; 3 weeks Oct; Christmas Eve - 5 Jan
Last
Orders: lunch (1.15pm); dinner (9.15pm)

This large cottage-style property is set in its own grounds, and as René Kaiser says, they grow as much of their own soft fruit, vegetables and herbs as possible. There's plenty of evidence of this in the vegetable and herb garden just to the left of the car park behind a delightful pond. They also have their own geese, chickens, and ducks, and smoke their own ham, meats and fish. Their intimate little restaurant has an interesting selection of dishes (although the menu is small) based on seasonally available produce. You might be offered home-smoked salmon served with a fresh horseradish cream, or a light mousse of home-pickled mackerel served on a tomato purée flavoured with raspberry vinegar, or kässler, Stane Street Hollow's home-smoked loin of pork served with a fresh pear filled with a mild mustard cream, or a casserole of wild rabbit cooked in white wine with mushrooms, fresh thyme and garlic.

There's a nice feeling to this homely cottage.

Ghyll Manor Hotel & Restaurant   Rusper

High Street, Rusper RH12 4PX
(029 384) 571

Last
Orders: lunch (2.00pm); dinner (10.00pm)

Ghyll Manor

This original Elizabethan house with later extensions has been carefully restored to provide about 25 bedrooms, some in the house itself, others in the sympathetically converted stable block. All are beautifully appointed, and most have antiques and oil paintings scattered around their pretty pink interiors. The dining room opens up onto a terrace overlooking the 30 acres of undulating Sussex countryside which form the setting for this

comfortable and well-loved hotel, which is a favourite place for Sunday lunch, or dinner on a summer's evening. Rusper is a charming little village and, situated opposite the Manor, is the Church of St Mary Magdalene, parts if which date from the 13th Century. Next door to the manor is the 300-year-old Plough Inn, which is worth a visit if you're a real ale drinker.

Little Thakeham   Storrington

Merrywood Lane, Storrington RH20 3HE
(090 66) 4416

— check, as this may have changed hands. £45

Closed: Christmas + New Year; all meals by reservation only

Last
Orders: dinner (9.30pm)

Tim and Pauline Ratcliff have been at Little Thakeham now for some 7 years, and their splendid Lutyens mansion is set in grounds and gardens after the style of Gertrude Jekyll. You can have an apéritif in the courtyard at the back of the hotel, which leads down to the formal gardens and orchards. The house itself has some fine examples of original furniture. The dining room is pleasant, and competently run by a team of smiling young ladies, under the watchful eye of Sue Jefferies.

The rack of lamb is good, as is the pheasant, and the partridge and wild duck when in season. The dinner menu at £19.50 consists of 4 courses with 3 choices for each, including Scotch salmon baked in pastry with white wine and tarragon, rack of South Down lamb, or simply but well-cooked grilled calves' liver and bacon. Good British puddings from the sideboard are followed by cheese. There's a fine choice of wines with plenty of clarets. If you can't make it in the evening, it's a superb place for Sunday lunch.

Altogether, the feeling is of warmth and comfort in this stylish country house.

Manleys   Storrington

Storrington RH20 4BT
(090 66) 2331   _the best in the area £45

Closed: lunch (Mon); dinner (Sun + Mon); 1 week Jan;
         1 week Sep; 2 weeks Aug
Last
Orders: lunch (1.45pm); dinner (9.30pm)

Karl Löderer, chef and proprietor at Manleys, has just finished
having an extension built to his neat, Queen Anne cottage-style
premises. The bar, with its furniture and timber beams, is totally
in keeping, but by now may have been incorporated into the
restaurant, itself run in a very efficient manner by charming
head waiter Gerard Basset. He is assisted by a young English
staff whose service complements the obvious professionalism in
the kitchen.

The comprehensive menu contains some 10 or so starters,
including some unusual choices and dishes that Mr Löderer has
made his very own. The short pastry filled with oyster
mushrooms, shallots, tarragon and lobster covered with a
lobster flavoured soufflé is quite superb. The fresh large scallops
provençale are served with lightly cooked peeled tomato pieces,
plump and juicy. The terrine of seafood - layers of mussels, crab,
lobster and spinach with a lightly cooked crêpe wrapped around
the outside, sliced and served with a watercress mayonnaise is
excellent. Amongst other stars on the menu are the whole boned
Dover sole filled with langoustine mousse served with a
langoustine sauce and red wine, and the salmon mille feuille
which we tried - layers of puff pastry interlaced with freshly
cooked salmon served with sorrel, Karl's version of the Louis
Outhier dish served at La Napoule in Cannes.

For the more carnivorous, there's a veal steak on a bed of
Savoy cabbage, garnished with tomatoes and a hint of sage, with
creamed Roquefort cheese and finished under the grill, and
fillets of venison in a piquant sauce served with a good selection
of wild mushrooms. The vegetables are fresh, crisp and plentiful,
with an excellent gratin savoyarde and rösti.

If you've enjoyed generous portions of first courses and main
courses, you might almost have made up your mind not to have a
dessert. But by the time you see the other guests tucking into
home-made sorbets in almond pastry with seasonal fruit and
spun sugar, or Karl Löderer's famous meringue du chef (which is
a meringue filled with vanilla ice-cream and hot chocolate
sauce), or the excellent French apple tart, individually cooked
and served in rum-flavoured cream among the 10 or so choices,
then you may as well decide to make a day or even a night of it!
You'll certainly go away feeling that some of the French dishes
cooked here truly reflect the warmth and character of this
generous Austrian chef.

Abingworth Hall Thakeham

Storrington Road, Thakeham RH20 3EF
(079 83) 3636/2257

Last
Orders: lunch (1.45pm); dinner (9.00pm)

Abingworth Hall is situated on the South Downs in about 10 acres of grounds, which are beautifully laid out with a lake, a 2-acre, 9-hole pitch-and-putt course, a heated swimming pool, and a tennis court. Reception rooms and restaurant are well decorated, and there's a peaceful air to the whole property and grounds. The staff are keen and interested in the customers, an attitude which stems from its owners, Philip and Pauline Bulman.

■■■■■■■■■■■■■ WEST YORKSHIRE ■■■■■■■■■■■■■

Restaurant Nineteen Bradford

Belvedere Hotel, 19 North Park Road, Bradford BD9 4NT
(0274) 492559

Closed: lunch (daily); dinner (Sun + Mon);
        1 week Aug; 2 weeks Jan
Last
Orders: dinner (9.30pm; 10.00pm Sat)

Without wishing to be unkind to Bradford, to find a restaurant of this calibre was a very pleasant surprise. Located on the northern side of the city just off the A650, this large corner house, which formerly belonged to a wealthy merchant, looks out over parkland. In fact, to find it you should turn alongside the park gates, which resemble the entrance to a castle rather than to a park.

Soft shades of apricot, starched white linen, mahogany woodwork and fresh flowers give the dining room a light fresh feeling. Robert Barbour runs the front of house and his partner, Stephen Smith, cooks in an accomplished modern style. His 4-course dinner menu is priced according to the choice of main dish, and the intermediate course offers a choice of 2 soups. To start you might like scallops in a lobster sauce - the scallops are perfectly cooked and served with a lightly creamed sauce which is well made and full of flavour. Yorkshire partridge sounds too good to miss. It is roasted then carved, and served on a bed of crunchy cabbage and bacon with a good gravy and bread sauce. Excellent vegetables arrive on a separate plate. Bread sauce can sometimes be badly made - left to stand until it resembles congealed cold porridge - but Stephen Smith has mastered the art. His is light, smooth and seasoned properly with just the right amount of nutmeg. For pudding, a poached peach filled with honey and brandy ice cream and a caramelised peach sauce is delicious. Sauces say a lot about a chef's ability, and each of these showed excellent skill and feeling for texture, flavour and consistency - a rare delight.

Service is a match for the kitchen. Robert commands the dining room quietly and efficiently with help from some charming staff. Wine and water are poured when needed, and there are reassuring pauses between courses. The wine list has good representation from around the world with fine Burgundy and claret and good value in other regions.

It must have taken a lot of courage to open in this location, as much perhaps as a decision to spend a weekend in Bradford. I hope that their aspirations will be achieved as quickly as my opinion of the city has been changed!

The Box Tree   Ilkley

29 Church Street, Ilkley LS29 9DR   £45
(0943) 608484

Closed: lunch (daily); dinner (Sun + Mon)
Last
Orders: dinner (9.30m; 10.00pm Sat)

*check, as changed
hands
December '86*

A history of recent English cooking would definitely have a long chapter devoted to the role of The Box Tree and its owners Colin Long and Malcolm Reid. In the grey days when a good meal in England was a rare and treasured thing The Box Tree stood out like a beacon. Pilgrimages were made from far and wide and sceptical southerners found themselves keen to visit West Yorkshire. Since those days, a lot of people have caught up with them and some may even have overtaken, but there is a timeless sense of quality when you enter the bar with its tinkling piano, and a picture or ornament in every available space. The menu is in French but the staff are English and will explain everything with a smile.

Cooking is modern now: clear and shiny mushroom consommé; and properly reduced sauces may accompany excellent quality meat or game from the neighbouring area. It is a restaurant for an occasion, you will never feel overdressed and the extensive wine list gives ample opportunity to celebrate in style.

Saturday evening takes 2 sittings for dinner, at 7.30pm and 9.45pm.

Kildwick Hall   Kildwick

Kildwick, Skipton, Near Keighley BD20 9AE
(0535) 32244

Closed: lunch (Mon - Sat)
Last
Orders: dinner (11.00pm)

This is an impressive stone house with views of the neighbouring towns and countryside and a real Jacobean feel inspired by
the dark and heavy panelling inside. By contrast, the dining
room is light, although dominated by several large portraits.
   The menu is more French than English, and the poached
quails' eggs with thick slices of field mushrooms and a properly
reduced sauce were good. The cheese trolley was proudly
displayed and the French cheeses were in good condition.
   You can stay at Kildwick Hall in large, solidly furnished rooms
which are reasonably comfortable.

Pool Court   Pool-in-Wharfedale

Pool Bank, Pool-in-Wharfedale LS21 1EH
(0532) 842288/9 and 842414

Closed: lunch (except by arrangement for parties of 10 or more); dinner
        (Sun + Mon); Christmas Eve for 2 weeks
Last
Orders: dinner (9.30pm)

In 20 years Michael Gill has created and run an impeccable
restaurant with rooms in this fine Georgian house. The
thoughtfulness and care of the whole operation are obvious
from the minute you enter the large, attractive, and superbly
furnished and equipped bedrooms. A combination of modern
science, (a drinks fridge, hair drier, etc) and traditional values of
hospitality are achieved to great effect. In the unlikely event you
have any problems, Mr Gill and his superbly drilled staff will
attend to everything with great charm.
   Chef Melvin Jordan has created a menu of modern cooking,
popular with locals and visitors alike. A soup of peas, lemon and
mint is refreshing and makes a perfect second course. You might
begin with a seafood slice in a light mustard sauce, and the
grilled baby chicken with fresh limes is perfectly executed.
Simpler tastes are taken care of with grilled liver and bacon, or
steaks. If you have never eaten rose petal ice-cream then here is
the place to try it.

The wines have been carefully collected over the years and there are some rare bargains at the top and bottom of the price range. Fashionable wines like Sassicaia, found usually only on the trendier New York and London lists, are also available here. Classic wines from France, Italy and the New World sit side by side - a Richebourg 1976, a Barolo Riserva 1961, and from Australia a Grange Hermitage 1978 - each exemplary in their way. Nearly a dozen wines from Châteauneuf du Pape, and a long list of clarets, give a wide range of choice, and the cheaper wines show an equal amount of taste and careful choice. Whether you stay overnight or just go for dinner, the quality and style of Pool Court shine through.

Over The Bridge   Ripponden

Millfold, Ripponden, Near Halifax HX6 4LD
(0422) 823722

Closed: lunch (daily); Sun; Bank Holidays
Last
Orders: dinner (9.30pm)

There are in fact 2 bridges - turn off the main road through Ripponden and after crossing the first bridge turn sharp left towards the church, then park in the car park on your right. As you leave the car park you will see the other small bridge, and the restaurant is just on the left up some stairs. As you enter you find yourself in the cosy little bar and you can have a well-earned apéritif and munch some crudités while reading the menu.

Seasonal produce is offered on the fixed price menu, and specialities include game during the season, spring lamb, and boned fowl such as ballottine of duck or guineafowl stuffed with spinach and ricotta. The restaurant is down another flight of stairs on the ground floor and is comfortably furnished with upholstered cane chairs and shades of blue and orange. Candles flicker on the tables and the smart young waiting staff are conscientious and attentive. By the way, if you do happen to cross the other bridge and find yourself in the pub, they will give you directions to the restaurant, which is not sign-posted.

■ WILTSHIRE ■

Beechfield House   Beanacre

Beanacre, Near Melksham SN12 7PH   £40
(0225) 703700

Last
Orders: lunch (1.30pm); dinner (9.15pm)

Beechfield House is one of the smaller, friendlier country house
hotels. Standing in its own grounds it is a fine example of a
Victorian country house, with all the grandness of that era:
mature gardens to the front, lawns and flowers at the back, a
fountain which leads you through to the swimming pool and
pleasantly converted coach house, which has been sympathetically restored and decorated. Its rooms overlook the pool at the
rear of the main house. Walk through a door in the wall on the
other side of the pool, and you'll find yourself amongst carefully
tended vegetable beds where there are also plastic cloches full of
herbs and lettuces - all of which are used to good effect by Peter
Crawford-Rolt, proprietor and chef.

The house itself is well furnished, and there are examples of
Georgian and Victorian antiques. The bedrooms are spacious and
have all the fittings and trimmings you would expect in a country
house of this standard. Of the 2 dining rooms, one is a garden
room in shades of green, with blue and green seated chairs with
cane backs, splendid garden views all around from the large
windows, and a very friendly, welcoming feeling. The second
dining room is more masculine and has polished mahogany
tables, with very much a Victorian feel to it. Drinks are served
from the massive dresser in the hall; there are crackling log fires
in the winter; and the whole atmosphere is one of staying in a
rather nice country house with some charming hosts to look after
you. The service is by local girls who really make you feel most
welcome, they're all smiles and always helpful.
    The food is regional English with French overtones, and there
is an excellent value lunch for around £10.00 or £15.00 on
Sundays, as well as some really good dishes on the à la carte
menu. Presentation is very good and large portions are served.
Choose from 8 or 9 starters which might include Beechfield
garden asparagus in pastry with a lime sabayon sauce, salad of
calf's tongue, mushrooms and artichokes with sauce ravigote,

and cream soup of Cornish crab and vegetables served with croûtons. Well worth a try if available is the chicken and pigeon terrine, a rough mosaic served with excellent kumquat preserve and chutney; or a generous portion of fish terrine, which is layers of sole and salmon trout set in vine leaves and served with herb mayonnaise. Main courses might include grilled délice of Dartmouth salmon with a champagne and chervil hollandaise; poached fillet of Cornish trout on a bed of leaf spinach, glazed with a cheese sauce and garnished with scallops; a whole roast Norfolk guineafowl with rosemary cream sauce garnished with asparagus; or fillet of Cotswolds lamb with a tomato and basil sauce amongst the 6 choices. The good lamb fillet is served pink, sliced, and accompanied by a mushroom timbale garnished with miniature sweet corn and turnips. There's an excellent side plate of crisp garden vegetables, a fine selection of English and French cheeses, and amongst the 6 or so excellent choices for dessert, try the hot caramelised pineapple and banana tartlet, flamed with rum. You might be offered a choice of 2 or 3 different types of home-made bread including a brioche.

Sensibly priced Bordeaux reds, 45 in total, range from £6.50 up to £85.00, and a good list of sweet white Bordeaux is again offered at affordable prices. If you really want to be over the top, there are even 2 from Château d'Yquem, a 1944 and a 1921 - and priced accordingly! The Burgundies aren't neglected and neither are the Beaujolais; and there is a good selection of half bottles.

I can promise you a pleasant stay at this friendly home.

The Sign of the Angel   Lacock

Church Street, Lacock, Near Chippenham SN15 2LL
(0249) 73230

Closed: 22 Dec - 5 Jan
Last
Orders: lunch (by arrangement); dinner (7.30pm)

Lacock, whose most modern building is 18th-Century, several in fact dating from Mediaeval times, is a delightful and pretty blend of whitewashed and timbered buildings housing inns, shops (including the National Trust), and a restaurant called The Sign of the Angel, which is an attractive stone timber-fronted building that was originally a 15th-Century wool merchant's house. It has beautifully beamed and panelled rooms, and a room on the first floor where drinks are served. The unique atmosphere is totally in keeping with the village, and reflects the type of food which the Levis family, who have been here for many years, choose to serve. This is cooking the way mother and grandmother used to cook. They use excellent local produce, and serve the food simply. Standard starters might be followed by roast beef and Yorkshire pudding, pork or lamb with 'The Sign of the Angel' stuffing and local vegetables; then puddings such as apple pie, home-made ice-cream or home-made meringues. You can also have Stilton or Cheddar cheese which will be included in the £16.50-a-head menu. Mr Levis looks after the wine list which has a good selection of housewines, starting at £6.40 a bottle. Charming, friendly service in the restaurant, which seats 40; and there are 6 bedrooms.

Before dinner, take time to explore this English gem, or walk up to the Abbey founded in the 13th Century, and breathe in some of the unique atmosphere. You might stop off at the George Inn, another traditional inn in the capable hands of Wadsworth's, or possibly stay the night at the Red Lion, which is perhaps the largest establishment in Lacock, an 18th-Century pub with earlier origins, roaring log fires, a long bar, old settles and lots of old bric-à-brac. There are lovely tubs of flowers and a nice garden area at the rear. Lacock must also have one of the nicest bus stops in England - a beautiful virginia creeper-clad shelter set right into the side of one of the houses!

A visit here can also be combined with lunch or dinner at the excellent Beechfield House, lying 3 miles down the road towards Melksham (see above).

Bishopstrow House   Warminster

Warminster BA12 9HH
(0985) 212312

Last
Orders: lunch (1.15pm); dinner (9.30pm)

An immense amount of money has been spent on converting Bishopstrow House, originally built in 1817, into an elegant hotel. The public rooms are furnished with English and Continental antiques and there's a welcoming log fire to greet you in the winter. The conservatory dining room, which has been added to the main house, has been done with great sympathy and care so as not to detract from the original building. The bedrooms themselves, including the ones in the modern converted stable block, are well equipped and have some items of antique furniture - several rooms even have jacuzzi baths. There is an outdoor pool, which is screened from the main house, and which houses a beautiful fountain. There's also a magnificent indoor pool, and both outdoor and indoor tennis courts.

There is a set price dinner menu with a choice of 7 starters and 7 main courses (with a soup of the day as a middle course) served either in the Buttery opposite the main dining room, or in the Conservatory.

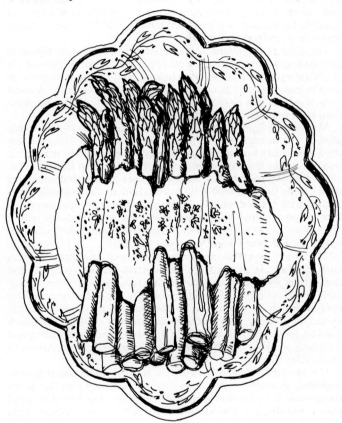

Scotland

For a land with lots of inhospitable craggy mountains and sometimes grim weather, Scotland has a surprisingly abundant array of culinary riches. As well as the national drink of whisky, the old favourites of haggis, porridge, and Dundee cake, there is fish, game, beef, cheese, interesting soups and all manner of tea-time treats. Maybe it's to keep out the cold, but they certainly know how to feed you up there!

The King of the Glens, a magnificent red deer stag, although not native to these parts (he was brought here from Exmoor for the King's pleasure) does now belong, and certainly figures on menus more often in Scotland than in the West Country. A roast or braised haunch or shoulder can readily be found on Scottish menus in season.

Aberdeen Angus is famous worldwide, a tribute to its reliable quality - from roast ribs of beef to meatballs and sausages, for the Scots waste nothing. Witness haggis, for instance, although it usually comes from the sheep rather than the beef farmer: offal, seasoning and oatmeal are mixed together and stuffed into a bag made from the stomach lining, then boiled. Traditionally, it is served with bashed neeps 'n' champit tatties (mashed swede or turnip and potatoes to you and me!), and washed down with a wee dram. You can buy good haggis from MacSween of Edinburgh, at 130 Brunsfield Place (031-229 1216).

The filler to these products, eking out the protein with carbohydrate, is of course that Scottish staple, oatmeal; and don't think you can avoid it by eating fish, for your herring may well come rolled in it! The king of fish, the salmon, needs no such dressing, however, nor do the smoked fish with romantic sounding names, like Loch Fyne kippers, Finnan haddock (served on its own, or as ham 'n' haddie), Eyemouth pales, and Arbroath smokies. Try R R Spink & Sons at 35 Seagate, Arbroath (0241 72023).

The Scottish cheese industry is making great inroads into southerly markets, with the mostly soft cheeses that the Scots themselves have been enjoying for centuries. Look for Crowdie, Caboc and Hramsa. The butterfat-rich milk of the Ayrshire herds is the ideal source of these cheeses.

Oatmeal mixed with bicarbonate of soda, melted bacon fat or lard and hot water, cooked on a griddle, makes oatcakes that are excellent with cheese; and oatmeal mixed with cream, honey and whisky is Atholl Brose (or Flummery, reputedly served by Flora MacDonald to Bonnie Prince Charlie); add Scottish raspberries and it's cranachan. Substitute almonds and ratafias for the fruit, and it's Edinburgh Fog.

Another tea-time favourite is shortbread, and there must be as many recipes for it as there are traditional designs baked into the finished product. Basically a very short, sweet pastry mixture of butter, sugar, flour and rice flour, this biscuit is baked in an oven not on a griddle, and is often shaped into fantails or fingers. A variation, with flaked almonds and lemon zest, comes out as slices of Pitcaithly Bannock.

Dundee cake and Dundee marmalade, the first distinguished from less regal fruitcakes by the pattern on top of whole almonds, the second being the first and original one to be made, need no advertising the world over.

There are hearty soups like cullen skink (smoked haddock and potato), cock-a-leekie (chicken and leek), lentil bro (lentils, ham stock and root vegetables). And when the protein runs low and you've already added oats to the diet, there are still stovies (potatoes and onions cooked in dripping on top of the stove) or rumbledethumps, a Scottish version of bubble and squeak. Some of the traditional tastes of Scotland can be purchased from The Scottish Gourmet, Thistle Mill, Station Road, Biggar (0899 21001); or Castle MacLellan, 10 St Cuthbert Street, Kirkcudbright (0557 30664) amongst others.

You can't leave Scotland without a wee dram. Derived from uisge beatha (water of life, just like the French eau de vie), it's a product of pure Scottish spring water, centuries-matured peat, and barley, the same recipe now as ever. Methods may have moved into this century, and new blends, now totalling over 2,000, keep appearing, but the depth of character of a fine, pure, single malt deserves the same attention as a grande fine cognac. Some would say even more. There are so many distilleries to mention that I thought we'd just mention the smallest: Edradour, at Pitlochry, Perthshire (0796 2095).

HISTORIC HOUSES OPEN TO THE PUBLIC

Borders Region
Abbotsford House, Nr Melrose
Bowhill, Nr Selkirk
Floors Castle, Kelso
Manderston, Duns
Mellerstain, Nr Melrose
Traquair House, Innerleithen

Dumfries & Galloway Region
Drumlanrig Castle, Nr Dumfries

Grampian Region
Braemar Castle, Braemar
Brodie Castle, Nr Nairn
Castle Fraser, Kemnay
Craigievar Castle, Nr Alford
Drum Castle, Nr Aberdeen
Haddo House, Nr Aberdeen

Highland Region
Cawdor Castle, Nr Nairn
Dunvegan Castle, Dunvegan

Lothian Region
Hopetoun House, Nr Forth
The House of the Binns, Nr Linlithgow
Lennoxlove, Nr Haddington
Palace of Holyroodhouse, Edinburgh

Strathclyde Region
Blair Castle, Blair Atholl
Culzean Castle, Nr Ayr
Inveraray Castle
Torosay Castle, Craigmure

Tayside Region
Glamis Castle, Nr Dundee
Scone Palace, Old Scone

323

The Cellar Restaurant   Anstruther

Anstruther, Fife KY10 3AA
(0333) 310378

Closed: lunch (Sun + Mon); dinner (Sun)
Last
Orders: lunch (1.30pm); dinner (9.30pm)

Don't let the uninteresting exterior to this restaurant put you off
- turn through the archway and you will find yourself in a pretty
little cottage-style restaurant. It has flagstone floors, beams,
open fireplaces and bits and pieces everywhere to create a
comfortable atmosphere. Polished wooden tables with mats,
and candlelight in the evening give a warm feeling to this small
dining room. Peter Dukes is the chef patron and his speciality is
fish - hardly surprising in this small fishing port which has
access to some of the best fish available to us. Crayfish and
mussel bisque, Crail crab, West Coast mussels, home-made
gravadlax, West Coast langoustine and fresh scallops are
amongst the first courses. Follow these with lemon sole,
perhaps turbot with scallops, Tay salmon, langoustine, or a
rendezvous of seafood, or maybe halibut. The menu naturally
revolves around the catches from the boats and will change
frequently. For those who don't like fish there are a couple of
alternatives available.

Peter's wife Vivien runs the dining room with some help, and
is a charming hostess. Sensibly for a fish restaurant, the wine list
concentrates on white wines with a large choice of Chablis and
of Alsace wines together with a few quality red wines from
Burgundy and Bordeaux. The Cellar Restaurant is thoroughly
enjoyable. Peter's cooking is extremely competent, sauces complement rather than kill the natural flavours and delicate tastes
of the fish, and the whole ambience of the restaurant is
absolutely right for a small seaside town.

Gleneagles Hotel   Auchterader

Auchterader PH3 1NF
(076 46) 2231

Last
Orders: lunch (2.00pm); dinner (10.00pm)

Gleneagles originally opened in 1924 and this grand old hotel is
now a totally different place, although its original splendour has

been very much retained. It has gone through a number of changes over the recent years and the team that really put Gleneagles back on the map now departed, leaving a new team working very hard to build up further this Scottish palace of 250 bedrooms and suites.

The hotel itself is set in some indisputably beautiful country-side, for lovely woodlands and the distant hills surround the more formal gardens. There is a sporting complex which they've cleverly added on, with its own lagoon-shaped swimming pool, saunas, Turkish baths, gymnasium, billiard room and squash courts. Within the estate they have no fewer than 4 golf courses, a selection of tennis courts, a bowling green and a couple of croquet lawns, as well as the Jackie Stewart Shooting School (wot, no cricket pitch?). You can't please some people!

The style of the public rooms is in the grand tradition: numerous bars are tucked away, with pleasant, helpful uni-formed staff available so that if you want to, you can hide yourself away in the well-stocked library and read a newspaper, or pick a book from the shelf, and still enjoy a quiet drink. In the afternoon you can take a full Scottish tea in the elegantly furnished drawing room. Restaurants include the Strathearn Restaurant, open for lunch and dinner, and the Eagles Nest, a more intimate restaurant which opens in the evenings only. There is a grand hotel wine list with grand hotel prices, operated by well-trained and professional staff.

Arisaig House   Beasdale

Beasdale, Arisaig, Inverness-shire PH39 4NR
(068 75) 622

Closed: lunch (daily); Nov - Easter
Last
Orders: dinner (8.30pm)

Without doubt Arisaig is one of Scotland's most lovely hotels, lying by the famous road to the Isles about 36 miles west of Fort William. John and Ruth Smither run an impeccable house which has spectacular views and wonderful walks around the coast-line, where Bonnie Prince Charlie first landed in 1745 and from where he later escaped with the help of the French. Originally built in 1864, the house was rebuilt in 1937 and retains a 1930s flavour. It is well furnished in country house style, the rooms being large and comfortable and staff quietly efficient. I reserved only the evening before arrival and was lucky to find a single room, which had its own bathroom located just along the corridor but secured with its own key. The menu is basically fixed although, sensibly, alternatives for each course are offered. A mousse of salmon with beurre blanc could be followed by cullen skink (a special soup made of smoked haddock, potato, celery and cream - delicious)! Main course might be a saddle of lamb stuffed with veal and herbs, accompanied by good fresh vegetables from the garden, with grapefruit sorbet and cheeses to finish. The hostess is charming and takes great trouble to ensure the guests' well-being, always being around at the right time in the right place.

Polmaily House Hotel   Drumnadrochit

Drumnadrochit, Inverness-shire IV3 6XT
(045 62) 343

Closed: lunch (daily); mid-Oct - Easter
Last
Orders: dinner (9.30pm)

Nick and Alison Parsons' comfortable hotel is in an ideal
position for those wishing to tour the beautiful Highlands, or for
aspiring monster hunters hoping to lay the Loch Ness mystery
finally to rest. It is furnished in homely rather than grand hotel
style and the hosts maintain this atmosphere with attentive,
caring service.

Alison cooks and produces daily menus based on the best
local produce obtainable, for example a warm salad of ham with
delicious chanterelles in tarragon dressing followed by wild
salmon in red wine sauce, which was perfectly cooked and full
of flavour. Other menus might have Kinloch Rannoch smoked
venison, baked Orkney scallops, Aberdeen Angus beef, Storn-
away mussels, Pennyghael oysters or Orkney crab roulade. A
good selection of Scottish cheeses is available, and sweets for
the diet conscious such as a blackcurrant leaf water ice or
home-made melon and mint sorbet contrast with those for heavy
appetites: rich chocolate and hazelnut cake with chocolate
fudge icing or Drumlanrig summer pudding - superb! Almost 100
very reasonably priced wines on the interesting list including
plenty of half bottles.

Young staff are well supervised by the patron in the dining
room and they smile a lot, which is always nice to see. There are
no private bathrooms, TV or telephone but there is a tennis court
and a swimming pool; plus the innovation of sachets of insect
repellant in each bedroom - for Nessie!?

Pomaily House is one of the best all round hotels in Scotland:
comfortable, excellent food and wines, and genuine service.

The Alp Horn   Edinburgh

167 Rose Street, Edinburgh EH2 4LS
031-225 4787

Closed: Sun + Mon; 3 weeks from Jun; 2 weeks from Christmas
Last
Orders: lunch (2.00pm); dinner (10.00pm)

Even the exterior of this cheerful and efficiently run restaurant
looks authentically Swiss. The interior is bright and clean with
red gingham curtains, light wood tables and chairs, and white
walls with pictures of Switzerland, the Alp Horn itself and
cowbells. The atmosphere is relaxed and informal with brisk
service in brasserie style. I would recommend the typically
Swiss dishes such as assiette des grisons (which is air-dried
beef, ham and sausages) to start, and then either venison or veal,
which are served with either spätzli or rösti. Both are perfectly
executed. Sweets tend to be ice-cream or meringue based, or
apfelstrüdel. The small wine list has a few Swiss wines, and
representatives from other well known areas.

Champany Inn Town   Edinburgh

2 Bridge Road, Colinton, Edinburgh EH13 0LF
031-441 2587

Closed: Sun; 2 weeks Jan
Last
Orders: lunch (2.00pm); dinner (10.00pm)

A converted butcher's shop in an outlying district of Edinburgh, this attractive restaurant could just as easily be in a provincial French town. The simple décor of plain walls with beams and paintings, a tiled floor covered with large rugs, and polished wood tables give a warm and comfortable feel to this small dining room.

The menu features Aberdeen Angus beef hung for a minimum of 3 weeks and then cut into a variety of steaks, and charcoal grilled. Alternatives are Scottish lamb, Dutch veal, chicken, salmon or lemon sole, and amongst the starters are dressed Scottish crab, prawns in garlic, dressed salmon, pickled fish and a few other items. Sweets are also simple and the accent is on the use of top quality produce throughout the menu. Vegetables are lightly steamed and served crisp, and the meat, perfect.

Housewines are South African from KWV and are hard to better at £5.50, though you could choose from 25 other Cape wines in addition to 100 better known European wines. Nigel Best cooks competently and his wife Fiona runs the dining room equally well, making this delightful restaurant a 'must' whilst in Edinburgh.

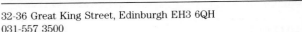

Howard Hotel   Edinburgh

32-36 Great King Street, Edinburgh EH3 6QH
031-557 3500

Closed: Christmas and New Year
Last
Orders: lunch (2.00pm); dinner (9.30pm)

Housed in an elegant Georgian terrace, the Howard Hotel is situated just a few minutes from Princes Street, which makes it a perfect place to stay while visiting the fascinating Scottish capital. Comfortable bedrooms have bathrooms, telephone and television; and thankfully, in such a central location, the hotel also has a car park. Public rooms at the hotel have been classically furnished and decorated to retain the style of the exterior, and the bedrooms are clean, well-kept and modern in furnishing. In the basement of the hotel are situated both a lively bar to enjoy a drink or the claret jug, and also the Number 36 restaurant, which has been decorated in shades of brown and gold. The menu offers the best of Scottish produce such as Seton sole, West Coast scampi, Tay salmon, and smoked mackerel. If you prefer the atmosphere of a smaller hotel, or perhaps if budgets don't permit the Caledonian, then the Howard must be one of the best places to stay in town.

Pompadour Room Edinburgh

The Caledonian Hotel, Princes Street, Edinburgh EH1 2AB £55
031-225 2433

Closed: lunch (Sat + Sun); dinner (Sun); 26 Dec; 1 + 2 Jan
Last
Orders: dinner (10.30pm)

The Scottish capital is justifiably proud of its 5-star hotel located in the shadow of the castle at the end of Princes Street. Almost £4 million has been spent in the last 5 years to achieve the standard in this internationally known hostelry, and luxurious comfort is the result.

The Pompadour Room is an elegant dining room in the style of Louis XV with huge carver chairs on thick carpet and sparkling cut glass and shining silver on the tables. A pianist plays in the evening, and waiters glide around with brisk efficiency, managing to arrive that split second before you need them. The menus are large both in actual size and in content. Alan Hill has created dishes in the nouvelle style for his main menu, and with "Legends of the Scottish Table" has researched old traditional Scottish fare, now offering dishes such as bawd bree (a hare soup), a Hebridean fish stew, Musselburgh pie, trout in oatmeal and so on.

At dinner, the menu Bonne Bouche is Alan's menu gastronomique, "6 light courses from today's market". Suffice it to say that they are light and they are delicious. A well-balanced menu using exceptionally good raw materials, which are cooked perfectly, with well-made sauces to complement them. Even at £25.00 this is good value. The wine list is also large and, naturally, is not cheap; though housewines are £7.50, prices climb gradually to a '70 Petrus at £295.00.

Luxury in this day and age is never inexpensive, but the Caledonian is a great place to spoil oneself occasionally.

The Buttery Glasgow

652 Argyle Street, Glasgow £30
041-221 8188

Closed: lunch (Sat + Sun); dinner (Sun)
Last
Orders: lunch (2.30pm); dinner (10.00pm)

Fine panelling, red carpeting, family portraits, engraved glass screens and period antiques add up to an Edwardian splendour that would do justice to a London gentlemen's club, and combine to create a warm ambience in this comfortable bar. There's more panelling in the dining room, with high-backed upholstered settles, crisp white linen, sparkling glass and silverware emphasising the care taken in running this well-established restaurant.

Brian Graham's menu offers an interesting variety of dishes. Parcels of crayfish in a pool of apple and ginger sauce, Oban mussels with shallots and white wine, green pasta with smoked ham and garlic, or watercress soup with chicken dumplings might be amongst first courses; and roast saddle of venison with blackcurrants and sour cream, breast of chicken with lobster sauce, piccata of veal with tarragon and lime or rendezvous of native seafood with saffron beurre blanc as main dishes. A set lunch menu is good value. The wine list offers around 70 good choices with reasonable prices.

The Belfry

Last
Orders: lunch (2.30pm); dinner (10.30pm)

In the basement is an attractive bistro called The Belfry with exposed stone walls, lots of timber and plastic tablecloths. Dishes such as navarin of lamb, charcuterie with salad or a port cutlet with noodles in apple and cinnamon sauce, provide a cheaper alternative to The Buttery.

A small wine list has some lesser known wines at economical prices, and the atmosphere is good.

One Devonshire Gardens   Glasgow

1 Devonshire Gardens, Glasgow G12 OUX
041-339 2001

Closed: lunch (Mon - Sat); dinner (Sun); Christmas Day; New Year's Day
Last
Orders: lunch (2.00pm); dinner (10.00pm)

Just a short distance from the centre of Glasgow, an elegant Victorian town house has been converted into a small luxurious hotel. Tasteful décor uses intense colour with dramatic wallpapers and fabrics, deep blue being the predominant shade in the hall, landings and dining room.

Each bedroom has been individually designed to offer variety of style, and the ambience makes one feel like a house guest. Staff are dressed in long grey dresses with starched white aprons and mob caps. They provide old-fashioned service - no tea-making equipment in the bedrooms of this residence!

Drinks are served in the drawing room where you can relax and choose from menu and wine list. Jennifer Koaker's daily fixed-price menu gives a choice of 2 dishes for each course, and a soup is included after the first dish. A typical menu might offer the choice of a rendezvous of seafood with saffron sauce, or asparagus salad with hazelnut dressing, followed by a cream of leek and potato soup. Main dishes of supreme of chicken with port wine, or braised sea trout with herbs and cream are served with vegetables or salad; and finally a dark chocolate pot or autumn fruits glazed with a passion fruit sauce. The wine list, though not large, has been carefully compiled with some lesser known items and a few magnums for sensible sipping.

At the time of writing, One Devonshire Gardens had only been open for 3 months but we have little doubt that under the guidance of Stephen Coupe, who helped to establish Cromlix House, this charming hotel will be a big success. It may well start a new trend for town house hotels which could become as popular as the country house variety.

Rogano Glasgow

11 Exchange Place, Glasgow G1 3AN
041-248 4055

Closed: Sunday
Last
Orders: 12.30pm

The ground floor bar and dining room have an almost decadent elegance, in superb Art Deco style using light timber, dark paintwork, and engraved mirrors on cream walls. You can just have a drink at the bar or eat in the dining room from the excellent, predominantly seafood menu. The ambience is 1930s but the cooking is very much in the 1980s with a small but well-judged variety of dishes using top quality produce.

The basement restaurant at Rogano serves meals throughout the day, and is ideal for catching up with lunch after a trip to the local shops, or for a pre-theatre dinner. The panelled walls are covered in monochrome photographs, and pretty waitresses in black and white serve with charm. The menu offers a choice of mussels marinara, seafood lasagne, steak frites, chilli con carne or smoked trout, prawn and avocado salad, and 100% pure beef hamburgers.

Sweets include crème brûlée, bread and butter pudding, apple and raisin crumble, and there is espresso coffee.

Rogano, with its option of dining rooms, provides a venue for entertaining or celebrating on the ground floor, or a good-value night out with friends downstairs.

The Ubiquitous Chip Glasgow

12 Ashton Lane, Glasgow G12 8SJ
041-334 5007

Closed: Sunday
Last
Orders: lunch (2.30pm); dinner (11.00pm)

Probably Glasgow's best-known restaurant, the Ubiquitous Chip is housed in converted stables in a Victorian mews off Byres Road. The glazed courtyard area has old cobble stones, whitewashed walls, a pool, waterfall and masses of trees, vines and creepers. The interior is similarly simple with tiled floor, beams, paintings and pine tables and chairs.

The kitchen specialises in fresh local produce cooked in a mixture of classic and modern styles. To start you could try venison haggis with neeps, wild mushrooms with pearl barley risotto, west coast squid and mussels in a tarragon bree, stuffed Loch Torridon mussels or Ardnamurcham queenies with garlic and parsley. For the main course there's Oban-landed monkfish with samphire sauce, saddle of Ayrshire hare, Loch Lomond line-caught salmon with cucumber sauce, creel-caught langoustines and, during the season, a Dalnacarroch grouse served blood-rare with Scots bread sauce. The cooking is sound and presentation is in simple family style. Vegetables are treated imaginatively - mushrooms in Malmsey and tarragon, purée of beetroot with cream of nutmeg, or perhaps mange-touts in sunflower oil.

The wine list is exceptional with representation from all over Europe and the New World. As a digestif, try one of the hundred or so single malt whiskies which are stocked!

The Willow Tea Room   Glasgow

217 Sauchiehall Street, Glasgow   £10
041-332 0521

Closed: Sunday
Last
Orders: 4.30pm

Between 1904 and 1926 Miss Cranston's tea rooms occupied these elegant premises designed by Charles Rennie Mackintosh, one of the most distinguished exponents of Art Nouveau in the U.K. At that time, whilst the City's ladies sipped their Earl Grey tea, their gentlemen were banished to a billiard room upstairs, as they were not allowed into the ladies' room. Times have changed, and no doubt eyebrows would be raised if the ladies of that era saw were to see the sexes taking tea together in that very room!

It is now called The Willow Tea Room, and is above Henderson's shop. One nonagenarian who knew the old tea room told me that the name 'Willow' came from the name 'Sauchiehall' which means 'avenue of willows'. Miss Cranston might recognise the style of the high-backed chairs like ecclesiastic sentinels, and she would approve of the crumpets, scones, pancakes and muffins with jam and cream. The menu is small with items suitable for morning coffee, snacks at lunch time, and of course various cakes for tea. Some traditions, I am glad to say, never die.

Just down the road at 283 Sauchiehall Street, is another old-established tea room and restaurant called Ma Brown's. I doubt that you will find another restaurant in the country that can offer you freshly made soup, followed by roast leg of lamb with vegetables, for the modest price of £2.80!

La Potinière   Gullane

Gullane, East Lothian EH31 2AA
(0620) 843214

Closed: lunch (Sat + Wed); dinner (Sun - Fri); Christmas;
        New Year; 1 week Jun; Oct
Last
Orders: lunch (1.00pm); dinner (8.00pm)

An unassuming cottage in the main street of this small holiday
resort and golfing centre provides the opportunity to taste some
of the most accomplished cooking in Scotland. Lunch is served 5
days a week, dinner on Saturdays only, and the menu changes on
each occasion but offers no choice - not that one could choose
better than Hilary Brown. As with any successful, small restaurant, bookings must be made well in advance. Service begins
promptly at 1.00pm for lunch or 8.00pm for dinner. David Brown
serves all the tables himself, offering apéritifs. When the wine
list arrives, it is a considerable document of some 40 pages
giving not just one good example of a wine, but sometimes a
choice of 10 or 12, as was the case with Chablis. An excellent
selection of half bottles always appreciated especially by the
lone diner, is also offered.

The quality of the cooking is outstanding. It is not hesitant or
contrived but gutsy and bold. Ingredients are used to full
advantage and speak for themselves: tomato and mint soup was
a thick purée with each flavour holding its own, a courgette
soufflé perfectly cooked, then farm chicken roasted and served
with a perfect tarragon cream sauce. A properly dressed salad
and gratin dauphinois accompanied the chicken and everything
was simple yet correct. It's good that some kitchens are still able
to produce natural food. To finish, I chose an orange parfait with
a caramelised orange sauce. Cheese was an alternative, but it
would have been a shame to miss something that Hilary had
cooked.

The décor is simple - you are here to eat and appreciate food,
not to be impressed by other diversions. Lunch is a civilised time
to enjoy La Potinière, and I can verify that there is no better
place to sustain oneself for the 400-mile trip back to London.

Tiroran House   Isle of Mull

Isle of Mull, Argyll PA39 6ES
(068 15) 232

Closed: lunch (residents only); mid-Oct - Easter
Last
Orders: dinner (one sitting at 7.45pm)

Wing Commander Blockey and his wife first went to Tiroran to
look at a cottage and ended up buying the estate! They have
converted the house into a hotel, and also have self-catering
holiday cottages. Tiroran is remote: to reach Mull you take a
ferry from Oban to Craignure, or from Lochaline to Fishnish, and
the drive is then some 20 miles along single track road to reach
the hotel; but don't let that deter you. The journey is an
enjoyable one and the effort worthwhile. The house is comfort-

able and homely, for Robin Blockey is a good host with a sense of humour and a friendly manner. He happily helps with cases, organises the service for dinner and will even arrange trips for his guests to the nearby islands of Iona and Staffa.

Dinner is competently cooked by Sue Blockey using the best of local produce including home grown vegetables. The main course is set but a choice of first courses and puddings is offered. Wines are well chosen and very reasonable in price, and I like the idea of putting a copy of the wine list in the bedroom so that you can choose well ahead, for with a large list there never seems enough time to decide at the last minute. At breakfast you may be lucky enough to see basking seals across the shining waters of beautiful Loch Scridain, whilst you tuck into your kipper.

Taychreggan Hotel   Kilchrenan

Kilchrenan, by Taynuilt, Argyll PA35 1HQ
(086 63) 211

Closed: mid-Oct - Easter
Last
Orders: lunch (2.15pm); dinner (9.00pm)

Loch Awe is Scotland's longest freshwater loch, being 24 miles from end to end, and Taychreggan sits on the waterside. The earlier part of the building was a drovers' inn where cattle would spend the night on their way to Falkirk Tryst. The building has had well-designed additions and now provides comfort and a warm welcome to human guests. The attractive central courtyard creates an interesting feature and is an ideal sheltered spot in which to relax with a drink on a summer's evening. The bar is a lively spot with locals as well as visitors, and many a fisherman's tale is exchanged over a wee dram before or after a day on the loch.

Décor is light and modern, simple lunches are served in the bar or there is a lunch time Danish cold table in the dining room. Dinner is a fixed price menu at a very reasonable £12.50. Not unnaturally, fish features prominently - Loch Etive prawns with garlic butter, turbot with crayfish sauce, Awe salmon with hollandaise, pan fried scallops or halibut in white wine sauce. Local meats are not neglected: roast venison, gigot of lamb with port and honey, or perhaps local duckling with kumquat sauce. A large wine list even offers 3 Scottish wines - one made from silver birch, one from elderflowers, and the other from meadowsweet - each at £5.00, while for the more traditional palate there are around a 100 French wines.

John and Tove Taylor's delightful hotel is ideal for a relaxing holiday or for fishing, stalking or sailing, for the more energetic.

The Cross Kingussie

25-27 High Street, Kingussie, Highland PH21 1HX
(054 02) 762

Closed: lunch (daily - except by arrangement); Mon in summer;
Sun + Mon in winter; 2 weeks May; 3 weeks Dec
Last
Orders: dinner (10.00pm)

This is a gem of a restaurant at the entrance to the Cairngorms, where Tony Hadley is front of house and his wife Ruth cooks: they each play their part extremely well. The Cross also has 3 bedrooms, which makes it a very worthwhile stopping point when touring around Scotland. Arriving mid-afternoon, you might find Tony busily preparing his new wine list; but he would still find time to make a pot of tea and join you for a chat after unloading the car. He is a genial host who thoroughly enjoys running the restaurant, which they purchased some 3 years ago. They have converted the old shop property into an unpretentious but comfortable dining room and the bedrooms have been furnished extremely well in a homely style, with impeccable bath or shower rooms.

Ruth changes her menu monthly. A delicious mousseline of Insh pike followed by fillet of roebuck in a sauce of port and redcurrants was excellent. Good fresh vegetables were served with it, and to follow, a peach terrine served with a coulis of raspberries and strawberries. Each Saturday a 7-course dinner is prepared and must be the best value in Scotland - if not the British Isles! The wine list, now complete, again shows Tony's tremendous enthusiasm for what he does. There are around 100 wines for under £6.00 each, and the list contains one of the most interesting selections to be seen.

As their brochure says, "the house has a delightful ambience and that lived-in feeling often lacking in larger hotels; a warm welcome, comfortable surroundings, excellent food and personal attention. All the ingredients for an enjoyable stay."

I couldn't have put it better myself. May they flourish and prosper.

Isle of Eriska Hotel Ledaig

Ledaig, by Oban, Argyll PA37 1SD
(063 172) 371

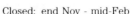

Closed: end Nov - mid-Feb
Last
Orders: lunch (1.45pm); dinner (8.30pm)

As Robin Buchanan-Smith, the genial owner of this delightful hotel says, "We are really a country house where peace and quiet are to the fore. About 50% of our guests are returns, and probably 85% are recommended by other guests." The statistics are not surprising. Though Eriska is an island it is joined to the mainland by road and it is well worth spending a few days in the relaxing surroundings. The host is most attentive, and even if you only have the opportunity to stop off for lunch he will make the effort to welcome you and to chat in the bar as though you were staying for a week. On this occasion, he was most concerned about the welfare of some guests who had just arrived after a transatlantic flight to Heathrow, thence a further flight to Glasgow before driving to the hotel. He had discussed with his staff the expected arrival time of all the other guests that day to ensure that the newcomers would be properly greeted - a lesson in hospitality that could change the British hotel trade, should we be lucky enough for it to spread.

"A dining room rather than a restaurant," was the explanation of the philosophy on food. And that is exactly how it is - staff on hand, but a help-yourself buffet lunch, which might have a deliciously mushroomy soup to start, and excellent cold roast beef and ham to follow with a selection of salads. Sweets or cheeses or both are available, and good coffee is served in the relaxed and homely atmosphere of the drawing room. Dinner is more formal with 6 courses, and breakfast is as it was at Eriska 70 years ago - chafing dishes on hot plates with silver covers. Take a leisurely walk around the estate after lunch and see the Jersey herd working on the day's milk production. Mine host would doubtless be rather indignant that the yield has to be pasteurised before serving it to guests, whilst the staff can drink it without such modification! Such is progress.

Fernie Castle Hotel   Letham

Letham, Cupar, Fife KY7 7RU
(033 781) 381

Closed: lunch (except by arrangement); Jan
Last
Orders: dinner (9.00pm)

This real Scottish castle, converted and set in its own grounds, is a popular spot for golfers wishing to play the renowned local courses. For the less energetic or ambitious there are lovely walks laid out around the lake and gardens where one can also see a wonderful example of an ice house. This was actually a functional forerunner to refrigerators and still consists of a stone-built cavern which would be filled with ice from the frozen lake, and stocked with meats or fish to be preserved for long periods of time.

The hotel is very comfortably furnished with elegant public rooms, and its bedrooms all have modern facilities such as trouser presses and hairdryers. Staff are very friendly and helpful, making guests feel welcome and at home. Lunch is served in the bar, and if you have never tasted the legendary haggis here's an opportunity, served of course with the traditional neeps.

In the evening the elegant dining room provides a more serious atmosphere in which to enjoy a leisurely dinner.

Champany Inn   Linlithgow

Champany, Linlithgow, West Lothian EH49 7LU
(050 683) 4532

Closed: Sun; 24 Dec - 13 Jan
Last
Orders: lunch (2.00pm); dinner (10.00pm)

The Champany Inn is proof that if a proprietor understands the commodity which he is buying and refuses to compromise on quality then he is well on the way to achieving perfection. Clive Davidson sets out to find the best available beef for his restaurant and succeeds, not just with beef but with all the produce that he serves to his customers. Lobsters and oysters are kept in a specially conditioned tank in the bar as are scallops and crayfish when available. They are proud to use Scottish farmed salmon which may alarm purists but salmon farming has made great strides and is now a good alternative rather than a substitute.

While reading the menu in the bar a basket of raw vegetables is shown to help selection: baby carrots with their foliage, young broad beans, French beans, baby new potatoes or leaf spinach; a gleaming whole salmon is also shown to demonstrate the quality, as if one would doubt it.

The menu concentrates mostly on first courses of fish, with 6 ways of preparing the farmed salmon - charcoal grilled, salmon hollandaise, gravadlax, smoked (especially by a Mr Buchanan of Otter Ferry), dressed salmon, or even a salmon soup. Other starters are Loch Fyne oysters, lobster, pâté, carrot and orange soup, North Sea prawns or Black Forest ham - remember these are just to start! Then, to the charcoal grilled steaks either plain or with sauce; duck, poussin or guineafowl from the spit; lobster or crayfish from the tank; and Scottish spring lamb also char-grilled.

The dressed salmon was a large suprême of salmon poached and then marinated in white wine with sliced onions and sugar - a very moist texture with a delicious sweet-sour flavour which complemented the flavour of the fish - served with a sharp cream sauce. The rib-eye steak was just the eye of meat seared on the outside and pink throughout, and you are offered a selection of home-made mustards, including the pungent local brew made from whisky and honey. Vegetables are steamed, and the baby leeks, spinach and carrots were all excellent. The ice-creams include strawberry, raspberry and even pineapple, all of excellent texture and flavour. Espresso coffee and 10 varieties of tea are available.

As if choosing the food was not enough to cope with, the wine list gives another 400 choices with over 30 from the Cape (Mr Davidson is South African), others from Europe, and some from other New World wine producers. Prices start at £7.50 and work their way up to £350.00 a bottle - take your pick.

Attached to the Inn is a Chop and Ale house which serves cheaper meals but still with the accent on quality. Champany Inn is good value and proves if you really want to serve the best it can be done; it just takes effort and determination.

For after dinner coffee of the highest quality.

Nestlé

The Melrose Station Restaurant   Melrose

Palma Place, Melrose, Roxburghshire TD6 9PR
(089 682) 2546

Closed: 5 Jan – 5 Feb
Last
Orders: 6.00pm Sun + Mon; 9.45pm Tue – Thu; 10.00pm Fri + Sat

Dennis Rodwell describes this restaurant as the handsomest provincial station in Scotland, and indeed it probably is, unusually located in this clever conversion. It is trying very hard to establish itself. For starters there's fettucini Alfredo, vegetable risotto, sardines or terrines. For seafood they have a swordfish steak poached in white wine rather than grilled, and there's salmon. From the stove comes a standard range of dishes, as well as some straightforward steaks. There's a vegetarian selection of mushroom and watercress pancakes, or seasonal vegetable pie, and some interesting home-made gâteaux and puddings. Their wine list covers most areas of France including Cahors and Haut Poitou, with a smattering from Australia and California, and a Château Musar 1978 from the Lebanon. On the same premises they have also established a craft centre, with workshops and a model railway, and it will be interesting to see how this place progresses during its first year.

The Clifton Hotel   Nairn

Viewfield Road, Nairn, Nairnshire IV12 4HW
(0667) 53119

Closed: lunch (except by arrangement); mid-Dec to mid-Feb
Last
Orders: dinner (9.30pm)

The Clifton is quite different to most other hotels both in its aspirations and its manner of operation. It is purely theatrical, and it comes as no suprise to learn that its flamboyant patron is indeed a man of the theatre and stages plays in his dining room during the winter. The house is decorated and furnished with great flair, dramatic wallpapers covered with portraits of the family or perhaps prints of costume design for Shakespearian plays. Mirrors abound to check one's make-up and the dining tables are draped with lace, and may have flower arrangements for greater effect. The dining room is arranged on a number of levels and looks out across the Moray Firth, which in the evening light is superb. Bedrooms show equal attention to detail: each is individually designed - mine provided a very high old bed around which was draped a fabric of pink and orange with lots of interesting books to hand.

Food is available at The Clifton and the choice of 200 world-wide wines provides something for all tastes, including no less than 30 varieties of Champagne and sparklers which, in this setting, is the only thing to drink.

Kirroughtree Hotel　　　　Newton Stewart

Newton Stewart, Galloway DG8 6AN
(0671) 2141

Closed: lunch (except by arrangement); 8 Nov - 1 Mar
Last
Orders: dinner (9.30pm)

An impressive drive leads up to the large brown and beige painted Georgian house and as I arrived I was greeted by a young, enthusiastic receptionist in a dinner jacket, which made me feel rather out of place, since I had just driven from London and was hardly a match for his impeccable appearance! The hotel is well decorated and comfortably furnished, and the large central drawing room leads off into 2 separate dining rooms, both with washed silk hangings, one in blue and one in red, picked up with white moulding. Comfortable carver armchairs, cut glass, shining cutlery and good quality china complete the image.

Ken MacPhee, who was at Inverlochy Castle for 6 years, cooks here now. His menus change daily and offer 5 courses. Amongst the many specialities from the kitchen are sole and salmon terrine, escalope of salmon finlandaise, apricot brandied pancakes and pistachio nut iced soufflé with a strawberry sauce. Noisettes of lamb with a mint béarnaise sauce and a light tarragon flavoured gravy were served on the evening that I dined, and were of good quality. In addition to the vegetables, a good Caesar salad was served which seemed a nice touch.

There are over 200 wines on the list which is strong in clarets, with no fewer than 40 half bottles for those who like small quantity or large variety. Situated in the extreme west of Dumfries and Galloway, the Kirroughtree Hotel makes an ideal base from which to tour the local places of interest. The nearby Logan Botanical Garden even houses a rare collection of plants and sub-tropical trees which flourish in a position sheltered by the Gulf Stream, defying popular opinion of Scottish weather.

The Peat Inn   Peat Inn

Peat Inn, By Cupar, Fife KY15 5LH
(033 484) 206

Closed: Sun + Mon; first 2 weeks Jan; 1 week Apr; 1 week Oct
Last
Orders: lunch (1.00pm); dinner (9.30pm)

A menu gastronomique with 6 courses is not the easiest thing to
serve well without a fairly large kitchen staff. Obviously David
Wilson is a talented chef and could not have built The Peat Inn
to its present position during the last 14 years without strong
direction and sheer dedication and hard work.

The restaurant is in a remote location and a full car park is the
first indication of other life in the area. On entering the
comfortable bar the atmosphere is most welcoming and Patricia
Wilson ensures that everyone is acknowledged. Attractively
dressed waitresses organise drinks, accompanied by a thin slice
of quiche to stimulate the appetite. The menu is small with
between 6 to 8 choices of each course – a pigeon breast with
wild mushrooms in pastry with a rosemary sauce, scallops in
lightly spiced sauce with barsac, and a smoked salmon salad
with warm mousse of Arbroath smokies are among the first
courses. Follow this with Tay salmon in pastry with a vermouth,
dill and cream sauce, saddle of venison in red wine and port
sauce or, for real indulgence, a whole lobster in crayfish sauce.
Expect to pay around £20.00 a head for food.

The wine list is extraordinary both in its content and its
pricing, the selection of almost 350 wines reading more like a
wine merchant's list, but prices are reasonable and there are a
few for under £10.00.

The cosy dining room buzzes with activity and has quite a
good atmosphere; and the staff combine friendliness with
efficiency.

Cringletie House Hotel   Peebles

Peebles EH45 8PL   £35
(072 13) 233

Closed: Jan + Feb
Last
Orders: lunch (1.45pm); dinner (8.30pm)

A long drive leads to an almost fairy-tale house with round
turrets and well maintained gardens all around it. Built in 1861
as a manor house, the hotel is tastefully decorated and comfortably furnished, retaining the feel of a country house rather than
a hotel. Food is ordered in the panelled bar where a log fire
burns on cooler days, and the dinner menu is 4 courses with a
soup halfway through the meal.

Aileen Maguire's kitchen uses freshly cooked local ingredients, with fruit and vegetables from their own garden. Wines
are mainly French and provide something for most palates -
Duboeuf housewines are £6.90 a bottle.

Even heavy rain cannot spoil the wonderful vista from the
first floor dining room, and the charming staff will brighten any
day with their attentive service.

The Coach House Restaurant   Perth

8 North Port, Perth, Tayside PH1 5LU
(0738) 27950

Closed: Sun + Mon; 2 weeks Jan; 2 weeks Jul
Last
Orders: lunch (2.00pm); dinner (10.00pm)

The Coach House is a perfect example of how to purchase top quality ingredients, handle them with care, cook them carefully and add a sauce to complement rather than overshadow the principal item. Tony and Betty Heath run this small restaurant which is just around the corner from the Fair Maids House and the River Tay, famous for its salmon. The décor is simple but comfortable, and the hostess supervises the service efficiently.

Soup of pea and lettuce could be followed by an excellent sole mornay, the fish perfectly cooked and the sauce light yet full of flavour. Vegetables are also superb, with cabbage that has been cut this morning. A home-made honey and whisky ice-cream confirms the patron's ability in the kitchen; and all that for a mere £7.50! There is a good selection of dishes on the fixed price lunch and dinner menus, and for £15.00 the evening menu includes an additional course of perhaps a sorbet or a soup.

There is something for all tastes on the list of around 70 wines, with plenty of half bottles for the modest drinker or the adventurous imbiber.

With the value which The Coach House offers at lunch time, I was amazed that there was not a queue. Perhaps the locals haven't yet heard of this restaurant, so simple and uncomplicated in both décor and food.

The Airds Hotel   Port Appin

Port Appin, Appin, Argyll PA38 4DF
(063 173) 236

Closed: lunch (daily); Nov - Mar
Last
Orders: dinner (one sitting at 8.00pm)

When so many Scottish hotels have spectacular views of mountains and water, it is hard to decide which has the best, but The Airds certainly ranks high amongst them. As I pulled into the forecourt a young waiter, who was re-laying tables after Sunday lunch, almost ran out of the dining room to help with my cases, and from then until the cases went back into the car, nothing was too much trouble. Mr and Mrs Allen do everything to ensure guests' well-being, (he front of house and she from the kitchen). It is not a pretentious hotel: it used to be the inn for the ferry which still goes between Port Appin and Lismore, but it is very comfortable and there is a sincere, homely atmosphere. At the back of the hotel a market garden has been created from what used to be a peat bog. A polythene tunnel shelters neatly arranged crops of vegetables and herbs, whilst hardier species fill the remainder.

Anyone who cares enough to go to this trouble would not spoil the produce in the kitchen. Betty Allen makes sure that this

341

is so and prepares a well-balanced menu of dishes. Delicious scallops in a light butter sauce could be followed by loin of well-hung venison with rowanberry jelly, served with lovely young leeks, new potatoes and fresh peas, then for pudding a well-made biscuit filled with home-made ice-cream and nectarines on a raspberry coulis. Everything is well prepared and cooked, and tastes as it should, and the large wine list has been carefully and sensibly composed.

The host dresses in kilt and black jacket, and waitresses wear long tartan skirts and crisp white blouses. Linen, glassware and cutlery are spotless, and when the sun sets over the water it would be difficult to find a more pleasant situation in which to dine in Scotland.

Don't miss the lovely walk around the point to ensure a good appetite.

The Grange Inn   St Andrews

Grange Road, St Andrews, Fife KY16 8LJ
(0334) 72670/72136

Last
Orders: lunch (2.00pm); dinner (9.30pm)

This small inn just outside St Andrews with wonderful views across St Andrews' bay provides a very reasonable place to stay whilst visting this lovely area of Fife. Unpretentious comfortable rooms and public areas with friendly service make this a popular venue for locals as well as visitors. The restaurant serves simple dishes using fresh local produce, and as an alternative one can eat in the busy bar with its typical old inn décor.

Kinloch Lodge   Sleat

Sleat, Isle of Skye, Highland IV43 8QY
(047 13) 214/333

Closed: lunch (daily); 4 days Christmas; 10 Jan - 28 Feb
Last
Orders: dinner (8.00pm)

The Lord and Lady Macdonald converted this old hunting lodge into a small hotel which makes an ideal base for the beautiful Isle of Skye. The hotel is situated at the head of a sea loch at the south of the island, and is reached by ferry from Kyle of Lochalsh or Mallaig. The house is comfortably furnished and retains the feeling of a family house with open fires, interesting books and paintings of previous members of the distinguished family. Lady Macdonald supervises the kitchen using local produce to good advantage, and everything is home-made, including lovely scones at breakfast and rich fudge with coffee after dinner. There is a choice of 2 dishes for each course at dinner, and typical offerings might be a roulade of smoked salmon, or spinach, apple and tumeric soup, or egg niçoise with cucumber relish, then perhaps roast haunch of venison, rack of lamb with minty hollandaise or monkfish poached in wine with lemon and parsley sauce. Puddings are rich and plentiful - good coffee and almond torte with chocolate cream, apricot roulade or chocolate and ginger cream vacherin - and a long walk the next day to compensate! The wine list and service are supervised by Lord Macdonald who makes sure that all is well with the guests in the elegant dining room. After dinner, coffee is served in either of the 2 drawing rooms, and provides a good opportunity to chat with other visitors and share the day's experiences.

A well run, comfortable and civilised hotel with a relaxing atmosphere, good food and wines, amidst beautiful scenery.

Portsonachan Hotel South Lochaweside

South Lochaweside, by Dalmally, Argyll PA33 1BL £30
(086 63) 224

Closed: Dec - Feb except New Year
Last
Orders: lunch (2.00pm); dinner (9.00pm)

This friendly hotel which Christopher and Caroline Trotter took over about 4 years ago has improved with their hard work and determination. The décor is basic but comfortable and private bathrooms are gradually being added to bedrooms. The hotel is at the side of Loch Awe and has its own fleet of small fishing boats which may be hired with or without an outboard depending on your energy. After a day's fishing Christopher's cooking will revive the body and even compensate for a luckless trip. Trained at The Savoy, he makes full use of the excellent local produce to create his Scottish menus including 4 courses which change daily.

Oban scallops, cock-a-leekie soup, or pigeon salad with sunflower seeds may feature as first courses, then a fish course of Loch Awe trout in oatmeal with gooseberries, or fillet of black sole in butter. The saddle of lamb served as a main course is superb, perfectly cooked, full of flavour and tender. Vegetables are fresh, properly cooked and grown in their own vegetable garden, together with herbs. Puddings include home-made ice-creams and sorbets, and rich treats such as walnut and rum pie or black treacle mousse. Cheeses are Scottish and come with home-made oatcakes, and the bread is also freshly made.

The wine list is small but good value with only about 4 wines over £10, and housewines are £4.20. Caroline supervises the dining room and is a charming hostess, while the young staff are all anxious to please. If you are an early riser, don't miss the sunrise over Loch Awe with the mists gradually rising to reveal Ben Cruachan - who knows, you might even catch some fish for lunch!

Wales

Wales is another Celtic region dominated by sea and mountains, with a history of people eking out an existence from the land. Mountains support sheep, and Welsh spring lamb is now much prized. Mountains also slope down to richer pastures, where a dairy industry plays a significant role. The concentration here is on butter rather than cheese, the butter usually quite strongly salted. Caerffili (or Caerphilly) is the traditional cheese most widely known, and it is the major ingredient of that famous offering, the Welsh Rarebit.

Often imitated and rarely perfected, the secret appears to be getting the right consistency to the mixture - grated cheese spiked with mustard, creamed with butter, moistened with milk AND beer - before spreading it thickly on the as yet untoasted side of your slice of bread, right to the edges of course, and then grilling it to bubbling point. Cheese is also the principal ingredient in a Glamorgan sausage, which has no meat at all.

What salmon is to the Scots, so sea trout is to the Welsh: a much prized main dish, at its best served simply, and generally poached. Herring appears again, along with cockles, but here the sea also yields something most particularly Welsh-laver.

Laver is a species of edible seaweed which also grows to some extent in Ireland and Scotland. Painstakingly gathered by hand, washed many times to reduce its saltiness, and cooked slowly and at length to soften it, the seaweed becomes a purée which is called laverbread and it is in this form that it is usually sold, either with or without some oatmeal mixed in. Reheated in bacon fat and served with bacon, it appears for breakfast; or else as a sauce for roast lamb.

The Welsh butter is the saltiest of the regional butters traditionally and commercially available; and in addition to this and the salty laver, the Welsh even prefer their ducks salted. Salt is rubbed into the cavity and into the skin of a cleaned duck, and left to penetrate for about 3 days, with a few turnings. It's a million miles away from the bird that is roasted and sometimes served with an orange or cherry sauce.

Leeks are indigenous to Wales and are its national emblem, alongside the daffodil. However daffodils don't make such good soups and cawls as leeks do! Leeks also go into pasties with bacon, or into pies with mutton or chicken.

Once again, it's at tea time that the full weight of Welsh cooking comes into its own. The Welsh cake is a small thick pancake, raised with soda and cooked on a planc or griddle. Bara brith, speckled bread, came about from kneading sugar and currants into the last bit of the week's batch of bread dough. Teisen lap is moist fruit cake, enriched with eggs and milk; teisen sinamon, a cinnamon-flavoured sponge topped with jam and meringue. Cacen gneifio's distinctive flavour comes from caraway seeds, and this cake was usually made on completion of sheep shearing.

With beer brewed at Brain's in Cardiff or Buckley's in Llanelli, the Welsh well know how to sustain you for a Saturday afternoon at the Arms Park.

VINEYARDS

Glamorgan
Croffta (3 acres)
Pontyclun

Gwent
Tintern Parva (4 acres)
Tintern, Nr Chepstow

HISTORIC HOUSES OPEN TO THE PUBLIC

Clwyd
Bodrhyddan Hall, Nr Rhyl
Chirk Castle, Chirk
Erddig, Nr Wrexham

Gwynedd
Penrhyn Castle, Nr Bangor
Plas Newydd, Anglesey

Powys
Powis Castle, Nr Welshpool

Porth Tocyn Hotel   Abersoch

Abersoch, Gwynedd LL53 7BD
(075 881) 2966

Closed: Nov; 1 week before Easter
Last
Orders: lunch (2.00pm); dinner (9.30pm)

Set at the end of a seemingly endless winding lane, the hotel perches over a bay and offers some breathtaking views. The Brewer family has run this place for nearly 40 years and built an enviable reputation during that time. The kitchens have seen a succession of cordon bleu girls, and the cooking reflects all the strengths and the occasional weakness of that discipline. The lamb with spinach was very sound and the raspberry meringues were definitely an indulgence. The smiling welcome is almost overwhelming, and you will feel at home very quickly. You can stay in some decent and affordable rooms, and might even choose to venture outside to the swimming pool.

The Philharmonic   Cardiff

St Mary's Street, Cardiff, South Glamorgan
(0222) 30678

Closed: dinner (daily); Sun
Last
Orders: 2.30pm

This carvery and cheese bar has a lovely exterior with curved windows and lots of brass. A traditional 'boozer' for young people, it is worth a visit.

345

The Cemlyn   Harlech

High Street, Harlech, Gwynedd LL46 2YA
(0766) 780425

Closed: lunch (except by arrangement)
Last
Orders: dinner (9.00pm, 9.45pm in summer)

You can see Harlech Castle from the window of chef Ken
Goody's unpretentious little restaurant, into which he will come
and take a bow after cooking dinner.

He uses some excellent local foods to produce some interesting dishes, and the thick cuts of gravadlax were as good an
example of this dish as I have had. Service, from family and
friends, can be a little casual, and you can't ignore the collection
of Chinese frogs. The Cemlyn has 2 letting bedrooms, for diners
who fall by the wayside or who don't want to drive home.

Y Bistro   Llanberis

43-45 High Street, Llanberis, Gwynedd LL55 4EU
(0286) 871278

Closed: Sun; Bank Holidays; 1 week Oct; 3 weeks Jan
Last
Orders: dinner (9.30pm)

Nerys Roberts cooks here. She uses top quality produce along
with local foodstuffs and lots of fresh herbs, and creates some
favourite dishes which are described as "low fat". Fish may be
caught and possibly even smoked locally, and the menus, which
are written in Welsh and English, offer some interesting dishes
for tasting: try the torgoch (char), and the Snowdon pudding.

The room is simply furnished, with rustic chairs and tables set
with crisp white cloths in this family run bistro.

La Chaumière   Llandaff

Cardiff Road, Llandaff, South Glamorgan
(0222) 555319

Closed: lunch (Sat + Mon); dinner (Sun + Mon)
Last
Orders: lunch (2.30pm); dinner (9.30pm)

Ex-fashion model Kay Morgan is an unlikely chef and the setting
of La Chaumière, behind a pub on the fringes of Cardiff, is an
equally unlikely setting. However the food served here would be
outstanding in any location – modern French cooking based on
sound techniques with interesting interpretations, such as fully-
flavoured mushroom soup under puff-pastry, fresh Welsh mussels encroûte, or a tender young partridge carefully roasted with
a light but strong red wine sauce. Home-made coffee ice-cream
is served in a block of ice and makes a good talking point.

Cliff Morgan supervises the very friendly and efficient waitresses and organises an interesting wine list which features

virtually no clarets. The décor is warm with pink tablecloths and trellis-backed chairs.

The Cobblers   Llandybie

3 Church Street, Llandybie, Dyfed SA18 3HZ   £25
(0290) 850540

Closed: Sun, Mon + Thu
Last
Orders: lunch (1.30pm); dinner (9.30pm)

What a surprise to find a restaurant called The Cobblers (it *was* an old cobbler's shop), on a windswept night in Llandybie! It's a restaurant which wouldn't be out of place in a French country village, with its very pretty lace curtains, a theme echoed in the lace cloths around the tables in the ground floor bar. Dark panelled walls are decorated with photographs of how the cobbler's shop used to be, with some authentic bills of sale dating back 100 years or so. There is a very friendly warm feeling to this family run restaurant. We sat there, trying the Welsh wine and wondering if the food would be as good as the initial impression, and where it would be served - we had been told that the restaurant was on the ground floor, but it is now upstairs.

It's a pretty pink dining room with floral tablecloths, where you might be treated to a beetroot salad with yoghurt and mint dressing, leek and yoghurt soup, a smoked salmon mousse in choux pastry with a red coulis of tomatoes, a whole lobster taken out of its shell, poached in fish stock and the sauce slightly thickened, the local salmon, or a lamb or beef dish simply cooked and served with excellent crisp vegetables. To follow, choose a chestnut pudding, plum bread and butter pudding, or perhaps some Welsh Cheddar cheese served with home-made wholemeal biscuits. There is excellent home-made bread, a good selection of wines on the list, and carbonated mineral water from Brecon. An absolute find for someone stranded a long way from home.

Meadowsweet Hotel   Llanrwst

Station Road, Llanrwst, Gwynedd LL26 0DS
(0492) 640732

Closed: lunch (Mon + Sun during winter)
Last
Orders: lunch (1.45pm); dinner (9.30pm)

Chef proprietor John Evans has taken a rather ordinary Victorian house and carefully furnished it to create a welcoming atmosphere and a good setting for his cooking. Tablecloths are crisp, glasses and cutlery well polished, and the wine list is enormous. Wine buffs will be amused for hours with this, and it is worth taking the time to try some excellent wine at basement prices.

English and French dishes are well cooked and the Welsh lamb with wine, garlic and black olives has a liberal dash of Elizabeth David. Try the unbelievably fluffy rum and brandy mousse as an alternative to the extraordinary collection of cheese from far and near.

Unassuming bedrooms are tidily furnished, and this would be an excellent place to spend a restful weekend.

The Abbey Hotel   Llanthony

Llanthony, Near Abergavenny, Gwent
(0873) 890487

Closed: lunch (daily except for bar snacks) dinner (Sun + Mon)
Last
Orders: by arrangement

It's best to arrive here in the daytime, as if you arrive in the dark you will not only miss the lovely view up to the Abbey but also have to negotiate some fairly hazardous single track double bends. On the way to it you pass the Skirrid pub, which informs you that it is the oldest inn in Wales. Llanthony Priory itself is splendid and although largely in ruins houses a 12th-Century chapel which is quite spectacular. The Abbey Hotel has only 4 bedrooms which are situated in a tower with only one bathroom between them. The room we had in fact had 2 4-poster beds in it and tiny little stained glass windows which looked over the Priory. To get to the restaurant or the rooms you go down two or three steps and find yourself in a bar with a low vaulted ceiling, and then you have to make your way up a couple of steps to the restaurant. It seats about 20 people either on settles or simple Welsh chairs, and has wooden tables with no cloths, stone-

flagged floors, dressers holding mostly odd pieces of beautiful old china, a grandfather clock and lots of polished copper and brass. The approach to the rooms is through a door off the restaurant, and you have to get to know your neighbours fairly well as there is only the one staircase, perhaps 4 foot at its widest point (limiting the number of people who can pass!), winding up to the 4 rooms.

The food itself is simple with French onion soup to start, a choice of one or two vegetarian dishes, local trout, poached salmon cooked simply, Caerphilly or Cheddar cheese to follow, and good local Welsh ham. Very good brown bread. A simple but adequate wine list includes some good clarets, all at good prices, which are kept in the room on the sideboard and brought to your table on request. This is not the place for a luxury stay, but if you are looking for some good honest food, a very pleasant welcome and service, by friendly local staff, or are into the Mediaeval life or fairy tales, and you happen to be staying with Rapunzel for the night, then this could be the place for you. You'll feel more at home in casual clothes and there is no need to dress up for dinner.

Llwynderw Hotel   Llanwrtyd Wells

Abergwesyn, Llanwrtyd Wells, Powys LD5 4TW
(059 13) 238

Closed: lunch (except by arrangement); Nov - Mar
Last
Orders: dinner (9.00pm)

Probably one of the most peaceful places to stay in Britain, this Georgian house, partly 18th Century with a Georgian front added in 1796, is set high up in the middle of a dense forest. There are no televisions or telephones to disturb the sound of the birds but if the weather will not allow you to walk around the genuinely unspoilt countryside, you can stay in the comfortable public rooms and read one of the old bound volumes, simply look at the very carefully chosen antiques or even play chess or dominoes.

LLWYNDERW

Bedrooms are light, spacious and comfortable and you could fit all the guests into the vast fireplace in the dining room! The tables are stout and solid, and local meat and game are features of a set menu. The wine list is worth exploring for such items as a Côtes de Jura '69.

Fairyhill House   Reynoldston

Reynoldston, Gower, Near Swansea, West Glamorgan SA3 1BS
(0792) 390139

Closed: lunch (Mon + Sat); dinner (Sun)
Last
Orders: lunch (2.30pm); dinner (9.30pm)

I admire anyone who opens a house and restaurant in this somewhat remote but beautiful countryside, a few miles or so from Swansea going towards Port Eynon, and Margaret and John Frayne do their best to make you feel at home in their hotel. Kate Spring in the kitchen produces farmhouse cooking, managing whenever possible to use fresh local produce. Starters might include laverbread in bacon parcels, and for main courses a wide choice from sea bass, calves' liver with sage and Madeira, suprême of chicken with spinach and garlic stuffing. There's a selection of gigantic portions of puddings or some locally made cheese from Pantyllyn, a cheese farm just north of Cardigan. Some reasonably priced wines include good Bulgarian house-wines. Not a grand country house hotel but a friendly farmhouse atmosphere in which to get away from it all.

Annie's   Swansea

St Helen's Road, Swansea, West Glamorgan
(0792) 55603

Closed: lunch (restaurant: daily); dinner (Sun + Mon)
Last
Orders: 10.30pm (restaurant); 11.00pm (café-bar)

Ann Gwilym runs this interesting little restaurant. She offers a set menu for £8.50, or a choice from the à la carte. It's been going for about 3 years, and they have just opened the café-bar in the basement which has a cheaper menu, offering some Mediterranean-style dishes in an informal atmosphere. The restaurant on the ground floor is a pretty pine room with furniture to match, happy cheerful service and some good rillettes of pork. There's spinach salad with crispy bacon and

Annie's BISTRO

stilton sauce, perhaps some sea bass with laverbread, suprême of duck with oyster mushrooms and roast garlic, or a rib of beef with tarragon, chive and cream sauce. A good selection of vegetables and a choice of some 40 wines from £4.90 a bottle to the most expensive, which is a Laurent Perrier. Annie's is a find in Swansea - we have to thank the people we were sitting next to at The Walnut Tree for recommending it to us.

Maes-y-Neaudd   Talsarnau

Talsarnau, Near Harlech, Gwynedd LL47 6YA
(0766) 780200

Closed: lunch (Mon - Sat except by arangement); mid-Jan - mid-Feb
Last
Orders: dinner (9.00pm)

There are views across Tremadoc Bay from this attractive 14th-Century Welsh manor house (with 16th- and 18th-Century additions) nestling on a hillside. It is run by two couples with fairly strong emphasis on a quiet, family holiday. Mrs Horsfall looks after the cooking, and the set menu offers several choices at each course. The menu is quite homely, with a few traditional and modern dishes too.

   There is a reasonable selection of mainly French wines and the dining room is pleasant with lace tablecloths and fresh flowers. Demi-pension rates are a bargain and bedrooms are comfortably furnished.

Minffordd Hotel   Talyllyn

Talyllyn, Tywyn, Gwynedd LL36 9AJ
(065 473) 665

Closed: lunch (daily); dinner (Sun + Mon to non-residents)
Last
Orders: 8.30pm

The Pickles family operates a quiet country hotel which discourages the many amenities of the 20th Century. The food prepared by Jonathan Pickles is equally honest and straight-forward and tends to be based, where possible, on local produce (though there are some classic dishes like duck with a bigarade sauce amongst them).

Mr Pickles Senior wrote me a very interesting letter explaining the life of a lone restaurateur and hotelier in Gwynedd, and as he says, there's no point in comparing standards you will find in a luxury hotel in London with those you will find in the middle of Wales, and the only way to judge is to bear in mind that he is catering in a sparsely populated area, with a per capita income far lower than that of the south-east England. He also points out that it's necessary to book unless you're staying there because a restaurateur just cannot function by wishfully thinking that someone will eventually turn up. So the restaurant is open only to non-residents by booking in advance, but whether or not you stay overnight, you should explore the wine list, which is very competitively priced, particularly for some classic wines.

If you're a lover of dramatic scenery, you'll like the Minffordd which is set at the top of the Dysynni valley, one of the most peaceful and little known valleys in Wales. You can enjoy a couple of days in this former coaching inn and get away from television, radio and telephones, by relaxing with the Pickles family.

Wolfscastle Country Hotel   Wolf's Castle

Wolf's Castle, Dyfed SA62 5LZ
(043 787) 225

Closed: lunch (Mon - Sat); dinner (Sun)
Last
Orders: lunch (2.00pm); dinner (9.30pm)

If you drive into west Wales, just before you reach Fishguard you will find Wolfscastle, a rather daunting grey slate house softened by a mass of red ivy.

The Stirling family offers a warm welcome and some very decent farmhouse style cooking. There is always lots of choice, featuring classics like duck à l'orange made more interesting by the use of duck from just down the road! Puddings are also a feature and worth saving some room for. There is a limited selection of wines and the better bargains are not always French.

Bedrooms are bright, basic and comfortable and the whole hotel has a refreshingly homely feel.

The original, and the best!

The reason **Branston** is Britain's No1 pickle is its original, distinctive and traditional character.

The crisp vegetable garnish, in a unique sauce, was specially created to be the perfect accompaniment to all kinds of cold meats, cheeses, salads and many other hot foods and snacks. (In fact, a 'Ploughman's Lunch' just isn't the same without the added bite of **Branston!**)

Make sure it's there for the asking and bring out the best ...

Bring out the Branston!

Ireland

I suppose if you ask anyone for their impressions about Irish cooking, the first thing that would spring to mind would be Irish Stew. Ireland's unspoilt countryside yields a wealth of good, natural produce which, in general, is simply cooked - why mess about with prime produce? Being an island means that there is no shortage of fish, and the waters yield superb quality fish and shellfish of all varieties. Dublin Bay prawns from the east, and lobsters from the west coast are both famous, crab and scallops are excellent, white fish abound, the lakes and rivers are well stocked with salmon, sea trout and trout.

Irish hams and bacon are amongst the finest available and dairy produce has always been one of the country's main industries; rich butter and cream for cooking and flourishing cheese production. Increasing interest has now seen the growth of the farmhouse cheese market with cheeses such as Milleens and Cashel Blue.

Poverty spawned many of Ireland's traditional dishes, several relying on the versatile potato as a means of filling hungry stomachs. Colcannon is perhaps the best known, a mixture of mashed potato and cabbage with a well of butter in the centre. At Hallowe'en it is a tradition to put a button, a ring, a thimble, a horseshoe and a silver coin into the colcannon when mixing it. Whoever receives the coin will become rich, the ring indicates marriage, the horseshoe good luck, and the finder of the button or the thimble is supposed never to marry. Champ is another potato dish, this time mashed with onions or leeks and enriched with butter and milk. Boxty pancakes are made with grated potato and flour, cooked as traditional pancakes and served with meats as a vegetable.

Soda bread is rather like a scone, made with sour milk, buttermilk or whey and using bicarbonate of soda as a raising agent. Barm brack is a yeast bread flavoured with spices and enriched with dried fruits, and the delicious Irish apple cake is similar to an apple pie, made with dough rather than pastry.

Looking at meat dishes we cannot neglect the Irish Stew which consists of mutton neck chops cooked slowly in the oven with potatoes and onions. There is even dispute amongst the locals as to whether carrots should be included or not! Stuffed pigs' trotters are called crubeens, and tripe is served with drisheen, which is Ireland's blood pudding.

Guinness or stout is the national drink and seems to taste so different in its country of origin. In cold weather try the scalteen if it's offered - it's a blend of hot milk with honey and Irish whiskey.

Restaurants in Ireland offer a wide variety of eating styles in an equally varied range of establishments. You can eat well in small bars in fishing towns where the seafood is magnificent, there is nouvelle cuisine in luxurious surroundings, and simple, homely cooking in some of the country house hotels. The independent hoteliers and restaurateurs work together to promote their businesses, and the best way to find good restaurants is to ask your host where to eat at your next destination. The Irish are hospitable people, and the majority of staff in their hotels and restaurants are local people. Should you wish to learn first-hand more about cooking in Ireland you could enrol for a course at the Ballymaloe Cookery School in Shanagarry. The school is run by Darina Allen whose mother, Myrtle, is fast becoming the Elizabeth David of Irish cuisine.

HISTORIC HOUSES OPEN TO THE PUBLIC

Co Clare
Bunratty Castle, Bunratty
Knappogue Castle, Quin

Co Cork
Bantry House, Bantry
Blarney Castle, Blarney
Charles Fort, Kinsale
Dunkathel, Glanmire
Riverstown House, Glanmire

Co Donegal
Donegal Castle, Donegal

Co Dublin
Casino, Marino
Dublin Castle, Dublin
James Joyce Tower, Sandycove
Malahide Castle, Malahide
Powerscourt Town House, Dublin

Co Galway
Dunguaire Castle, Kinvara
Kylemore Abbey, Connemara
Thoor Ballylee, Nr Gort

Co Kerry
Derrynane Historic Park, Nr Waterville
Muckross House, Killarney

Co Kildare
Castletown, Celbridge

Co Kilkenny
Kilkenny Castle, Kilkenny
Rothe House, Kilkenny

Co Limerick
Castle Matrix, Rathkeale
Glin Castle, Glin

Co Monaghan
Castle Leslie, Glaslough

Co Roscommon
Clonalis House, Castlerea

Co Sligo
Lissadell House, Lissadell

Co Tipperary
Cahir Castle, Cahir
Carrick-on-Suir Castle, Carrick-on- Suir
Damer House, Rosecrea

Co Wicklow
Russborough, Blessington

Doyle's Seafood Bar

Dingle

John Street, Dingle, Co Kerry
010-353-066 51174

Closed: Sun; mid-Nov - mid-Mar
Last
Orders: lunch (2.15pm); dinner (9.00pm)

Locals underestimated John Doyle's tenacity when they thought that trying to open a fish restaurant in a back street of Dingle was a waste of time. He soon proved them wrong, and John and Stella's seafood bar has become known internationally as a vital stopping point when visiting County Kerry. Once in Dingle, signposts guide you to the bright red and white painted house, and inside is a cosy pub-like atmosphere. Flagstone floors, polished wood tables, a black kitchen range in one corner, unusual chairs and stone walls give a comfortable feel to the dining room.

The menu is all fish, and depends - for white fish - on local landings, while a tank keeps the shellfish alive until required. Hot trout smokies, scallop mousse with lobster sauce, oysters, smoked salmon with home-made tagliatelli, crab cocktail, tara-masalata or crab soup might be available for first courses; while to follow might be mussels with garlic stuffing, salmon with sorrel sauce, fillets of Dover sole with prawns, hot buttered crab claws, John Dory in lobster sauce, or you could even choose a lobster and have it poached while you wait. Home-baked bread, and good fresh vegetables or salad are served with the main course. Puddings, like an apple tart, orange cheesecake, lemon ice-box cake or meringue with raspberry purée, are irresistible.

There are also a few items for non-fish eaters, and at lunch time there is a blackboard menu, featuring lighter dishes such as smoked salmon or crab sandwiches.

John's wine list has about 100 white wines from Europe and California, and 16 reds from Spain which, as he rightly says, offer good quality and character at a realistic price. Stella looks after the cooking, and like Catherine Healy from Dunderry, has spent time in the kitchen of Roger Vergé's Moulin des Mougins, and with Albert Roux at Le Gavroche.

After a testing drive across the mountains from Kenmare, and then along the coast road from Castlemaine to Dingle in a strong gale during late October, the warm welcome and excellent food were precisely what was needed!

If the local planning officers look favourably upon the Doyles' application, they will convert the house next door so as to provide 8 bedrooms, which should be ready for the summer of 1987.

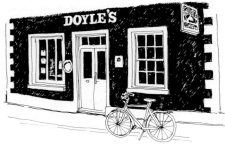

Restaurant Patrick Guilbaud — Dublin

46 James Place, Dublin 2
010-353-01 764192

Closed: lunch (Sat + Sun); dinner (Sun)
Last
Orders: lunch (2.00pm); dinner (10.15pm)

Situated in custom-built premises in a small mews directly behind the vast Irish Bank offices, Monsieur Guilbaud's restaurant offers style at a price. The brick-built exterior has a round stained glass window, and the patron's name is etched in glass on the front door. Inside there's the feel of a conservatory, with plants cascading from the glazed roof above the small bar. The restaurant has 2 areas, one with a low ceiling, the other opening out in similar style to the bar, with well-ordered creepers encircling the room. There are a few prints and large plaster reliefs on the high walls, with tiny spotlights forming pools of light on each table. Décor is grey and pink, seats are upholstered in mauve tweed, and floral patterned china sits on pink tablecloths. It is well designed, and has the ambience of a serious French restaurant.

Food receives the same attention to detail as the dining room, with dishes being presented in the nouvelle style. Cheeses come from Androuët in Paris, and arrive in a special trolley made of wicker to keep them in good condition. The wine list has an excellent selection of good clarets and Burgundies at high prices; some of the regional wines offer better value. Service is attentive and discreet from smart French staff.

Dunderry Lodge Restaurant — Dunderry

Dunderry, Navan, Co Meath
010-353-046 31671

Closed: lunch (Sat, Sun + Mon); dinner (Sun + Mon);
        Dec - mid-Feb; 5 days Easter
Last
Orders: lunch (2.00pm); dinner (9.30pm)

About 30 miles north west of Dublin on the outskirts of the small village of Dunderry, Nicholas and Catherine Healy converted some old farm buildings into a restaurant which provides some of the best food in Ireland. You enter a long lounge which is comfortably furnished with big sofas and armchairs. The ceiling is covered with hessian, the stone walls have been whitewashed, and on cold days a large wood-burning stove soon removes the chill.

An apéritif is served with perhaps a small piece of onion tart and a tiny crescent of puff pastry, stuffed with a creamy mushroom and anchovy filling. Catherine's menu gives the choice of a small à la carte selection, or a 4-course set menu. A feuilleté of mussels and leeks, Swiss chard with an oyster sauce, terrine of two fish, duck livers with a warm vinaigrette, or carpaccio are typical first courses on the carte. Escalopes of turbot with champagne sauce, papillote of river and sea, magret of wild duck with a confit of pears, escalope of venison with a damson sauce, rack of lamb with bitter orange sauce or mignonettes of beef with Cabernet sauce might follow.

The first of these, the feuilleté of mussels and leeks, was a small quantity of pastry filled with lightly-cooked young leeks and small mussels in a creamy sauce. It was a perfectly judged dish, and the combination of flavour and texture in the ingredients was a delight: sweet, fresh mussels and slightly crunchy leeks in a punchy sauce - a larger portion would have sufficed for dinner!

If you ask Nicholas if the venison is good, he might even proceed to tell you the animal's history! Some came from an unfortunate buck who had been shot on a local estate as he had been terrorising the does during the rut! Since his demise, he had been marinated and was now ready for eating - how could you refuse? The escalopes were served in a deep red, shiny sauce made from a reduction of damson juice, and, presumably, the marinade with a touch of acidity to balance it. This was accompanied by the last of the mange-touts from their garden, small florets of broccoli (side shoots, which seem so much nicer than the ungainly head of the plant), and a plain boiled potato in its jacket. As with the first course, this dish seemed to combine honest farmhouse cooking with the best of modern cuisine. Flavours were natural but sauces had been composed very much in the new style, and were light and delicious.

The cheeseboard is irresistible, with a good showing of Irish, Scottish and English cheeses, together with a few French favourites, all in perfect condition. They are served after the main course with a small salad and some more of Christine's bread, made from wheat grown locally and stone ground just a few miles away.

The sweet trolley has homely puddings - a chocolate roulade, damsons in port, strawberries in dessert wine, oeufs à la neige, or a wonderfully rich ginger ice-cream. Excellent cafetière coffee and petits fours round off a wonderful dinner.

The dining room is also a long room with a high ceiling, an exposed stone wall on one side, a white wall on the other, a deep red carpet and crisp white linen laid with silver and elegant tall glassware. Nicholas is an accomplished host who seems to be everywhere in the room. He is very ably assisted by charming, mature staff who serve caringly, with friendliness and discretion.

Dunderry Lodge is a tribute to dedication, and the care shown by the Healys is reflected in all that they do. They plan to cultivate an extra acre of land for vegetables, to overcome the difficulty of supplies. Catherine spends part of her holiday working in the kitchens of people like Roger Vergé, Albert Roux and Raymond Blanc, so that she can learn new techniques and be stimulated with new ideas.

If you are in Ireland, don't miss this unique restaurant. Without doubt, it is worth a detour!

Marlfield House   Gorey

Gorey, Co Wexford
010-353-055 21124

Closed: Christmas
Last
Orders: lunch (2.30pm); dinner (9.30pm)

Dating from around 1850, this elegant stone-built mansion was
the dower house of the Courtown estate, and was latterly used
as the Earl's principal residence in Ireland. Mary Bowe has now
converted the house into a hotel with 12 bedrooms, each
tastefully decorated in individual styles, and furnished with
antiques. A magnificent 19th-Century conservatory has been
added to the rear of the building to overlook the gardens, and
this forms an extension to the dining room. Green and white
décor, mirrored walls with trellis work, and a profusion of plants
and flowers emphasise the feeling of a conservatory.

At lunch an à la carte menu is offered, and at dinner a fixed
price menu has 5 courses. Fish features strongly, with good
fresh Kilmore crab salad, or mussels marinières amongst the
first courses, and sea bass, turbot or scallops as main dishes.
Breast of chicken might be served with a smoked salmon soufflé
veiled with tarragon sauce, a stuffed pork steak with honey and
madeira sauce, or sirloin with mellow mustard and burgundy
sauce. Puddings might be lemon tart, profiteroles with chocolate
sauce, chocolate cheesecake with mint sauce, or fresh fruit with
coconut cream.

The wine list has a fine range of clarets, with vintages from
1945 to 1983, and representative bottles from most of Europe
and the New World. Mary is a good hostess, and her young staff
are pleasant and attentive.

Park Hotel   Kenmare

Kenmare, Co Kerry
010-353-064 41200

Closed: Nov to Easter (but open 14 days Christmas)
Last
Orders: lunch (2.00pm); dinner (8.45pm)

Francis Brennan must rank as one of Ireland's premier hotel-
keepers for the exemplary way in which he runs his superb hotel
overlooking the Kenmare estuary. The impressive stone building
was custom-built as a railway hotel at the turn of the century,
and retains a classic hotel style with every modern amenity.

Service from the young Irish staff is friendly but very efficient, and they appear from nowhere to carry a case, park a car, or top up a glass. The hotel is full of good antiques and paintings. Well-proportioned rooms have been tastefully decorated, and there is not a speck of dust to be seen.

Matthew d'Arcy is the chef, and his menus are based on a modern style of cooking, using good quality produce. Being near to the sea, fish is a popular item, either as a first course or a main dish. You could start with salmon in a champagne and basil sauce, local Kilmakillogue mussels with white wine and a hint of curry, a poached pear with leek and cheese mousse in a watercress cream sauce, or a cream of spinach soup with sea urchin quenelles. Fish dishes include monkfish cooked with tomato and garlic, baked turbot with crabmeat and apple in a saffron sauce, scallops with leek purée and grape sauce, or a lobster from Kenmare Bay, cooked to your liking. Amongst meat and poultry dishes, there is roast Kerry lamb with garlic potatoes, duck breast in pastry with port and orange sauce, or fillet of beef with mustard and rosemary. If you have room after the main course, try the grand choix des desserts du Park, which is a huge plate with small portions of each of the puddings. The massive wine list offers a choice of the best of the world's wines, with prices ranging from £12.00 up to £120.00.

The elegant dining room has an open fire burning on cold nights, and candles on the tables help to create a warm atmosphere. Gerry Browne's team of waiting staff are charming.

Longueville House   Mallow

Mallow, Co Cork
010-353-022 27156

Closed: lunch (daily); mid-Nov - end Mar
Last
Orders: dinner (9.00pm)

The Longueville estate has a colourful history, dating back some few hundred years, but the most interesting event occurred when the father of the current owners bought the property in 1938. The wheel had by then turned full circle, for it was his ancestors who had been deprived of the property by Cromwell in 1650! Times have changed, and Michael and Jane O'Callaghan now run the magnificent house as a hotel with 18 bedrooms. The Georgian building has some wonderful features - a Portland stone floor in the hall, ornate plastered and decorated ceilings, a

white marble Adam fireplace in the dining room, inlaid mahogany doors with superb brass locks, and a fine staircase. A large, curved iron-work conservatory was added to the house in 1866 and makes a delightful flower-filled room from which to see the Blackwater valley.

Menus are based on good local produce, with such items as wild salmon, Longueville lamb, and lovely home-made bread. The wine list has some fine selections, with an excellent range of wines from Rioja shown separately. At the side of the house is Ireland's only vineyard, but the Irish weather has been unkind for the last 2 years and no wine has been produced. There may still, however, be the odd bottle of '84 hidden in the cellar!

Arbutus Lodge Hotel   Montenotte

Montenotte, Cork, Co Cork
010-353-021 501237

£40

Closed: Sun (bar food available for residents)
Last
Orders: lunch (2.00pm); dinner (9.30pm)

The Ryan family keeps a watchful eye on this converted town house perched high above Ireland's southern capital. The Gallery Bar seems to be the meeting place for locals at lunch time, and here you can have everything from Galway oysters with a glass of Champagne to tripe and drisheen with black velvet.

The restaurant meanwhile combines the traditional with the modern, with such dishes as Irish nettle soup, Cork crubeens (stuffed pigs' trotters), or Irish smoked salmon being offered alongside a pigeon breast and walnut salad, grilled scallops with beurre blanc, or salade landaise. Fillet of brill with sea urchin sauce is excellent. Other main courses include a breast of duck with garlic and ginger, rack of lamb with garden herbs, veal kidney with sherry vinegar, and veal cutlets with chervil sauce. A 7-course 'tasting menu' provides an opportunity to sample a variety of dishes, and is good value at around £22.00.

The wine list has received much acclaim, and this is not surprising, as there are around 300 carefully chosen wines from all principal regions of the world. Several vintages of some of the clarets and Burgundies are listed, which might give a larger party a chance to taste and discuss their relative merits.

Best Country House Hotels

Country house hotels are perhaps the greatest breakthrough in areas outside major cities for many years. The term 'Country House Hotel' is used extensively by many establishments throughout the country but we have endeavoured to include only those whose style of food, service and décor (and in the majority of cases, beautiful gardens and grounds), qualify them for the top category, and we have put the best into this section in random order.

Gidleigh Park Chagford

Chagford, Devon TQ13 8HH
(064 73) 2367/2225

Last
Orders: lunch (2.00pm); dinner (9.30pm)

Without doubt one of the country's most beautiful country house hotels, Gidleigh Park looks out over the magnificent Teign valley, the nearest road being over a mile away. You have to follow the instructions on how to get there very carefully, and signs along the private drive advise, "Keep going, you're not too far away now." The detour is worthwhile. Landscaped gardens surround the black and white timbered house which nestles in 40 acres beside the Dartmoor National Park. Décor and furnishings are impeccable, and the Hendersons and their staff make guests very welcome. A log fire burns in the lovely panelled hall more as an added comfort than a necessity.

The dining room at Gidleigh is almost its raison d'être and the hosts are justifiably proud of their achievements. Shaun Hill is now in charge of the kitchens and everything, including bread, is made fresh daily. His cooking is precise and imaginative. A typical set dinner menu might consist of a chilled pepper soup, grilled monkfish with Meaux mustard sauce, roast Challans duck breast with wild mushroom essence, followed by cheese and pudding. If you are not happy with that there are always equally delicious alternatives - rules are made to be broken.

The wine list makes interesting reading, starting with a page on policies and prejudices, and continuing by offering 400 selections, and the option of 250 bin ends: "these must be ordered before 5.00pm so that we can try to find them."

As Paul Henderson has said, they bought Gidleigh Park in 1977 and had no experience in running a hotel or restaurant, but they had travelled extensively, so they set out to make it a place where *they* would like to stay and eat. If lecturers in some of our catering colleges in this country could add that simple philosophy to their curriculum, there might be hope for us yet.

Bodysgallen Hall — Deganwy

Deganwy, near Llandudno, Gwynedd, Wales LL30 1RS
(0492) 84466

£40

one of the best in Wales

Last
Orders: lunch (2.00pm); dinner (9.45pm)

Apparently Bodysgallen means 'house among the thistles' - we didn't see many thistles but we did see a beautifully kept country house, its rooms warm and inviting with huge fireplaces and comfortable furniture. The house, dating from the 17th Century but with a 13th-Century tower, has been restored with care by Historic House Hotels. It stands on its own on the side of a hill looking down on Conway Castle, and offers spectacular views of Snowdonia.

Inside there are some fine antiques and oil paintings, and the large entrance hall and first floor drawing room - both oak panelled - look out through stone-mullioned windows. The terraced gardens are lovingly maintained and include a water-lily garden, a walled rose garden and the rare sight of a 17th-Century knot garden of box hedges and sweet scented herbs. In addition to the rooms within the Hall, self-contained accommodation is provided in cottages arranged around a courtyard. There is a conference facility but the additional numbers do not seem to detract from David Harding's cooking, which is a blend of classic dishes mixed with some local and Welsh specialities like the tart of Anglesey crab, tomatoes and seaweed. The cooking is never too ambitious and blends in with the house rather than dominates it. The cheese board has local Welsh cheeses and the breakfasts are recommended for their range and quality. Like its sister hotel, Middlethorpe Hall, Bodysgallen has a large cellar, and offers some interesting wines and vintages at fairly affordable prices as well as Californian wines and a good selection of Bordeaux and Burgundies. Housewines from £6.60 a bottle.

Ballymaloe House   Shanagarry

Shanagarry, Midleton, Co Cork, Republic of Ireland   ♣ £40
010-353-021 652531

very friendly relaxed, the best in these parts

Closed: 3 days Christmas
Last
Orders: lunch (2.00pm); dinner (9.30pm; 8.00pm Sun)

Friends had told me that Ballymaloe was something rather special, and after visiting this delightful country house, I would say "very special". It has all the facilities of a hotel, yet doesn't feel like one. You have the impression of being a house guest of the Allen family, who do everything possible to make your stay enjoyable. It is very much a family concern, Ivan and Myrtle Allen and their children running the hotel together with a 400-acre farm, a cookery school and a farm shop.

The house has great character - it is actually part of an old Geraldine castle which has been rebuilt, while retaining the original 14th-Century keep. Rooms are tastefully decorated and comfortably furnished. Some bedrooms are in the main house, while others are in the courtyard or the 16th-Century gatehouse. The Wedgewood blue dining room with its collection of modern Irish paintings is the hub of activity at Ballymaloe, and Myrtle's cooking has become internationally famous. She uses fresh local produce, much of which is in fact home produced. In the foreword to her cookbook she expresses the style of her cooking perfectly: "If I could start a fashion, it would be to recapture some forgotten flavours, or to preserve some that may soon die." She achieves her objectives daily with everything that she cooks.

At breakfast time there is freshly squeezed juice, a delicious fruit salad of prunes, apricots, bananas and raisins, hot freshly baked scones, home-made muesli or porridge made of locally ground oatmeal, free-range eggs with smoked bacon, fresh fish, home-made preserves, and toasted Ballymaloe brown bread. You could survive on breakfast alone, but dinner is too good to miss.

A thick watercress soup was delicious, with the true pungent flavour of really fresh watercress. Fish from the nearby Ballycotton Bay was made into a light mousse, served with a crayfish butter sauce; and this was followed by a main course of roast duck with apple sauce and sage and onion stuffing. The duck was cooked traditionally, which was a welcome change from the hackneyed magret of most modern menus. It was crisp-skinned and succulent, and accompanied by braised red cabbage, duchesse potatoes and a purée of spinach. A green salad was served next, and then a selection of Irish farmhouse cheeses and home-baked oatcakes.

The sweet trolley had crème brûlée, a praline gâteau, caramel ice-cream with sticky caramel sauce, fruit salad or almond meringue gâteau, sandwiched with chocolate and rum cream. Good coffee and hand-made truffles or fudge rounded off an exceptional meal. There are choices of items for each course on the fixed price menu, and they all sound so good that it is hard to decide which to try. The service is as honest and attentive to detail as the cooking, and the charming staff always ask you if you would like more of anything before they clear a plate. The wine list is impressive, with a good selection of fine vintages, chosen by Ivan Allen and his son-in-law, Jim Whelan.

There is a swimming pool, a few holes for golfers, a tennis court, or a croquet lawn for the less energetic. It was also good to see that children are welcome. There is a sandpit, pool and slides for them, and I believe that the tea-party at 5.30pm is quite something!

Chewton Glen — New Milton

New Milton, Hampshire BH25 6QS
(042 52) 5341

Last
Orders: lunch (2.30pm); dinner (9.30pm)

The drive leading up to Chewton Glen is not perhaps what you would expect as the approach to a grand house, but in fact when you arrive you do reach an ivy-covered red brick country house of quite huge proportions. The main house is cleverly connected to the main bedroom suites in an adjacent wing, the whole covered with ivy, and set in beautifully kept lawns with herbs, pots of flowers and 3 sets of steps leading down to a heated outdoor swimming pool. In fact the aspect of the house from the pool at 8.00am on a September morning, with wisps of warm air rising from the heated water, is probably the best view of all. Great care and attention have been paid to detail. They've even cleverly managed to hide all the pumping stations and the odd buildings you don't want to see behind carefully maintained box hedges.

Certainly no expense has been spared on the lavish interior either, which is also very professionally done. It will not take you long to realise why this place is internationally known on the

European circuit. The management will even arrange to pick you up from the airport, if you like, and give you a guided tour on the way back to Chewton Glen.

The dining room, though large still manages to maintain an excellent standard of cuisine and the management is justifiably proud of its German cheese-holding fridges and new wine-dispensing chiller. Few people would be disappointed by the choice offered on the menu, which might include a delicious shellfish soup flavoured with basil and garnished with strips of cucumber, a tartare of salmon with chopped avocado and flavoured with tarragon, followed by an excellent plate of assorted seafood including grilled fillets of sea bass, Dover sole served with fennel and butter sauce, an escalope of salmon with fresh sorrel sauce, rabbit served on a bed of peppers, baby marrows, onion, garlic and eggplant as well as a more orthodox treatment of lamb, veal and beef - all accompanied by an excellent selection of well cooked crisp vegetables and good salads.

The very good wine list has lots of bargains to be found in the Rhône and the Bordeaux sections, and a reasonable choice of half bottles. They really manage exceptionally well in this quite large hotel to purvey a homely yet overall professional service to make you, the customer, feel very welcome.

Cromlix House   Dunblane

Kinbuck, Dunblane, Perthshire, Scotland PK15 9JT
(0786) 822125

Last
Orders: by arrangement

Grant Howlett, whom we last saw under the eye of Gerald Milsom at Maison Talbooth, is now firmly established at the front of house here, either with an attentive staff in the dining room or in one of the other grand reception rooms. Stephen Frost with his team in the kitchen turn out some excellent dishes, taking advantage of the availability of some of the finest beef in Great Britain, but a good selection is offered across the board with interesting fish dishes, beautifully flavoured and served with crisp vegetables. The kitchen also turns out its own bread and puddings. The whole ambience is of a grand country house - no menu is formally offered, dishes are proposed, although you can have alternatives if you request them.

The tranquil surroundings are magnificent and the house is set in an estate approaching some 500 acres. The house itself was built in 1880 and still retains a Victorian character both in style and

service. You feel that everything revolves around you, and the staff appear from nowhere to fulfil your needs.

There are 14 bedrooms, each with private bathroom, and no fewer than 7 sitting rooms. Bedrooms and reception rooms contain some of the original furnishings, and there is exquisite porcelain, glass and silver. During the respective seasons, fishing and shooting can be arranged; there is a tennis court in the grounds; and no shortage either of golfing facilities, with Gleneagles a mere 20 minute drive away.

If you wish to make an entrance, you can even drop in by helicopter!

Hambleton Hall   Hambleton

Hambleton, Oakham, Leicestershire LE15 8TH   £60
(0572) 56991

Last

Orders: lunch (1.30pm); dinner (9.30pm)

Nick Gill is no longer in the kitchen but they're still producing good food.

It's taken me a long time to realise why people go on so much about the countryside in this part of the world: it *is* rather spectacular; and Oakham, where Hambleton is situated, is actually on a peninsula, jutting out into Rutland Water. The approach to Oakham is spectacular in itself, with a few fishing boats bobbing up and down on the water on both sides of the road, and some lovely countryside stretching away into the distance. As you rise up the hill into this picturesque village, you see houses covered with ivy, Virginia creeper, climbing roses and geraniums. Go on past The Finch's Arms which sells John Smith's ales, and follow the road through to Hambleton Hall, a huge Victorian house set in its own grounds with beautiful rooms.

Although large, the house has a pleasant, welcoming and friendly atmosphere about it. The staff are pleased to see you, and you immediately feel at home. In winter, as you enter the front door, there's a nice fire; beyond that a small bar, and then straight through to the large lounge which overlooks the gardens and Rutland Water. Some lovely furnishings, good solid English furniture, some nice antiques and some beautiful touches, including exquisite flower arrangements. The restaurant itself, again overlooking the gardens, is solid and Victorian, all crisp linen and sparkling glassware which together with well-informed and obliging staff, lift the ambience.

Dishes on the menu taste as good as they sound. For starters you might pick from a tartlet of morels and pigeon with a salad of baby leeks, fillet of eel in a chardonnay jelly encircled with cucumber, or as a first or middle course you might try a puff pastry pillow of sweetbreads, which is exactly what it sounds like, or perhaps a poached fillet of John Dory with saffron and samphire, or maybe a poached fillet of Rutland Water trout with a champagne sauce (you'll get no fresher fish than that!). From the 7 or 8 main courses you might pick the pot roast chicken in a morel sauce, or a pot roast squab with port and foie gras, or maybe a whole sea bass with amontillado sauce. A good selection of farmhouse cheese is offered, served with walnut bread. A nice idea is the symphony of puddings for 2; or you might prefer marinated strawberries served in a brandy snap basket with a Grand Marnier mousse, or profiteroles filled with coconut ice on a sauce of dark chocolate laced with rum. Alternatively, maybe you'll opt for Hambleton's own toasted rice pudding. All in all you'll find some interesting and exciting presentations of very good local produce.

The bedrooms are as well thought out as the public rooms, each with its own individual style and flair, and if you're lucky enough to get a room at the rear of the house - I know this is getting boring but - overlooking Rutland Water, it is quite spectacular. It's a beautiful place to stay, in either summer or winter. If you're there for a weekend or so, there are wonderful walks, lovely things to look at, a museum in Oakham itself, and a rare breed park of animals from an earlier age.

Homewood Park   Hinton Charterhouse

Hinton Charterhouse, Bath, Avon BA3 6BB
(022 122) 3731

Closed: Christmas - 14 Jan
Last
Orders: lunch (2.00pm); dinner (9.30pm)

- exceptional cooking in friendly comfortable surroundings

Homewood Park is very special. We had been recommended to go there by numerous people including Richard Shepherd and Bob Payton, and we thank them, as well as the others who have recommended Penny and Stephen Ross's excellent country house hotel. Architecturally the exterior is not my favourite style, I must admit. But forget all that, the interior offers you some 15 luxurious bedrooms with bathrooms, well decorated, friendly public rooms and a restaurant split into 3 sections. There are 10 acres of informal gardens and woodlands and the house is situated opposite the ruins of the Carthusian Hinton Priory.

The food is what this place is about. Stephen Ross, who worked with Ken Bell at Thornbury Castle years ago, turns out - to my mind - the very best country house cooking. Again, the menu is easy to read and makes you really want to try every dish on it. Superb tomato and basil soup, and delicious venison rissoles in a juniper sauce, followed by a pot au feu of fish with scallops, salmon, lobster, mussels and turbot, all cooked perfectly and served with a selection of crisp fresh vegetables. I chose - hesitantly - the quail stuffed with Stilton and walnuts, and when it arrived it was excellent. The Stilton was in a subtly flavoured mousse stuffed inside the quail, which was served in an excellent reduction. Soup, casseroles and pots au feu are brought to the table in cast iron pans; a serving is ladled into your dish, and the pan is left at your side for seconds, if you can manage it.

The puddings, as simple as you could imagine, are absolutely delicious: a light puff pastry tart with fresh figs served on a clear syrupy base; a very pretty, cleverly woven pastry basket served in 3 different sauces of mango, raspberry and guava and filled with fresh fruits - sensational! I could go on, in fact I wish we could have stayed for a week so I could have tried every dish on the menu. I bet they were all as good as the ones we did try. A good selection of wines has no fewer than 12 housewines all exceptionally priced around the £7.50 mark. It's also nice to be offered no fewer than 4 dessert wines served by the glass, including a Sauternes, a Loire and a Californian.

The service is friendly and efficient from young staff who are enthusiastic, and with Stephen in the kitchen and Penny Ross in the front of house, you enjoy the experience from the moment you enter to the moment you leave this friendly and professional establishment.

369

Hunstrete House   Chelwood

Chelwood, Near Bristol, Avon BS18 4NS   ♣ £50
(076 18) 578

Last   *one of my very favourite*
Orders: lunch (2.00pm); dinner (9.30pm) *country houses.*

The approach to the house is bordered by beautiful trees on either side, and on the main drive you pass a small deer park. The hotel is beautifully situated with pleasant English country views all around, and the house itself is built of mellow Bath stone. To the left of the main house is a beautiful walled garden with a croquet lawn, bordered hedges leading through into massed flowers, old-fashioned herbaceaous borders and a most wonderful selection in the vegetable garden.

Many of the paintings are by owner Thea Dupays and the whole style of the interior is very much her own: well-matched colours, comfortable furniture, ruched drapes, as many flowers inside as outside in the garden, and lots of objets d'art around the house, the whole mixture making you feel as if you are in someone's home. The feeling is very much like a house party although no-one intrudes on your privacy. All the main reception rooms have beautiful sash windows that reach to the ground giving lovely views of the gardens, which seem to overflow into the house. The courtyard at the rear is surrounded by the bedrooms, all beautifully and individually styled and furnished. The courtyard itself has a central fountain and lily pond, surrounded by huge terracotta pots and wooden tubs containing a profusion of flowers, olive trees, geraniums and fuchsias. One side of the restaurant looks out onto this courtyard and in summer spills out through the large french windows. Inside, the restaurant is cool in décor, with pastel shades, and the service is friendly and helpful by a mainly young, local staff.

The food turned out by Robert Elsmore's team in the kitchen costs £22.00 per head for a 3-course dinner inclusive of service.

The 8 selections might include warm salad of chicken and lobster served with sherry vinegar dressing, a red lettuce salad, a mousse of scallops served with a hot port sauce, fresh crab, avocado with pink grapefruit salad, a terrine of wild salmon garnished with pistachio nuts and green peppercorns. Main courses, out of a choice of 7, can vary from saddle of venison cooked pink and served on a bed of celery confit with a port sauce and spätzli, wild salmon served with a light stew of cucumber and asparagus, flavoured with dill, breast of chicken sliced and served on a bed of green noodles surrounded with herbs and white butter cream sauce, or perhaps fillet of beef garnished with a slice of goose liver sautéed with madeira sauce and chopped truffle. A good selection of desserts is offered and a wine list to suit most pockets, the clarets ranging from £7.80 a bottle.

It must be a joy to cook in such a wonderful atmosphere with a vegetable garden that can give you the variety that the Dupays obviously plant and nurture through the year. Did I mention the swimming pool or the tennis court, which are hidden away beyond the herb garden? Did I mention the views, you can see for miles around without another house in sight? I really do like Hunstrete: for comfort, warmth and welcome it is well worth a visit.

For a healthy appetite

Inverlochy Castle   Torlundy

Torlundy, Fort William, Inverness-shire, Scotland PH33 6SN
(0397) 2177/8

Closed: mid-Nov - mid-Mar
Last
Orders: lunch (1.45pm); dinner (9.00pm)

Once in a while Inverlochy Castle should be visited to remind you
of how life can be: it is a place for indulgence, a place to celebrate
or be tranquil. Though the castle has a craggy granite exterior, the
interior is warm and gives a sense of well-established security.
The large hall with its beautiful staircase, high ceilings and solid
furniture, looks like a Scottish castle should. Nestling below Ben
Nevis, the grounds of the hotel are well maintained, and there is a
lake and more mountains to admire - and there is peace.

Having absorbed the setting and the atmosphere, your taste-
buds should be ready to take over and revive the inner self. The
menus are as substantial as the castle - dinner is 5 courses, and
might tempt you with a terrine of fish or duckling followed by a
soup, main dishes of wild salmon en papillote with champagne
sauce, roast Aberdeen Angus with bordelaise sauce, or saddle of
lamb stuffed with mushrooms and spinach. Cheese precedes the
desserts, which might include a pear and rhubarb parfait, figs
poached in raspberry syrup with cinnamon ice-cream, or perhaps
a peach and nectarine tulip with lemon sorbet. The Loch Linnhe
prawns are not to be missed; without doubt, they were the best I
had eaten, and served with sauce aux fines herbes they were a
meal in themselves.

Wines are all that you could wish for, but are at the top end of
the price range. Service is professional and well trained, the staff
are polite and friendly, and in true baronial manner they appear
when required and withdraw when not. Inverlochy offers a taste
of a lifestyle to which one could become accustomed, at least
once in a while.

Sharrow Bay   Ullswater

Howton Road, Ullswater, Cumbria CA10 2LZ
(085 36) 483

— out of the first and still going strong

Closed: Dec, Jan + Feb
Last
Orders: lunch (1.30pm); dinner (8.30pm)

What new can you say about Sharrow Bay? The team of owners, Francis Coulson and Brian Sack, have been dispensing hospitality for over 30 years in this location, picturesquely set in woodlands and perched on the edge of Lake Ullswater which laps against the terrace wall. Such spectacular views - what a way to live! The house, built in 1840, has the owners' personalities stamped throughout. Dare I say it, it's a bit like going to stay with a wealthy auntie who plies you with large portions of irresistible food, ranging from very good local fish to superb roast game and excellent sticky puddings. They do have lighter dishes on the menu, but after being dragged for a 3-mile hike, albeit in the most beautiful countryside, I always seem to plump for the more English of their dishes. There is a fantastic wine list with a good choice and price range.

The Bank House is separate - nicely decorated rooms, each in its own individual style, and in the breakfast-cum-conference room is a fireplace from Warwick Castle... I must mention the time when people were snowed in under 7 feet of snow, doing exercises and their own washing-up under the watchful eye of Mavis, the housekeeper! If I was going to be snowed in anywhere, this is where I'd choose it to be. Don't be put off by the fact that it says dinner between 8.00pm and 8.30pm; and note the twinkling lights from buildings on the other side of the lake and the separate VIP suite away from the main hotel.

How could Francis and Brian bear to have people staying in their marvellous house? You realise why, when you see the even more marvellous house they have themselves, terraced down to the lake!

Welcome
Bienvenue
Willkommen
ようこそ
Bienvenidos

The first choice around the world.

A hot drink says welcome in any language. When you are welcomed by the brands that are recognised world-wide for their quality and taste, the welcome is complete. Wherever you seek the best, ask for the best by name – **Nescafé, Nescafé Gold Blend, Nescafé Gold Blend Decaffeinated** and **Carnation Liquid Coffee-Mate** and **Tea-Mate.**

Your first choice around the world.

Nestlé.

A general comment on the Lake District: it doesn't matter what the weather is like when the scenery is this spectacular and so different from anywhere else in the British Isles - one *has* to make a pilgrimage here. Sharrow Bay was one of the first in the Country House Hotel game some 25 years ago, and although others have sought to emulate them with their own styles, this remains one of the best places in the country.

When we were paying the bill, there were people begging them to find a cancellation so they could stay the following year.

Middlethorpe Hall   York

£55

Bishopthorpe Road, York, North Yorkshire YO2 1QP
(0904) 641241

Last
Orders: lunch (2.00pm); dinner (9.45pm)

Once upon a time Malcolm Broadbent used to take time off from his studies at the Oxford Polytechnic to help me in various outside catering events around Oxfordshire. Since then he has made the long journey up the A1 from the excellent Stafford Hotel in London to establish Middlethorpe Hall, in almost record time, as one of the leading hotels in the North. Just outside the town centre, this imposing house, built in 1699, offers comfort on a grand scale. The lounge is vast with generous furnishings to match and some wonderfully chosen antiques which suit the setting perfectly. From the minute you walk in you can sense the professionalism and you know that you are in safe hands. The bedrooms are attractively and thoughtfully furnished; the ones in the adjoining stable block have been sympathetically converted, but do try to get a room in the main house. The gardens and parkland have been carefully tended and restored to their original style.

Chef Aidan McCormack came from Chewton Glen and has brought with him its style of precise, modern cooking which presents English cuisine with a liberal dash of French flair. The quails' eggs, which were suitably mollet, were served with a strongly flavoured mushroom mousse and some strips of smoked duck. Top quality lamb is cooked to good advantage in the main course, as are the mille feuille of scallops with champagne sauce, and the roast saddle of rabbit with apples and cream sauce. Try the soufflé of eau de vie to finish.

Service is informed, formal but not stiff, and the wine list is as imposing as the surroundings. The tightly packed list of clarets and Burgundies may well tempt you to part with a little more money than intended and you will have to hunt for bargains.

Such a splendid country house, converted and furnished so superbly, and so carefully run, is well worth a visit.

NESCAFÉ®

GOLD BLEND®

freeze dried instant coffee

The promise of pure gold.

Nestlé®

Robert Carrier's Paris

When I am in Paris I always stay on the Left Bank in the area immediately surrounding the Place Saint Germain-des-Prés, where I spent (misspent, perhaps?) 5 golden years of my life. It was at this colourful juncture of the old Boulevard St Germain and the narrow Rue Bonaparte with its famous cafés (les Deux Magots and the Café de Flore), illustrious hangouts (at that time of existentialist writers Camus, Sartre, and de Beauvoir, singers Juliette Greco and the lovely Annabel, the black American writer Jimmy Baldwin and a host of other talented independents), that I received my first taste of French intellectual and gastronomic life.

It is in the streets of this fascinating quarter that I feel most at home today. I like to shop on the short strip of the Rue de Buci that runs from St André des Arts to the Boulevard St Germain. This open-air street market, with its stalls of fresh fruits and vegetables that we cannot equal in this country, is backed by little, open shop-fronts lining each side of the market with some of the best purveyors of country breads, cheeses, butters, poultry and game in the city.

The area is full of enchanting restaurants as well. My locals - Le Petit Zinc, and Chez Allard (right on the street where I live), and the nearby Brasserie Lipp (just opposite les Deux Magots and the Flore) are my regular stopping-off places; unless, of course, I am overcome by a sudden 'coup de folie' and choose to dine in regal splendour at one of the best and certainly one of the most prestigious restaurants of Paris - Tour d'Argent - just a few blocks from my apartment.

The restaurants that I have picked are all living examples of a new active style, whether it is the 'born again' interest in fish dishes and lighter sauces of Le Bernardin; the miraculous purées of butter-rich potatoes and the traditionally correct tête de porc in the grand manner of Joel Robuchon; or the refreshingly original, even unorthodox creations of Robert Vifian with his 'cuisine de Vietnam intellectualisée' that strives to create the classic recipes of a mythical Vietnam that exists only in the memory of Robert Vifian.

But to get my restaurant preferences in perspective, let's get one thing straight. In general, I am not mad about 'temples' of haute cuisine where one is expected to approach the gastronomic altar with reverence and awe. I go to restaurants for enjoyment and to experience new flavours, new pleasures. Restaurants for me are made by the memories that they evoke; truly outstanding dishes that remain in my subconscious, jogging my senses for days, weeks, and even years. So don't look for ecstatic paragraphs from me only about the great show-place

restaurants of Paris, Taillevent, Pavillion de l'Elysée, or the Pré Catalan. You will find, however, Alain Senderens at Lucas-Carton, Alain Dutournier at the Carré des Feuillants and Domini-que Bouchet at the Tour d'Argent. Though I must admit that I far preferred Senderens, one of the undisputed innovators of French modern cooking, when he was in his little bistro on the Rue de l'Exposition near the Eiffel Tower (one had a sense of glorious discovery). Michel Guérard was at his height for me (long before Eugénie les Bains) when he cooked alone in his tiny restaurant in Asnières, a forgotten suburb of Paris (I went 4 times in as many weeks). And I even preferred Alain Dutournier (most interesting forerunner of the new 'return to the land' cooking that is rapidly out-distancing nouvelle cuisine) at Au Trou Gascon before he went on to finer things at the rich and glamorous Carré des Feuillants in the shadow of the Place Vendôme. That is why you will find, nestling among my choice of the 'greats' some of my favourite restaurants that operate on a more intimate - but no less exciting scale: Robuchon (perhaps Number One restaurant in Paris today), Le Bernardin (my first choice for fish), Beauvilliers (Bocuse's favourite Paris restaurant), Le Clodenis (up-and-coming young 'Turk' cook), and yes, even a Vietnamese one, Tan Dinh, reputed to have one of the most interesting wine lists in Paris.

It was Alain Dutournier who reminded me, by his vibrant and highly personal style of cooking and his revolutionary return to natural flavours, that nouvelle cuisine, if not dead, is on its crutches. And that the new movement in French culinary history is a step backwards into the recent past - to the cuisine bourgeoise of the 19th Century, a long awaited return to the homely, comfortable dishes of grandmêre or tante Léonie - but with all the best lessons of nouvelle cuisine, finesse and subtlety, retained.

Tour d'Argent   Paris

15-17 Quai Tournelle, 75005 Paris
(010-331) 43 54 23 31

Closed: Mon
Last
Orders:10.00pm

The Tour d'Argent, like Maxim's, has to be counted one of the most famous restaurants in the world. It has held this high rank in the world's esteem - with only an occasional dormant period - since the 14th or 15th Century. For the last 20 years or so it has been the gastronomic showpiece and responsibility of Claude Terrail, who inherited it from his father and has been refining and beautifying it for as long as I can remember. As a result it is probably the most beautifully appointed restaurant in Paris, and perhaps the world. I can think of no other that comes near to it. It has the grandest entrance hall, the most 'perfect' lift, the most beautiful (and well-kept) wine cellar (on view to privileged guests) and private dining rooms in Paris. And certainly it has the most spectacular view: flood-lit Notre Dame, a duck leg's throw across the river Seine. Indeed duck - canard rôti à la Tour d'Argent - has been the great speciality of the house for over 100 years. Specially reared ducks from Challans, each and every one hand picked and numbered since the restaurant began - sounds difficult to believe but it's absolutely true. Until fairly recently there were a number of duck recipes on the menu. But today, under the expert guidance of young chef Dominique Bouchet, who joined Terrail in 1981, the cooking has become lighter, less traditional and more in keeping with the new French style. Today duck figures on the menu only 3 or 4 times.

I first dined at the Tour d'Argent when I was twenty-three and have still not forgotten my first view of the glamour of the setting, the ballet of the service, and the excellence of the food. I can even tell you what I ate - a traditional choice so I could taste at first-hand the great dishes that I had heard about all my life: pâté de foie gras, a fat slice of fresh goose liver pâté served with its own amber-tinted gelée, followed by the famous canard à la Tour d'Argent, the breast served first in thin even slices, beautifully rare with its justly famous sauce made from the bird's crushed liver, its pan juices, wine and the blood and juices from the bones of the carcass (crushed in a special silver duck press), served with the Tour's world-famous pommes soufflées (little pillows, crisp and golden, as light as air, their gossamer-thin veils enclosing magical puffs of heated air). Ethereal; I had never had anything like it in my native America. And to this day I am grateful for what was for me, at that time, an earth-shattering experience. The meal ended with a soufflé aux fraises de bois (a creamy cognac-scented soufflé of tiny wild strawberries so full of flavour). Another first.

Years later I celebrated my 35th birthday there with great friends who were frequent and fêted patrons of the restaurant - again a symphony of intoxicating savours and equally intoxicating wines, and I have been visiting this august establishment ever since. To my mind, for a first visitor to Paris, it is a must. It is undeniably one of the great dining experiences of this century. A restaurant to dress up for, an event to look forward to, and to savour for many years after.

Jamin (Robuchon)   Paris

32 Rue Longchamp, 75016 Paris
(010-331) 47 27 12 27

Closed: Sat + Sun; 28 Jun - 27 Jul; 28 Mar - 5 Apr
Last
Orders: 10.15pm

Robuchon (or Jamin as it is still called) is at this moment in time probably the best restaurant in Paris, with Alain Senderens (Lucas-Carton) running almost neck to neck. It is certainly the most difficult to get into. I was recently in Paris for 4 days to refresh my memory on other visits to this famous restaurant and could not get a reservation for any evening in that period. Robuchon is a hot property right now so don't think you can just drop in. Booking at least a month in advance is advisable.

Recently termed the 'most successful innovator' of the new French cooking, Joel Robuchon gained his 3 stars in only 3 years. A rapid rise for a young chef (he is 39) who made his name - and his first 2 stars - at Nikko hotel. Not content with his success, he goes on playing with new flavours, new presentations, his kitchen staffed with 16 chefs. He is a man obsessed with his search for culinary perfection. The restaurant is small (40 seats); beautifully appointed (warm pink walls hung with period prints on decorative silk ribbons); green plants, huge pots, and delightful glass screens to ensure a feeling of privacy, enliven this charming 'intimiste' décor of refined elegance.

Robuchon himself is never in sight; he, unlike many chefs today, prefers to devote his attentions and his energies to his kitchen. The welcome is left to maître d'hôtel Jacques Caiment who takes you deftly through the menu's delights and ably directs the service of the professional, young, dining room staff. Madame Robuchon is hidden away, in French fashion, at the caisse, and is reportedly very pretty. Perhaps it would be a good idea for her to come out to add her charms to the reception.

Robuchon's menu changes every 3 months giving him ample opportunity to experiment with new ideas and new ways of cooking old favourites. His own personality is much in evidence in every dish he serves: unpretentious, dedicated and gifted with a rare sense of proportion, genius perhaps, which adds extraordinary lightness and delicacy to his authoritative natural flavours. Among my favourites are dishes such as his ragoût d'huîtres et de noix de St Jacques au caviar (minced raw scallops, oven-poached in spinach-lined dariole moulds served with a delicate oyster cream scented with saffron and fennel, each shining green mould topped with an extravagant dollop of caviar), or the handsome lobster salad garnished with minute balls of crisp white apple, soft green avocado and ripe tomato, the whole bathed in a truffled aromatic vinaigrette sauce. I liked too his simple but different way with fresh cod, a fish often looked down upon in the tonier French restaurants where turbot, sole, brill, lotte and rouget seem to head the stakes. His morue fraîche aux fins aromates lards fresh cod fillets with thin threads of smoked salmon, sears them in oil, garnishes them with glittering vegetables and serves them with a subtle butter sauce enriched with a hint of soy. Canette rosée aux épices is another imaginative case in point, this gives a subtle touch of the orient, the duck is half roasted, then braised en cocotte with oriental spices and served with caramelised fried apples. Rôti d'agneau aux herbes en croûte de sel bakes the tender lamb with thyme in a thyme-flavoured crust of salt and flour to serve it pink, moist and flavoursome. Robuchon has a way too with vegetables, elegantly thin strips of colourful red and green peppers, courgettes and mushrooms decorate many of his dishes, and his simple (but butter-rich) purée of potatoes has become a Parisian watchword for the fresh new cooking style, served as it is in soft swirls of piped perfection. His salads are another key to this subtle sense of colour, texture and flavour. Each one is a masterpiece and desserts are as exciting as the rest of the menu; superb sorbets, crêpes soufflées, crisp, thin tuiles of orange and raspberry, and a wonderful crème caramelisée à la cassonnade, the best vanilla crème brûlée I have ever tasted, the cream flecked with tiny black dots of vanilla grains trembling under its crisp crackling of caramel.

Lucas-Carton   Paris

9 Place de la Madeleine, 75008 Paris
(010-331) 42 65 22 90

Closed: Sat + Sun
Last
Orders: 10.30pm

I first lunched at Lucas-Carton more than 30 years ago as the guest of Princess Fawkia, sister of the late King Farouk of Egypt, just months before that unfortunate monarch's death. The setting was superb, the conversation heady (we were plotting the foundation of a Royal Ballet of Egypt), and the food and service everything one could desire. But it was dead, somehow lacking in that high-keyed sense of bustle and pleasure that a truly great restaurant can have. There was no spark, no life, no excitement. It seemed as if the old lady, content with her reputation and her art nouveau splendour had just dozed off, dreaming no doubt of past glories. In later years, Lucas-Carton fell on even more difficult times.

But now all that has changed, and Lucas-Carton, at the instigation of (and financed by) Rémy Martin and under the direction of Alain Senderens, has come to life again, its fabulous décor refurbished, its private reception rooms refitted and its mouldy kitchens brought miraculously up to date.

Alain Senderens, well known and respected as one of nouvelle cuisine's most imaginative creators, started out totally unknown in a simple little restaurant with café windows and red checked tablecloths, on the Rue de l'Exposition under the Eiffel Tower. I still remember the fantastic dishes he prepared from his inspired researches in French cookbooks of the 17th and 18th Centuries: turbot à la nage de Bouzy, served with a delicious beurre rouge; smoked lamb as an intriguing first course, garnished if my memory serves me correctly with a cranberry mousse; followed on my first visit by a thunderously good gibelotte de lapereau aux quenelles de lapereau.

He then moved to a more elegant, but still simple restaurant l'Archestrate on the Rue de Varenne, on the Left Bank, where international fame caught up with him. Here he received the highest accolades of the French and International food press with his wonderfully subtle culinary creations. Senderens is a poet and philosopher of the kitchen, an ex-Sunday painter who now puts his art into his inspired dishes, an intrepid voyager who brings back the Orient and the Caribbean to his kitchens. He was one of the first restaurateurs in France to highlight the exotic new fruits and flavours recently arrived from the Pacific. Thin threads of hot pepper and orange and ginger and mint began to enliven his dishes, to be followed by combinations of crayfish with peaches, turbot with raisins, curry of lamb with apple. In Sri Lanka he discovered that vanilla was used throughout the meal to bring a touch of magic to every dish. In France this fragrant spice is used only in desserts and sweets. Senderens created homard rôti à la coque, sauce au vanille. One of his most delicious dishes was a chilled dessert of pineapple, mango and kiwi in a vanilla, ginger and citrus-flavoured passion fruit sauce.

His cooking has not changed; it has moved boldly in a continuous straight line from the early days of the Rue de l'Exposition to full fruition in the luminous sauces of his painter's kitchen palette. He is more than a cook; he above all others seems to be able to blend, faultlessly and effortlessly, dishes as different as his famous chou farci au foie gras (foie gras steamed in a cabbage leaf, served with coarse salt and cracked pepper) - criticized by some, loved by me - and the sophisticated salade d'homard aux mangues (tender moist rounds of lobster, firm and sweet, with their freshly sliced mango accompaniment set against a décor of vari-coloured wild lettuces and garnished with fried sticks of home cured fat bacon, or was it confit of duck?), lightly seasoned with a vinaigrette graced with a subtle touch of the Orient. The majestic côte de boeuf à l'ancienne he garnishes with deep fried strips of baked potato peel - a Chicago touch! Or there's his pigeon désossé aux ragoût de poivrons (grilled pigeon with a pink peppercorn-flavoured ragoût of fresh peppers). Magic, as is the tarte tatin aux mangues - an impressionist painting on a plate of individual upside down tart of caramelised mango slices, set like an island in a wild red sea, with a soft coloured 'moon' of mango sorbet on the horizon. Crisp fried sugared banana strips seem to be setting off in the blood-stained waters. Or there's the pure contrast of the wonderful creamy simplicity of an old-fashioned rice pudding served with consummate style.

Carré des Feuillants   Paris

14 Rue Castiglione, 75001 Paris
(010-331) 42 86 82 82

Closed: Sat + Sun
Last
Orders: 10.00pm

The Carré des Feuillants, Alain Dutournier's newest restaurant venture, located a truffle's throw from the Place Vendôme, is destined for great things. Especially so since Alain Dutournier has already placed himself high in the ratings of innovative young chefs in the new French style (post-nouvelle cuisine) with his much talked about 'return to the land' dishes of his native south-west France.

It is rare for a young chef to run 2 top class restaurants with equal success as Alain Dutournier is doing. French food critics are divided in their loyalties between the original 1900s bistro style of his first restaurant - now run by his wife Nicole, and the newer, grander style of the Carré des Feuillants. And I am no exception. My heart is with Au Trou Gascon but that does not prevent me including the newer, grander Carré among my top Paris favourites. Praise indeed.

But now for the restaurant; located at the end of a super 'super market' gallery of chic shops (not all of them filled on my last visit), the restaurant is a glittering jewel with an elegant, almost masculine decor by Slavik, one of Paris' best known restaurant decorators, in Mitterand/Chirac 1986 style. From the moment you enter the spacious light-coloured entrance hall you have the feeling of the restaurant: cool, modern, cold even, with its high glass ceiling and huge bunches of glass (or are they plastic?) grapes hung in trellised arbour effect and lit at night; its belle epoque fountain complete with refraîchoir for cooling bottles of champagne and white wine; its wide, flat-topped buffet and handful of tables artfully set out - stage-like - for guests to enjoy a drink or perhaps a light informal meal, at lunch time or when the restaurant is full.

To the right of the entrance hall is the busy kitchen, to the left the main dining room (there are 3), business-like, impersonal, rather reminiscent of an ocean liner or an international hotel, its tables set well apart so that businessmen of the quarter can talk without fear of being overheard. The main items of décor here are the huge super-realist paintings of giant edibles - asparagus, artichokes, aubergines - but don't be put off, smiling maître d'hôtel Jean-Guy Lousteau will take you in hand. Warm, friendly and extremely helpful, especially with the wines, he is an old friend of Dutournier's, and partner in the new venture I believe, having transferred from the other restaurant along with a few others on the staff.

The clientele on the two nights I was there seemed almost equally divided between native Parisian and internationals - the latter, no doubt, fugitives from the neighbouring grand hotels: the Ritz, Inter-Continental, Loti and Meurice. While the former come from banks, maisons de mode and jewellers in the nearby Place Vendôme. In other words, this is a 'rich' place for a 'rich' clientele. In fact, on my last visit, my bill was £175 for a dinner for two.

Dutournier's cooking at the Carré des Feuillants still draws upon his prowess with French country dishes of his native Gascony, but dresses them up with touches of modern sophistication for his new clientele. A carpaccio de thon aux piments, for instance, serves thin slices of raw tuna fish cooked in the nouvelle cuisine manner of many restaurants with virgin olive oil and a spark of citron and then tops it off (country cooking) with 3 mousses of rustic green peppers. Raviolis de foie gras à la truffe is comfortingly rural in its execution with foie gras and fresh truffles for its rich stuffing and a well-flavoured consommé as a moistening agent. Pastilla de morue à la vinaigrette d'oursins is a triumph; the homely salt cod cooked in the southern way with Moroccan pastry, the delicately acid sauce of sea urchins bringing a fresh modern note to this very original dish. There are other Moroccan touches on the menu at the Carré, such as deliciously light warkha pastry casings for little galettes of wild mushrooms and touches of Moroccan spices in some of the sauces. I like, too, his lotte grillée (monkfish, nailed with thin strips of anchovy, grilled and served with thin leaves of endive and threads of ginger).

Le Bernardin   Paris

18 Rue Troyon, 75017 Paris
(010-331) 43 80 40 61

Closed: Sun + Mon; Aug
Last
Orders: 11.30pm

One enters the restaurant directly into a long bar with a comfortable corner near the door for lengthy conversations. Beyond, the restaurant is a deep sea blue, with marine engravings. But don't let the idea of a cold décor put you off; the blue is rich and distinguished, like the colour of a private dining room in some great house or, perhaps, the grill room of a '30s paquebot on the French line. The food here is marine too; the Le Cozes (Gilbert is in New York master-minding their new Bernardin in mid-town Manhattan - see review - and Maguy's at the helm in the original Paris restaurant) serve everything from the sea fresh, and with unequalled verve.

Maguy is wonderfully thin, elegant, electric - her smile a brave red gash in a stylish French face. This Bretonne is a Parisienne through and through. It is she who gives the restaurant an electric air as she darts from table to table, flashing around her deep blue lagoon like some beguiling underwater princess. But I found, dining unannouced as a good critic should, that she sailed by more times than she hove to. It looks as if you have to become a regular before you are treated to the bright charms of the maîtresse de maison. When she finally does come over though - and she did - she is kindness, French chic and charm itself.

Chef Serge Polito, in charge of the kitchens now that Gilbert Le Coze is in New York, continues the marine theme of the house: Breton sea dishes enhanced by a new feeling for the delights of the Mediterranean.

First courses to note are le Saint Pierre cru au basilic et à la coriandre (cool thin slices of raw John Dory marinated in virgin olive oil with basil and coriander), oursins chauds au beurre d'oursins (sea urchins - delicate little sea porcupines - with a creamy topping of beaten butter and orange roe) and raie rôtie en papillote à l'ail (skate, minimally cooked en papillote with garlic and aromatics).

Of our table's main courses, I particularly liked filet de turbot au curry (turbot cooked perfectly, à point, like all the fish in this restaurant, and served with a deliciously light curry sauce) and perhaps, best of all, the most perfect turbotin au persil (chicken turbot, pure white and moist, on bright leaves of flat-leafed parsley). A delicate sauce à la minute added moistness and flavour to the parsley.

Top prize of the evening went to the feuilleté de chocolat aux pistaches (literally 3 paper-thin leaves of powdered chocolate filled with a pistachio flavoured crème pâtissière).

Au Trou Gascon   Paris

40 Rue Taine, 75012 Paris
(010-331) 43 44 34 26

Closed: Sat + Sun; 12 Jul - 10 Aug; 24-31 Dec
Last
Orders: 10.00pm

Au Trou Gascon, with its 'brasserie de banlieue' décor in tones of rose-tinted cream, is one of the best little restaurants in Paris. The 1900s setting with its cosy brass lamps, its brasserie banquettes and its door opening onto the street makes you feel comfortable from the moment you cross the threshold into the little entrance bar. And there is Nicole Dutournier - tiny, smiling and completely French - to welcome you.

Claude Teyssier is the maître d'hôtel - left over in the great move of Dutournier's staff to the new and possibly more exciting Carré des Feuillants. He has doubled in stature and charm with his new responsibilities and leads his young team of waiters (few for the number of diners and the succession of delicious dishes that come out of the kitchen) with easy efficiency. The kitchen is in the hands of young (25-year-old) Bernard Broux who worked under Robuchon before moving to Dutournier.

Dutournier comes from south-western France; his cuisine is that of the terroir (back-to-the-land cooking) with a modern touch of Parisian sophistication. Here too a taste of Morocco is in evidence, with exciting accents of ginger, cinnamon, saffron, hot red pepper and coriander; the use of warkha (mille feuille) Moroccan pastry, for some dishes and vegetable accompaniments; luscious country puddings of marinated dried fruits flavoured with cinnamon and a charlotte of chestnuts enhanced with a hint of orange flower water. Persillé de lapereau au vin de jérès - one of his first courses - combines earthy country flavours with sophisticated modern touches - it's a country terrine of young rabbit in a sherry-flavoured jelly; the rabbit moist and tender, the jelly a miracle of flavour; the whole lined in leaves of flat-leafed parsley and wrapped in paper-thin bands of crisp carrot. A wonderful idea and beautifully executed.

On my last visit I chose as a starter les petites crabes au piment doux - 4 little crab shells stuffed with the white meat of crab seasoned with notes of hot red pepper, ginger and coriander, followed by a taste of cassolette de premiers cèpes (wild mushrooms). For my main course, rôti de lotte en gasconnade (a centre 'roast' cut of monkfish coated with a subtle flavouring of anchovies and aromatics); and for a pud, tourtière chaude et glacée aux pruneaux (a delicious combination of hot and cold with a prune ice-cream).

On an earlier visit this last spring (when Dutournier was still in his kitchen) I had one of the best dishes I've ever tasted - a gigotin d'agneau also en gasconnade (leg of tender baby lamb set on a bed of chopped anchovies and aromatics wrapped in flakey pastry and baked until the pastry was crisp and golden and the lamb was pink and moist). Perfection.

Beauvilliers   Paris

52 Rue Lamarck, 75018 Paris
(010-331) 42 54 54 42

Closed:lunch (Sun + Mon); dinner (Sun); 1-25 Sep
Last
Orders: 10.30pm

Beauvilliers - one of the most exciting small restaurants in Paris - is named after the famous 18th-Century chef who was France's first great restaurateur. Formerly 'officier de bouche' of Monsieur, the future Louis XVIII of France, author of one of France's first cookbooks, he opened a series of elegant restaurants in the Palais Royal, lending his sumptuous style to the cuisines of both the Revolution and the Empire. Beauvilliers was a name to conjure with, and eating at Beauvilliers is an experience. The one-time baker's shop off the Butte de Montmartre, dating from the second Empire, is decorated with a profusion of 19th-Century paintings, prints, collection pieces and huge table arrangements on pedestals that separate the tables.

Flowers, flowers, flowers...are the keynote of the restaurant. Whether you are sitting in one of the 3 beautifully appointed dining rooms or, weather permitting, out on the flowered terraces which hang precariously over the steep, narrow stairways to the Butte. Edouard Carlier - blond, tubby-figured proprietor and genius behind Beauvilliers, is as full of charm as the restaurant itself. His personality which is warm and theatrical, though perhaps a trifle overblown, sets the style of the restaurant, its poetically written menu and the food itself. Without him there would be no Beauvilliers; he is its image, its myth. The first time I met Carlier was when he was wandering around his restaurant late one evening, going from table to table talking to the late diners with an enormous grey cat in his arms. He is an interesting man to talk to, wonderfully knowledgeable about food, and happy to impart his enthusiasms and his knowledge. The second time we met it was I who was wandering from table to table one Sunday lunch at my Hintlesham restaurant, to find that Edouard and his associate and maître d'hôtel, Mike, had flown over for the day to sample Carrier fare. The third time was a luncheon with photographer John Stewart and editor Michael Bateman (we were doing a series on the Great Dishes of Our Time for the *Sunday Express* and of course Beauvilliers had to be included).

Beauvilliers is full to bursting point every evening (you have to book 2 weeks in advance) but at lunch it's never busy. At lunch that day there were only a few tables occupied: veteran actor Jean Marais and a few friends at one table, a gaggle of fashion editors and models down one wall, and French restaurant critic and champagne buff George Prade, a friend from my youth, accompanied by his lovely wife Gyp, at another. In minutes, thanks to the extravagant, generous personality of Edouard Carlier, it was a party, one of the pleasantest, and most delicious meals I can remember. I can still recall the menu: minute de rougets en escabehce, fillets of fresh rougets grilled for only an instant on each side and allowed to cool in a dressing of virgin olive oil flavoured with a tiny graines de paradis - hot little chilli peppers - and the slightly smokey tones imparted by a little bouquet of charcoal grilled red pepper in strips. The dish itself was a poem, the rouget fillets cut on the bias into lozenge shapes formed the pink 'leaves' of a pretty little 'tree' whose green 'flower' was an arrangement of thin slices of pan-fried courgette, the stem a long strip of leek. The main course was rognonnade de veau (a whole veal kidney wrapped in a thin sheet of pounded veal with a farce of foie gras, fresh bread-crumbs and truffles, roasted until the veal was tender and the kidney still moist and pink), served with its own truffle- and sherry-scented jus.

Dessert was a series of sublime sorbets; delicate frozen essences of lychee, mango and coconut cream all piled into tall, elegant towers of silver that take diners right back to 'la belle epoque', as in some way do both the restaurant and Carlier himself.

Le Clodenis   Paris

57 Rue Caulaincourt, 75018 Paris
(010-331) 46 06 20 26

Closed: Sun
Last
Orders: 10.30pm

Clodenis is a small restaurant located in a forgotten suburb barely a stone's throw from Paris' Place Clichy. A charming little restaurant with its own terrace - closed in during the winter months, open to the street in the summer - has become one of those 'in' places definitely off the beaten track - where Paris 'locomotives' and the international food buffs take their lovers and friends to dine.

Warmly lit and welcoming, the restaurant is like a comfortably appointed small country inn, a calm oasis furnished with round tables, French provincial chairs with cane seats, antique wall brackets, tall potted plants and old mirrors.

The colours are soft and soothing. Long undercloths of printed material emphasise the country look of the restaurant. Not busy at lunch time - it's too far from commercial Paris, the little restaurant is packed full in the evenings.

The cooking, by Denys Gentes himself and a young chef, in one of the smallest professional kitchens in Paris, is wonderfully light: classic in feeling, yet modern in presentation, with more than a touch of good country common sense that makes this interesting young cook a forerunner to the new French feeling for 'country foods like grandmère used to make'.

I remember with great affection a deliciously light brandade de morue (mousse of salt cod) set in a pool of light cream sauce. 'Toasts' of crisp golden fried bread with a hint of garlic were the perfect foil for the rustic freshness of the salt cod purée. I remember trying a lapin rôti à la moutarde served with fresh noodles and a splendiferous charlotte aux framboises.

Gentes cooks fish, steams them, rather, over seaweed or a court bouillon flavoured with thyme and ginger. He serves them - slightly undercooked, moist and fresh tasting - on a bed of ginger flavoured, tomato purée arranged around gleaming white fillets of brill or turbot in a wavy pattern reminiscent of the briny deep from whence they came. A delicate pat of puréed celery and another of puréed carrots accent this dish.

His chiffonade de homard aux truffes is a triumph of texture and flavour; a small half lobster shell is filled with finely sliced lobster tossed in a light vinaigrette. The lobster is served at room temperature, and garnished with a lightly dressed bed of corn salad, finely sliced lettuce and bitter wild salads.

Assiette du pècheur (a fisherman's catch of one quenelle of pike, three goujonettes of sole and a nugget of steamed brill) is highlighted by 3 delicate sauces: a light purée of ginger-flavoured tomato for the brill, celery root for the sole, and beurre blanc for the quenelle. Canard rôti aux fruits served with a colourful garland of fresh figs and wild strawberries in a tangy fruit and wine sauce is another Gentes speciality of note.

Tan Dinh   Paris

60 Rue de Verneuil, 75007 Paris
(010-331) 45 44 04 84

Closed: Sun; 15-31 Aug
Last
Orders: 11.00pm

It might seem strange to include a Vietnamese restaurant among my top favourite restaurants in Paris, but such is the case. The Vifian family - brothers Robert and Freddy, and M Vifian, père - have created a most enchanting little restaurant decorated with Japanese lacquered panels of a warm rich coral bordered in black wood; mirrors, screens and exotic plants complete the Eastern setting in this quiet backwater of St Germain-des-Prés. The street floor restaurant (seating only 30 covers) is the one to aim for; the downstairs room (30 more covers) seems more claustrophobic somehow. And make sure, like for all the other restaurants in this round up, that you book in advance. Tan Dinh is deservedly popular.

Robert Vifian is the mentor of the family, constantly experimenting with flavours and choosing new wines (Tan Dinh has one of the most interesting wine lists in Paris with 120 white Bourgognes and over 180 Pomerols). When I asked him in London recently to explain to me his unique style of cooking - Vietnamese-based with Japanese and Thai overtones, and a freshness of flavour that owes much to modern French cooking - he explained that for him Vietnam has not existed as a country since 1975 and that his aim is to create a magical, modern Vietnamese cuisine as it might have been if his country still existed.

The cooking at Tan Dinh is imaginative, innovative and well suited to modern Parisian palates.

One of my favourite dishes on a recent visit to Tan Dinh is rouleaux Vietnamiens (deliciously crisp spring rolls, fatter than we are used to, cut in half to display their cargo of raw and poached vegetables, beansprouts and mint leaves served with a light soy flavoured sauce). The excellent raviolis Vietnamiens is of interest too, with its filling of minced smoked goose. Another favourite house speciality is emincé de boeuf Tan Dinh (a strip fillet of beef grilled in one piece western-style, instead of in thin strips in the classic Vietnamese manner). Robert marinates it in oriental savours - badiane, lemon grass, cinnamon, nutmeg and a splash of nuoc nam (Vietnamese fermented fish sauce) and then slices it to serve it well-browned, highly flavoured on the outside, meltingly rare on the inside; a delicious invention. Or try champignons sèches farcis (large, flat, dried mushrooms soaked in hot water and stuffed with finely chopped scallops and coconut cream, spiked with finely chopped red chilli pepper, ginger, garlic and citronelle). And for dessert; beignets de mangue (fresh mango fritters).

Robert Carrier's New York

New York City is a great melting pot of food in all its myriad forms. Its thousands of restaurants - there are over 12,000 new licences granted each year - represent virtually every type of cuisine known to the world.

New Yorkers today are obsessed with the art of dining...and dining well. Yet until fairly recently most people ate out only on special occasions, or limited their excursions to an inexpensive local restaurant in their own neighbourhood. Today it is the meal cooked at home that has become the special occasion, while dinners for two (with pick-up tabs of over $100.00) have become commonplace.

According to a recent New York survey, people are spending more on eating out than ever before; new restaurants are jammed, and talking about food is the great excitement for New York's new food trendies. Of course, the expense account (at this writing, 80% tax allowable) is responsible for a great deal of this new obsession. Business entertaining is important business in New York where making a deal is king and hosting one or two dinners in town is a legitimate - and necessary - part of every executive's life. But there is another, more practical side to this new phenomenon: the small size of the average New York apartment and its kitchen. It is the high cost of real estate and the low vacancy rate in Manhattan that are forcing people into restaurants. As families grow and living quarters diminish in size, public spaces for entertaining - restaurants - are taking on a new importance. The result is a social revolution: dining out has become a necessary social ritual; and restaurants today have become the best entertainment in town: at once an artistic experience and the outward manifestation of worldly success. Brillat Savarin's 19th-Century dictum, "You are what you eat," has become New York's 20th-Century counterpart, "You are *where* you eat!"

The restaurant scene in New York is ever-changing: the 'in' places (the restaurants New Yorkers like to see and be seen in) termed by trendies the 'hottest tickets in town', are in constant movement. A few - Lutèce, Le Cirque, Le Cygne, the Four Seasons - are glamorous New York constants; others - Aurora, Le Bernardin and Lafayette - are exciting newcomers, jostling avidly for first place. The following are my firm favourites - all of them outstanding, all of them difficult to get into (you will have to book) and most of them, I am afraid, expensive. But no trip to New York would be complete for me - no matter how short the duration - if I couldn't wangle my way into one, or more, of them during my stay.

The Four Seasons   New York

99 East 52nd Street
(010-1) 212-754 9494

Closed: Sun

The Four Seasons - now in its 27th year - is a New York landmark, considered by some to be the greatest American restaurant of our time.

Created by Joe Baum (see Aurora below) in the 1950s as a glittering restaurant expressive of an equally glittering New York, it has turned into a media meeting place for New York's power élite.

The clientele of the Grill Room at lunch time is the most distinguished of its kind in the city. These regular customers aren't socialites or even café society as they are at Le Cirque and Le Cygne, or serious eaters as they are at Lutèce or the Quilted Giraffe - they are the New York achievers. In fact, at lunch, the Grill Room is almost a private club for New York's top professionals.

The ground floor entrance hall is all travertine marble, unfurnished, cold, relieved only by 4 photographic blow-ups. It is not until you start mounting the broad marble stairs that you get a feel for the modern majesty of the place. The upper floor level, with its 20-foot-high ceilings, its huge Richard Lippold hanging sculpture of 3,000 bronze rods, the seasonal planting of trees, the score of well-dressed waiting staff, and the elegant reservations desk, where co-owners Tom Margittai and Paul Kovi stand together or singly, to welcome you. The solid charm of this serious restaurant operation is built on equally solid efficiency: as soon as you give your name, a seating card with your name on it will be given to a young captain, and from then on you will be addressed personally throughout the meal. A little down the hall (hung with a huge Picasso theatre curtain) is the Pool Room - the restaurant's most glamorous dining room with its rosewood walls and great windows festooned wih ever-rippling strands of bronzed aluminium. Here square tables are set in majestic fashion around the 20-foot lit pool, placed strategically in the centre of the room, its hard corners softened by towering rubber trees.

Chef Seppi Renggli, pencil slim and grey-haired, is one of the highest paid chefs working in America today. With his team of 32 kitchen staff, he serves over 1,000 meals daily to the restaurant's discriminating diners. The Four Seasons is completely fresh-food-orientated, and although the big kitchen contains several walk-in refrigerators, the freezer is only used for ice-creams, sorbets and frozen desserts. Swiss-born Renggli, married to an Indonesian, has worked in Amsterdam, Lucerne, Stockholm and the Caribbean before coming to the Four Seasons kitchen. His cooking is eclectic, international, imaginative and sound with no hint of nouvelle cuisine. Excited by new combinations of flavour, he scours the world for new ingredients to add colour and excitement to his cooking, and uses sun-dried tomatoes, lemon grass, jalapena peppers, and the zest of not only orange and lemon, but lime and kumquat in his recipes. His food is real food, substantial stuff, but with a bow to what the Four Seasons calls 'spa' cuisine for those diners who eat out frequently, or who have a weight problem, and must look for something lighter on the menu.

Look for American-style dishes such as blackened red fish served with re-fried Mexican beans wrapped in poached cabbage leaves; veal Four Seasons (tender fillet of veal served in its own reduced jus with an artichoke stuffed with crabmeat); Chinese wontons filled with wild mushrooms; sautéed calves' liver with avocado (one of the original creations of the Four Seasons 27 years ago and still on the menu) is a classic: the thin slices of delicate liver cooked over a high heat so that the exterior is beautifully browned on the outside, with the inside wonderfully moist, pink and tender; the brilliant green of the sliced avocado, a perfect foil. Grilled gravlax with a dill and mustard flavoured sauce is a great favourite with Grill Room regulars, as is the crisp shrimp filled with mustard fruits, (the huge prawns battered and deep-fried, the sauce made of the famous mustard fruits of Cremona).

Four Seasons desserts are not as exciting perhaps as the rest of the foods available on the menu. The famous chocolate cake is a good bet as are the fruit-fresh sorbets. And for those in search of a truly American sweet, the walnut tart is of interest.

Great things are afoot in the Grill Room at the Four Seasons and by the time you read these pages, the famous room will have a super new look with hand rubbed walnut walls, a muted silver ceiling, a deep blue carpet studded with multiple colour bursts and intimate new table settings (small lamps at each table, new china, silver, glassware and linen) to personalise this formerly austere setting. And a glossy new menu has been commissioned from designer Emil Antonucci, which is reportedly a reworking of the splendid rice-paper menu of the restaurant's early days: a design collectors' piece for the cognoscenti.

Le Cirque   New York

58 East 65th Street
(010-1) 212-794 9292

Closed: Sun

Le Cirque - elegant eating place for the rich, the chic, the powerful and the famous - is the kind of restaurant that could only happen in New York. Under the leadership of suave, John Wayne look-alike, Sirio Maccione, it has held its place as one of the city's top restaurants for the past twelve years. No mean feat when you consider that Maccione serves about 200 dinners a night, 6 nights a week, with lunch times that are equally crowded. Everybody and his cousin, seem to want to squeeze into the coral, velvet-covered, elbow-to-elbow banquettes that ring the cool, classically decorated room.

This is a restaurant that has carefully allotted celebrity tables: on my last visit (one of my guests was a famous New York theatre critic) we had the Nixon table, the corner table in a line-up of 8 to 10 that overlook the soft grey trellised room with its painted panels in warm browns and corals depicting elephants and monkeys at play in French 18th-Century style. Imposing wall lights, like great bouquets of tulips fashioned in black-painted tole, are set between the panels and create an immediately recognisable symbol of fantasy and elegance.

Mirrored columns, dotted strategically about the restaurant, make sure that wherever you sit, cameo views of the restaurant are visible and you can catch the action. And action there is: head waiters pass, proudly carrying trays of chilled beluga caviar from table to table; silver baskets of Italian white truffles or porcini mushrooms are displayed, and there is a constant stream of captains, waiters, wine waiters and Mr Maccione, or one of his 3 sons called in to help, not to mention the guests themselves.

The intimate little bar to the left of the restaurant, where bar man Rudi officiates, making the best iced Kir Royale imaginable, served in an equally iced tall tulipe glass, is a good place to spend your evening.

The bar serves as backstage hub of the busy restaurant. From there, as you comfortably sip your cassis-flavoured Champagne, you can watch head waiter Renato lovingly prepare the Cirque's famous pasta con tartuffi (fresh pasta tossed in a chafing dish with butter, and then in chicken stock, until the pasta has absorbed the concentrated flavours; then a quick twist of the pepper mill, a sprinkling of grated parmesan and the dish is whisked off to the table where generous amounts of razor-thin slices of fresh white truffle are shaved over the hot pasta). Le Cirque has always been famous for its pasta dishes: one of the best known, imitated in every Italian restaurant in New York, is pasta primavera (an elegant combination of fresh pasta simmered in butter and then in chicken stock as above, garnished with jewel-bright segments of fresh asparagus, broccoli, cauliflower, mange-touts and petits pois). Pasta primavera is never on the menu (regulars ask for it) for the simple reason that when you are serving as many covers a meal as they do at Le Cirque, it is very difficult to prepare this dish properly; it must be made strictly to order - and from scratch.

The menu at Le Cirque is extensive. The food - under the direction of Daniel Bulod - is of the highest quality; classical French with Italian and modern overtones, well suited to the restaurant's aristocratic clientele. Influenced by the general luxury and hi-jinks of the restaurant, we decided to try three of the dishes made with American fresh foie gras (a relative newcomer to restaurant fare): coeur de truffe sous le cendre au foie gras (a whole black truffle robed in New York State foie gras and served hot in a puff pastry shell); medaillons de foie gras aux pommes (pan sautéed fresh foie gras served with caramelized apple slices) and a lobster and foie gras salad in a light vinaigrette dressing, garnished with thinly sliced green asparagus spears, artichoke heart and quartered quails' eggs.

Main courses at Le Cirque feature milk-fed veal - selle de veau farci aux pistaches (roast veal served in its own jus, with thin leaves of Belgian endive and thin slices of artichoke heart). The saddle is boned, stuffed with chopped cooked spinach, mushrooms and pistachio nuts. Or a fine fat veal chop, pan-seared and served with a pastry case piled high with wild mushrooms. Game - pheasant, quail or pigeon -and sole prepared in many different ways and a delicious sautéed chicken served in a rich wine sauce enhanced with chopped tomato, mushroom and ginger are restaurant favourites. And Le Cirque, thanks to Maccione's Italian background, was one of the first New York restaurants to offer carpaccio, served here as a main course, thinly sliced with a salsa verde and freshly grated parmesan - delicious.

Chef Daniel Bulod and his pastry cooks obviously have a thing about country sweets; we particularly liked the old-fashioned apple pie with custard and fresh fruits in syrup, the hot lemon soufflé, intense in flavour, served with fresh raspberries in syrup, a special flourless soufflé of passion fruit, and the feuilleté of pear with its accompanying praline ice-cream and crème chantilly. What is reputed to be Le Cirque's most famous sweet, crème brûlée Le Cirque, a cooked custard cream with a glazed caramel covering, was served with an intriguing Italian dessert wine, Malvasia delle Lipari Tipo Passito from Salina.

Lutèce   New York

249 East 50th Street
(010-1) 212-752 2225

Closed: Sun; 26 Jul - 5 Sep

The restaurant is located in a small brownstone on East 50th Street just west of 2nd Avenue, and has been called the finest French restaurant in New York. The entrance is cramped; you enter right from the street, down two steps to the tiny entrance hall-cum-bar with its zinc-covered bar and four café-style tables, the kind you might find in any small provincial restaurant or café in France.

There are two rather formal upstairs dining rooms and a covered 'garden' room in the rear of the bar with a high vaulted glass ceiling, pink washed walls behind white trellis and columns of brick supporting green palms in huge pots. This is an elegant room with a fresh 'party' feel about it.

If the restaurant is comparatively modest, there is nothing modest about the cooking. Chef/proprietor André Soltner has been in charge of the kitchens at Lutèce since the famous restaurant opened 25 years ago. Today, he and his assistant, Chef Bertrand, create food that is classically orientated, but with a light, modern feeling.

Soltner cooks with love, buying the finest ingredients available and cooking them with imagination and flair. He loves his small restaurant with its limited seating capacity, its French porcelaines and crystal, its Christofle silver and its spanking new décor by famous restaurant decorator Sam Lapota. He feels it gives him the possibility of maintaining personal contact between kitchen and dining room, and the opportunity of producing his perfect renditions of classical French food.

Look out for famous first courses - timbales d'escargots à l'alsacienne (snails served in minute porcelaine pots, the snails simmered in a wine-flavoured butter accented with fresh herbs) and pelerines à la meridionale (bay scallops, lightly browned in butter, served in a rich concentrate of tomatoes and mushrooms spiked by a hint of Mediterranean flavour). I like, too, the ethereal quenelles de brochet (feather-light turrets of fish fillets, cream and egg white, bathed in a delicate saffron sauce and accompanied by crescents of flaky pastry).

Main courses at Lutèce include poussin aux herbes (a whole young poussin roasted with herbs in a rich herby sauce); medaillons de veau aux morilles (medallions of veal served with wild mushrooms). Try, too, Mr Soltner's magic ways with fish and game when in season. Cooked to just the right point and served with delicate sauces that confirm his award, Meilleur Ouvrier de France, in 1968. And I almost forgot to mention his magnificient côte de boeuf au beurre rouge (a superb surloin cooked to crusty perfection - rare beneath its charred crust - served with a delicious red wine butter and meaty wild mushrooms). Delicious.

Desserts at Lutèce are famous: try the admirable soufflé glacé aux framboises (a skilful combination of chilled layered raspberry cream and genoise sauced with fresh raspberries) and the fresh-tasting French apple tart with its crumbly pastry base.

Le Bernardin   New York

155 West 51st Street
(010-1) 212-489 1515

Closed: Sun

It seems that the electric, eclectic sister-and-brother team, Maguy and Gilbert Le Coze of Paris restaurant fame, always dreamed of conquering 'sea city' New York with a cross-the-Atlantic version of their starred Parisian restaurant Le Bernardin. Well, here they are (Gilbert that is; Maguy, except for a brief stint at the launching early in 1986, holds the fort in Paris). And here I am, too, ready to be stunned by the décor so bountifully provided by Equitable Life in their great new 7th Avenue building at a reputed cost of $4,000,000.

From outside, the restaurant is most impressive, a long clean bank of huge plate glass windows with modern, high-tech awnings, each with its own soft spotlight shining from underneath to give brightness and authority to the cool façade. Inside is cool, too, with a spacious entrance hall and bar separated from the warmly-lit dining room by a handsome glass screen. The room is clearly visible from the entrance hall and the bar, but protected in a sense by the folding glass panels of the screen.

The restaurant is a sea symphony of warm, sand-stoned woods, greyed blue, cut velvet walls and underwater green upholstery. It is a huge, handsome, softly lit room with a lofty coffered, light wood ceiling; great sways of sand-coloured drop Venetian curtains, and huge paintings lit by grey-blue vistas of some distant Breton shore. The whole room is like the great hall of some noble house near the sea of Brittany; yet almost startlingly modern in feeling with its coffered ceiling and bank of pale curtains.

The tables are set generously apart and about 1½ inches lower than usual for extra dining comfort, a sign that Philip George, designer of the American Festival Café and Aurora has been here. The restaurant - thanks to its generous size and high ceilings - is the perfect setting for what is possibly the best restaurant in the city. The night we were there, it literally buzzed with the happy murmur of success, everyone supremely happy to be there and wanting everyone to know it. We met in the bar for a quick Champagne before dinner and had a moment to talk briefly to the brilliant, young master chef/proprietor who had just popped out of his spotless kitchens to share for a moment in the general bubble of the restaurant. Gilbert Le Coze is the movie star of young chefs; his gallic good looks and presence - not to mention his culinary flair and excitement - will make him number one this side of the Atlantic. His cooking gives fish a new dimension of freshness of flavour. A magnificently rich fish soup for example, intense, tomatoey, rouille-flavoured and served with crisp rounds of French bread and freshly grated cheese, is a refreshing breath of the Mediterranean in New York. Both of the raw fish appetisers - carpaccios of raw fish, really - are out of this world. How, you might ask me, can raw shavings of sea bass brushed with virgin olive oil and a fine swathe of finely sliced fresh coriander leaves be so different? But the slivered sea bass with coriander leaves, served at Le Bernardin, is so elusive in flavour, so subtle in texture, so different from its more mundane versions, that I've almost come to think of it as the only one in existence. The same, though to a lesser degree, is true of pounded tuna (not a brandade as I had thought, but pounded super-thin like a carpaccio); brushed with olive oil and spinkled with cracked pepper and chopped chives.

Other appetisers of special interest: fresh oysters, just poached rather than cooked, served with a truffled cream sauce and (when in season) sea urchins, those salty little spiked meteors of the sea: M Le Coze cooks the orange oursin roe with beaten butter and the warm nectar of the shellfish and serves it in the shell. Delicious.

Main courses include poached lobster with basil butter - served with the shell split in half and slivers of fresh basil; and thin strips of pink salmon presented on a red-hot dish, its elegant sorrel and white wine sauce still bubbling. I like, too, the roasted monkfish, served in slices on the crisp-sautéed shredded green of Savoy cabbage, with a hint of lemon in the butter sauce.

Fillets of pan-seared pompano served on a light beurre blanc sauce flecked with leaves of bright green Italian parsley do not equal, I am afraid, the superb version of this dish made with chicken turbot that I enjoyed two weeks before in the Paris-based Le Bernardin. But this is the fault of the fish, not the cooking, the flesh a little too oily for the delicately simple, 'country-style' parsley sauce.

It was almost a relief - after all this excellence - to see that the sweets served in the New York restaurant are not as good as those I had tasted in the Paris Le Bernardin just two weeks before. The chocolate mille feuille with pistachio cream and chocolate sauce is but a shadow of its Parisian original - the pastry thicker and correspondingly less crisp, the piped pistachio filling too pronounced in flavour. Another mille feuille - this time filled with diced green apple and raisins, was frankly disappointing. Top favourite had to be warm mousse of passion fruit with raspberries - which we all tasted - the hot mousse with raspberries hiding under a crackling brown sugar glaze.

The $55.00 fixed-price dinner is a bargain in New York terms, including coffee, tiny cookies and crisp, chocolate coated truffles.

Aurora   New York

60 East 49th Street
(010-1) 212-692 9292

Closed :Sun

Joe Baum is the most important food personality in America today. Creator of some of New York's most famous restaurants - The Four Seasons, The Fonda del Sol, The Forum of The Twelve Caesars, Windows on the World and the whole exciting complex of restaurants at the World Trade Centre - he is the moody, generous, neurotic, obsessed near-genius who has done more to make dining out an exciting adventure in America than any other man alive today.

I have known Joe Baum ever since my *Sunday Times* days in the early '60s when I came to New York to feature the first 3 restaurants listed above for the then new colour supplement. At that time they were quite simply the 3 most exciting restaurants in the world. Baum had his finger on the pulse of a whole new movement: restaurants were going to gain a surprising new importance in America. And the Baum restaurants - great themed extravaganzas combining flair for food with theatrical presentation, great art and great architecture - were there to astound and delight a new-found public, ready for new experiences and new sensations.

Baum has always been a restless perfectionist, compulsively nagging and niggling his way through countless tastings and testings, with endless re-appraisals and soul-searchings until the formula was finally just right. He is still doing this today. But this time, the new restaurant, Aurora, is his own, designed and built with the help of old friends, Milton Glaser, New York's top graphic-arts designer, and restaurant architect, Philip George - a tried and true team that have worked with him on other projects and will undoubtedly continue doing so for some time to come. (There are rumours that the trio are already working on a revamp of the Rockefeller Centre's famous Rainbow Room).

The basic theme behind the restaurant was to create a great bar-grill-restaurant like the great dream places of Europe - London's old Savoy, Vienna's Demels, the Paris Ritz - playgrounds for adults where one could lunch and dine in a variety of ways in a variety of moods; where the food would be classic with modern overtones, memorable but not pretentious, and where men and women could effortlessly play host in a setting of soft, honeyed woods and fresh, muted colours.

Aurora, named after Baum's favourite goddess, Goddess of the Dawn, is a 'new beginning' restaurant, a place to create your own future, according to Baum. It celebrates Baum's new beginning as restaurant creator/proprietor; French Chef Gerard Pangaud's new beginning as top chef in America after owning his own Michelin 2-starred restaurant in Paris; and is a warm, sensuous setting for all new beginnings, whether new friendships, new loves or new business deals.

There is a feeling of comfort and ease immediately you enter the restaurant and are greeted at the door by Ray Wellington, Aurora's young knowledgeable manager; and there's a great sense of space. This is a serious room for serious diners: large square tables, and comfortable, caramel leather and steel 'swing' chairs that rotate easily on their axis to allow an unusual amount of flexibility for the diner. Giove leather sofas are placed back-to-back at tables set around the periphery of the room: each sofa faced by 2 comfortable leather covered chairs of the same design. Other tables for four are spaced throughout the restaurant.

There are none of the usual restaurant touches - no candles, no spotlights, no flowers - no drama, except for the luminous setting of the central bar with its smooth polished pink, grey and black granite counters and the irridescent glow of its down-turned 'bubble' lights which, with the honeyed wood panelling of the walls, give a turn-of-the-century Viennese coffee house look to the restaurant. And what could be more timely with the Vienna 1900 exhibition drawing record crowds all over the world? Lunch is served daily at the bar from noon to 5.00pm. I'd like to have breakfast there...or even supper when the restaurant is full.

There are 'bubbles' everywhere in soft tones of cream, cinnamon, pink and pale blue (shades of dawn and new beginnings?) rising through the mid-blue carpeting; on the plates specially commissioned from Villeroy and Boch; etched on the glasses; and stiched onto each waiter's jacket. The silver from France is heavy, well-balanced, set inexplicably on the right of the plate (an eccentric Baum touch!) Menus are surprisingly simple for a restaurant of this calibre: men's club 'no-nonsense' printed sheets inserted into the simplest of card holders.

Chef Gerard Pangaud (now 33) opened his own restaurant in Paris in 1976, earning 1 star from Michelin and a 16/20 rating from Gault Millau when he was only 23 years old (something of a record). His second restaurant gained him his second Michelin star and a hefty 17/20 from Gault Millau in 1982, before he was enticed away by Joe Baum for the new restaurant project that was to become Aurora. The two creators obviously get along well, are comfortable together and enjoy working together. They spent a year touring the world's great restaurants before settling down to the serious business of creating the menu at Aurora. Pangaud is an inventive cook, very much at home with the classic; it is obvious that he and Baum will be doing great things together. A new dawn.

The food at Aurora is already most impressive: I particularly like the sumptuous, colourful Napoleon of layered vegetables (3 paper-thin rectangles of cheese-flavoured pastry with a cargo of crisp, crisp vegetables - brilliant green mange-touts, haricots verts and garden peas (almost raw) - the 2 bottom layers of pastry spread with a thin herby green purée, the top layer garnished with 1-inch spikes of fresh chive, the whole served on a sauce of finely grated carrot in a lemony beurre blanc. Other robust starters of note: short-smoked salmon (a handsome turn of phrase) with lentils (a fat pink rectangle of salmon set on a bed of crisp, well-flavoured lentils); and cream of pumpkin soup with julienne of sorrel (a creamy golden soup laced with threads of brilliant green), the sharp acid note of the sorrel setting off the creamy richness of the pumpkin to perfection.

Main courses: sautéed sea scallops, red wine sauce, (a ring of pan-fried golden scallops served on a pool of red wine sauce enriched with finely chopped shallots and beef marrow). Sautéed veal chop with chanterelles, a great thick veal chop, moist and tender with the exterior surfaces brushed with a rich-tasting butter glaze, served with a delicious slew of wild mushrooms. But my favourite and a truly great dish is the red snapper antiboise - a fillet of red snapper lightly grilled and served on 3 rounds of toasted French bread, one spread with a garlicky topping, one with tapenade and the third with a green herby mixture. The dish is garnished with 2 square-cut batons of red pepper, courgette and aubergine, sautéed quickly so that the colour and texture remain fresh, rustic, delicious. On the other side of the fish are 2 oval garlic quenelles, a tiny pile of thinly sliced olives and fresh herbs, brushed with imported French olive oil (L'Olivier).

The desserts excel each other: we tasted 13 of them on the evening I was there - an orgy of Pangaud delights, they kept arriving at the table, each more delicious than the last. My favourites: hot plum tart on a circle of paper-thin crumbly pastry; the thinly sliced plums brushed with a light, almost sugar-free glaze and accompanied by a delicious vanilla ice-cream; a sumptuously rich chocolate Napoleon with preserved fruit; a flour-less chocolate pudding with pistachio ice-cream and a lovely granita of Zinfandel with berries, the tart, sweet, winey flavour and crisp crackle of the frozen wine crystals a great foil for the summer fruits.

Lafayette   New York

65 East 56th Street
(010-1) 212-832 1565

Closed: Sat + Sun

Swissotel, owners of The Drake Hotel on Park Avenue at 56th Street, have lured Louis Outhier (La Napoule-based French momentarily three star chef) away from his other two nouvelle cuisine-inspired restaurants - 90 Park Lane in London's Grosvenor House Hotel, and the Lafayette Hotel in Boston - to open New York's latest restaurant find, Lafayette. Outhier transferred young chef Jean-Georges Vongerichten from his Boston restaurant to reveal his sunny Mediterranean-style food at The Drake.

The low-ceilinged locale that used to house the famous Drake Room in the '30s and '40s has been transformed at a reputed cost of 1.5 million dollars into a dining room of great charm - with soft lighting, cream panelled walls, a mirrored central ceiling, pale shaded brass wall appliqués in the shape of swans, and Art Deco black metal railings at each of the 4 central columns that separate tables in the centre of the room from others. The effect is like a dream version of a French provincial hotel, 'ho-hum' perhaps in Aix-les-Bains or Nancy, but refreshingly different in New York. The room is decorated in soft flower colours with comfortable French provincial armchairs covered in faded rose velvet with checked material backs. And for those who like additional comfort, there are 4 semi-circular banquettes in rust-coloured leather, large enough for three people. Widely spaced square tables fill the rest of the room.

Food at Lafayette is modern French - cuisine actuelle - with the added touches of Louis Outhier's nouvelle cuisine garnishes. In addition to the à la carte menu there are 3 interesting 'tasting' menus: one composed of seafood dishes at $53.00, a second a little more adventurous at $60.00 and a 'surprise' 7-course special at $75.00. All begin with tasty 'on-the-house' morsels designed to put you in the mood for the treats to come. On the evening we were there, it was a tiny cassolette of John Dory in a creamy sauce, garnished with tiny dice of cucumber and tomato. At other times it might be fragile raviolis filled with chopped crayfish in a herb-flavoured broth, or a chilled soup of cucumber garnished with prawns and fresh dill.

Specialities to look out for: shirred egg served with a vodka and lime flavoured chantilly, topped with a generous dollop of beluga caviar - nouvelle cuisine elegance at its best. A delicate skewer of pieces of langoustine set in a lightly breaded fish mousse, sautéed in butter until faintly crisp outside and served with a creamy langoustine sauce sparked with finely chopped fresh oyster. Another winner is the luxurious marjolaine de foie gras et son consommé: a smooth mousse of fresh foie gras packed between crisp thin layers of sugarless almond pastry and served with a richly flavoured game consommé. A house speciality that I shall have to return for (I just didn't have room) is red snapper en écailles de courgette et son aïoli (red snapper with courgettes, tomatoes and aïoli).

Perhaps one of the most truly original and delicious dishes at Lafayette is Outhier's expertly fashioned selle d'agneau en robe de pomme croustillante (a fat medallion of lamb cut from the saddle and wrapped in an unusual crust made of thinly sliced potato, held together with hair-like threads of raw potato and butter, the lamb in its crisp golden potato case served like a rich golden pear with leaves of red tomato slices and a stem of rolled basil leaf). A delicious contrast of flavours and textures.

Game is to be particularly recommended at Lafayette. Of particular note are tender venison with wild blueberries, and aiguillette de canard de Barbarie à l'armagnac (a fan of thinly-sliced breast of duck in a butter and armagnac glaze, served with caramelized apple slices and superb duck-shaped golden croûton: a wonderful contrast of complementary textures).

Anyone who has been to Louis Outhier's other establishments doesn't need me to tell him that the meal will end with an overwhelming tasting of mousse-topped cakes and creams that are as dazzling to look at as they are to eat: try the rich chocolate mousse cake, the lemon cake, the rich caramel ice-cream or the refreshingly tart orange sabayon.

The wine list of mainly French wines has some well-priced bottles at the lower end a selection of rather high-priced Bordeaux, should the desire take you. Swiss wines (the hotel group's Swiss influence showing here) and American wines round out the selection.

The Quilted Giraffe   New York

955 Second Avenue
(010-1) 212-753 5355

Closed: lunch; dinner (Sat + Sun)

Barry and Karen Wine's restaurant in New York, The Quilted
Giraffe, is one of the hottest tickets in town, according to food
buffs in the know (others are Montrachet, Le Bernardin, and the
perenially green Le Cirque and the Four Seasons.) Wonderful
clear soups are served in square Japanese dishes with attractive
mosaics of seafood and artfully cut vegetables; pan-seared,
almost raw, cubes of tuna fish are set on a delicate bed of Chinese
vegetables; the finest slices of lightly grilled polenta are coupled
with black truffles; Mr Wine's beggar's purses - delicately thin
crêpes filled with beluga caviar and a dollop of crème fraîche and
tied with threads of raw green onion ($30.00 supplement) - have
become a noose signature. But perhaps the most deliciously
startling dish is the hot chocolate soufflé into which an icy cold
bitter espresso ice-cream is tossed in front of the diner. The rich,
hot chocolate soufflé contrasting to perfection with the cold,
bitter ice-cream.

Each year, Barry Wine and his wife Karen visit the best
restaurants in Europe or the East and bring back ideas for their
New York restaurant. Wine presents such delights as ravioli
stuffed with wild mushrooms, rose pink rack of lamb with
Chinese mustard, and marinated chicken breast, grilled, sliced
and served on a bed of sweet potato chips and accompanied by
lightened aïoli sauce.

The restaurant's 2 dining rooms are filled nightly (the restaurant is open evenings only, Monday through Friday) with an
elegant crowd willing to book weeks in advance for the pleasure
of spending $150 a head for an evening's gastronomic entertain-
ment. And entertainment it is. This is no plain and simple food
operation: Barry Wine, American-born and self-trained, is one of
the most brilliant and imaginative young chefs in America. His
food is charismatic, different, delicious: his conjunctions of
texture and flavour at once daring and infallible; his new-found
interest in the cooking of the Orient bringing new delights to
dining possibilities in New York.

The restaurant is arranged on 2 floors with the main dining
room on the ground floor and a more intimate room on the first
floor. I like to dine in the ground floor room where the action is: a
long, narrow room with warm, cream-toned walls and ceiling, and
a panelled mahoghany wainscot. It has Art Deco wall and ceiling
lights and stainless steel-framed mirrors and service tables which
give a charming 1930s look to the room. Enamelled metal
Chinoiserie designs from a silk factory in Lyons make interesting

wall panels. But to me, the most interesting feature of the room is an inspired room divider which separates the small professional kitchen from the dining room. Its etched glass panels slide back easily to allow waiters to pass through orders and receive dishes from the kitchen, a clever change from the obtrusive swinging doors of most restaurants.

The restaurant - since the Wines opened a new, more casual verison of The Giraffe nearby - is under the capable management of Wayne, the personable young front-of-house host who communicates his dedication, energy and pride in the place, making guests comfortable from the moment they enter.

On my last visit we tried Mr Wine's new Oriental Tasting Menu (7 delicious Orient-inspired dishes served on hand-made Japanese pottery dishes plus a staggering array of house sweets costing $100.00 per head). Sounds expensive? Not when you try it. It is overwhelming in its variety of texture and delicate balancing of subtle flavours.

The menu begins with a slender rectangular pottery plate, commercial envelope size, with one claw of lobster, lightly poached; a cluster of the thinnest game chips I have ever seen, deep fried to a translucent orange gold in rich nutty flavoured butter; and a tiny pile of peeled, sliced cucumber crescents dotted with poppy seeds and dressed with a smoke flavoured sesame vinaigrette.

Our second course was a wasabi pizza (the thin individual bread pastry-based pizza spread with a fiery-flavoured wasabi pommade topped with a thin slice of raw tuna) followed by caramelized sweetbreads (two firm pyramids) served with an accompanying fried egg set in a creamy purée of potatoes ringed by a meat flavoured glaze. Different and delicious in its home-spun simplicity.

Our fourth course was a wide pottery mug of rich tomato consommé topped with a round (geranium-like) Chinese apple mint leaf under which swam tiny perfectly-cut, razor-thin fish-shaped slices of crisp carrot, radish, red and yellow pepper. An inspired dish.

Fifth course: a thinly-sliced poached chicken breast set in a richly coloured quince sauce with a diminutive pile of diced pink quince as its only accompaniment, followed by confit of duck with creamy garlic potatoes (a super moist magret of duck simmered until tender in duck fat, then drained and coated with bread crumbs and pan grilled, served with crisp-cooked scalloped potatoes in a puréed garlic cream). Attractive touch: 2 glazed slices of American butternut squash and sugar peas in the pod. A winner.

Seventh course: 1 baby lamb chop, cooked to perfection, pink and moist, served with a purée of celeriac and tiny green asparagus spears.

The meal ended with an amazing succession of The Quilted Giraffe's superb house sweets - the orient left aside for this final course - which are all-American in inspiration. The details are lost in a mist of delight except for an astounding chocolate terrine with pistachio sauce and a trio of strawberry slices for colour: a hazelnut waffle with vanilla ice-cream and maple syrup sauce and a homely pecan brownie served warm with whipped cream.

The Quilted Giraffe - now in its eighth year in New York - is one of the most exciting restaurants of the city - vying for the top place with new-comer Le Bernardin and old-timer Lutèce.

Montrachet   New York

239 West Broadway
(010-1) 212-219 2777

Closed: lunch (daily); Sun

Do you want to get lost even if you have been supplied with meticulous directions on how to get there; venture below New York's Canal Street into the stark hinterlands of TriBeCa (the triangle below Canal Street); have your taxi driver back up for 3 blocks when he misses the right turning and look as if you are mad when you get out, chortling with adventurous glee at finding the unfindable?

Of course you do; that is, you do if you are food-orientated and out to find one of the hottest new restaurants in town. New Yorkers - foodies, trendies and people-in-the-know - are cramming into the place every evening as if there were no tomorrow. On the night we were there, 2 rival New York restaurateurs were sitting at nearby tables, a well-known uptown socialite was holding forth at her table of 8 on the suave subtleties of the lobster sauce, and the chief taster/writer from the Gault Millau Guide was sitting at the table next to ours.

Montrachet seems to have caught the food mood of the moment: French modern cooking at its most perfect, twinned magically with American no-nonsense presentation. The restaurant itself is simple and comfortable and definitely without frills. Don't expect a 4 million dollar décor; Montrachet cost nearer $15,000: the ceilings are too high; the colours - eggshell blue and a sort of pinky mauve - too pale; the lighting guaranteed to turn any reasonable complexion muddy grey. But none of this matters for at Montrachet the food is the thing. Well worth a trip downtown.

The very simplicity of the place is a plus. It is the kind of restaurant where you see the bare bones of the operation, where the young owner (33-year-old Drew Nieporent) is dressed in black trousers, black shirt and tucked-in black tie, just like the rest of his enthusiastic team of young waiters - and where, when the service is over, members of the kitchen staff leave by the front door in blue jeans and heavy jacket, and stop for a drink at the bar with the boss.

Owner Drew Nieporent (the name is French; papa was Parisian) has been interested in good food ever since early childhood when he and his parents used to visit the top restaurants of the day, and young Drew used to visit the kitchens to see how his favourite dishes were made. This early interest led him to 4 years at Cornell University and then on to work in the kitchens and then front-of-house in such well-known New York restaurants as La Reserve and La Grenouille. Today he hosts and runs his own restaurant with panache and easy charm. And although the restaurant is open only in the evenings, he and his young chefs, led by Brian Whitmer and Bruce Lim, are hard at work in the restaurant from 1.00pm creating the basics and ideas for some of the most interesting dishes in town.

Usually, my top restaurants boast one - or, more rarely two - dishes whose 'savant' combination of flavours, texture and appearance hit the top notes: dishes that seem to explode in the consciousness, to remain in my taste memory long after I have left the restaurant. My last visit to Montrachet gave me 3 such moments. The menu - all in plain spoken English - is deceptively simple. Not so the execution. Starters and sweets are the keynotes here - with some remarkable main courses set happily in between. The sweetbread appetiser is dazzling in its tender/crunchy, piping hot/chilled virtuosity: twin pyramids, diminutive in size, of tender sweetbreads, browned lightly in hazelnut butter, are served hot on a crackling crisp bed of chunky-cut mange-touts and diced roasted sweet red pepper and tomato, with a sprinkling of toasted hazelnuts added for extra crunch.

Roasted lobster floats in a heady bath of saffron and tomato-scented crème fraîche with a reduction of lobster essences; the dish accented with a light garnish of fresh peas and a fragile plume of fresh chervil. An individual tart shell is filled with lightly poached oysters and sautéed fennel, brushed with the reduced oyster juices and a splash of crème fraîche.

Made-in-America fresh foie gras de canard (a recent addition to American fare) is a 'must' in any self-respecting New York restaurant. Montrachet is no exception. Their version sautés the tender lobes of duck liver briefly; sits them on a concealed mound of slivered shallots and blends the pan juices with a red wine glaze. Delicious.

Memorable main courses for you to try: red snapper with roasted peppers and lemon (sautéed red snapper with batonnets of red and yellow peppers in a herb and lemon-scented sauce, served on a bed of green spinach leaves); roast chicken with sweet garlic (the chicken breast served sliced on a bed of colcannon - creamy potato purée spiked with leek and Savoy cabbage - the chicken thigh boned and wrapped around a foie gras and spinach stuffing, sliced like a miniature ballotine, and set on a pool of sweet garlic-flavoured pan juices); roast kidney with chiroubles wine (the kidney, rare-roasted whole, sliced and served with little mounds of fava beans and a trio of glazed shallots in a chiroubles wine sauce). Delicious.

Montrachet is famous for its desserts, too; a flat oval dish of delicious crunchy-topped crème brûlée (a New York favourite); a rich chocolate dacquoise with a praline Bourbon flavoured sauce. Winner for me: little hot dollops of chocolate and citrus soufflé mixtures baked on tiny rounds of genoise, the twin soufflés handsomely risen, light and moist with a full, rich flavour, served with a folded tuile of ice-cream. The 3 sweets set in a pool of fresh raspberry purée and garnished with fresh fruits.

Felidia   New York

243 East 58th Street
(010-1) 212-758 1479

Closed: Sun

As your taxi arrives at the door, somehow you know that this is a very special restaurant; the elegant façade of earth-toned wood and attractive windows of etched glass spell privacy and prestige. And when you enter the small ante-room with its warm mahogany panelled walls and proud collection of fine, fat bottles (Methusalahs) of choice Italian wines set out proudly on an antique chest, you know you have arrived in a bastion of good living.

Just ahead of you is the long comfortable bar where they serve the best dry martini in one of the most sumptuous, jumbo-sized,

Martini glasses in town. This is a restaurant that, in spite of the eager diners attempting to crowd into the small premises, seems more like a private home than a public eating house.

On my last visit, platters of elegantly presented prosciutto canapés (the prosciutto thinly cut and palely gleaming, is home-cured, I later learned, by two members of the restaurant staff) passed over our heads as we followed a happy foursome of well-dressed New Yorkers past the bar to the small dining room where at a round table crowded with platters of colourful Italian antipasti, fruits, wild mushrooms and cheeses, a smiling lady of ample but elegant porportions awaited us: Lydia Bastianich, who with her husband Felice, owns and runs this popular restaurant. Lydia is a warm-voiced, sparkling-eyed, clear-complexioned lady whose formidable talents - both in front of house and in the kitchen - have made Felidia such a success. A casting director's dream of the archetypal 'mamma mia', she is a warm, loving earth mother who dispenses her generous hospitality and love of good food along with the comforting, robust dishes of her native land, Istria, on the south-eastern shore of what was once Italy (a region annexed by Yugoslavia in 1946 and located geographically about 80 miles across the Adriatic from Venice).

The cuisine is an ethnic mix of Venetian, Austrian and Slav dishes with fascinating overtones of Byzantium and the East: hints of finely grated orange peel, cinnamon and raisins in one intriguing first course pasta dish, pomegranate seeds and orange in another. Pasta dishes with names no self-respecting Italian has ever heard of - fuzi, pasutice and fragi, to mention my favourites, I tasted for the first time in Felidia.

Wild foods there are in abundance - splendid game dishes of pheasant, rabbit, venison and elk - served poached in novel country-style appetiser salads, raw and thinly sliced carpaccio shavings, or pan seared, finished off in rich barolo wine sauces, served piping hot with individual purées of turnip, carrot and chestnut, and wild rice. Wild mushrooms - cèpes, porcini and chanterelles - are served either alone or as sumptuous garnishes for risotto and polenta dishes. And white truffles, on the evening we were there, seemed to be the speciality of the house, so abundantly were they shaved over dishes at every table in the restaurant.

Mrs Bastianich has becomes something of an authority on her native cuisine in New York and gives courses on food anthropology at Pace University, appears on television and has conducted wine seminars on Italian wines. There are many notable dishes at Felidia. On a recent visit in the game season, we enjoyed fresh porcini (fleshy wild mushrooms, sautéed in olive oil with aromatics); fuzi alla fortuna del cacciatore (bow-tie shaped pasta with a rich game sauce; pasutice all' Istriana (diamond shaped pasta with lobster and a rich seafood sauce) and krafi all' Istriani (3-inch rounds of stuffed pasta, the creamy filling flavoured with finely grated orange peel) followed by a rabbit salad (the poached rabbit thinly sliced and served with a light vinaigrette spiked with raisins and pomegranate seeds). Thin, thin shavings of home-cured prosciutto, pale pink and slightly sweetened, and a truffled risotto bianco, set the scene for a sumptuous serving of wild boar and elk in rich gamey sauces, served with tiny purées of root vegetables and chestnuts, and wild rice. Delicious. Felidia's food is unusual. Soul satisfying.

To my mind it is the best Italian restaurant in the city.

406

Great Chefs and their favourite restaurants

Simon Hopkinson of Hilaire:

Ajimura
51-53 Shelton Street London WC2
01-240 0178

If you want to get away from the strict formality of most Japanese places then Ajimura is for you. 'Japanese Bistro' may be a term that's been used before, but it's correct. It's got a pleasantly laid back feel to it and it's noisy, always busy (do book), full of potted plants and greenery, and there is a great bar in one half of the restaurant which I think is the nicest place to be. Here you can watch the chefs at work grilling superb mackerel fillets, slicing raw tuna and salmon of prime quality for sashimi or sushi. Meanwhile you sit and become wildly intoxicated on delicious saké or kirin beer. It's not the sort of place where you find personalised bottles of Suntory whisky. In fact you don't see that many Japanese here at all. It's the only time I've seen "mix the wasabi into the soy" printed on the menu under the raw fish heading! They might have the odd slip-up, but it does not seem to bother you that much. It's altogether too nice a place for that.

Ikkyu
67 Tottenham Court Road London W1
01-636 9280

For me this has to be one of the most pleasurable Japanese places in London. There are plenty of establishments where some dishes are measurably better - but finally that is the only difference. (You may think that that is damning enough!) It's the tremendously good atmosphere that is unique. The place is slightly 'stuffy' with the smell of good frying and boiling, cigarette smoke and much chatter from the predominantly Japanese customers. Yakitori is a speciality and here you can enjoy a medly of crunchy chicken 'variety' bits - at least that's what I call it! Yakitori could consist of gizzard, heart, liver, meat and wings. Terrific. Also try the grilled mackerel - equally as good as at Ajimura.

The mixed sashimi (raw fish) gives you a greater choice of varieties than most places (eg tuna, salmon, octopus, bass, mackerel and a type of abalone). Eat at the bar, which incidentally, seems also to accommodate the restaurant's office and accounts department!

Ikeda
30 Brook Street London W1
01-629 2730

Ikeda is one of the smallest Japanese restaurants I know. There are only 3 tables and one long bar, where you can watch the bandanna'd chefs working with extraordinary dexterity. This again, like Ajimura, is the place to be. I like Ikeda when I am feeling thoroughly adventurous. On more than one occasion I have left it to them and eaten several courses of really special treats. Memorable dishes have been aubergine grilled with miso paste, salted cuttlefish guts (yes really), omelette stuffed with salted eel, and cold buckwheat noodles with nori (seaweed). You may take a risk with a 'leave it to them' meal, for prices are not discussed and you may get a shock - but the experience can be memorable. It's open on Sundays, which is useful to know - especially for chefs.

Le Caprice
Arlington Street London SW1
01-629 2239

Le Caprice is a brilliant formula. And that formula is good, stylish food, carefully cooked, minimum of fuss and decoration and served by the best waiters in town. Jeremy King and Chris Corbin are the perfect hosts, work incredibly hard and are admirably supported by their chef, Charles Fontaine.

It has to be the most reliable place in town and I think that's the secret of its enormous success. I am afraid that after much 'umming and aahing' each time I look at the menu, more often than not I end up having Caesar salad followed by grilled spring chicken with terrific almondine potatoes and the best spinach in the world. (The chips come a close second.) Also, it is incredibly good value for money and sports an interesting and well-chosen wine list.

The bar is one of the nicest around and is always dominated by the most extraordinary flower decorations. It's open on Sundays and I think I could quite easily eat there every Sunday night for evermore. I love it.

Michel Bourdin of the Connaught:

Michel Bourdin is a man of straightforward tastes, and rarely has the time to eat out but when he does in London, Langan's Brasserie is his favourite place for the ambience, the cooking and Richard Shepherd's character; and the fact that perhaps half a dozen or so other chefs or restaurant people are likely to be there, makes it a place to say hello to friends in the trade.

In Paris, his favourite is Robuchon, for the overall style of the food, service and atmosphere, and going Oriental, he loves to have an Imperial Chinese breakfast at the Regent Hotel in Hong Kong.

Peter Kromberg from the Inter-Continental:

Having worked for 4 years in the Far East, I very much enjoy Malay, Indonesian and Thai food, and will enjoy a Chinese meal in Gerard Street when out at the cinema or theatre.

I am not a great 'eater out' and basically prefer small brasseries and bistros. But in France, it is different - this last summer I visited Le Gendreau in Catus near Cahors, run by Monsieur and Madame Pelissau. They have converted an old school house with a huge open fire in winter. It is set in the middle of the country, and my favourite dishes there are cul de lapereau or os de canard. With my family I also enjoyed the creative cuisine and hospitality of Michel Trama; chef patron of L'Aubergade at Puymirol. On another occasion whilst staying with Monsieur Peybeyre, the truffle king, we enjoyed some beautiful trout which he'd just caught from the Dordogne, followed by a clafoutis made with fruit from the garden, some soft farm cheese, a loaf of fresh baked bread and some local red wine - perfect.

Finally, when in my native Germany on Lake Constance, I always aim to find a country farmhouse-style restaurant which would, for example, do its own butchery and make its own sausages - and then have to diet on returning to England.

Anton Mosimann of The Dorchester:

Like most chefs I tend to eat at hours different to the general public, and normally want to eat something which is interesting, light and basically different from the food I am involved in in my everyday cooking. Quite often Chinatown gets a visit - places like the Chueng Cheng Ku in Wardour Street where, I think, they do perhaps the best dim sum; and Mr Ken always gives you a warm welcome at the New World, where I particularly enjoy their crisp duck and their chicken with black bean sauce. The Diamond is always a particular favourite where I was first taken by my friend Nico Ladenis, and the fish always seems to be the thing there: garlic prawns, fresh garlic scallops served with ginger and their marvellous selection of crab and lobster. I can never seem to find these things on the menu, but if you ask for them they are only too pleased to oblige.

I think, perhaps, my other ethnic favourite must be The Bombay Brasserie. It always seems to be full of people and there is a good atmosphere, and food of great excellence. One of the benefits of being a chef is that knowing people in the kitchen they'll often make a selection for you and serve you with an excellent combination. My preference is for the lighter, spiced and seasoned curries, rather than the hotter variety, and I enjoy the sensation created by the different textures and flavours that can be created out of the same base sauce.

If I'm travelling in the country I'm a particular admirer of the country house style of hotels, their setting, furnishings and the way they have developed over the last few years. When I'm travelling on the Continent, I normally like to eat at some of the top restaurants such as Girardet, Troisgros, Bocuse, Alain Senderens, Alain Chapel; or Witzigmann and Winkler in Munich.

Richard Shepherd of Langan's:

I think I look for variety when I eat out, with perhaps lots of small dishes or choices rather than a standard 3-course meal. After being behind the stove for a few hours, your appetite sometimes becomes jaded, and you need variety of tastes and flavours to start you into food again. One particular place I like for this is the Phoenicia in Abingdon Road and I enjoy the selection of 30 or so mezes, hot and cold. They offer some unusual dishes, all served on separate plates, with a constant supply of hot pitta bread. I enjoy the aubergine purée with garlic and the tabbouleh, I quite like their version of steak tartare which is made with minced lamb, very fresh, and a little spice and wheat added to it. They also serve little sheep and goat cheeses marinated in oil, and small pieces of spicy grilled sausage. If you've got room for it you could have some simple grilled meat to follow. You can choose from many more things on the menu but I always opt for the meze as I tend to be eating with friends, and it means that everyone gets a taste of what they enjoy eating, and it's quite easy to order another dish of something you particularly like.

I am also a fan of Lou Pescadou. It's handy because it's got a late closing time too, so if you do get out of the kitchens early you can stop in and have either a choice of some excellent seafood in the normal Pierre Martin style or, if you prefer, a pizza with seafood or some other topping, or a filling pasta dish. It's got a great atmosphere, a cross between a brasserie and a bistro really. I think it offers good value, and there are normally one or two other people in the catering profession eating there to say 'hello' to, if Pierre's not there himself. I like the fact that if you want to eat lightly and the person you're with wants to eat a larger meal, or vice versa, it doesn't present any problem with a menu of this style.

My third choice must be The Bombay Brasserie, a place I particularly enjoy on Sunday lunch times, and there always seem to be tables full of family and friends around the room. They do an excellent buffet of hot and cold dishes where you can choose to eat as much or as little as you would like, accompanied by some excellent naan bread. I normally have a choice made for me if I go during the week and I have yet to be disappointed with what comes to the table. The restaurant really couldn't be much simpler with lots of green plants, some wicker chairs and a lovely conservatory at the rear. It occurred to me when I was setting my thoughts down that what is as important to me as the food is the greeting you get when you enter. And although I know the people concerned in the 3 restaurants I mentioned, in a restaurant where I am not known the greeting can often make or mar my overall impression of the evening.

Prue Leith of Leiths

Punter's Pie
183 Lavender Hill, London SW11
01-228 2660

My favourite restaurant is Punter's Pie - the fact that it's owned by my brother who will, if his arm is twisted, give me half a glass of free Beaujolais, has of course absolutely nothing to do with it.

Seriously, though, Punter's Pie is an off-duty cook's dream. Old-fashioned pies like granny used to make (not my Granny - she couldn't boil an egg - but someone's Granny). You can get as-light-as-air Cheddar soufflé and a heap of delicate salad leaves in a perfect French dressing, banana and toffee pie and half a bottle of very drinkable French wine all for £8.00. The place is packed with London's youth of course, and the management tend to want your table if you linger but it is a really great time-off treat.

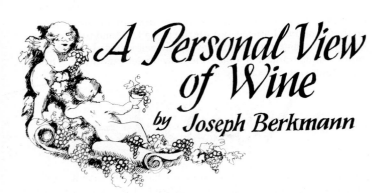

A Personal View of Wine

by Joseph Berkmann

In 1985 there arose a strange sect who called themselves 'the foodies'. For them food no longer stilled hunger but had become a religious experience. Instead of contemplating the wisdom of holy books and the *Financial Times*, they would immerse themselves in delightful cookery books until late in the night, and then, after a secret breakfast of eggs, bangers, chips and tomato ketchup, spend their days in restaurants that serve colour photographs instead of real food.

As a result, restaurants, once judged by the feeling of well-being and happiness they could give you, turned into cinemas for the sole benefit of Michelin stars, *Gault Millau* toques and *Good Food Guide* pestles. They forgot that good food should be well balanced and contain the necessary roughage to keep their customers regular and alive; that their customers came to restaurants for an evening out, to see the famous and the infamous and generally have a good time. One would have thought that wine had an important part to play (making the extraordinary bill palatable). Alas, as chefs gained in ascendance, wine fell into disrepute: jealous that a good bottle might upstage their culinary art, chefs multiplied the cost of each bottle by four and five, and sold mineral water instead.

The foodies are disappearing. Their high priest, a man of great writing ablity but confused by massive doses of baby food he had to prepare for his growing horde of infants, regained his earlier taste for gefillte fish and resigned. This greatly benefited old-fashioned restaurants who had never quite taken to beurre blanc and sculptured carrots, and customers gave a sigh of relief at the reappearance of such favourites as braised oxtail, steak and kidney pie and coq au vin. The wine lists of these splendid establishments are usually simple. As to content, one glance will tell you if they really care for their wines: they not only list the name of a wine, like Gevrey Chambertin, but also the vintage and - most importantly - the name of the producer.

I personally cannot admire restaurants that list 1,900 wines, but I admire the restaurateur who manages to hit a balanced selection of wines which are at their peak, that is to say, neither too young nor too old. This is far more important than is generally recognised. Sadly, too many people still consult plastic vintage charts, an abomination since very many good wines are made in bad vintages, just as too many bad wines are made in five-star vintages. Today a growing number of producers make wines that are perfect if drunk within the year of their vintage: Loire wines ranging from Muscadet to Sauvignon de Touraine and Sancerre; the wines of Beaujolais including the village wines like Brouilly and Chiroubles (although a good Moulin-à-Vent will be even better after a year or two in bottle); inexpensive Rhône wines; the wines of Alsace, Valpolicella and virtually all Italian white wines. And then there are others who need their time to achieve perfection, but even here, more modestly priced wines rarely benefit from excessive cellerage. 1982 Burgundies are at their best now and, apart from the likes of Richebourg, will hardly improve. Clarets of the 1979, 1980 and 1981 vintages are quite ready for drinking now and even 1982 petits châteaux are starting to open up. Britain is a country that somewhat overrates senile wines, a taste dictated by two generations deprived of fresh shipments during the wars. (The French by contrast err on the side of youth and often serve immature wines.)

Outside Bordeaux, where the name of the château is all important, one must learn to remember the names of producers. Hugh Johnson's pocket guide is of invaluable help here and I strongly recommend the modest investment, unless you only drink well-thought-of clarets. Gevrey Chambertin, to cite it once more, is made and bottled by a host of people and the variations in quality are quite staggering. Wine people think therefore not just in terms of Gevrey Chambertin but Gevrey Chambertin Phillipe Rossignol, Charles Rousseau, Jean Trapet, etc.

Once you have selected your wine, keep an eye on the wine waiter. In his book *Wine*, Hugh Johnson described a man who would whisk an ancient bottle from the shelf, push it into a basket and then arrive on tip-toes to convey an impression of totally undisturbed deposits while the bottle was actually still palpitating. Insist, therefore, that wines from old vintages be decanted in front of you: carefully handled wine is crystal clear; badly handled wine will be muddy.

My most common complaint in restaurants is wine served at the wrong temperature: white wines iced so that you might as well be drinking water, red wine at the temperature you wish they had served the soup. Be firm and complain. Your wine waiter may not like the idea of Richebourg in an ice-bucket (it also diminishes the wine's aroma) but at least it makes it drinkable. Red wine should be served at cellar temperature, so that it can warm up and develop in the glass. Asking for a wine 'chambré' is an invitation for disaster.

As the wine waiter or 'sommelier' offers you a first sip of each bottle you may wonder why he doesn't take this responsibility from you - after all, he carries a well-polished 'tasse' around his neck for precisely that purpose. Alas, I was a wine waiter once myself, and whilst tasting some 60 wines a day was most attractive, alcoholism would have followed inevitably, since restaurant proprietors do not like it if you spit out on their carpets. So it's up to you to approve the bottle with a first sip. Sometimes a corky wine does not show its off-flavour until it has been in the glass for a few minutes, but you need not fear that that nod of approval constituted a contract to drink a tainted wine: ask for it to be changed. If you (and the wine waiter) have doubts, order another half bottle of the same wine and compare. Any defect will show up at once.

Good wine is one of the great pleasures of life. It deserves to be taken seriously, but it should not become a religion: its main purpose is to make you feel well and happy. And help you to digest a meal.

General Listing of Other Establishments

This section lists by area other establishments which have not been reviewed, or have been visited only once - hotels, restaurants and historic inns - which hopefully can provide alternatives, and in some cases rooms where the establishment reviewed has none.

Almost all of this country's Trust House Forte (THF) and Holiday Inns (HI) feature in those area lists, and a few details about some of the other hotel groups are additionally given below:

Crest Hotels
Nearly 60 in the UK and another 30 in Europe. Mostly modern and in major cities. Average price for a double room: £55. Central reservations: 01-236 3242.

Embassy Hotels
Modern and character hotels in England, Scotland & Wales, in major cities. Average price for a double room: £50.

Holiday Inns
1,700 hotels worldwide, including 16 in the UK. Average price for a double room: £70. Central reservations: 01-722 7755.

Ladbroke Hotels
Over 50 hotels in the UK and 7 in Europe. International hotels in city centres and tourist hotels in leisure destinations. Average price for a double room: £70.

Stakis Hotels
31 hotels in England, Scotland & Wales in major cities. Average price for a double room: £50.

Thistle Hotels
Over 30 hotels in the UK with over 300 affiliated Supranational Hotels worldwide. Average price for a double room: £70. Central reservations: 01-937 8033.

Trust House Forte
800 hotels worldwide, including 200 in the UK and some of London's grander hotels. Price range for a double room: £40 - £150. Central reservations: 01-567 3444.

AVON
Bath
H Aspley House, Newbridge Hill
   (0225) 336966
   Small hotel just outside the town
   The Canary, Queen Street
   (0225) 24846
   Licensed restaurant serving lunch, afternoon tea
H The Francis, Queen Sq THF
   (0225) 24257
   Classic façade, 95 bedrooms
H Royal York Hotel, George St
   (0225) 61541

   Bristol
H Holiday Inn Bristol HI
   (0272) 294281

   Michael's, Hotwell Rd
   (0272) 276190
   Small, comfortably furnished French restaurant
H Unicorn Hotel, Princes St
   (0272) 294811
   Large modern hotel
   Farrington Gurney
H The Old Parsonage, Main St
   (0761) 52211
   Queen Anne house, restaurant with rooms
   Hutton
H Hutton Court, Church Lane
   (0934) 814343
   Small hotel furnished with antiques

Weston-super-Mare
H   The Grand Atlantic, Beach
Parade THF
(0934) 26543
Large seafront hotel

BEDFORDSHIRE
Bedford
Woodlands Manor Restaurant, Green
Lane, Clapham
(0234) 63281
*Victorian manor house in wooded
gardens*

Clifton
Reuleaux's, Shefford Road
(0462) 811911
French restaurant

Leighton Buzzard
H   Swan Hotel, Mr Swan's Restaurant,
High St
(0525) 372148
Georgian coaching inn

BERKSHIRE
Ascot
H   Royal Berkshire, London Road,
Sunnyhill
(0990) 23322
*Elegant, well furnished Queen Anne
mansion*

Newbury
H   Elcot Park Hotel
(0488) 58100
Period country house
H   The Chequers, Oxford St THF
(0635) 38000
Coaching inn, Georgian facade
Swan Inn, Lower Inkpen
(048 84) 326
Old inn with restaurant

Reading
H   Post House Hotel THF
(0734) 875485
Modern low-rise hotel

Streatley
H   Swan Hotel, High St
(0491) 873737
Thames riverside hotel

Windsor
H   Holiday Inn Slough HI
(075 35) 44244
H   The Castle Hotel, High St THF
(075 35) 51011
Georgian coaching house
The House on the Bridge, High St
(075 35) 60914
*Converted Victorian boathouse
overlooking river & castle*

Yattendon
H   Royal Oak Hotel Restaurant, The
Savane
(0635) 210325
Village inn

BUCKINGHAMSHIRE
Aylesbury
H   The Bell, Market Sq THF
(0296) 82141

Buckingham
H   The White Hart, Market Sq THF
(0280) 815151
19 bedrooms

Marlow
H   The Compleat Angler, Marlow
Bridge THF
(062 84) 4444
Riverside setting, character hotel

Milton Keynes
H   Post House Hotel, Saxon Gate
West THF
(0908) 667722
Hotel & fitness centre

Rickmansworth
H   Bedford Arms Thistle, Chenies
(092 78) 3301
Modern hotel

CAMBRIDGESHIRE
Cambridge
H   The Blue Boar, Trinity St THF
(0223) 63121
Small hotel
H   Post House Hotel, Impington THF
(022 023) 7000

Eaton Socon
The Old Plough, Great North Road
(0480) 72815
*So named as the first iron plough was
made here in 1738*

Huntingdon
H   The George, George St THF
(0480) 53096
*Posting house, once owned by
Oliver Cromwell's grandfather*

Melbourn
The Pink Geranium
(0763) 60215
*Pretty thatched cottage with well-
kept gardens*

CHESHIRE
Bucklow Hill
H   The Swan, Chester Road
(0565) 830295
De Vere hotel

Chester
Abbey Green, Northgate St
(0244) 313251
Vegetarian restaurant
H   Chester Grosvenor, Eastgate St
(0244) 24024
Built in 1860 in city centre
H   Queen Hotel, City Road THF
(0244) 28341
Secluded garden
H   Post House Hotel, Wrexham Rd THF
(0244) 674111

Disley
The Ginnel, Buxton Old Road
(066 32) 4494
Restaurant in converted cottage

Knutsford
H La Belle Epoque, King St
(0565) 3060
Art nouveau décor
H The Swan, Bucklow Hill
(0565) 830295

Nantwich
Pentangle Restaurant, Beam St
(0270) 629875
*Rooftop restaurant in restored manor
house*

Prestbury
H Mottram Hall Hotel, Mottram St
Andrew
(0625) 828135
Georgian mansion

Warrington
H Lord Daresbury Hotel, Daresbury
(0925) 67331
Modern De Vere hotel

CHANNEL ISLANDS
Alderney
H The Georgian House, Victoria St, St
Anne
(048 182) 2471
Nellie Gray's, Victoria St, St Anne
(048 182) 3333
Seafood restaurant

Guernsey
H La Frégate, St Peter Port
(0481) 24624
*18th C manor house, now hotel &
restaurant*
H St Pierre Park Hotel, St Peter Port
(0481) 28282
*Luxurious modern hotel with sports
facilities, set in spacious grounds*

Jersey
Apple Cottage, Rozel Bay, St Martin
(0534) 61002
*Seafood restaurant in converted
cottage, also serving cream teas*
H Sea Crest Hotel, Corbière
(0534) 42687
Modern hotel with sea view

CLEVELAND
Stockton-on-Tees
H Parkmore Hotel, Eaglescliffe
(0642) 786815

Thornaby-on-Tees
H Post House Hotel, Stainton
Village THF
(0642) 591213

CORNWALL
Bodinnick
H Old Ferry Inn
(072 687) 237
16th C inn

Bude
H Reeds, Poughill
(0288) 2841
Small country house
H The Strand Hotel, The Strand THF
(0288) 3222
Modern seaside hotel

Falmouth
H Budock Vean Hotel, Mawnan Smith
(0326) 250288
Sports facilities
H Meudon Hotel Restaurant, Mawnan
Smith
(0326) 250541
Gardens by Capability Brown

Fowey
H Cormorant Hotel, Golant
(072 683) 3426
French restaurant specialising in fish

Looe
H Talland Bay Hotel Restaurant, Talland
Bay
(0503) 72667
Cliff-top views

Lostwithiel
Trewithen, Fore St
(0208) 872373
*Specialises in fish dishes &
international evenings*

Mousehole
H Lobster Pot, South Cliff
(0736) 731251
Harbourside setting

Padstow
H The Metropole, Station Rd THF
(0841) 532486
*Overlooks the harbour and Camel
estuary*
H The Old Custom House Inn, South
Quay
(0841) 532359
Character inn on quayside

Polperro
Kitchen at Polperro, Fish na Bridge
(0503) 72780
Small restaurant specialising in fish

St Columb Major
H The Old Rectory & Country Club
(0637) 880656
*15th C rectory, now a restaurant with
rooms*

Veryan
H Treverbyn House, Pendower Rd
(0872) 501201
*Turn of the century house now a
seafood restaurant with rooms*

CUMBRIA
Ambleside
H Kirkstone Foot Hotel, Kirkstone Pass
Rd
(0966) 32232
Comfortable 17th C manor house
H Nanny Brow Hotel, Nr Clappersgate
(0966) 32036
*Charming house in large gardens with
spectacular views*
H The Swan THF
(09665) 551
H Grizedale Lodge Hotel
(096 66) 532
*Comfortably furnished hotel in the
heart of the Grizedale forest*

Borrowdale
H Lodore Swiss Hotel
(059 684) 285
At the side of Derwent water

Bowness on Windermere
Jackson's Bistro West End
(096 62) 6264
Chef/patron cooks good local produce

Carlisle
H Crosby Lodge Hotel, Crosby on Eden
(022 873) 618
Elegant hotel in parkland and gardens

Cockermouth
H Pheasant Inn, Bassenthwaite
(059 681) 234
Typical English inn with beamed bars and log fires

Crook
H Wild Boar Hotel
(096 62) 5225
Comfortable rooms with exposed stone and beams

Kendal
H Woolpack Hotel, Strick Pandgate
(0539) 23852
18th C coaching inn

Keswick
H The Keswick THF
(0596) 72020

Melmerby
Village Bakery
(076 881) 515
A bakery, restaurant and craft shop using natural local produce

Newby Bridge
H Swan Hotel
(05395) 31681
Old coaching inn

Ravenstonedale
H Black Swan
(058 73) 204
Country hotel with fishing on the River Eden

Temple Sowerby
H Temple Sowerby House
(07683) 61578
Old Cumbrian farmhouse overlooking Cross Fell

Underbarrow
H Greenriggs Country House Hotel
(044 88) 387
18th C family run hotel with 14 bedrooms

Windermere
H The Belsfield THF
(096 62) 2448
H The Old England THF
(096 62) 2444

DERBYSHIRE
Bakewell
H Hassop Hall Hotel, Hassop
(062 987) 488
Elegant 12 bedroomed family run hotel

Derby
H Pennine Hotel, Macklin St
(033 20) 41741
De Vere hotel

Dovedale
H Peveril of the Peak, Thorpe THF
(0335 29) 333
11 acres of grounds

Matlock Bath
H New Bath Hotel, New Bath Road THF
(0629) 3275
Swimming pool and leisure centre

DEVON
Barnstaple
H The Imperial, Taw Vale Parade THF
(0271) 45861
Overlooks the River Taw

Branscombe
H Bovey House Hotel
(029 780) 241
Elizabethan country house
H Masons Arms
(0203) 542571
14th C inn

Bampton
H Huntsham Court, Huntsham
(039 86) 210
Comfortable Victorian mansion

Chagford
H Mill End Hotel, Sandy Park
(064 73) 2282
Old flour mill
H Teignworthy, Frenchbeer
(064 73) 3355
Lovely stone-built house in landscaped gardens – good restaurant

Croyde
The Whiteleaf at Croyde
(0271) 890266
1930s house

Exeter
H White Hart Hotel, South St
(0392) 79897
15th C hostelry

Exmouth
H The Imperial, The Esplanade THF
(0395) 274761
Family hotel close to Lyme Bay

Huxham
Barton Cross
(039 284) 245
16th C converted cottage with thatched roof and lots of beams

Lifton
H Arundell Arms Restaurant
(0566) 84666
Fishing hotel

Loddiswell
Lavinia's
(0548) 55306
Converted coach house serving French cuisine – speciality seafood hors d'oeuvres

Milton Damerel

H Woodford Bridge Hotel Restaurant
(040 926) 481
Thatched, 15th C building

Paignton

H The Palace, Esplanade Rd THF
(0803) 555121

Plymouth

H Holiday Inn, Armada Way HI
(0752) 662866
H Mayflower Post House Hotel, The
Hoe THF
(0752) 662828
Mister Barrett's, Admiralty St,
Stonehouse
(0752) 221177
*Small restaurant specialising in
seafood and game in season*

South Molton

H Stumbles, East St
(076 95) 4145
*Small hotel with restaurant and wine
bar*

Tavistock

H The Bedford, Plymouth Rd THF
(0822) 3221
On the site of a Benedictine Abbey

Tiverton

Hendersons, Newport St
(0884) 254256
*Comfortably furnished restaurant
with good food and excellent wines*

Torquay

H The Imperial Hotel, Park Hill Rd THF
(0803) 24301
*Luxury hotel, sub-tropical gardens,
sea views*

DORSET
Bournemouth

H Carlton Hotel, East Overcliff
(0202) 22011
*Comfortable hotel with leisure
facilities*
H Marsham Court Hotel, East Cliff
(0202) 22111
Outdoor pool
H Palace Court Hotel, Westover Rd
(0202) 27681
103-roomed, comfortable hotel
H Royal Bath, Bath Road
(0202) 25555
*Victorian hotel with pool &
gymnasium*
Sophisticats, Charminster Rd
(0202) 291019
Small intimate French restaurant

Bridport

H Chideock House Hotel, Chideock
(029 789) 242
*Thatched roof & beams in this 15th C
hostelry*

Christchurch

H Avonmouth Hotel, Mudeford THF
(0202) 483434
Private landing stage
Splinters, Church St
(0202) 483454
*Small friendly French restaurant with
excellent wine list*

Dorchester

H King's Arms, High St
(0305) 65353
Coaching inn
H Maiden Newton House, Maiden
Newton
(0300) 20336
*Lovely converted priory in 21 acres of
gardens*

Ferndown

H Dormy Hotel, New Road
(0202) 872121
De Vere hotel with leisure club

Gillingham

H Stock Hill House, Wyke
(074 76) 3626
*19th C manor house, with Austrian
chef/patron*

Lyme Regis

H Mariners Hotel, Silver St
(029 74) 2753
Spectacular views of Dorset coast

Poole

The Warehouse, The Quay
(0202) 677238
*Converted warehouse overlooking the
harbour*

Shaftesbury

H The Grosvenor, The Commons THF
(0747) 2282
18th C modernised hotel

Sherborne

H Post House Hotel, Horsecastles
Lane THF
(0935) 813191

Wareham

H Kemps Country House Hotel
(0929) 462563
*Victorian rectory with additional
rooms in the Coach House*

Wimborne Minster

H The King's Head, The Square THF
(0202) 880101
*Georgian hotel overlooking the
minster*

DURHAM
Chester-le-Street

H Lumley Castle Hotel
(0385) 891111
9th C castle

ESSEX
Brentwood

H The Post House Hotel, Brook St THF
(0277) 210888

Brightlingsea

Jacobe's, High St
(020 630) 2113
Specialises in seafood

Buckhurst Hill

H   The Roebuck, North End   THF
01-505 4636
18th C inn, originally a small ale-house

Coggeshall

H   White Hart Hotel Restaurant, Market End
(0376) 61654
Characterful old hostelry with an exceptional wine list

Colchester

Bistro Nine, North Hill
(0206) 576466
Cheerful bistro with daily vegetarian dishes

H   Rose & Crown Hotel, East Gates
(0206) 866677
Heavily beamed historic posting house

Epping

H   Post House Hotel, High Rd, Bell Common   THF
(0378) 73137

Great Dunmow

H   The Saracen's Head, High St   THF
(0371) 3901
Georgian with Tudor features

Harwich Pier at Harwich, The Quay
(0255) 503363
Seafood restaurant overlooking estuary – piano music in evenings

Leigh-on-Sea

Christine's Restaurant, The Broadway
(0702) 76111
Pretty décor with daily changing menu

Maldon

Francine's, High St
(0621) 56605
Small friendly bistro

H   The Blue Boar, Silver St   THF
(0621) 52681
Beamed inn with 24 bedrooms

Old Harlow

H   Green Man Hotel, Mulberry Green
(0279) 442521
Old timbered building facing village green

Saffron Walden

H   Saffron Hotel, High St
(0799) 22676
Good base for visiting local places of interest

Wethersfield

Rudi's, The Green
(0371) 850723
Austrian & French cooking in an old bakery

EAST SUSSEX
Alfriston

Moonrakers Restaurant, High St
(0323) 870472
Pretty 16th C cottages once used by wigmakers

Battle

The Blacksmith's, High St
(042 46) 3200
Hungar

H   Netherfield Place
(042 46) 4455
Georgian brick manor house

Brighton

H   The Dudley, Lansdowne Place, Hove THF
(0273) 736266
Set in a Regency square

French Cellar, New England Rd
(0273) 603643
Brasserie and classical French restaurant

Restaurant Chardonnay
(0273) 672733
French chef/patron – attractive dining room

Eastbourne

Byrons, Crown St, Old Town
(0323) 20171
Small French restaurant offering fresh produce

H   Cavendish Hotel, Grand Parade
(0323) 27401
Large De Vere hotel on sea front

H   Grand Hotel, Grand Parade
(0323) 30327
Elegant Victorian seaside hotel

Lewes

The Sussex Kitchen, High St
(0273) 476149
Pub with restaurant serving English fayre

Lower Dicker

H   Boship Farm Hotel
(0323) 844826
17th C building

Mayfield

Old Brew House, High St
(0435) 872342
16th C timbered building with inglenook fireplace

Peasmarsh

H   Flackley Ash, London Rd
(079 721) 381

Rye

Landgate Bistro, Landgate
(0797) 222829
Small bistro with imaginative menu

H   The George, High St   THF
(0797) 222114
400 year old coaching inn, timbers from Elizabethan ship

Three Legged Cross

The Bull
(0580) 200586
Pub with simple menu served in the bar

Uckfield

Sussex Barn, Ringles Cross
(0825) 3827
Small restaurant owned by former restaurant manager of Brown's Hotel, London

Wadhurst
H Spindlewood Hotel, Wallcrouch
(0580) 200430
Victorian country-style hotel

GLOUCESTERSHIRE
Bibury
H The Swan Hotel
(0285 74) 204
*Charming Cotswold hotel overlooking
River Coln*

Bishop's Cleeve
Cleeveway House
(024 267) 2585
*Ivy clad, stone built house just outside
Cheltenham*

Blockley

H Lower Brook House
(0386) 700286
*Small country hotel offering fresh local
produce in the dining room*

Bourton-on-the-Water
Rose Tree, Riverside
(0451) 20635
*Attractive old cottage with Anglo-
French cooking*

Cheltenham
H Hotel De la Bere, Southam
(0242) 37771
Tudor mansion with leisure complex
Number Twelve, Suffolk Parade
(0242) 584544
Attractive modern French restaurant
H The Queen's, Promenade   THF
(0242) 514724
Classical building
Redmond's, Suffolk Rd
(0242) 580323
*Chef/patron cooks in modern French
style*
The Retreat, Suffolk Pde
(0242) 35436
Busy bistro with homely cooking

Chipping Campden
H Noel Arms Hotel
(0386) 840317
*14th C coaching inn in lovely
Cotswold village*

Cirencester
H Fleece Hotel, Market Pl
(0285) 68507
*Old world atmosphere in part Tudor,
part Georgian coaching inn*
The Kings Head, Market Pl
(0285) 3322
14th C coaching inn with 70 bedrooms

Ewen
Wild Duck Inn
(028 577) 364
*Well-kept pub with restaurant and
garden*

Forest of Dean
H The Speech House, Coleford   THF
(0594) 22607
*Character hotel with timbered
restaurant*

Lower Slaughter
Manor Hotel
(0451) 20456
Mid-17th C building

Moreton-in-Marsh
H Manor House Hotel, High St
(0608) 50501
*Charming Cotswold stone manor
house with indoor pool*
H The White Hart Royal, High St   THF
(0608) 50731
*15th C inn, half-timbered, cobbled
entrance*

Tetbury
Chiswick's, Long St
(0666) 53796
*Newly-opened cheerful international
restaurant*
The Snooty Fox, Market Pl
(0666) 52436
*16th C coaching inn with oak panelled
restaurant*

GREATER MANCHESTER
Birtle
H Normandie, Elbut Lane 061 – 764 3869

Manchester
H The Grand, Aytoun St   THF 061 – 236
9559
Traditionally styled hotel
Isola Bella, Booth St
061-236 6417
Long-established Italian restaurant
Market Restaurant, Edge St
061-834 3743
Weekly changing menu
H Piccadilly Hotel, Piccadilly 061-236
8414
International executive hotel
Truffles, Bridge St
061-832 9393
*Elegant Victorian dining rooms
serving modern French cuisine*

Northenden
H The Post House Hotel, Palatine
Rd   THF
061-998 7090

Wythenshaw
H The Excelsior, Ringway Rd   THF
061-437 5811
Manchester Airport hotel

HAMPSHIRE
Beaulieu
H The Montagu Arms
(0590) 612324
Old coaching inn

Botley
Cobbett's, The Square
(048 92) 2068
*16th C cottage restaurant with beamed
bar*

Buckler's Hard
H Master Builder's House Hotel
(059 063) 253
On the edge of the estuary

Havant
H Post House Hotel, Hayling Island   THF
(0705) 465011

Hurstbourne Tarrant
Esseborne Manor Restaurant
(026 46) 444
Features game in season

Lymington
Limpets, Gosport St
(0590) 75595
Specialises in fish

Portsmouth
H Holiday Inn Portsmouth HI
(0705) 383151

Romsey
H The White Horse, Market Place THF
(0794) 512431
Historic building in central location

Rotherwick
H Tylney Hall
(025 672) 4881
Magnificent 19th C manor house, now a country house hotel set in 66 acres

Southampton
H The Dolphin, High St THF
(0703) 226178
13th C coaching inn
H Polygon Hotel, Cumberland Pl THF
(0703) 226401
Modern hotel with 119 bedrooms
H Post House Hotel, Herbert Walker Av THF
(0703) 228081

Southsea
Bistro Montparnasse, Palmerson Rd
(0705) 816754
Friendly bistro with menu changing monthly
H Pendragon, Clarence Parade THF
(0705) 823201
Close to the sea with pleasant views

Stockbridge
Game Larder, New St
(0264) 810414
Specialises in game!

Sway
H Pine Trees, Mead End Rd
(0590) 682288
Comfortable Victorian hotel

Winchester
Below Stairs, St Cross Rd
(0962) 55135
British & French cooking
H Lainston House
(0962) 63588
17th C manor house set in parkland
H The Wessex, Paternoster Row THF
(0962) 61611
Modern hotel close to the cathedral

HEREFORD & WORCESTER
Abberley
H The Elms, Nr Worcester
(029 921) 666
Elegant country house built in 1710 by a pupil of Wren

Broadway
H Collin House, Collin Ln
(0386) 858354
Comfortable family-run hotel with good English cooking
H Dormy House, Willersey Hill
(0386) 852711
17th C Cotswolds hotel with beams, open log fires & comfortable rooms

Droitwich
H Château Impney
(0905) 774411
French style château in an old Spa town

Evesham
H Evesham Hotel, Cooper's Lane, off Waterside
(0386) 49111
16th C mansion house modernised in 19th C!

Hereford
H The Green Dragon, Broad St THF
(0432) 272506
Old posting inn with some 16th C panelling

Kington
Penrhos Court Restaurant
(0544) 230720
Dating from 13th C, restaurant occasionally offers Mediaeval evenings

Malvern Wells Cottage in the Wood, Hollywell Rd
(068 45) 3487
Set amongst the Malvern Hills with superb views

Ross-on-Wye
H Pengethley Hotel, Harewood End
(098 987) 211
Georgian country house hotel, restaurant offers nouvelle cuisine
H The Royal, Palace Pound THF
(0989) 65105
150 years old, views over River Wye

Worcester
Brown's, Quay St
(0905) 26263
Converted grain mill overlooking river, serving good fresh produce
H The Giffard, High St THF
(0905) 27155
Modern Hotel, close to River Severn and cathedral

HERTFORDSHIRE
Chipperfield
H The Two Brewers THF
(09277) 65266
Late 17th C building

Hemel Hempstead
H Post House Hotel, Brakspear Way THF
(0442) 51122

Hertingfordbury
H The White Horse THF
(0992) 56791
Originally the local manor house

421

Hitchin
H   Redcoats Farmhouse Hotel, Redcoats Green
(0438) 729500
Beamed house furnished with antiques

Old Hatfield
Salisbury Restaurant, The Broadway
(070 72) 62220
French restaurant with imaginative menus

Puckeridge
White Hart, High St
(0920) 821309
16th C inn with restaurant

Royston
Sheen Mill Restaurant, Station Rd, Melbourn
(0763) 61393
Restored water mill overlooking mill pond
The Chequers Inn, Fowlmere
(076 382) 369
17th C inn, visited by Samuel Pepys

Stevenage
H   The Roebuck, Broadwater   THF
(0438) 65444
15th C inn with modern amenities

HUMBERSIDE
Driffield
H   The Bell Hotel
(0377) 46661

Hull
H   Waterfront Hotel, Dagger Ln
(0482) 227222
Converted old warehouse

Little Weighton
H   Rowley Manor Hotel, near Hull
(0482) 848248
Georgian country house

Stamford Bridge
Three Cups
(0723) 71396
Beamed, panelled pub with stained glass

ISLE OF WIGHT
Newport
Lugleys, Lugley St
(0983) 521062
Charming restaurant offering fresh seasonal produce

Ryde
H   Yelf's Hotel, Union St   THF
(0983) 64062
Once a coaching house

Seaview
H   Seaview Hotel, High St
(098371) 2711
Edwardian-style hotel, restaurant features local produce

Ventnor
H   The Royal Hotel   THF
(0983) 852186

KENT
Biddenden
Three Chimneys
(0580) 291472
Pub offering seasonal dishes on blackboard menu

Canterbury
H   Slatters Hotel, St Margaret's St
(0227) 463271
Modern hotel in town centre
H   The Chaucer, Ivy Lane   THF
(0227) 464427
Close to cathedral and Marlow Theatre

Cranbrook
H   Kennel Holt Restaurant, Goudhurst Rd
(0580) 712032
Elizabethan manor house
H   Willesley Hotel Restaurant
(0580) 713555
Character hotel

Eynsford
Malt Shovel Inn, Station Rd
(0322) 862164
Pub with seafood restaurant

Faversham
Read's, Painter's Forstal
(0795) 535344
Competent cooking & fine wine list

Folkestone
Emilio Restaurant Portofino, Sandgate Rd
(0303) 55762
Long established Italian restaurant
La Tavernetta, Leaside Ct, Clifton Gdns
(0303) 54955
Italian restaurant
Paul's, Bouverie Rd West
(0303) 59697
Bistro with weekly changing menu

Goudhurst
H   Star & Eagle, High St
(0580) 211512
14th C inn

Hawkhurst
H   Tudor Arms Hotel, Rye Rd
(058 05) 2312
Small family run hotel

Hayes
Guests, Station Approach 01 – 462 8594
Fresh food on fixed price menus

Herne Bay
L'Escargot
(0227) 373876
Cheerful bistro-style restaurant

Ightham
Town House
(0732) 884578
Interesting 15th & 16th C building housing restaurant which serves nouvelle cuisine

Maidstone
H   Chilston Park Hotel, Sandway
(0622) 859803
16th C manor house
Leeds Castle
(0622) 65400
Norman castle (functions only)

St Margaret's at Cliffe
H Wallett's Court, West Cliff
(0304) 852424
Built in 1627

Tonbridge
H The Rose & Crown, High St THF
(0732) 357966
Jacobean panelling

Tunbridge Wells
H The Spa Hotel, Mount Ephraim
(0892) 20331
Victorian hotel

Winchelsea
Manna Plat, Mill Road
(0797) 226317
Café-style rooms & gallery

Wrotham Heath
H Post House Hotel, London Rd THF
(0732) 883311

Wye
The Wife of Bath, Upper Bridge St
(0223) 812540
Reliable cooking in this plain French restaurant

LANCASHIRE
Bolton
H Pack Horse Hotel, Bradshawgate
(0204) 27261
De Vere hotel

Lancaster
H Post House Hotel, Caton Rd THF
(0524) 65999

Slaidburn
H Parrock Head Farm
(020 06) 614
17th C farmhouse

Thornton-le-Fylde
H River House, Skippool Creek
(0253) 883497
Small Victorian hotel with homely cooking

LEICESTERSHIRE
Leicester
H Holiday Inn Leicester HI
(0533) 531161
H Post House Hotel, Brawnstone Ln THF
(0533) 896688

Lutterworth
H The Denbigh Arms Hotel, High St
(0455) 53537
18th C coaching inn

Market Harborough
H Three Swans Hotel, High St
(0858) 66644
Old inn with 17th C sign

Melton Mowbray
H Harboro' Hotel, Burton St
(0664) 60121
18th C coaching inn

Shepshed
Turtles, Brook St
(0509) 502843
French restaurant, seafood menu on Wednesdays

Sileby
Old School Restaurant. Barrow Rd
(050 981) 3941
English cooking in the old school house, complete with desks!

Uppingham
H Lake Isle, High St East
(0572) 822951
Old rustic style restaurant

LINCOLNSHIRE
Boston
H New England Hotel, Wide Bargate
(0205) 65255

Bourne
H Black Horse Inn, Grimsthorpe
(077 832) 247
Georgian coaching inn

Grantham
H The Angel & Royal, High St THF
(0476) 65816
One of England's oldest inns
H George Hotel, High St
(0476) 63286
18th C coaching inn

Lincoln
H Eastgate Post House Hotel, Eastgate THF
(0522) 20341
Harvey's Cathedral Restaurant, Exchequergate
(0522) 21886
A la carte lunch & fixed price dinner menus
H The White Hart, Bailgate THF
(0522) 26222
Traditional hotel
White's, Jews House, The Strait
(0522) 24851
Claims to be the oldest dwelling house in Europe

LONDON
E1
H Tower Thistle Hotel, St Katharine's Way
01-481 2575

EC1
Baron of Beef, Gutter Ln
01-606 6961
Old established atmospheric city restaurant
Nosherie, Greville St
01-242 1591
City Jewish restaurant open 8am-5pm

EC2

Bill Bentley's, Old Broad St
01-588 1635
One of London's oldest group of oyster bars & seafood restaurants
Corney & Barrow, Old Broad St
01-638 9308
Gallipoli, Bishopsgate Churchyard
01-588 1922
Originally a Turkish bath, now a Turkish restaurant!
Mr Garraways Wine Bar & Restaurant
01-606 8209
H Great Eastern Hotel, Liverpool St
01-282 4363
Wheelers, Foster Ln
01-606 8254
Old established fish restaurant

EC3

City Tiberio, Lime St
01-623 3616
Mario & Franco
Wheelers, Fenchurch St
01-481 2362
Popular seafood restaurant
Wheelers, Great Tower St
01-626 3686
Massive seafood restaurant

EC4

Corney & Barrow, Cannon St
01-248 1700
A new addition
Villa Augusta, Queen Victoria St
01-248 0095
Muralled Mario & Franco restaurant
Ye Olde Cheshire Cheese, Fleet St
01-353 6170
Old London pub from Dickensian times with English food

N1

H Great Northern Hotel, King's Cross Stn
01-837 5454
Minogues, Theberton St
01-354 5220
Irish specialities
Portofino, Camden Passage
01-226 0884
Popular Italian restaurant

N6

Wheelers Highgate, South Grove
01-341 5270

NW1

Bill Bentley's, Baker St
01-935 3130
Le Routier, Chalk Farm Rd
01-485 0360
H The White House, Albany St
01-387 1200

NW3

H Holiday Inn, King Henry's Rd
01-722 7711
H Ladbroke Hotel, Primrose Hill
01-586 2233

NW6

La Frimousse, Fairfax Rd
01-624 3880

NW11

La Madrague, Finchley Rd
01-455 8853

SE3

Wheelers Blackheath, Montpelier Vale
01-318 9164

SE19

Luigi's, Gipsy Hill
01-670 1843

SW1

A l'Ecu de France, Jermyn St
01-930 2837
Old, established French restaurant
H Belgravia Sheraton, Chesham Pl
01-235 6040
Elegant hotel & restaurant, indoor pool
H Berkeley Hotel, Wilton Pl
01-235 6000
H Cadogan Thistle Hotel, Sloane St
01-235 7141
H Cavendish Hotel, Jermyn St
01-930 2111
H Ebury Court Hotel, Ebury St
01-730 8147
Ebury Wine Bar, Ebury St
01-730 5447
Popular wine bar with good atmosphere
Ken Lo's Memories of China, Ebury St
01-730 7734
Long established upmarket Chinese restaurant
Locketts, Marsham St
01-834 9552
Popular with MPs, English food
Mr Chow, Knightsbridge
01-589 7347
Expensive, but good, Chinese food
Overtons, St James' St
01-839 3774
Overtons, Victoria Buildings
01-834 3774
Long-established fish restaurants
Parco's, Knightsbridge
01-584 9777
Spaghetti Opera
H Sheraton Park Tower, Knightsbridge
01-235 8050
Stockpot, Basil St
01-589 8627
Stockpot, Panton St
01-839 5142
Good value from breakfast to a late snack - basic décor
Suntory, St James' St
01-409 0201
Classic Japanese restaurant
Villa Claudius, The Broadway
01-222 3338
Mario & Franco
Wheelers Carafe, Lowndes St
01-235 2525
Popular with local residents
Wheelers St James', Duke of York St
01-930 2460
The smallest Wheeler's with fish bar on ground floor
The Upper Crust, William St
01-235 8444
Traditional English puddings & pies

SW3

Bill Bentley's, Beauchamp Pl
01-589 5080
Don Luigi, Kings Rd 01-352 0025
Mario & Franco
Henry J Beans, Kings Rd
01-352 9255
*American style bar and American
style food*
Meridiana, Fulham Rd
01-589 8815
*Stylish Italian restaurant under new
management*
Ports, Beauchamp Place
01-581 3837
Attractive Portuguese restaurant
Wheelers, Kings Rd
01-730 3023
Good local following
Zen, Sloane Avenue
01-589 1781
*Very popular up-market Chinese
restaurant*

SW5

H London International Hotel, Cromwell
Rd
01-370 4200
Tiger Lee, Old Brompton Rd
01-370 2323
Szechuan fish restaurant

SW6

Perfumed Conservatory, Wandsworth
Bridge Rd
01-731 0732
Nouvelle British cuisine
Pigeon, Fulham Rd
01-736 4618
Reasonably priced bistro food

SW7

Chicago Rib Shack, Raphael St
01-581 5595
*Large American restaurant with good
ribs*
Daquise, Thurloe St
01-589 6117
Polish café open all day
H Embassy House Hotel, Queen's Gate
01-584 7222
H Gore Hotel, Queen's Hotel
01-584 6601
L A Café, Knightsbridge
01-589 7077
*Bustling bar and diner in American
style*
Montpeliano, Montepelier St
01-589 0032
*Cheerful Italian restaurant near
Harrods*
H Number Sixteen, Sumner Pl
01-589 5232
*Tastefully furnished B&B hotel
without restaurant*
H Rembrandt Hotel, Thurloe Pl
01-589 8100
Shezan, Cheval Pl
01-589 7918
Authentic Pakistani food
Texas Lone Star Saloon, Gloucester Rd
01-370 5625
Western films and Mexican food

SW10

Brinkleys, Hollywood Rd
01-351 1683
French restaurant with pretty garden
Garden Restaurant, Fulham Rd
01-736 6056
Hungry Horse, Fulham Rd
01-352 7757
Busy bistro with English food
Jakes, Hollywood Rd
01-352 8692
Red Pepper, Park Walk
01-352 3546
Modern Szechuan restaurant
September, Fulham Rd
01-352 0206
Village Taverna, Fulham Rd
01-351 3799
*Friendly, family-run Greek
restaurant*

SW11

The Inebriated Newt, Northcote Rd
01-223 1637
American dishes, good atmosphere
Maggie Brown, Battersea High St
01-228 0559
*Simple décor, stewed eels or meat pies
with mash*

SW13

The Old Rangoon, Castelnau
01-741 9655
*Trendy pub with large terrace and
garden for the summer*

SW19

Le Parc, Arthur Rd
01-946 6518

W1

Al Harma, Shepherds Market
01-493 1954
Comfortable Lebanese restaurant
Bentleys, Swallow St
01-734 4756
H Berners Hotel, Berners St
01-636 1629
Le Bistingo, Old Compton St
01-437 0784
Le Bistingo, Trebeck St
01-499 3292
Good value simple bistros
Brewer St Buttery, Brewer St
01-437 7695
H Britannia Hotel, Grosvenor Sq
01-629 9400
Cafè Loire, Gt Marlborough St
01-434 2666
H Chesterfield Hotel, Charles St
01-491 2622
Chez Victor, Wardour St
01-437 6523
Cranks, Marshall St
01-437 9431
*Vegetatarian restaurant – English
country wines*
L'Epicure, Frith St
01-437 2829
*Long established French restaurant –
popular with media people*

Fortnum and Mason, Piccadilly
01-734 8040
Adam Faith Dining Room
Choice of 3 in-house dining areas, one
open until 11.30pm
Granary, Albermarle St
01-493 2978
Self-service buffet of homely food –
open 11am-8pm
Hard Rock Café, Old Park Ln
01-629 0382
Rock music, long queues and
hamburgers
H   Hilton Hotel, British Harvest
Restaurant, Park Ln
01-493 8000
Specialising in English dishes
H   Hilton Hotel, Trader Vic's, Park Ln
01-493 7586
Vast cocktails and Polynesian cooking
Justin de Blank, Duke St
01-629 3174
Good size portions of wholesome food
Mirabelle, Curzon St
01-499 4636
Old style classic French restaurant
H   Park Lane, Piccadilly
01-499 6321
Pâtisserie Valerie, Old Compton St
01-437 3466
Good for breakfast, morning coffee or
afternoon tea
H   Portman InterContinental Hotel,
Portman Sq
01-486 5844
Smollensky's Balloon, Dover St
01-491 1199
Swiss Centre, New Coventry St
01-734 1921
Terrazza, Romilly St
01-437 8991
The original Mario & Franco
Tiddy Dols, Shepherds Market
01-499 2357
Victorian atmosphere, English food
Veeraswamy, Regent St
01-734 1401
One of London's oldest Indian
restaurants
H   Westbury Hotel, New Bond St
01-629 7755
Wheelers
Antoine, Charlotte St
01-636 2817
Sovereign, Hertford St
01-499 4679
Vendome, Dover St
01-629 5417
H   White's Hotel, Lancaster Gate
01-262 2711

W2
H   Montcalm Hotel, Gt Cumberland Pl
01-402 4288
H   Royal Lancaster Hotel, Lancaster Terr
01-262 6737
Wheelers, Kendal St
01-724 4637

W4
Mirage, Chiswick High Rd
01-995 1656

W8
Geale's, Farmer St
01-727 7969
H   Kensington Close Hotel, Wrights Ln
01-937 8170
H   Royal Garden Hotel,
Kensington High St
01-937 8000
Rooftop restaurant with beautiful
gardens
Trattoo, Abingdon Rd
01-937 4448
Attractive Italian restaurant
Wheelers, Alcove, Kensington High St
01-937 1443

W11
L'Artist Assoiffè, Kensington Pk Rd
01-727 4714
Popular restaurant with French
cuisine
H   Hilton International, Holland Park Ave
01-603 3355
H   Portobello Hotel, 22 Stanley Gardens
01-727 2777

W12
Balzac Bistro
01-743 6787

WC2
Le Beaujolais, Litchfield St
01-240 3776
Long established, well run restaurant
& wine bar
Beotys, St Martin's Ln
01-836 8768
One of London's oldest established
Greek Cypriot restaurants
Bertorelli's, Floral St
01-836 3969
Popular Covent Garden Italian
restaurant on 2 floors
Café du Jardin, Wellington St
01-836 8769
Bistro style food on two floors
Chez Solange, Cranbourn St
01-836 0542
Old established well run French
restaurant
Cork & Bottle, Cranbourn St
01-734 6592
One of London's busiest wine bars
l'Entrecôte Café de Paris,
Upper St Martin's Lane
01-836 7272
Flounders, Tavistock St
01-836 3925
Bistro-style seafood restaurant
Food For Thought, Neal St
01-836 0239
Busy vegetarian restaurant closes
early evening
Giardino's, Long Acre
01-836 8529
Bustling New York/Italian restaurant
Last Days of the Raj, Drury Ln
01-836 1628
North Indian restaurant in theatre-
land
L'Opera, Great Queen St
01-405 9020
Old style French restaurant

Poons & Co, Leicester St
01-437 1528
*Chinese restaurant specialising in
wind-dried meats*
Le Renoir, Charing Cross Rd
01-734 2515
R S Hispaniola, Victoria Embankment
01-839 3011
*Converted paddle steamer with two
restaurants*
Smith's Restaurant, Shelton St
01-379 0310
*Busy bistro, good atmosphere at lunch
time*
H Strand Palace Hotel, Strand
01-836 8080
Thomas de Quincey's, Tavistock St
01-240 3972
*Once the home of Thomas de Quincey,
now elegant French restaurant*
Tourment d'Amour, New Row
01-240 5348
H Waldorf Hotel, Aldwych
01-836 2400

MERSEYSIDE
Haydock
H Post House Hotel, Newton-le-Willows
THF
(0942) 717878

Liverpool
H The Adelphi Hotel
051-709 7200
*Refurbished Edwardian hotel with
amazing period features*
La Grande Bouffe, Castle St
051-236 3375
*Basement bistro with live jazz on
Tuesdays & Saturdays*
H Park Hotel, Park Ln, Bootle
051-525 7555
Modern hotel
H St George's, Lime St THF
051-709 7090

MIDDLESEX
Harrow Weald
H Grims Dyke Hotel, Old Redding
01-954 4227
Attractive country house

Hayes
H The Ariel, Bath Rd THF
01–759 2552
H The Skyway, Bath Rd THF
01-759 6311

Pinner
La Giralda, Pinner Green
01-868 3429
*Long established Spanish restaurant
specialising in fish & paella*

Twickenham
Cezanne, Richmond Rd
01-892 3526
French restaurant with modern décor
Quincey's Restaurant, Church St
01-892 6366
Fixed price menus, French cuisine

West Drayton
H The Excelsior, Bath Road THF
01-759 6611
H Holiday Inn Heathrow Airport HI
(0895) 445555
H Post House Hotel, Sipson Road THF
01-759 2323

NORFOLK
Brockdish
Sherrif House Restaurant
(037 975) 316
17th C timbered restaurant

Dereham
H The Phoenix, Church St THF
(0362) 2276

King's Lynn
H The Duke's Head, Tuesday Market Pl
THF
(0553) 774996
*Georgian building overlooking market
place*

Guise
Tollbridge Restaurant, Dereham Rd
(036 284) 359
*Converted toll house offering
freshwater fish & game*

Norwich
Brasted's Restaurant, St Andrew's Hill
(0603) 624044
French restaurant using local produce
H Maid's Head Hotel, Tombland
(0603) 628821
13th C inn
Marco's Restaurant, Pottergate
(0603) 624044
Well-established Italian restaurant
H Park Farm Hotel, Hethersett
(0603) 810264
*5 miles S of Norwich on A11 – indoor
pool*
H Post House Hotel, Ipswich Road THF
(0603) 56431

Thetford
H The Bell, King St THF
(0842) 4455
16th C half-timbered building

Wells-next-the-Sea
The Moorings, Freeman St
(0328) 710949
Small menu with emphasis on fish

NORTHAMPTONSHIRE
Kilsby
Hunt House Restaurant, Main Rd
(0788) 823282
17th C building

Northampton
H Post House Hotel, Crick THF
(0788) 822101

Oundle
Tyrrells, New St
(0832) 72347
Homely cooking in cosy dining room

Roade
Roadhouse Restaurant, High St
(0604) 863372
Modern cooking in a converted pub

427

Stoke Bruerne
The Butty, Canalside
(0604) 863654
Italian restaurant in lovely canalside setting

NORTHUMBERLAND
Belsay
Highlander Inn
(066 181) 220
Pub with a restaurant

Corbridge
The Ramblers Restaurant, Farnley
(043 471) 2424
Country house with German specialities

Hexham
H Langley Castle, Langley-on-Tyne
(0434 84) 8888
14th C castle

Morpeth
H Linden Hall Hotel, Longhorsley
(0670) 56611
Georgian country house

Otterburn
H Otterburn Tower Hotel
(0830) 20620
Originally a border fortress in 1066

Powburn
H Breamish House Hotel
(066 578) 266
Georgian country house

Wall
H The Hadrian Hotel
(043 481) 232
Adjacent to Hadrian's Wall

NOTTINGHAMSHIRE
Barnby Moor
H Ye Olde Bell, Retford   THF
(0777) 705121
Leaded windows and oak panelling

Langar
H Langar Hall
(0949) 60559
Country house

Nottingham
Les Artistes Gourmands, Wollaton Rd
(0602) 228288
Good value French restaurant
H The Albany, St James's St   THF
(0602) 470131

Plumtree
Perkins Bar & Bistro, Old Railway Stn
(060 77) 3695
Set in a converted railway station

Sandiacre
H Post House Hotel, Bostocks Ln   THF
(0602) 397800

NORTH YORKSHIRE
Bolton Abbey
H Devonshire Arms, Skipton
(075 671) 441
Converted coaching Inn with modern additions

Boroughbridge
Fountain House Restaurant, St James Sq
(090 12) 2241
18th C building, fresh local produce

Great Ayton
H Ayton Hall, Low Green
(0642) 723595
House of architectural & historic interest

Harrogate
H The Crown, Crown Place   THF
(0423) 67755
Situated in the old part of town
H Hodgson's, Valley Dr
(0423) 509866
Overlooking Valley Gardens
H The Majestic, Ripon Rd   THF
(0423) 68972
Victorian hotel in 12 acres of ground
Oliver, Kings Rd
(0423) 68600
French restaurant in terraced house

Helmsley
H The Black Swan, Market Place   THF
(0439) 70466
Comprises 3 houses, 1 Georgian, 1 Tudor & 1 Elizabethan

Hetton
H Angel Inn
(075 673) 263
Historic country inn

Kirkbymoorside
H George & Dragon, Market Pl
(0751) 31637
Stone-built oak-beamed hotel

Knaresborough
H Dower House Hotel, Bond End
(0423) 863302

Leyburn
Bolton Castle, Castle Bolton
(0969) 23408
Historic site in Wensleydale

Malton
H The Talbot, Yorkersgate   THF
(0653) 4031
18th C country-style house

Northallerton
H The Golden Lion, Market Place   THF
(0609) 2404
Restored Georgian inn

Ripon
H Old Deanery, Minster Rd
(0765) 3518
Near the cathedral

Thirsk
H The Golden Fleece, Market Place   THF
(0845) 23108
Coaching inn in cobbled square

Whitby
H Mallyan Spout Hotel, Goathland
(0947) 86206
Trenchers, New Quay Rd
(0947) 603212

York

H Crest Hotel
(0904) 648111

H Dean Court Hotel, Duncombe Pl
(0904) 25082
Beneath W tower of York Minster
Judge's Lodging, Lendal
(0904) 38733
Georgian town house, once the Assize Judge's residence

H Post House Hotel, Tadcaster Rd   THF
(0904) 707921
Tullivers, Good Ramgate
(0904) 51525
Vegetarian restaurant
Russells of Coppergate
(0904) 644330
Russells on King's Square
(0904) 36592
Russells of Stonegate
(0904) 641432
Huge joints of meat on display in these well run carveries

OXFORDSHIRE

Abingdon

H Abingdon Lodge Hotel, Marcham Rd
(0235) 35335
Modern hotel

Banbury

Three Conies, Thorpe Mandeville
(0295) 711025
Pub with restaurant

H Whatley Hall, Banbury Cross   THF
(0295) 3451
17th C building with secret staircases
Wroxton House
(029 573) 482
Part-thatched, Cotswolds stone-built hotel

Brightwell Baldwin

The Lord Nelson Inn
(049 161) 2497
Inn of architectural & historic interest

Burford

H Bay Tree, Sheep St
(099 382) 3137
16th C home of Elizabeth I's Lord Chief Baron of the Exchequer

H The Inn for all Seasons, The Barringtons
(04514) 324
Old stone-built coaching inn with buffet and restaurant

Chipping Norton

H The White Hart, High St   THF
(0608) 2572
Founded during Richard II's reign

Chislehampton

H Coach and Horses, Stadhampton Rd
(0865) 890255
16th C inn

Clanfield

The Plough
(036 781) 222
Elizabethan manor house

Faringdon

H Bell Hotel, The Square
(0367) 20534
16th C posting house
Sinclairs, Market Pl
(0367) 20945
Traditional English food

Henley-on-Thames

Walnut Tree, Fawley
(049 163) 360
Pub with restaurant & bar food

Horton-cum-Studley

H Studley Priory Hotel
(086 735) 203
12th C priory with oak panelling

Kingham

H The Mill Hotel & Restaurant
(060871) 8188
Converted mill

North Stoke

H Springs Hotel, Wallingford Road
(0491) 36687
Attractive mock-Tudor style house overlooking lake

Oxford

H The Randolph, Beaumont St   THF
(0865) 247481

Shipton-under-Wychwood

H Lamb Inn, High St
(0993) 830465
Popular for Sunday lunches

SHROPSHIRE

Bridgnorth

The Haywain, Hampton Loade
(0746) 780404]
6-course set menus

Clun

H Old Post Office, The Square
(058 84) 687
Converted Victorian post office offering local produce

Ellesmere

H The Grange, Grange Rd
(069 171) 3495
Georgian country house

Ludlow

Penny Anthony, Church St
(0584) 3282
Good bistro in town centre

Newport

Scholars Bistro, High St
(0952) 812362
Cheerful bistro in the old school house

Oswestry

H The Wynnstay, Church St   THF
(0691) 655261
Georgian inn

Shrewsbury

H Lord Hill Hotel
(0743) 52601
Modern De Vere hotel

H The Lion, Wyle Cop   THF
(0743) 53107
At the top of the town's oldest street

SOMERSET

Bishop's Lydeard
Rose Cottage
(0823) 432394
Simple homely cooking

Dulverton
H Ashwick House
(0398) 23868
Edwardian country estate overlooking Barle valley

Dunster
H The Luttrell Arms, High St   THF
(0643) 821555
Ivy-clad coaching inn near Castle

Minehead
H Beach Hotel, The Avenue   THF
(0643) 2193
Close to waterfront

Nunney
The George Inn, Church Street
(037 384) 458
14th C freehouse

Taunton
H The County Hotel, East St   THF
(0823) 87651
Coaching inn

Trull
Wrexon Farmhouse Restaurant, nr Angersleigh
(0823) 75440
Beamed cottage with antiques

West Bagborough
H Higher House
(0823) 432996
Country guest house running gardening courses in Spring & Autumn

Williton
H White House Hotel
(0984) 32306
Attractive Georgian house with courtyard and good restaurant

Yeovil
H Little Barwick House, Barwick Village
(0935) 23902
Comfortable Georgian dower house with restaurant specialising in local produce

STAFFORDSHIRE

Burton-on-Trent
H Riverside Inn, Riverside Drive, Branston
(0283) 63117
Well-run hotel overlooking River Trent

Newcastle-under-Lyme
H Post House Hotel   THF
(0782) 625151

Rugeley
The Old Farmhouse, Armitage
(0543) 490179
Popular restaurant in converted cottages

Stoke-on-Trent
H The North Stafford   THF
(0782) 48501

Tutbury
H Ye Olde Dog and Partridge, High St
(0283) 813030
Attractive 15th C timbered inn

Waterhouses
H Old Beams, Leek Road
(053 86) 254
18th C house with conservatory & attractive garden – good restaurant

SUFFOLK

Aldeburgh
H Brudenell Hotel, The Parade   THF
(072 885) 2071
Seaside hotel
H Uplands Hotel, Victoria Rd
(072 885) 2420
Comfortable hotel near sea front
H Wentworth Hotel, Wentworth Rd
(072 885) 3212
Medium-sized family hotel overlooking sea

Bury St Edmunds
Bradleys, St Andrews St South
(0284) 703825
Small restaurant with open plan kitchen, French cuisine
H The Angel Hotel, Angel Hill
(0284) 3926
Ivy-covered Georgian building, where Charles Dickens used to stay
H The Suffolk, Buttermarket   THF
(0284) 3995
Reconstruction of ancient inn

Cattawade
Bucks Restaurant, The Street
(0206) 392571
Converted pub offering small menu of well-cooked dishes

East Bergholt
Fountain House
(0206) 298232
15th C house in village where John Constable was born

Framlingham   H The Crown, Market Hill   THF
(0728) 723521
16th C with magnificent beams

Ipswich
H Belstead Brook Hotel, Belstead Rd
(0473) 684242
Well-run hotel with large grounds and attractive interior
H Post House Hotel, London Rd   THF
(0473) 690313

Ixworth
Theobalds Restaurant, High St
(0359) 31707
Chef/patron offers monthly changing French menus

Long Melford
H Bull Hotel   THF
(0787) 78494
Timbered building dating back to 1450

Orford
H The Crown & Castle   THF
(0394) 450205
Once a smugglers' haunt

Woodbridge
H The Crown, Thorofare   THF
(039 43) 4242
*Old coaching house with family
bedrooms*

SURREY
Bagshot
H Pennyhill Park, College Ride
(0276) 71774
*Conference hotel, member of the
Prestige group*

Camberley
H The Frimley Hall, Portsmouth Rd   THF
(0276) 28321
Victorian country house

Chipstead
Dene Farm, Outwood Ln
(073 75) 52661
*French restaurant set in wooded
valley*

Croydon
Dijonnais, High St 01−686 5624
French bistro
H Holiday Inn Croydon   HI 01−680 9200
La Flambée, High St 01−688 0763
French provincial cooking

Dorking
H The Burford Bridge, Box Hill   THF
(0306) 884561
Riverside gardens
H The White Horse, High St   THF
(0306) 881138
*Once a regular haunt of Charles
Dickens*

East Molesey
Bastians, Hampton Ct Rd
01-977 6074
*Hunting lodge atmosphere, French
cuisine*
Langan's at Hampton, Palace Gate Pde
01-979 7891/2
*Restaurant with collection of
paintings*
Le Chien Qui Fume, Walton Rd
01-979 7150
*Popular, well-established French
restaurant*
The Lantern, Bridge Rd
01-979 1531
Small French restaurant by the river

Elstead
Bentley's Restaurant, Elstead Mill
(0252) 702310

Farnham
Frensham Pond Hotel, Churt
(025 125) 3175
Tranquil lake-side setting
Tirolerhof, West St
(0252) 723277
*Austrian food & wine in 16th C
beamed restaurant*

Gatwick
H Post House Hotel, Horley   THF
(0293) 771621

Godalming
Inn on the Lake
(048 68) 5575
*Attractive Georgian inn in landscaped
gardens with lake*

Guildford
H Angel Hotel, High St   THF
(0483) 64555
Restaurant in 13th C crypt

Haslemere
H Lythe Hill Hotel, Petworth Rd
(0428) 51251
*Originally a Tudor farmhouse with
modern additions*

Leatherhead
The Pilgrims Rest, Guildford Rd
(0372) 373602
Heavily-beamed old alehouse

Ottershaw
Foxhills Country Club, Stonehill Rd
(093 287) 2050
*Jacobean manor house restaurant,
open to the public*

Peaslake
H The Hurtwood, Walking Bottom   THF
(0306) 730851

Richmond
Eleven Hill Rise, Hill Rise
01-948 7473
Restaurant with river views
The Captain Webb, Bridge St
(0932) 248105
*River boat hotel & restaurant for
private charter only*

South Godstone
La Bonne Auberge, Tilburston Hl
(0342) 892318
Victorian manor house

Walton-on-Thames
Octavia's Restaurant, Queens Rd,
Hersham
(0932) 227412
*French restaurant overlooking the
green*

West Clandon
Onslow Arms, The Street
(0483) 222447
*Old beams, copper pans, huge
fireplace*

SOUTH YORKSHIRE
Barnsley
H Brooklands, Barnsley Rd, Dodworth
(0226) 299571
Motel & restaurant

Sheffield
H Grosvenor House Hotel, Charter
Sq THF
(0742) 20041
H Hallam Tower Post House Hotel,   THF
(0742) 686031
Manchester Road

TYNE & WEAR
Newcastle-upon-Tyne
CJ's Restaurant, Higham Pl
091-232 4949
Small restaurant offering English menu

Fisherman's Lodge 091-281 3281
Specialises in fish & shellfish

H Gosforth Park Thistle Hotel, High Gosforth Park
091-236 4111
Large modern hotel with leisure facilities

H Holiday Inn Newcastle–upon–Tyne HI
091-236 5432

Le Roussillon, St Andrew's St
091-261 1341
Chef/patron offers large à la carte menu

Washington
H Post House Hotel, Emerson District THF
091-416 2264

WARWICKSHIRE
Kenilworth
H Clarendon House Hotel, Old High St
(0926) 57668
15th C inn built around an oak tree!

H De Montfort Hotel, The Square
(0926) 55944
Modern De Vere hotel

Stratford-upon-Avon
H The Alveston Manor, Clopton Bridge THF
(0789) 204581
Manor house with 110 bedrooms

H Chase Hotel, Ettington
(0789) 740000
Victorian Gothic style building

H Stratford House Hotel, Sheep St
(0789) 68288
Small comfortable hotel & restaurant

H The Swan's Nest, Bridgefoot THF
(0789) 66761
Close to Royal Shakespeare Theatre

H Welcome Hotel, Warwick Rd
(0789) 295252
Elegant Jacobean style hotel with golf course

H The White Swan, Rother St THF
(0789) 297022
15th C building

Warwick
Randolph's, Coten End
(0926) 491292
Converted 16th C cottages – good restaurant

Wishaw
H Belfry Hotel
(0675) 70301
Large hotel & leisure complex near 2 golf courses

WILTSHIRE
Aldbourne
Raffles Restaurant, The Green
(0672) 40700
French restaurant with à la carte & fixed price menus

Chippenham
H Manor House, Castle Combe
(0249) 782206
Situated in own grounds in Dr Doolittle's village

Malmesbury
H Whatley Manor Hotel, Easton Grey
(066 62) 2888
Country house hotel with swimming pool, tennis court & putting green

Marlborough
H The Castle & Ball, High St THF
(0672) 55201
17th C coaching inn

H The Ivy House, High St
(0672) 53188
Georgian house with cobbled courtyard & matured walled garden

Melksham
H King's Arms Hotel
(0225) 707272
Old coaching inn built of Bath stone

Salisbury
H The White Hart, St John St THF
(0722) 27476
Opposite the cathedral

Swindon
H Post House Hotel, Marlborough Rd THF
(0793) 24601

Warminster
Dove at Corton, Corton
(0985) 50378
Pub with restaurant, 5 miles SE of Warminster

WEST MIDLANDS
Berkswell
Nailcote Hall, Nailcote Ln
(0203) 466174
Elizabethan country house in 8 acres

Birmingham
H The Albany, Smallbrook Queensway THF
021-643 8171

Chez Julien, Stratford Rd, Shirley
021-744 7232
Chef/patron specialises in fish, shellfish and dishes from S France

Birmingham National Exhibition Centre
H Metropole & Warwick Hotel
021-780 4242
Large comfortable hotel in the exhibition centre complex

H Holiday Inn Birmingham HI
021-643 2766

Michelle, High St, Harborne 021–426 4133
Bistro offering French provincial cooking

Birmingham Airport
H The Excelsior, Coventry Rd THF
021-743 8141

432

Coventry

H The Brandon Hall, Brandon   THF
(0203) 542571

H Herbs, Trinity House Hotel,
Lower Holyhead Rd
(0203) 555654
Vegetarian restaurant

H Post House Hotel, Allesley   THF
(0203) 402151

Edgbaston

Le Mange Tout, Strathallan Hotel,
Hagley Road
021-455 9777

H Plough &'Harrow, Hagley Road
021-454 4111
*Small luxury hotel with good
restaurant*

Great Barr

H The Post House Hotel, Chapel
Lane   THF
021-357 7444

Meriden

H Manor Hotel
(0676) 22735
Attractive Queen Anne manor house

Solihull

Liaison, Old Lode Ln
021-743 3993
*Modern cuisine in attractive
restaurant*

WEST SUSSEX
Arundel

H Norfolk Arms Hotel
(0903) 882101

Chichester

H Clinchs', Guildhall St
(0243) 785121
*Elegant town house near Festival
Theatre*

Chilgrove

White Horse Inn
(024 359) 219
Pub with restaurant – good wine list

Climping

H Bailiffscourt, Nr Littlehampton
(0903) 723511
Comfortable hotel near the coast

Cuckfield

H Ockenden Manor Hotel, Ockenden Ln
(0444) 416111
Converted 16th C manor house

H The King's Head
(0444) 454006
Village pub with restaurant

Lower Beeding

H South Lodge
(040 376) 711
Member of the Prestige group

Midhurst

H Spread Eagle Hotel, South St
(073 081) 2211
15th coaching inn with 17th C hall

WEST YORKSHIRE
Bradford

H The Victoria, Bridge St   THF
(0274) 728706

Elland

Bertie's Bistro, Town Hall Bldgs
(0422) 71724
*Blackboard menus of international
dishes*

Farnley Tyas

Golden Cock, The Village
(0484) 661979
Pub with restaurant

Halifax

H Holdsworth House Hotel, Holdsworth
(0422) 244270
*Comfortable hotel in converted 17th C
house*

Haworth

Weavers Restaurant & Bar, West Ln
(0535) 43822
*Converted weavers' cottages with
traditional English food*

Huddersfield

H The George, St George's Sq   THF
(0484) 25444
Weavers Shed, Knowle Rd, Golcar
(0484) 654284
18th C cloth-finishing mill

Ilkley

H The Craiglands, Cowpasture Rd   THF
(0943) 607676
Set in its own parklands

Leeds

H Post House Hotel, Bramhope   THF
(0532) 842911

H The Metropole, King St   THF
(0532) 450841

H The Queen's, City Sq   THF
(0532) 431323
1930s building 198 bedrooms

Pontefract

H Wentbridge House, Wentbridge
(0977) 620444
*18th C house with large grounds, set
in Went Valley*

Wakefield

H Post House Hotel, Ossett   THF
(0924) 276388

Wetherby

L'Escale, Bank St
(0937) 63613
French restaurant in town centre

SCOTLAND

Aberdeen Airport
H Holiday Inn HI
(0224) 770011

Aviemore
H Post House Hotel THF
(0479) 810771

Ballater
H The Green Inn, Victoria Rd THF
(0338) 55701
Bistro with rooms
H Tullich Lodge
(0338) 55406
Victorian mansion overlooking River Dee

Callander
H Roman Camp Hotel
(0877) 30003
Old hunting lodge of the Dukes of Perth

Canonbie
H Riverside Inn
(054 15) 512
Modernised inn on the River Esk

Crinan
H Crinan Hotel, by Lochgilphead
(054 683) 235
Hotel and seafood restaurant

Cullipool
Longhouse Buttery & Gallery, Isle of Luing(085 24) 209
Salad & sandwich restaurant on small island

Cupar
Ostlers Close, Bonnygate
(0334) 55574
Small restaurant specialising in seafood & game

Dirleton
H Open Arms Hotel
(062 085) 241
8 golf courses nearby!

Drybridge
The Old Monastery, by Buckie
(0542) 32660
Fabulous views of Moray Firth, good local produce

Edinburgh
H Braids Hills Hotel, Braid Road
031-447 8888
Views over city
H Prestonfield House, Priestfield Rd
031-668 3346
17th C building in parkland
H Post House Hotel, Corstorphine Rd THF
031-334 8221

Glasgow
H Albany Hotel, Bothwell St THF
041-248 2656
Charlie's Basement Restaurant, Royal
041-221 0798
Exchange Sq
Rustic décor and French provincial cooking

Charlie's Diner, Royal Exchange Sq
041-221 0798
Tex-Mex and Anglo-French cuisine in club atmosphere
The Colonial, High St
041-552 1923
Good cooking from chef/patron in basic surroundings
The Fountain, Woodside Crescent
041-332 6396
Comfortable French restaurant with large à la carte and fixed price menus
H Holiday Inn, Argyle St HI
041-226 5577
Poachers, Ruthven Ln (off Byres Rd)
041-339 0932
French cuisine in an old stone-built mews house

Glasgow Airport
H Excelsior Hotel, Paisley THF
041-887 1212

Glenborrodale
H Glenborrodale Castle, Acharade THF
(097 24) 266

Grantown-on-Spey
H Tulchan Lodge, Advie
(080 75) 200
Old hunting lodge converted to a comfortable small hotel

Gullane
H Greywalls, Muirfield
(0620) 842144
Lutyens-designed house with gardens by Gertrude Jekyll

Inverness
H Culloden House
(0463) 790461
Member of the Prestige group
H Dunain Park Hotel
(0463) 234317
Country house & gardens

Isle of Harris
H Scarista House
(085 985) 238
Georgian dwelling, formerly the Church of Scotland manse for Harris – good restaurant

Isle of Mull
H Ardfenaig House, by Bunessan
(068 17) 210
Small country hotel with competent cooking

Kelso
H Sunlaws House Hotel, Heiton
(057 35) 331
Victorian mansion owned by Duke of Roxburghe

Kilchrenan
H Ardanaiseig, by Taynuilt
(086 63) 333
19th C mansion house with beautiful landscaped gardens

Kirkmichael
H The Log Cabin
(025 081) 288
Hotel and leisure centre

Moffat

H Beechwood Country House Hotel,
   Harthope Pl(0683) 20210
   *100-year old grey stone hotel
   overlooking Moffat*

Oban

H Knipoch Hotel, Knipoch
   (085 26) 251
   *Attractive Georgian house overlooking
   Loch Feochan*

Old Meldrum

H Meldrum House
   (065 12) 2294
   Seat of the Lairds of Meldrum

Peebles

H Tontine Hotel, High St THF
   (0738) 24455
   Built in 1808

Perth

H Royal George Hotel, Tay St THF
   (0738) 24455
   Overlooking River Tay

Pitlochry

H Atholl Palace Hotel THF
   (0796) 2400
   Baronial hotel, 48 acres of woodland

St Andrews

H Old Course Hotel
   (0334) 74371
   *Comfortable hotel overlooking the
   home of golf*

Scone

   Balcraig House
   (0738) 51123
   Country mansion, 5 miles from Perth

Selkirk

H Philipburn House Hotel
   (0750) 20747
   Family hotel with poolside restaurant

Stewarton

H Chapeltoun House
   (0560) 82696
   *Victorian house with oak-panelled hall
   & good restaurant*

Stirling

   Broughton's, Blairdrummond
   (0786) 841897
   *Converted farmhouse specialising in
   local game & fish*

Turnberry

H The Turnberry
   (0655) 31000
   *Luxury hotel overlooking famous
   championship golfcourse*

Tweedsmuir

H The Crook Inn, Biggar
   (089 97) 272
   Small family run hotel

Whitebridge

H Knockie Lodge
   (045 63) 276
   *Originally a hunting lodge,
   overlooking Loch Nan Lann*

WALES

Abergavenny

H Angel Hotel, Cross St THF
   (0873) 7121
   Originally a private home

Bala

H Palé Hall Hotel, Llandderfel
   (067 83) 285
   Secluded country house hotel

Betwys-y-Coed

H Royal Oak Hotel, Holyhead Road
   (069 02) 219
   Restaurant offers health food menus

Cardiff

H Post House Hotel, Pentwyn THF
   (0222) 73121

Carmarthen

H Ivy Bush Royal Hotel, Spilmen St THF
   (0267) 235111

Conwy

H Castle Hotel, High St THF
   (049 263) 2324

Glyn Ceiriog

H Golden Pheasant Hotel
   (069 172) 281
   Wonderful views of Ceiriog valley

Haverfordwest

   Jemima's Restaurant, Puddleduck Hill,
   Freystrop
   (0437) 891109
   Specialises in fresh fish

Llandudno

   The Floral Restaurant, Victoria St,
   Craig-y-Don
   (0492) 75735
   *Attractive restaurant serving good
   local produce*

H Marine Hotel, Vaughen St THF
   (0492) 77521
   on seaside promenade

Llanelli

H Stradey Park Hotel, Furnace THF
   (0554) 758171
   Overlooks the town

Llangollen

H Royal Hotel, Bridge St THF
   (0978) 860202
   Own fishing stretch on river

Machynlleth

   Janie's Restaurant, Maengwyn St
   (0654) 2126
   Bistro open from Easter to October

H Wynnstay Hotel, Maengwyn St THF
   (0654) 2941
   Former mid-Wales coaching inn

Newport

H Celtic Manor Hotel, Coldra Woods
   (0633) 413000
   17 bedroomed converted manor house

Porthmadog

H Royal Sportsman Hotel, High St THF
   (0766) 2015
   Close to sea and beaches

Presteigne
H Radnorshire Arms Hotel, High St THF
(0544) 267406

Pwllheli
The Dive Inn, Tudweiliog
(075 887) 246

Swansea
H Dragon Hotel, Kingsway Circus THF
(0792) 51074

NORTHERN IRELAND
Belfast, Co Antrim
Strand, Stranmills Rd
(0232) 682266
Wine bar and bistro

Dunmurry, Belfast, Co Antrim
H The Conway, Kingsway THF
(0232) 612101

Holywood, Co Down
H Culloden Hotel, Bangor Rd
(023 17) 5223
*Comfortable hotel with tennis and
squash courts*

Portrush, Co Antrim
Ramore, The Harbour
(0265) 824313
Competent cooking by chef/patron

REPUBLIC OF IRELAND
International Code
(010-353)

Adare, Co Limerick
H Dunraven Arms, Main St
(061) 94209
Well-run inn

Ballina, Co Mayo
H Enniscoe House, Castlehill, Nr
Crossmolina
(096) 31112
*Georgian country house on shores of
Lough Conn – good shooting and
fishing*
H Mount Falcon Castle
(096) 21172
*An Irish castle base for local fishing or
shooting*

Ballinascarthy, Co Cork
H Ardnavaha House Hotel
(023) 49135
*Set in 40 acres of grounds, outdoor
pool, tennis court and own stables*

Ballylickey, Co Cork
H Ballylickey House, Nr Bantry
(027) 50071
*Serviced accomodation in cottages –
poolside restaurant*
H Sea View House Hotel, Nr Bantry
(027) 50462
*Small comfortable hotel overlooking
Bantry Bay*

Ballyvaughan, Co Clare
H Gregans Castle Hotel
(065) 77005
*At the foot of Corkscrew Hill with
wonderful views over Galway Bay*

Borris, Co Carlow
Step House
(0503) 73209
*Late Georgian house on what was once
the estate of the kings of Leinster*

Bunratty, Co Clare
MacCloskey's, Bunratty House Mews
(061) 74082
*Restaurant in restored cellars of
17th C Bunratty House*

Caragh Lake, Co Kerry
H Caragh Lodge
(066) 69115
*Country house furnished with
antiques and beautiful gardens*

Cashel, Co Galway
H Cashel House Hotel
(095) 21252
*Secluded country estate, tasteful décor
and furnishings*

Cashel, Co Tipperary
H Cashel Palace Hotel, Main St
(062) 61411
18th C mansion house
Chez Hans, Rockside
(062) 61177
Restaurant in converted chapel

Castledermot, Co Kildare
Doyle's Schoolhouse Restaurant
(0503) 44282
*Restaurant with rooms in area of
historic interest*

Clones, Co Managhan
Hilton Park, Scotshouse
(047) 56007
*Mansion house in parkland with
private lake*

Cong, Co Mayo
H Ashford Castle, Claremorris
(094) 71444
*19th C turreted castle on shores of
Lough Corrib*

Connemara, Co Galway
Crocnaraw House, Moyard
(095) 41068
*Georgian house overlooking
Ballinakill Bay*
Currarevagh House, Oughterard
(091) 82313
*Mid-19th C house with trout fishing
on Lough Corrib*

Cork, Co Cork
Lovetts, Churchyard Ln, Douglas
(021) 294909

- Seafood restaurant

Culleenamore, Co Sligo
H Knockmuldowney Restaurant
(071) 68122
*Ivy clad Georgian house in the heart of
Yeats country*

Dublin, Co Dublin
Le Coq Hardi, Ballsbridge
(01) 689070
Georgian house, French cuisine

Ernie's, Mulberry Gardens
(01) 693300
Renovated cottage with attractive décor

H Sherbourne Hotel, St Stephen's Gn
(01) 766471
Elegant 19th C hotel

H Westbury Hotel, Off Grafton St
(01) 791122
148 bedroomed modern hotel
White's on the Green, St Stephen's Gn
(01) 751975
Elegant French restaurant overlooking The Green

Dublin Airport
H International Hotel THF
(0001) 379211

Durrus, Co Cork
Blairs Cove Restaurant
(027) 61127
Converted stable with enormous fire for grilling meats and fish

Ennis, Co Clare
H Old Ground Hotel, Station Rd THF
(0353) 28127

Kanturk, Co Cork
H Assolas Country House
(029) 50015
Small hotel with beautiful gardens on riverside

Kinsale, Co Cork
H Acton's Hotel THF
(0353) 772135
Overlooks fishing port

Letterfrack, Co Galway
H Rosleague Manor
(095) 41101
In the centre of Connemara, a Georgian house overlooking Ballinakill Bay

Maynooth, Co Kildare
Moyglare Manor, Moyglare
(01) 286351
Elegant Georgian house overlooking park and mountains

Moycullen, Co Galway Drimcong House Restaurant
(091) 85115
17th C lakeland house with good restaurant

New Ross, Co Wexford
Galley Cruising Restaurants
(051) 21723
River cruises around New Ross and Waterford with restaurant on board

Newmarket-on-Fergus, Co Clare
H Dromoland Castle
(061) 71144
Romantic turreted castle

Parknasilla, Co Kerry
H Parknasilla Great Southern Hotel, Nr Sneem
(064) 45122
Superb Victorian mansion overlooking Renare Bay

Rathmullan, Co Donegal
H Rathmullan House
(074) 58117
Overlooks the sea on the shores of Lough Swilly

Rathnew, Co Wicklow
H Hunter's Hotel
(0404) 4106
Old coaching inn on banks of River Vartry
H Tinakilly House Hotel
(0404) 9274
Well-furnished Victorian mansion

Riverstown, Co Sligo
H Coopershill House, Coopershill
(071) 65108
Georgian mansion with just 5 bedrooms, set in 500 acres

Rossess Point, Co Sligo Reveries
(071) 77371
Overlooks Sligo Bay

Schull, Co Cork
Ard na Greine Inn
(028) 28181
18th C farmhouse

Waterville, Co Kerry
H Huntsman
(0667) 4124
Restaurant with rooms
H Smugglers Inn, Cliff Rd
(0667) 4330
Converted farmhouse. Restaurant offers good seafood

Wicklow, Co Wicklow
H The Old Rectory
(0404) 2048
Charming rectory with 5 bedrooms

Youghal, Co Cork
Aherne's Seafood Bar, North Main St
(024) 92424
Excellent seafood in a converted pub

Index of Establishments Reviewed

Place names are set in italic

R

Styles of Restaurants and Cuisines

Bistro
Normally smaller type of establishment, with checked tablecloths, bentwood chairs, cluttered décor, friendly and mostly informal staff. Honest, basic and robust cooking, possibly coarse pâtés, thick soups, casserole dishes often served in large portions.

Brasserie
Largish, styled room, often with long bar; can be variety of styles ranging from Art Nouveau/Art Deco through to the 1980s. Normally serving one plate items rather than formal meals (although some offer both). Often, licensing hours permitting, it is possible just to drink wine or eat a small amount or just drink coffee. Normally offer one-plate items throughout the day and more extensive menu at lunch and dinner. Traditional brasserie dishes include charcoterie, moules marinières and steak frites. Service generally by waiters in long aprons and black waistcoats.

Farmhouse Cooking
Usually simply cooked with generous portions of basic, home-produced fare.